InJUSTICE

From LOISAIDA to the New York State Police[1]

Pedro Perez

PAGE PUBLISHING
Conneaut Lake, PA

First originally published by Page Publishing 2024

ISBN 979-8-89157-133-4 (pbk)
ISBN 979-8-89157-141-9 (digital)

Printed in the United States of America

Pamela Ortiz Perez's unwavering dedication to our partnership and family paved the way for our journey out of poverty. Even in the face of her struggle with Lupus, she gave everything she had to keep our family together. Her legacy of love and sacrifice will continue to inspire us as we strive to honor her memory. Her valiant efforts to survive her struggle with Lupus ended in 2019. This book would not have been possible without her. Of all the titles I have had throughout my life, Papi is the one I cherish the most. I love Yasmine and Aramis; their joyous smiles when I returned from patrol always inspired me and reminded me of the most essential thing in my life: family.

Contents

Prologue

It was midnight on Thursday, July 16, 1992. Hundreds of protesters were burning tires and other debris on the New York State Thruway, Southern Tier Expressway, and other New York State roads that crossed the Seneca Nation of Indians' territories.[2] The Seneca and their allies are protesting the imposition of tobacco and gas taxes on their land. Seneca Nation President Calvin John was setting up a committee of Indian leaders to decide how to fight New York's tax efforts. "For two hundred years, New York state has attempted to infringe upon our sovereignty," John said.[3]

Figure 1. Tire fires on New York State Thruway.[4]

The New York State Police (NYSP) was the primary law enforcement agency responsible for responding to calls for service, investigating traffic accidents, and enforcing the law on this major highway. The NYSP was also authorized to enforce criminal statutes but not New York State regulations in certain areas, like hunting and fishing, on the Native American territories in New York. In this case, we responded to protect the innocent motorist from being killed in a fiery crash. State police arrived to extinguish the tire fires and remove protesters from the overpasses.

The New York State Police troopers holding the line on either side of me were nervous, tense, and some were scared. I told them to relax and focus on our mission and that we will get through this together. A car speeds toward us, honking its horn and flashing its lights before the driver hits the brakes and skids to a stop a few feet short of a vehicular assault charge. The trooper beside me was angry and scared, and I said I was too. I told him we had to focus on protecting citizens using the highway and each other. I also told him I would be at his side throughout this ordeal. He visibly relaxes until the next car barks its tires and bears down on us, honking and flashing its lights like the last one. At the last minute, the driver pulled a hand brake, causing the car to spin 180 degrees, which spat gravel at us before speeding off in the opposite direction, back toward the line of protestors. I prayed we would hold firm and not lose control of our emotions and the situation. The protestors on the highway have been blocking traffic, burning tires, and throwing rocks at us for hours.

This was a desolate and dark part of the New York State Thruway. We had marched onto the overpass to stop the protestors from throwing debris upon the main traveled part of the New York State Thruway. They were endangering the lives of innocent motorists. We had no vehicles to protect us from the dangerous tactics some protestors used to intimidate us with their cars. Some protestors stopped directly in front of us, exiting to attack us. When things got ugly, the skirmish line we formed held through the sporadic periods of hand-to-hand combat before the protestors fell back and stopped fighting us up close. I had asked the command post to send us several more troopers with their vehicles to create a protective barrier, but the incident commander said it would take a while. We arrested several of the individuals. We seized their cars temporarily to make our barricades; once the protest ended, we returned the vehicles to the owners.

Another car came through the line of protestors and headed our way, slowly this time, with no screeching horns or blinding flashing headlights. The driver reached us, saying he lived on the other side of the roadblock and needed to get home to his family. The address on his driver's license matched his story, and we let him through. A few more cars came through, and checking addresses worked. As a bonus, the protestors are no longer sending cars to play chicken with us, scared they might hit one of the people trying to drive home. Then, a pickup loaded with people from the front line of protestors came toward us. The front passenger flashed a peace sign out the window as they approached, and when they reached us, the driver claimed they lived on the other side of the bridge.

I leaned back against one of the cars we commandeered and looked the driver in the eye. "Can you prove that? Got some ID with your address on it?" "Yeah, hang on," the driver says, but then he hits the gas, pinning me between the truck and the commandeered car. The truck spins me like a pencil between praying hands and takes off. I stumble after being spun, and the truck breaks the line of troopers. The ones in front jump to get out of the way. As I regained my balance, I was amazed I was not hurt. The riders in the truck's bed had bats and were swiping at the troopers they passed. I saw and heard the troopers defending themselves, and then I heard a thud. The truck sped away.

Half a second later, some troopers are rushing toward an injured officer. We did not know whether he got hit by the truck or by a bat the riders were swinging. His face was bloody as he lay splayed on the highway, and he appeared to be in shock as he writhed in pain. We summoned a medevac evacuation, and he was loaded onto it and taken to the Dunkirk Hospital. I knew we had to regain control of the situation. The supervisors and I ordered the troopers to reform the line, and we radioed for reinforcements. During the next few hours, I wondered, what am I doing here? I am fighting my Indigenous cousins to serve the same colonial powers that murdered, enslaved, and marginalized us in the first place. Was this their continued work to actualize their Civil Rights Movement, in which factions of frustrated and angry protesters, like in the 1960s, allowed themselves to turn toward violence and rioting?

Since then, I have had a lot of time to think about "what I was doing there" and why I stayed with the NYSP through that incident, a severe injury I sustained in the line of duty, and many other hurdles, both professional and personal. I was trying to get my family out of poverty, staying true to my ideals, and effecting change from within. In my time as a trooper, I called out racism when I saw it, encouraged women and people of Color to strive for leadership positions, and tried to emphasize "justice" over the "criminal" about my role in the criminal justice system. In its 246 years as a nation, I recognized that the United States only reluctantly began to accept itself as a multi-racial nation in 1964 after the enactment of the Civil Rights Act. I understood this meant that before that, there were portions of this country where citizens essentially experienced apartheid because of "Jim Crow" laws.[5] And just as egregious was the forced displacement and nearly successful genocide of the Indigenous people of this nation before the passage of the Indian Civil Rights Act of 1968. As a multiethnic person in the state police, I had a duty to serve all the people justly and equitably while enforcing the law.

When I first applied for the job, though, I thought only of the paycheck, the benefits package, and the potential for career advancement, and I did not even realize I was joining the state police. I wanted to belong, but on my terms, finding that middle path was continuously complicated.

Introduction

My family and I began our journey out of poverty over eighty years ago on the Island of Borinquén. My mother's trauma began when she was two years old; her mother died from tuberculosis during the 1930s tuberculosis outbreak in Puerto Rico. This loss would have crushed a less formidable spirit. This experience severely tested her inner strength as she "couch-surfed" from family to family. Her father worked on merchant vessels and was nearly always at sea, making my mother's situation all the worse. No one recognized the depth of her resilience and resourcefulness, yet her inner voice knew. She was not and is not alone. Millions of women, mothers, daughters, and sons worldwide have shown the same determination to change their lives for themselves and their families. She passed that strength, resilience, and resourcefulness not just to me; she shared it with anyone who needed it and would listen. My mother and the millions of female-headed households struggle every day to work their way out of poverty. In the United States, over twenty-one million women are in poverty, sadly outpacing men. This means that if they have children, their children are experiencing poverty too. That is over eleven million children under eighteen years old.

According to the US census analysis, "In 2019, there were 34.0 million people in poverty, approximately 4.2 million fewer people than in 2018."[6] Many families in the Black, Brown, Native American, and other marginalized communities, based on their population, are still poor and overrepresented in these statistics.

The global pandemic has made this reality worse in those communities. The crucial public health strategy to save lives caused an unprecedented economic downturn globally and nationally, forcing many businesses to reduce hours of operations or close entirely. In turn, these businesses reduced employee hours or laid off their employees. This impact has been felt most severely in communities mentioned above, specifically, women and the children of these communities. If there was a "silver lining" in the pandemic, it shone an even brighter light on the structural inequities existing before COVID-19 emerged as a global catastrophe. The preexisting healthcare access and affordability gaps, education, employment, career, and entrepreneurial opportunities have devastated poor communities. Even middle-class families, who may have been "living from check to check," were battered by the downturn. Chairman Alan Greenspan, former chair of the Federal Reserve Board, at a symposium sponsored by the Federal Reserve Bank of Kansas City, Jackson Hole, Wyoming, on August 28, 1998, said this about income inequity:

> "The study of income inequality its causes, its consequences, and its potential policy implications has a long history in economics, although it has not always had a high profile among researchers and policymakers… 'One particularly notable change was an apparent rise in the share of wealth held by the wealthiest families at the expense of other wealthy families; most of the change occurred within the top 10 percent of the distribution."[7]

The pandemic has revealed the fragility and vulnerability of individual, national, and global economies. My children were both laid off from their jobs; luckily, I was able to help them during this period. Had they not found other jobs, they could have fallen from the upward socioeconomic mobility ladder we had worked hard to access. People worldwide and millions of Americans journeying to a better life were on their bridges out of poverty that began crumbling beneath them. Increased homelessness and food insecurity among already marginalized communities are evidence of this collapse.

My mother's experience as a child, I believe, yielded the incredible woman who was determined not to allow her children to experience the instability she did. She had unyielding devotion and love for her two boys. Had she remained with my abusive father, we might not have survived, let alone thrived. Her example of hard work and education was the path I followed. She was the person who modeled the behavior I needed to engage in if I wanted to be successful.

My mother's lessons encouraged me to pursue a career that would provide me with a living wage, health care, and a pension. Joining the New York State Police was serendipitous in many ways. My family and I experienced fear, joy, and many other emotions on our trek out of poverty. We gained access to a better life because I became a trooper and forged a career in the New York State Police, whose trajectory many people, including myself, would not have predicted. I succeeded in the state police despite the organization's history of discriminatory culture and practices. I had the help of mentors and others who performed their jobs justly and with integrity. They stood by their convictions while holding steadfast to the central vision of the New York State Police: "To serve, protect, and defend the people of New York, while preserving the rights and dignity of all." This mission statement has expanded significantly since I served.[8] I also served beside some colleagues who were biased toward men of Color, women in general, and those experiencing poverty, even though some of those troopers came from poverty themselves.

The New York State Police championed itself as a leading law enforcement agency recognized throughout the nation and the world as such. There were, and still are, many good reasons to celebrate the institution. But it is also an agency stained by bigotry and sexism. My story has triumphs and failures, moments of joy and pain. Some may applaud my telling of it, and others will resent what I want to bring to light. I offer my story not from a place of bitterness about the New York State Police and the criminal legal system but from a place of hope. Although my rise in the NYSP was, at times, excruciatingly painful, both literally and figuratively, because of some of its policies and bigoted members, I loved being a trooper who served the people equitably without bias. In the state police, I met some bigots, but fortunately, I also met many individuals in the state police who treated me and other members of marginalized groups with respect. Most troopers I met were helpful, welcoming, and focused on serving their community with integrity and honor. Some state police members saw themselves as "color-blind" but remained silent in the face of discriminatory police practices. The idea of racial "color-blindness" is an intellectually and emotionally flawed approach to the complex social construct of race and the resulting racism.[9] Many of these troopers did not see themselves as being affected by prejudice even though they were.[10] Some of the things and people I worked with during my tenure described herein will be painful and embarrassing for some to relive. While empathically understanding, not including them would fail to show how they impacted my journey.

I joined the state police in 1981, not knowing its history of discrimination toward men and women of Color and women in general. I was unaware of its history of ugly and unprofessional enforcement efforts, like its recapture of Attica, New York State's maximum-security prison, after the inmate uprising in 1971. The rebellion ended four days later in a barrage of gunfire. Twenty-nine incarcerated men and ten hostages died, and a further eighty-nine people were wounded.[11] In an accurate depiction, the 2021 documentary "Attica" describes the underlying cause of the uprising of the inmates and the NYS troopers responding in gas masks overlooking a prison yard littered with the dead and dying.[12]

I was also unaware that a United States Department of Justice investigation had begun in 1977 and led to a lawsuit that forced the New York State Police to hire men of Color and women in general. All I knew was that I needed a job with good health care, a pension plan, and opportunities for career advancement; the state police offered these benefits, which mattered to me.

Even though I didn't know about the affirmative action case, once I joined the state troopers, many in the organization never let me forget their true feelings. They said I was only there because of the lawsuit. This is one way that affirmative action policies can have both positive and negative effects. The positive impact is the partial mitigation of the centuries of discrimination and inequities that African Americans, Asian Americans, Hispanics, Native Americans, women, and other marginalized groups have suffered and continue to suffer. While immigrants from Ireland, Italy, and Eastern Europe suffered discrimination initially, many of these new citizens avoided further bias by anglicizing their names and conforming to the ever-expanding definition of "Whiteness." Moreover, helped by their skin color and facial features, they were able to be included in the expanding definition of the "White race."[13]

After World War II, returning military veterans and their families advanced economically because of the GI Bill. This affirmative action plan for soldiers who rightfully earned because of their heroic service. However, veterans of Color and their families, who also rightfully earned and deserved to benefit from the GI Bill, were systematically prevented from fully taking part. The program allowed low-income and undereducated European Americans to enter the middle class by subsidizing their college educations and mortgage loans. Still, only a tiny number of African Americans or other people of Color received these benefits. Together, these programs enabled White veterans to buy the American dream: owning one's own home.[14] The affirmative action programs of the 1960s and beyond began to offer some redress of the gaps in education, employment, and wealth in America. It moved beyond the notion of equality toward equity. The following pictorial metaphor helped me understand equality, equity, and liberation.

Figure 2. Merely giving a box to each boy does treats the kids equally, but more is needed to solve the smallest boy's problem, and the tallest boy does not need the box in the first place. However, while giving the shortest boy the tallest boy's crate allows everyone to see the game, the boxes do not eliminate the barrier. When we remove the fence, there is no need for the boxes at all.[15]

I wanted this for my family: removing obstacles that would prevent us from escaping poverty and all its accompanying trauma. The state police job gave me a path out of poverty, and as high as I climbed in the ranks, I always remembered rummaging through garbage cans for empty bottles to cash in. I knew being a trooper would mean my children would not have to experience the trauma my mother, brother, and I did. For that, I am deeply grateful.[16]

Use of Terminology
The Language of Race and Its Origins

Words have meaning; meanings have words; you should say what you mean and mean what you say. As I stepped onto the path that I hoped would lead my family and me out of poverty, I began to reconsider the words used to describe the various ethnicities that made up what had been mistakenly called races. The terms I want to discuss here are labels for social constructs full of complexity, controversy, and tragedy. In the United States, the terms race, biracial, and multiracial describe people with parents of African, Afro-Caribbean, Latinx, Hispanic, American Indian, or Asian descent. The dominant European-American population sometimes uses terms like Irish-American or Polish-American to describe themselves ethnically. Still, until recently, there has only been one identifier for them in governmental and other forms: White. Whiteness is a social construct that has expanded over the years to include ethnic groups not considered White when they first arrived in the US.[17]

There is no genetic or other biological evidence for so-called racial differences. Yet, race artificially puts people into subgroups claimed to have defining characteristics (that is, they are assigned stereotypes, "scientifically," of course).[18] The racist pseudoscience eugenics seeks to delineate these differences and promote only the "best" genetic traits; Hitler called it "racial hygiene."[19] In actuality, individuals of different races often have more in common genetically than many members of the same "race."[20] Pointing out this socially constructed concept, I "am not downplaying the importance of "race." These social constructions have a real-world impact on your life, especially in the United States, where if you are not White, you will experience racial discrimination and may face racially motivated violence; if you are White, you have privileges not available to other races, freedom from racial discrimination and violence being first among them. Deeply entrenched in historical fact, labels like Black and White have no basis in scientific fact.[21]

One historical adherent to this pseudoscientific approach to race was also one of our founding fathers, Thomas Jefferson. Jefferson had quite a bit more to say about African Americans: "Blacks are in reason much inferior...and in imagination they are dull, tasteless, and anomalous...never yet could I find that a black had uttered a thought above the level of plain narration." Jefferson ended his thought with a slight equivocation: "The opinion, that they are inferior in the faculties of reason and imagination, must be hazarded with great diffidence." So, Jefferson acknowledged that he might be wrong, but ever dedicated to reason, imagined that racial difference was a suitable subject for scientific investigation.[22]

Jefferson's complex and conflicted views reflected America's complicated and torturous relationships with slavery and the conceptions of race used to justify it. Jefferson's hypocritical view of slavery is clear in a case he accepted early in his career as a Virginia lawyer. Defending a man born into slavery, Jefferson said, "Under the law of nature, all men are born free, everyone comes into the world with a right to his own person."[23]

Jefferson also immunized some of his enslaved workers to protect them from smallpox.[24] This was a business decision, however, not a humanitarian gesture. In another move that seems on the surface like a kindness, Jefferson released from slavery some of the children he sired after raping Sally Hemings multiple times, a woman he enslaved. According to some historians, though, this was a quid pro quo in return for her "consenting" to be his enslaved sex partner.[25] How could she have given uncoerced consent, she was forced into slavery? Jefferson did not grant freedom to members of the other families he enslaved, and he did not free Sally Hemings. Thomas Jefferson's daughter, Martha Jefferson Randolph, freed Sally Hemings not long after Jefferson died in 1826.[26]

Of the nine presidents who enslaved people, George Washington was the only one who wrote in his will that upon his death, his heirs should release the people he held in slavery. Tragically, that was not what happened. Many remained enslaved.[27] Jefferson, at the urging of Thomas Paine, included anti-slavery language in the original draft of the Declaration of Independence.[28] He laid the blame for slavery on King George III, writing, "He has waged cruel war against human nature itself, violating its most sacred rights of life and liberty in the persons of a distant people who never offended him, captivating and carrying them into slavery in another hemisphere or to incur miserable death in their transportation thither." Yet, in the end, Jefferson had to remove the anti-slavery language because New York and Rhode Island were the major financiers of the slave trade in the colonies, and the Southern colonies would also vigorously object to such language because their agricultural model would fail without the free labor of enslaved people. He understood that the economy, including his wealth, was bolstered by enslaved labor.[29]

In 1801, ironically as the newly elected president, Jefferson ordered the US Navy and Marine expedition to North Africa to free people of European descent enslaved by Barbary pirates, memorialized in the Marine Corp hymn, "…To the shores of Tripoli…" Regrettably, he was unwilling to use the power of his presidency to do the same for people of African descent enslaved here.[30] Jefferson's inconsistent support of liberty and democracy around the world revealed his views of who was worthy of freedom. In the 1790s, Jefferson championed the French Revolution. Still, he feared the Haitian Revolution might encourage a similar revolt among enslaved people in the newly formed United States.[31] Jefferson then leveraged the near bankruptcy of Napoleon's government in the wake of the successful Haitian Revolution by buying the Louisiana Territory from the French. This land grab nearly doubled the size of the United States and secured its trade routes, but once again, Jefferson missed an abolitionist opportunity. He tried to set aside regions in the newly purchased territory where slavery would be illegal, but his efforts failed.[32]

This devastating dual standard of freedom and who is entitled to it has poisoned America's body politic ever since. The United States continues to pay with its soul for the Faustian bargain of slavery. As a nation, we are ready to break this contract. Fueling America's current moral reawakening: Me Too,[33] Black Lives Matter,[34] and Native

Lives Matter,[35] three powerful movements focused on ending centuries of systemic sexism, racism, and other intersectional forms of discrimination. Native Lives Matter gets less media attention than the other two movements, but by some measures, police shoot Native Americans more often than any other group.[36] The same CNN article reported:

> "For every 1 million Native Americans, an average of 2.9 of them died annually from 1999 to 2015 as a result of a "legal intervention," according to a CNN review of CDC data broken down by race. The vast majority of these deaths were police shootings."[37]

Still, and tragically, African American males are still at the top of the list of those most likely to be shot and killed by police, according to numerous studies.[38] There are some social justice efforts are trying to bring lasting law reforms in many arenas, including the law enforcement community.

Stephen L. Carter said in his book Reflections of an Affirmative Action Baby, "My comments are about people, not colors."[39] But, our complexions are an essential driver of the discrimination, often within a given racial group where lighter skin is often valued, and thus, we must address colorism as well.[40]

American descendants of slavery (ADOS) are Black, and many people who are part of the African diaspora are also considered Black. Still, each group had vastly different experiences in the Americas. Sometimes, the complexity of our lived experience as people of Color in the Americas can seem overwhelming.[41] Some of us create new ways to self-identify, express these different experiences, and hold on to our uniqueness.[42] Many people considered part of the Latinx community identify as White. While many are more accurately members of this hemisphere's Indigenous population, a large segment of this population is also part of the African diaspora.[43]

I understand some concerns about the labels people of Color and person of Color. They can conceal the individualized and specific trauma different ethnicities have suffered.[44] The phrase Black, Indigenous, and People of Color (BIPOC) has come into favor recently as the most inclusive label.[45] Still, despite this, I use the phrase people of Color a lot because, as a teenager, I heard and periodically reread Reverend Martin Luther King's "I Have a Dream" speech, in which he used the phrase citizens of Color.[46] It called to me directly; I was a "citizen of Color" as a Nuyorican.

The individualized racial labels applied to people of Color have undergone several changes over the centuries, and I generally prefer to use the term individuals use to describe themselves. Latino, Hispanic, and, more recently, the gender neutral Latinx have generated controversy. I use the terms interchangeably. Latinx is considered by some to be more inclusive since Spanish uses the gender-specific word Latino for boys and men and Latina for girls and women, leaving no room for those who don't identify as either of those genders. However, many members of the Hispanic community do not use this term.[47]

The United States Department of Justice and the New York State Police use the term minority to describe people they have discriminated against: Black, Indigenous, people of Color, women of all races and ethnicities, and members of the LGBTQ community. Like all the other labels for race and ethnicity, the term minority is fraught with condescension, oppression, and pain. Applying the term minority expresses and reinforces the dominant group's belief system. It creates in some groups a false sense of inferiority and gives the group in the majority a corresponding illusion of superiority. It damages both groups.[48] I am not less than any other human being, even though being called "a minority" might make me feel that way. The term makes some sense if we are talking about numbers in aggregate, but the term minority has devolved into a racialized phrase used to describe any non-White individual. Since childhood, I have been referred to as "a minority" by White teachers, social workers, and others. Their words and actions told me they saw me as less important and less valued than the White children in the class. I struggled for years to cleanse myself of the trauma it caused, and that struggle continued in nearly every endeavor I pursued. Today, I have come to a stage where I no longer feel less than others, but the scars on my psyche and soul where the concept that I was "a minority" was drilled in are still there. Moreover, according to the US Census Bureau, soon, no group of US residents will form an ethnic or racial majority.[49]

When referring to the Indigenous people living in New York State, I have used the terms Native American, American Indian, and Indian interchangeably when necessary but prefer to refer to specific groups by their name: Mohawk, Oneida, Onondaga, Cayuga, Seneca, and Tuscarora nations. When writing about these nations as a group, I use their endonym, Haudenosaunee, meaning "the people of the Longhouse."[50] I recognize that Christopher Columbus mistakenly used the term Indian to name the Arawakan-speaking Taíno people he met on his Atlantic voyage.[51] Columbus thought he had arrived in India; instead, he had landed on one of the islands of the Lucayan archipelago near Bahama in the Caribbean.

In 1993, I took part in the FBI National Academy's 173rd session and found that the FBI also used the minority label for people of Color. I was amused and saddened by my academy cohort leader's superficial attempts at inclusiveness and diversity. There were officers from large and small police departments, rural and urban communities, officers from around the world, and officers from seemingly every ethnicity in the US. The special agent in charge said he and the FBI agent counselors took pride in including minorities in their training sessions. I knew, however, that this wasn't true of the whole organization. I was amused and disappointed because I knew some African American and Latino special agents. They told me they understood the racism I faced in the state police culture because they were experiencing a similar culture of discrimination in the FBI.[52] Less than thirty years earlier, the FBI under J. Edgar Hoover investigated, surveilled, and infiltrated Martin Luther King's organization, the Southern Christian Leadership Conference. They sought to dig up information that could destroy Dr. King and the Civil Rights Movement. The FBI even anonymously sent what is now known as "the suicide letter" to Dr. King's wife, Coretta, revealing King's many affairs and strongly suggesting King kill himself. The letter concludes:

> "There is only one thing left for you to do. You know what it is. You have just 34 days in which to do [sic] (this exact number has been selected for a specific reason, it has definite practical significant [sic]. You are done. There is but one way out for you. You better take it before your filthy, abnormal fraudulent self is bared to the nation."[53]

For me, the FBI's continued use of racialized terms and their attempts to sabotage the Civil Rights Movement tarnished the unique opportunity the FBI National Academy presented. The FBI's culture suffered from the same structural racism the state police engaged in, and that Judge Foley forced them to eliminate; however, glacially, it was a process I was determined to speed up as soon as I could.[54]

What is the nature of position and privilege? Why do we discriminate against "other" people who are different from us, whether that difference is class, caste, or race? Class is mutable; with considerable effort and some luck, you can move up in class. Caste and race are paradigms that are nearly impossible to change, and race especially so given America's "one drop" rule first codified in Virginia in 1662. This law held that if you had any Black ancestry, however far back in your gene pool went; you were Black.[55] Consider the six children of Thomas Jefferson and Sally Hemings. They grew up enslaved because of that 1662 Virginia law.[56]

When do we acquire prejudice? Is racism inherent in our genes, or is it taught? Research shows that it is learned early in childhood and causes lasting emotional and psychological damage. A test to show the impact of prejudice was developed in the 1940s by psychologists Kenneth and Mamie Clark. The "doll tests" studied the psychological effects of segregation on African American children. These psychologists used four dolls in pairs that were identical except in color. In each pair, one was White and the other Black to test children's racial perceptions. The test also showed how racism, colorism, and self-worth were intertwined. The psychologists asked the children which doll was "good" and which doll was "bad." The African American children often saw the White doll as the "good" doll and rejected the Black one.[57] Another study conducted by Professor Kang Lee of the University of Toronto, Canada, determined racial bias may arise in children as young as six to nine months of age. Lee states:

> "Implicit racial biases tend to be subconscious, pernicious, and insidious…it permeates almost all of our social interactions, from healthcare to commerce, employment, politics, and dating. Because of that, it's very important to study where these kinds of biases come from and use that information to try and prevent racial biases from developing. Can racial bias be unlearned? Lee suggests that exposing infants to people from other ethnicities, cultures, and socioeconomic classes is one way to correct this early in the culturalization of our children."[58]

Furthermore, we can face and possibly unlearn our biases when we recognize them arising in our relationships. We can engage in implicit bias training, enhance cultural competency, and ensure awareness of racism, misogyny, and colorism. These biases are especially dangerous in police culture, given the power we have granted police, and calls for reform have been made for decades. Most recently, legitimate and peaceful protests for police reforms have included calls for greater diversity among police forces. However, increasing the diversity of law enforcement officers to better reflect the community is not enough. It will not in and of itself create more significant equity and justice for the community a police agency serves if these officers' opinions, cultures, and experiences are not seriously considered and incorporated into the agency's culture and policing practices. Suppose they have instead accepted the racist culture of policing in America. In that case, police officers of Color will continue to kill unarmed people of Color, as we saw in the case of Tyre

Nichols. A Black man was beaten to death by five Black Memphis police officers, which resulted in a murder charge. The Black Lives Matter and Me-Too movements awakened the world to the urgent need for structural and systemic reforms to eliminate racism and sexism from our institutions.

Diversity is one of many reforms needed to create policies and practices that foster fairness and justice as law enforcement agencies patrol our streets. Intelligent recruitment strategies, complete background checks, psychological and integrity tests, implicit bias training, and de-escalation training are some of the other changes that will help refocus criminal justice priorities.

Henceforth, I will capitalize the following words despite capitalization conventions in this treatise.[59] Notwithstanding these terms, racialized individuals or groups Black, White, Color, and other similar racialized words to describe the ethnicity of individuals or groups of individuals is the accepted lexicon.[60]

The New York State Police uses several titles: New York State Troopers, Troopers, the Division of State Police, or the Division. I will use these terms interchangeably. It also uses the term Field to describe its statewide patrol areas.[61]

Regrettably, I experienced being called offensive racial slurs. Sadly, I will use them not to offend but as they occurred in my life.

Chapter 1 - My Daughter's Eyes

My heart pounded as I held my newborn daughter on my forearm and saw her look at me with a beautiful, toothless smile. But while her smile filled me with joy, it nearly paralyzed me with fear. Could I support my young family and get us out of poverty? It was 1980, and autumn was just beginning. I stared intensely into her smiling brown eyes in our Brooklyn apartment and worried about the future. As I gazed at her, the fear turned into determination and a joyful urgency. I would put all my energy into creating a good life for her and my growing family. I would move us out of poverty and into a life filled with opportunities for her and my unborn son, still nestled in his mother's womb.

I did not want my daughter to feel about me the way I felt about my father, who had not been a part of my life when I was a child. My father was a proud yet troubled Afro-Taíno Puerto Rican who was abusive and who struggled with alcoholism. His deep anger, which grew from years of discrimination and poverty, led to domestic violence. Eventually, he abandoned my mother, my brother, and me, a decision that left us in dire poverty. At the end of each month, my mother had only enough money to feed us white rice with ketchup. Those terrible days filled her with despair. I knew she went hungry, so my brother and I could eat. I remember walking to a building in our low-income housing project to pick up cartons of powdered milk and bricks of government cheese.[62] This food subsidy, supplied by the U.S. Department of Agriculture, was the predecessor of the Supplemental Nutrition Assistance Program (SNAP). It is one of my favorite memories of those difficult days. Biting into the hot, gooey grilled cheese sandwiches, they were filling and delicious. Or at least that is what I told myself.

I remember wanting to help my mother as a boy by not asking for money or complaining about hunger. My mother did not have enough money for all our needs and certainly not for any of the frivolous things I wanted to do, like go to the local Winston Theater

1

to see a double feature and a cartoon with my brother. On Saturday mornings in the early 1960s, between the ages of eight and twelve, I walked around our neighborhood with my mother's shopping cart, rummaging through garbage cans for empty glass bottles. One Saturday, I was so hungry I ate half a packet of chocolate cake I found in the trash. Fortunately, I did not get sick. I took the bottles I found to the supermarket on Grand Street for the deposit refund, two or three cents depending on the bottle's size. Then, I would stand outside the store and ask folks if they needed help carrying their groceries home. Usually, older White women would accept my offer and give me a nickel or two for helping them. After several trips, I had enough to enjoy taking my younger brother to the movies.

I promised myself I would not pass this trauma on to my children. I swore I would never leave my kids. No matter how difficult, I would be there for them into adulthood. Today, I understand that my father's desertion caused significant emotional damage to me, my brother, and my mother. I would break the cycle of our family history of violence and abandonment; my father's father had treated him abusively, causing my father emotional trauma, which he passed on to my brother and me. This sad birthright would stop with me. Gazing into my daughter's eyes, I made that vow.

Figure 3. My daughter, son, and their abuelo are playing on the beach on the Island of Borinquén.[63]

Later, in a psychology course at LaGuardia Community College, I read about Erik Erikson's work on the epigenetic principle. It reinforced my intuitive understanding of emotional inheritance and its potentially harmful effect on families generationally.[64] When my kids were a little older, I reached out to my father and had a frank and highly charged discussion about our failed relationship. I told him I wanted him to have a chance to be a better abuelo (grandfather) than he was a father. He said he would try, and he succeeded. My children remember him as a loving grandfather with mischievous humor. We traveled together to the island of Boriquén (the Taíno name for Puerto Rico) to visit our extended family so that my children could learn about their heritage. During that trip, while we were all at the beach, my father pretended to be the creature from the Black Lagoon. He walked out of the Caribbean covered in seaweed and howling, scaring the kids at first before their fear turned into cackles of delight.

My father may have been in and out of my life, but I am also the son of a diminutive Puerto Rican woman who arrived in this country at fourteen, not having completed high school or being able to speak English. By the time she was seventeen, she was the mother of two boys. Soon after turning nineteen, she divorced my father. His behavior had been terrible, and he abandoned us often. One afternoon, when I was around three years old, he had left my younger brother and me alone. I opened the apartment door and played with the other children in the hallway. It was locked when I pulled on the apartment door to get back inside. The neighbor's kids took me into their apartment and left a note on my door. My father returned drunk and went into a rage when he found out I was not in the apartment. He went to the neighbor's apartment, banged on the door, and dragged me back home. Once we were inside, he began beating me with a garrison belt. I only remember the first few blows and him screaming. The next day, my mother took me to her aunt's house and had me stand on the toilet so she could show her aunt all the welts and bruises on my little body. These swollen welts hurt, yet I was distracted by the glass bowl full of beautiful marbles in the bathroom, and I paid no attention to my aunt and mother except when they started to apply salve to prevent scarring. I remember my mother saying she was leaving him. When it happened, I cried. For several years after that, whenever I thought he was coming to see my brother and me, I sat at the window of the sixth-floor apartment waiting, and I would cry when he did not show up. Eventually, I stopped waiting and crying.

My mother was determined to get beyond the circumstances where she found herself. Her mother died in Puerto Rico when she was only two, and because her father was at sea a lot as a merchant mariner, she couch-surfed from one relative to another, all of whom were poor. Her father remarried and sent for her when she was fourteen. She was excited, but when she arrived in Spanish Harlem, it became clear he only wanted her to care for her new half-siblings, which she resented.

Undaunted, she found success through arduous work, education, and self-sacrifice. She got her GED, her associate degree, and her bachelor's degree, all while raising my brother and me. She became a licensed practical nurse, then a registered nurse, and later a nursing administrator in a prominent New York City hospital after earning a master's degree. I was incredibly proud of my mother and have tried to emulate her refusal to let others determine what her life would be. She was a feminist before that word was fashionable and instilled in me a feminist fervor. She died from COVID-19 in November 2020. Like other US nursing homes during the height of the pandemic, my mother's facility did not allow in-person family visits. I said my final goodbye to her via a Zoom call; she took her last breaths as I watched with tears streaming.

Despite how proud I am of my mother, we all paid the price as she strove to improve our station in life. She worked long hours, usually at multiple jobs, and went to school at night. This meant my brother and I were "latchkey kids" from an early age. I had no choice but to care for my little brother, mainly while we were in grade school. I learned to cook, wash and mend clothes, and do many other things to help my mother. Because we were poor and lived in one of the most impoverished areas of New York City, there weren't many resources we could access to improve our circumstances. In addition to redeeming bottles and carrying groceries, I kept a constant eye on the gutter while walking around the city, hoping to find spare change. I jabbed a finger into the coin return slot of every pay phone and vending machine I passed to see if any coins were there. This habit stuck with me, and I kept doing it even when I was old enough to get part-time jobs during the summer. The family always needed more money at the end of the month.

I spent a lot of time on the streets unsupervised, including commuting to Haaren High School, six miles away in Midtown. In middle school, a social worker had labeled me "incorrigible" because I was bored and got into mischief to entertain myself. Haaren High School had a unique program for gifted children identified as incorrigible. I had to ride a bus and then a train to get there. When I attended this former vocational high school, it had become an all-boys school. With the Urban Coalition's help, Haaren began using smaller class sizes with more personalized instruction, in line with the 1970s trend toward modernizing public education.[65] I was part of the so-called College Bound program, but the school was rife with violence. At the start of each school year, I had to prove myself by fighting. And it wasn't just at school. I had to defend myself against all the dangers found in communities like the one I grew up in because of bullies, child predators, gangs, and sometimes cops. Fortunately, I was fast on my feet and started learning Karate around age eight. Karate saved my life, literally and figuratively.

I first discovered Karate when I was very young before I started kindergarten. My mother and her friend were going for a girls' night out, and my younger brother and I were to sleep over with the friend's children, who were also young. My mother jokingly told me I was in charge and should watch my brother and the other woman's kids. She would often tell me that I was the man of the house. This admonition meant nothing to me when I was five years old, but as I got older, I began to resent it because the responsibility it implied was overwhelming. They had placed us down to sleep that night, but I did not sleep. When they left, I got up and found a book on the bookshelf with incredible photos of a man fighting a bull using only his hands and feet. I could not read it, but the pictures transfixed me. I finally fell asleep with the book open across my chest.

In the morning, my mother's friend said, "How much should I pay you for babysitting?"

"No thanks," I said.

She said, "Okay, what do you want?"

I told her I wanted the Karate book. She said I could have that book along with all the rest of her ex-husband's books, but I only wanted the Karate book.

I learned years later that the book was "What Is Karate?" It was Masutatsu Oyama's first book. "Mas" Oyama was a skilled martial artist whose story of resiliency as a Korean raised in Japan inspired me, given Japan's turbulent and oppressive relationship with Korea.[66] I have the book to this day. The book made me eager to learn Karate, but my mother could not afford the training fees. She finally found a brown belt at a YMCA in Brooklyn who would teach me for $5 a month. I kept up my training throughout my childhood and teen years, eventually earning a black belt and began teaching. The American Shotokan Dojo on Grand Street was a storefront converted into a martial arts gym headed at the time by Sensei Hector Martinez. It had an open loft but no shower. I used to sleep there sometimes in my late teens and early twenties when I became homeless because I couldn't afford an apartment.

Those periods of homelessness ended when I found a steady job working at a butcher shop in the Essex Street market, six days a week, ten hours a day. It was hard work. I knew I needed another line of work. My experience teaching Karate could help me become a schoolteacher. With this goal in mind, I enrolled at La Guardia Community College and earned an associate degree in human services with a concentration in child development. One of my courses included an internship at a local daycare center that allowed me to apply what I had learned. I played with the toddlers, helping them satisfy their curiosity and gain a love for learning. After this internship, and having taught Karate for several years, I knew I enjoyed teaching and wanted to pursue it as a career.

I wanted to earn a bachelor's in early childhood education through a federal program that offered jobs and tuition waivers. However, the newly elected president, Ronald Reagan, was a fiscal conservative opposed to "big government." Unfortunately, reducing the "size" of the government meant cuts to consumer and environmental protections and public education at all levels. Many of us looked away as the Cold War military budget grew.[67] Among the many changes it brought, Reagan's election meant the end of the program I sought to be a part of and would have placed me in a teaching job. Instead, I continued my back-breaking work as a non-union butcher.

Spurred on by the needs of my growing family, I redirected my ambition toward finding a job that paid a sustainable income, obtaining medical benefits, and having opportunities to pursue a career. Upon learning Pamela and I would have another child, I asked my boss for a raise to help pay for health insurance. Because I was a hard worker, he reluctantly granted the increase. I was very appreciative, but I knew it might not last. The boss periodically laid workers off for vague reasons. He even fired me once for arguing with his son, who occasionally worked at the butcher shop as a laborer but acted like he was in charge because his father owned the shop. On the day of the argument, he ordered the workers to change how we did our work and started yelling at us. Some workers did not speak English well and couldn't understand what he was saying. When I told him his new system went against what his father had taught us to do, he got in my face and yelled, "When my father is not here, I'm the fucking boss!"

"I work for your father, not you. Go fuck yourself!" It was not a smart move on my part, even if I was right. While it felt good at the moment, I got fired the next day. I returned to the shop a few days later and asked for my job back. I got it but knew I had to find a more stable career.

I had always been passionate about Afro-Caribbean music, and I began supplementing my modest income as a percussionist for Afro-Caribbean folk dance troupes. I also taught Karate at the Pitts Street Boys Club and started a Karate dojo. But none of these jobs offered health insurance, opportunities for advancement, or a retirement plan. I was determined to find a way out of poverty. I searched for a job that would be my passage into the life I wanted for my family. I bought the Chief Leader, a local paper, from the newsstand at the corner of Essex and Delancey and scoured the job postings for career opportunities.[68] I applied for every government job but one. I would not work for the New York City Police Department because of the way some of its officers mistreated people of Color and people experiencing poverty, mistreatment I had experienced firsthand. I could not see myself serving in the NYPD.

While on the job search, my sister-in-law showed me a job posting that showed men in broad-brimmed hats that reminded me of Smokey the Bear. I had lived in low-income housing projects on the Lower East Side of Manhattan or Loisaida, as activist and poet Bimbo Rivas Latinized it in 1974. I had never even seen the New York State Park Rangers, I assumed, donned those hats. But I completed the application anyway with little understanding of how it would change my life and family. To my surprise, the application was not for the park rangers but for the New York State Police, a very different organization with a complicated history and culture. At the time, I didn't know anything about this organization's history, so I laughed, thinking that if I got the job, I could chase Yogi Bear and Boo Boo when they stole picnic baskets after all.

The laughter hid my doubt about whether this was the right move. I had never seen a trooper and knew nothing about the agency. Still at this point, I felt desperate to make a career move, so I steeled myself for what my life would be like if the police hired me. I did not know whether the state police were as racist in their policies as I knew the NYPD was, but if they were, I told myself I would find ways to deal with that. I would also have to pass their written exam and a battery of physical tests before I entered the six-month training academy far away from my family's home in New York City. My heart raced. I laughed it off again and thought that at least chasing bad guys would be more exciting than chasing Yogi and Boo Boo.

Chapter 2 - Leap of Faith

When I applied to the NYSP, I stepped off the edge of the world known to me. I did not have a map. Still, I trusted my sense of direction and leaped in the only open direction. I hoped the chance I was taking would lift my family into a better life, fulfilling my promise to them and myself.

The fact that I saw the state police job posting in the first place was an indirect result of Chief Judge James T. Foley's 1979 decision in the case of United States v. State of New York No. 77-CV-343. The outcome of that early affirmative action case ordered the New York State Police to hire men of Color and women of any ethnicity. The state police began recruiting aggressively in New York City and the other major cities of New York to obey the mandate. Their job postings appeared in NYC's Chief Leader and other urban publications across the state because most people of Color in New York State lived in urban areas.[69]

The next available entrance exam was in June 1981 at City College of New York (CCNY) in Harlem. I am unsure whether knowing about Judge Foley's decision would have changed my decision to join the state police. My growing family and my dream of making my children proud of me would probably have overcome any misgivings I would have had. The starting salary was less than I was bringing home, working multiple jobs. Regardless, the benefits, potential salary increases, and promotional opportunities represented a path out of poverty. Also, I was young and idealistic about social justice. I thought that if the state police were like the NYPD, I could be an agent of change. And while New York City cops had harassed me more than once, I had never experienced bigotry at the hands of the NYSP. I had never even seen a trooper until I took the entrance exam. That changed upon meeting my very first trooper. As I arrived at the examination site, I asked where I was to go within the college building. The officer pointed to the entrance and said gruffly, "Follow the others." As I turned to walk away, I heard him respond

9

patiently to the same question from a White man and woman. "Go through the doors, turn left, and you'll see another trooper who will direct you from there."

I may not have known about Foley's decision or the NYSP's history of discrimination when I arrived at CCNY. Yet, I sensed that bigotry was deeply seated in some of this agency's members. Some troopers were visibly uncomfortable to be in Harlem around so many people of Color, and their disdain for the men of Color and the women who were there to take the examination was palpable. An overweight staff sergeant barked orders at the applicants filing into the gymnasium. He stood at the entrance, playing with the bullets on his belt, looking like he would prefer to shoot us than help us find our seats. Like the first trooper I'd met, he was polite only to the White applicants and responded rudely to any person of Color who asked for directions. The NYSP's racist attitudes ran more profound. I noticed that increasingly once I entered the police academy. Judge Foley may have ruled that the NYSP needed to be more inclusive, but I quickly realized some organization members deeply resented the judge's decree. Many troopers did not accept Judge Foley's assertion that women, African Americans, Latinx people, and other members of marginalized groups deserved our **"turn in the sun."**[70]

Part of Judge Foley's ruling included revising the police academy entrance exam because the earlier exam was an obstacle to diversity.[71] He instructed the state police to formulate another test, writing that the NYSP needed to overhaul the hiring process. While my recruit class was not the first class hired under the new mandate, it was the first class that used the revised entrance exam. Because we had taken the new exam, some senior troopers said the women and people of Color in my class were only there because Judge Foley made the NYSP lower their standards, which he did not.

As I began my journey in policing, I braced myself for what was to come because of my own experiences with the New York City police. I had seen NYPD officers be disrespectful and sometimes brutally violent toward people in my community. My gut told me the police were the cause of the hostility they faced when they interacted with communities of Color in America. I began researching issues in policing to understand better what lay ahead of me. I was determined to stay in the state police and change it from within. I explored how some police systematically keep "law and order" in such a way as to maintain racial and economic divides, often most harshly affecting communities of Color and communities with high rates of poverty. I began to understand that the police enforce local legislation and social norms, even when the laws and norms are unjust. Both discriminatory legislation and the inequitable enforcement of just laws were common throughout the nation's history. Growing up in a poor community mainly made up of people of Color, I experienced unfair enforcement firsthand.[72]

In the summer of 1965, I was 13 years old. I walked with a friend to Kozy Korners, a candy store on the Lower East Side at Madison and Grand Streets. Grand Street was the dividing line between poverty and affluence in that neighborhood. On the north side of Grand were expensive co-ops populated exclusively, as far as I could tell, by White tenants. On the south side of Grand was the low-income housing project where I lived. My friend and I were crossing the street when a driver screamed from his car window, "Niggers, get off the street!"

I already knew I was "other;" neither society nor my family would let me forget it. To my mother's light-skinned family, I was "café con leche," coffee with milk, while to my father's bronze-hued Afro-Taíno family, I was "leche con café," milk with coffee. I rejected the colorism underlying these descriptions and proclaimed my humanity. In discussions with my young friends, I would describe myself as a human being, not by race or color.

Figure 4. Pedro Perez, my father, is on the far left. He
is seated with his brothers Junior Perez, Carmelo Perez,
Angel Perez, and Willie Perez (standing).[73]

Moreover, although school during those early days reinforced
that notion of otherness, I had not understood it as racism per se.

Some of the kids in my school called me "spic," which sometimes ended in fistfights. And I was aware that the teachers viewed
me not as an American but as an outsider because of my Puerto
Rican heritage. I remember telling my mother how I was treated. She
would say, "Oye hijo, ignore them; you're an American." But every
day at school, on the street, and in the movies, the message was that
I was not.

The incident on Grand St. burned into my consciousness the
reality of otherness—especially discrimination based on ethnicity,
skin color, and class. Since then, I have fought internally to rid myself
of this disease and externally to fight against the injustices carried out
personally and systemically by others who have contracted it. Was I
too, serving a life sentence, as Carl Douglass Upchurch so eloquently
describes it in his book Convicted in the Womb, because of poverty
and who my parents were? Before I drew my first breath, America
had defined me as unworthy of the American Dream.

A politically racist cartoon from Puck magazine, published January 25, 1899, captures the mindset of American imperialists.[74]

This political cartoon shows how the United States viewed, and still views, the people of the Islands of the Philippines, Hawaii, and "Porto Rico," [sic Puerto Rico], and Cuba. The Puck magazine cartoonist drew the images of the people from these colonized nations in an insultingly infantile, dark-skinned, frightened, and vile manner. Uncle Sam is standing over these images with a menacing expression. The colonialist mindset views the people of these islands as less than human and in need of "care" and oversight because they were considered incapable of caring for themselves. I felt the disdain, sense of superiority, and dehumanizing attitude shown in the cartoon from the first day I entered public school by some of my teachers and guidance counselors. This attitude among the dominant class created a perverse desire to live up to the standards the colonialists said we would never reach. I shared the same pain of trying to be a "good enough American" my father must have struggled with as we tried to gain a foothold in the United States.

The reality was that we would never be considered fully American by everyone, but my father and I managed that reality in different ways. He tried to live up to what the dominant culture considered acceptable, even allowing himself to be called Peter instead of Pedro. I refused to let that happen and would correct anyone who called me Peter. After we reconciled, my father said part of his anger was that no matter what he did, White people still treated him as less than worthy, so he drank alcohol to deal with all his pain. I told him I accepted that many White people would not consider me a "true" American, but because I knew I was one, I fought for equity at every opportunity.

I understood and experienced Evelyn Brooks Higginbotham's notion of "the politics of respectability" from her book Righteous Discontent: The Women's Movement in the Black Baptist Church, 1880–1920.[75] I heard this in my mother's hopeful reassurance that I was just as much an American as the White kids who called me a spic.[76] Yet I rejected the charge that being educated and adhering to high professional standards meant one was trying to deny their heritage and culture. Racism is as real as it has ever been, and colonialist attitudes and respectability politics. They are encouraged and expressed by politicians today. Consider the former president's question, "Why do we want all these people from shithole countries coming here?"[77] Hearing that took me right back to Grand Street.

On April 5, 1968, we had seen the horrific news about Dr. Martin Luther King Jr.'s assassination the night before. We walked out of school chanting "bang, bang, beep, beep, ungawa, Black power," marching from Fifty-Ninth Street and Tenth Avenue to Central Park. This protest chant used the tune of the Joe Cuba Latin Boogaloo hit "Bang Bang."[78] My fellow Haaren High School students and I wondered how do we change the world. Sadly, our screams and tears changed little. I became determined to learn more and do more. I was a teenager and easily distracted, yet the memory of that moment never left me. I was thinking of it a couple of years later when I boarded an Amtrak train bound for Philadelphia to hear Huey P. Newton speak at Temple University's McGonigle Hall. Newton, the co-founder of the Black Panther Party, struck me as brilliant and courageous.[79] His insightful message that day was like the following passage from his memoir Revolutionary Suicide is as valid today as it was then:

> "The democratic capitalism of our early days became caught up in a relentless drive to obtain profits until the selfish motivation for profit eclipsed the unselfish principles of democracy. Thus 200 years later we have an overdeveloped economy which is so infused with the need for profit that we have replaced democratic capitalism with bureaucratic capitalism. The free opportunity of all men to pursue their economic ends has been replaced by constraints (confinement) placed upon Americans by the large corporations which control and direct our economy. They have sought to increase their profits at the expense of

the people, and particularly at the expense of the racial and ethnic minorities…

Generation after generation of Black people in America have been born, they have worked, and they have seen the fruits of their labors in the life, liberty, and happiness of the children and grandchildren of their oppressors, while their own descendants wallow in the mire of poverty and deprivation, holding only to the hope of change in the future. This hope has sustained us for many years and has led us to suffer the administrations of a corrupt government."[80]

Huey P. Newton raised his clenched fist behind the podium as he spoke that Saturday, September 5, 1970. Security guards of the Party surround him. About 6,000 people attended, with another thousand outside the crowded hall.[81] Newton and other Black Panthers spoke about revolution, feeding hungry children, and other activities designed to help the Black community in Oakland, California. I listened intently and considered joining the New York Chapter of the Black Panthers or their Puerto Rican counterpart, the Young Lords.[82] I bought Elaine Brown's record album "Seize the Time," an album of songs and poems whose proceeds Brown returned to the Black Panther Party. I memorized nearly every cut on that record. I was seventeen years old and had graduated high school a few months earlier.[83] I was young, naive, and idealistic about what it would take to effect the change I knew was needed to create a fair and just America. Ultimately, I went to rallies and protests but never joined the Panthers or the Young Lords. I was more focused on girls, Karate, and playing my congas. Then, I married and became a father. Yet the desire to be a change agent for justice and equity was never far from my heart. I decided change could only happen if I educated myself, my family, and others about the history of racism and valiant resistance in this country.

Now, fifty years later, people are still rising to protest racism and oppression. Two powerful movements, MeToo, and Black Lives

Matter, are focused on countering the intersecting forces of misogyny and racism. I pray my grandchild does not have to continue the struggle fifty years from now. We must act with Dr. King's admonition to end the oppression with, "the fierce urgency of now."[84] We can ensure our grandchildren's children live in a just and inclusive country. We can strengthen voters' rights so all citizens can vote and know their votes will count. We can enact legislation that supplies universal healthcare and childcare. We can codify the right to bodily autonomy. We can impose term limits on Supreme Court justices and federal judges serving for life.[85] We can reform the criminal legal system. We can teach US history in a way that includes the contributions of everyone who has lived here.[86] We can cut so-called benefits cliffs. The cliff effect occurs when working low-income families eligible for programs like Medicaid, the Earned Income Tax Credit, SNAP, Temporary Assistance to Needy Families, and subsidized public housing make one dollar more in their hourly wage, which can significantly reduce benefits. The tragic outcome is that the added dollars will not compensate for the loss of food stamps, childcare, or other benefits designed to help people in poverty or near poverty.[87] These efforts will make the United States fairer, healthier, and more financially beneficial. It takes more than a belief that America can live up to its promise; we must act to ensure it does.

Chapter 3 - Affirmative Action Trooper

While studying to become an early childhood educator, it took me longer than some of my peers to complete the first phase. I became homeless when I was fifteen and couch-surfed for a few years because I had no safe place to live. Despite this, I graduated high school in 1970 with a Regents' diploma. My lack of income and housing insta-bility delayed my college education. Eventually, I did attend, and in 1980, I graduated with an associate degree. While working on that degree, I married, became a father, and worked in a butcher shop. While the job at the butcher's helped pay for my tuition, it was not something I could depend on, nor was it a career I wanted to pursue long-term. I felt sure that my dream of affording a decent life for my children would die if I stayed.

I began taking civil service entrance exams. I learned I passed the state police's written test in the summer of 1981. Then, one day, in early August, the butcher shop's phone rang as I cut steaks for a customer. The owner picked up the receiver and yelled that the police wanted to talk to me. I couldn't afford a phone for my home and had left the butcher shop's phone number as my contact number. The owner didn't know I was looking for another job and assumed I was in trouble with the police. I wiped my bloody hands, took the phone, and said, "This is Pedro Perez." The caller told me the second phase of the hiring process for the fall trooper recruit class would occur soon. Did I still want to be a trooper? The caller asked for an immediate decision, and I accepted the opportunity.

"Are you going to jail?" my boss asked when I hung up.

"No," I laughed. "I'm going to become a New York State Trooper."

"No fucking way," he said. "When?"

"In October," I said to him and the other workers. "If I pass the next test."

The lady I was serving before the call yelled that she was wait-ing, and I went back to cutting the steaks for her.

I had never been to Albany, New York. I drove to the police academy, not knowing what to expect. I had a wreck of a car, an eight-cylinder Gremlin hatchback with one hundred thousand miles on it that I had bought for $200, "The Death Trap," so dubbed by the recruits I ferried to and from the city to Albany. They quit riding with me that winter because of the Gremlin's defective heater. I have fond memories of that car, which lasted through the academy. The Gremlin finally quit working when I arrived at my first training station in Western New York.

The academy was on a sprawling campus with other state office buildings for different departments and agencies. It was next to the State University of New York at Albany (SUNY Albany), another large campus. I didn't know it then, but the road circling SUNY Albany would be the path we'd run on every morning, rain, snow, or shine. Sometime in late August or early September, I arrived at the State Police Academy for other examinations. The second phase of examinations included a medical exam, a few physical agility tests, and a set of interviews. The physical agility tests included running a mile and a half, pull-ups, push-ups, and sit-ups. I also had to lift a dumbbell over my head. The recruit's weight and gender determined the weight of the dumbbell used. I was in good shape and had no problems.

The interviews included a written integrity test that asked questions about my moral character, including highly personal matters. The integrity interview was understandable; they needed to evaluate my moral character and truthfulness in answering. Once I completed the test, a state police investigator interrogated me to decide whether I had been honest. They used my written answers and the interrogation transcript to conduct a background investigation of everything I claimed. They verified my places of employment and my academic credentials. They also asked my employers, coworkers, and neighbors what they thought of me; their investigation into my life to discover what I might be hiding from them. Yet I wondered whether it might also be a way to avoid implementing Judge Foley's edict by disqualifying women and people of Color. Years later, when I became a technical sergeant in the affirmative action office, I learned that some investigators were often less forgiving of irregularities in the backgrounds of men of Color than of similar issues in the backgrounds of White men.

Fortunately, I had no debt, criminal history, or other issues that would be of concern. My landlord mentioned that an investigator called and asked whether I had paid my rent, fought with my wife, or used drugs. Several of my fellow recruits of Color told me their friends did not get accepted because of their credit card debt, or because they had experimented with marijuana, or because they had moved several times. In passing, a few White recruits mentioned that they had similar histories, but there they were in the class of recruits. Years later, when I was the head of the Bureau of Criminal Investigation (BCI) and oversaw background investigations, I knew we would accept candidates who had experimented with cannabis, had minor credit card debt, or faced similar issues. We would consider the candidate holistically using the standards of recency and frequency when the dereliction occurred, how often it happened, and how long it lasted. I still doubt whether candidates of Color had this kind of holistic consideration when I was entering the academy.

Figure 5. The construction of the New York State
Police Academy was completed in 1970.[88]

This second phase of the hiring process was a two-day ordeal. Troopers barked orders at us, and I felt the same disdain emanating from some of the White officers that I had first sensed from the sergeant at CCNY. We completed a series of documents on the first day, including a questionnaire about your ethnicity. At the time, just like now, I celebrated my multiethnic heritage. I am a Nuyorican, Afro-Caribbean Taíno Indian with a Spanish surname, a Puerto Rican born and raised in New York. I did not use the term race to define myself other than to say I am part of the human race. Their application, in contrast, had a very narrow set of categories next to boxes one could check: White, African American, Hispanic, or Other. I checked Other.

When I handed in my documents, the officers at the table said that I could not use the category Other because my name made it clear that I was Spanish. I insisted that I was not from Spain and that my Spanish name was only one part of my identity. I explained I was a Native American (Taíno Indian) and part of the African diaspora. My explanations and refusal to change my answer to Hispanic annoyed and befuddled the investigator; he called his supervisor. The supervisor looked at me, instructed the investigator to put down Hispanic, and told me to move on. I considered arguing the point but chose to wait. I needed this job for my family; it gave me great benefits, a career path, and union protection, none of which I had at the butcher shop. I also thought that someday I would change this ridiculous process.

Judge Foley's affirmative action decree influenced many decisions throughout my career. When I first learned about it, I considered the current and incumbent troopers' reactions to my presence and pondered my future as a trooper. I weighed my response to the label "protected-class person" as defined by Foley's decree.[89] I realized it meant I needed protection from the discriminatory hiring practices of the state police because I was a man of Color. It also told me I might need protection from discriminatory disciplinary practices inside the organization. But how could Judge Foley's orders protect me from bigotry expressed to me personally by my fellow recruits, incumbent troopers, or the citizens I vowed to protect?

I assumed the poorly staffed affirmative action office dealt only with the most egregious violations. I would have to fend for myself in handling any bigots I met. I had already met racist troopers who did not want me to succeed, and it seemed the organization felt the same way but had to pretend it was making strides to be inclusive and welcoming. My response to this climate was to perform at such a high level that I could not reasonably be considered unfit to do the job.

As for the state police's treatment of citizens of Color, I would ensure that I, for one, perform equitably and justly. I would also hold my fellow troopers accountable. How the community would react to me as a trooper remained a mystery, although I suspected it would depend on their views of affirmative action and people of Color. I also worried about how joining the police would affect my relationships with my family and friends. My immediate family and some friends were proud of me, but I had other friends who believed I had lost my way and sold out.

Having completed the final phases of the New York State Police hiring process, I received the second call at the butcher shop in late September. The caller said I could attend the police academy in October and asked if I was still interested in joining the New York State Police. I replied yes. The caller instructed me to arrive at the academy on Sunday, October 18, 1981, to begin the six-month training. It gave me and my family three weeks to prepare for this new job.

One challenge my family faced was a significant pay cut. The annual salary of a recruit trooper in 1981 was $13,606. I was making about $15,000 a year, working six days a week, ten hours a day. I also made a small amount of money teaching Karate at the Pitt Street Boy's Club and taking drumming gigs. Taking the state police job was a financial risk in the short term, but the payoff seemed worth it. The salary I earned at the state police placed me only $3,744 above the poverty line, but it was well worth the cut in pay because my family now had guaranteed health insurance and other benefits. Also, I became a member of the Police Benevolent Association union, which meant my salary would go up eventually, and it did.

We gave up our apartment to ensure we had enough money for food and other necessities while I trained. We moved into my mother in-law's railroad apartment, a two-bedroom walkup in the tenement building on Essex Street. I had given the butcher shop's owner my notice, and to my surprise, he was genuinely happy for me. He had inherited the shop from his dad, and although he was not poor, he had seen what it was like to live in poverty. He knew the salary and benefits he could provide were insufficient to lift me or any other workers into the middle class. Not the way police work would if I succeeded. His reaction surprised me because he often treated his workers indifferently in our day-to-day interactions with him. He rarely showed concern for how we felt or what happened in our lives unless it affected our work. My coworkers were happy for me as well. They viewed the butcher shop as a dead-end job and expressed their hope that I would deliver more fairness and justice than the average police officer, particularly to people of Color.

As I said earlier, some friends expressed their disappointment and a sense of betrayal when they found out I was joining the state police. Like me, they had grown up in New York City during the Civil Rights Movement. They had experienced the racism of the NYPD and our fellow New Yorkers, mainly when we traveled through the wealthier parts of the city. My friends asked if I had compromised my principles. We had long debates about how to make things better and how to deal with the racism we experienced. One friend challenged my assertion that I could influence the way the police acted toward Black and Brown folks. He asked, "How are you, by yourself, going to make policing fairer?" I replied I would make it fairer by treating anyone I had to arrest the way I would want my mother treated under similar circumstances. That is treating people fairly, acknowledging their constitutional right to the perception of innocence, and protecting them from verbal or physical abuse when they were in my custody. This was the attitude I continued to have and share with fellow troopers, and later in my career, I would emphasize this when training and supervising troopers.

As a young man, I had read many Civil Rights Movement-era memoirs and novels, such as The Autobiography of Malcolm X,

Eldridge Cleaver's Soul on Ice, Ralph Ellison's Invisible Man, Piri Thomas's Down These Mean Streets, and others. My friends and I had spent long hours discussing the Civil Rights Movement and our responsibility to support it and carry its vision forward.

One of my closest friends, Tito, was the most critical of my decision to join the police. He said, "Have you completely lost your fucking mind? Why have you gone over to the other side?" These comments concerned me, yet what was most important to me was my family's well-being and the hope that once my daughter grew up, she could look at me with pride. Keep in mind also that at the time, I did not know about the state police's reputation as a racist organization, but once I realized they were not the park rangers, I assumed some of them would be as racist as some of the New York City police. But when I first applied, I did not fully understand who they were; all I knew was they offered medical insurance, a pension plan, and a career path.

I argued that not only was this best for my family but also that if the state police organization was as racist as other police departments, I believed I could effect change from within. If I acted equitably and justly when dealing with the communities I policed and the individuals I met in small ways, I could help move policing toward keeping the peace and achieving justice in society rather than rigidly enforcing "law and order." Was I overly idealistic? Or worse, foolish? I genuinely believed I could do what I proposed and still do the best for my family. I thought I could be a peace officer for social justice and that this was a more sustainable way to change the system than marching in the streets.

On October 18, 1981, I drove to the state police academy in Albany. All the way there, I kept wondering whether I had made the right decision. I entered the academy scared and excited. I looked at the other recruits reporting on the same day and saw the same emotions in their eyes. The only thing I knew to expect was a grueling six months of training; given my goal of improving my family's circumstances, I had no choice but to succeed at the academy. As I entered, several troopers were barking out orders, sometimes shouting different commands simultaneously, making them difficult to understand.

Another set of officers took my name and told me to enter the main hall, the academy's auditorium. Troopers told me where my assigned seat was and said I would sit there whenever we were in the auditorium for lectures, informational sessions, and class-wide disciplinary actions. For the first time but not the last, I heard the voice of the civilian receptionist over the academy's intercom system, a voice the entire cadre of recruits and I would come to dread.

"All recruits, all recruits, auditorium, five minutes." Later, the commands became far more menacing: "All recruits, all recruits, back parking lot, physical training clothes, five minutes." That voice of the civilian receptionist intoning over the loudspeakers eventually prompted a Pavlovian response in all recruits.

The major in charge of the academy class took the stage and issued his expectations and instructions. Then, he ordered us to report by cohort designation to our cohort's counselor, Tpr. Furney was a White woman with just a couple of years as a trooper. Tpr. Furney was very helpful when my newborn son got gravely ill midway through the academy. She helped arrange my being able to leave the training for a couple of days to help care for him. At the time, only a small number of women, all White, and a couple of troopers of Color were serving in the academy. Five years earlier, in 1974, four women became the first in the history of the New York State Police Academy to graduate and become troopers.

On October 19, 1981, I swore an oath to defend the United States and New York State Constitutions. I did not realize I would be an affirmative action trooper for the rest of my career, no matter what rank I attained in the eyes of some of my colleagues.

And so it began; on a typical day at the academy, they had us up by 5:00 a.m. for the mandatory morning run before breakfast. The rest of the day consisted of academics and periodic calisthenics for infractions, whether yours or another recruit's. The day did not officially end until 9:00 p.m. If recruits made errors throughout the day, they kept all of us late and put us through what they called "esprit de corps" exercises, such as random room changes, extra running, and calisthenics. Every Friday at 5:00 p.m., we reported to the main hall, where the major told us the expectations for the following week.

On some Fridays, the instructors administered disciplinary action for errors one, some, or all of us recruits might have committed. They would hold us longer than usual in the auditorium before ordering us out to the parking lot for punitive calisthenics. They told us these "esprit de corps" disciplinary actions created a sense of camaraderie; in fact, they bred resentment as the troopers laughed at our discomfort. One snowy Friday, I heard the order over the intercom. "All recruits, all recruits, back parking lot, PT clothes, five minutes." I ran back to my dorm room, conjugating fuck in English and Spanish, preparing myself to run some more. As I circled the parking lot, stopping to do pushups and other calisthenics when ordered, I watched one of the troopers in charge shove the recruits as they passed him for no other reason than that he could. I wondered how he treated civilians when he was on patrol.

That night, they kept us two and a half hours past our usual dismissal. I got home well past midnight and felt terrible for the recruits returning to Buffalo. We only got part of the weekend; we had to report back to dorms before 9:00 p.m. Sunday, and at that time, recruits did not qualify for overtime pay. They could delay us on any day, but most annoyingly, on Fridays. Because of this, they forced us to work exceedingly long hours. They would often extend these punitive exercise sessions late into the evening on weekdays, and sometimes, they woke us in the middle of the night to conduct them. The academy used these practices to get recruits to quit, targeting women and recruits of Color in particular, and they were likely encouraged by their win in a court case challenging their use of the same tactics with the recruit class just before mine.[90] My experience was that while they were careful when using ethnic humor, they increased the use of late-night physical exercises and random changes to the room assignments, ensuring they stayed within the parameters of the court's decision.[91] These practices just made me angry and more determined not to quit.

The academy class just before mine was the first class with significant diversity because of Judge Foley's ruling in 1979. According to a lawsuit filed by recruits of Color, the discriminatory tactics they faced included racist jokes and even live snakes placed on the auditorium seat of a recruit of Color. Judge Foley heard this case, too, and dismissed it. New York Times reporter Michael Oreskes interviewed him in September 1984 and quoted from the decision:

> "Racial and ethnic jokes,' he said, were told at every level of society. 'Many give humor, and many are offensive,' he wrote. 'I find that the alleged jokes included ethnic jokes other than those relating to blacks and Hispanics. The stated purpose was to ease tension and to break the monotony of the classroom. I found those purposes acceptable."[92]

Whose tension? Acceptable to whom? I do not find racist jokes acceptable, and hearing them does not ease the tension for me; on the contrary, I find them insulting and infuriating, and they elevate the tension I experience. Judge Foley ruled in favor of the state police in this discrimination case, yet the academy staff only refined these practices after the lawsuit. They were more careful in applying their esprit de corps punishments; my experience was that the protected-class troopers from Judge Foley's 1979 decision, women and people of Color, were singled out for punishment more often than the White men in my class.[93]

Chapter 4 - Stories of Interpersonal Racism

Systemic racism can be hard to pin down. When exclusionary attitudes form the bedrock of an institution and permeate its culture, it can be challenging to point out. NAACP President Derrick Johnson put it this way in a 2020 USA Today article: "This is about the systemic and pervasive nature of racism in this nation that must be addressed…" "Johnson went on to define systemic racism, also called structural racism or institutional racism, as 'systems and structures that have procedures or processes that disadvantages African Americans."[94] The gaps in outcomes are often easy to see. Yet, overtly racial slurs are not written into any of the statutes, not anymore, anyway, and that's part of what makes the very existence of systemic racism a contentious issue in some circles. As Judge Foley's two very different rulings illustrate, systems more readily acknowledge disparities like inequality in hiring than subjective disparities like an institutional culture that uses racist humor as a tool. Foley couldn't ignore the recruitment numbers like he could the dignity of people he didn't mind making the butt of the joke. Both kinds of racism are systemic, but in the latter case, the system hides behind the individual instances of bigotry while claiming they are not its responsibility.

Whether you think a racist system encouraged them or they were just random acts of bigotry, I have experienced many overtly racist interpersonal exchanges in my lifetime. Maybe you have, too, and if you have, this chapter is not for you. This chapter is for the people who want to downplay the prevalence of racist attitudes in the United States. It's for the people who think we live in a "post-racial" society, people who don't see racism because they do not face it every day.

During my first course at the academy, titled Rules and Regulations, I learned that I was what Stephen L. Carter called an "affirmative action baby."[95] This course was also when it became apparent that some White troopers resented affirmative action and those of us who had gained entry to the state police because of it.

27

As we got underway, the lieutenant leading the course, Lieutenant Heritage, asked recruits what they thought about affirmative action. One of the White recruits said he had a friend who scored 100 on the entrance exam, bumped by an unknown minority candidate who scored 84. This recruit felt Foiley's decision unfairly punished his friend for the discrimination he did not cause.

Yes, I replied and added that for a long time, White men bene-fitted from the state police's discrimination even though they did not directly cause it, and so it was only fitting they share the privilege of fair hiring practices. The debate got heated, and Lieutenant Heritage, a Black man, stepped in, telling us he did not get promoted to lieu-tenant based only on the fact that he was not White. He admonished us to follow the court order and learn to work together. The lieu-tenant also said affirmative action may have opened the door wider, but it did not guarantee anyone in the class would become a trooper, whether they scored 100 or 84, or 184 on the entrance exam. Unlike the entrance exam, he said, this first course's final test would have no affirmative action applied to the final assessment. Getting a passing grade would decide whether we would stay in the academy or risk dismissal. Lieutenant Heritage's speech was inspirational; it created a heated debate that day, but the resentment that bubbled up into recriminations and occasional outbursts of rage toward the recruits of Color remained intense. It made me renew my commitment to prove I deserved to be there. I did belong. And I could do it on my terms by finding the middle path between adhering to the just rules, regulations, and culture of the NYSP without surrendering my own culture, heritage, and values. It also showed me I could work success-fully to make the NYSP a fairer organization while knowing it would take work.

In 1973, the New York City Police Department abolished its height requirement, and in 1977, the United States Supreme Court ruled that employment requirements for height and weight illegally discriminate against women. Police agencies that wanted to maintain such requirements had to prove that they had an objective relation to a person's ability to handle the job.[96] The New York State Police changed its height requirements around the same time. Whether directly related to Judge Foley's mandate or not, the timing of the change made it an excellent counter to colleagues who said I only qualified to be a trooper because of affirmative action. I would ask these troopers how tall they were; if they were shorter than five feet ten, I would say, "See? Affirmative action helped you become a trooper, too." This question usually stopped them from complaining further about affirmative action. They typically walked away, cursing me out. These were small victories, but I savored them, nonetheless.

I passed the Rules and Regulations exam and continued my journey to becoming a trooper. I felt triumphant and made sure my fellow recruits knew it. Some congratulated me, but others were unimpressed. One guy said, "That doesn't mean shit. You're only here because of the judge's order, and there's still a long way to go before we graduate."

I replied, "Stay tuned because I will walk across that stage at graduation."

The second commissioned officer of Color I met was the late Technical Lieutenant Theodore Cook III. He had not taken part in any of the lawsuits. The NYSP leadership chose Cook to fill the newly created role of officer in charge of affirmative action. He explained to me years later that his experience in the state police had been very different from mine. He had been an officer with the New York City Transit Police before joining the NYSP. During his training at the academy, his wife became gravely ill and died. Compassionate White troopers had rallied around Cook and helped him get through the academy. While he was aware of the bigotry experienced by other men of Color in the state police, the White troopers treated him differently. Many believed Cook's refusal to participate in the lawsuits got him his promotion. Lieutenant Heritage felt this way and resented Cook for accepting a promotion he did not think Cook deserved. Heritage had passed the sergeant's and lieutenant's examinations while Cook had not. Each man had broken down barriers for those who came after him, yet Heritage's misgivings created a career-long rift between these two men. This rift was private, known only to a few close confidants.

During the academy training, recruits of Color and I discussed the hidden and overt biases we were enduring. We talked about what to do about the interpersonal racism we faced. Some went to speak with Lieutenant Cook, who was always ready with a sympathetic ear and sound advice. I confronted the biases on my terms and proved them wrong through my performance. I dealt with any biased comments or behaviors immediately and directly. I ended up in a few heated debates, one nearly ending in a fistfight with a particularly racist and sexist recruit. During a pickup basketball game, this six-foot-five White recruit fouled me deliberately. When I confronted him and asked him to be more careful, he glared at me and began yelling obscenities instead of apologizing. I put down the ball and began to walk toward him. He backed up and said, "I am not going to fucking fight you. All you people carry knives." It was a ridiculous, ignorant thing to say, but what made it more absurd was that we were both dressed in academy-issued gym clothes with no pockets to hold a piece of gum, let alone good places to conceal weapons. It was such a stupid statement that I stopped being angry and started laughing. That made him furious, but I walked away. I had to do something about the racist attitudes in this place, and I realized that the only way to change attitudes would be to become a commander and change policies first. Even at the academy, I was forming a long-term plan to address the bigotry of the state police on both the individual and systemic levels.

The training included a week of Field training outside the academy. I went to a station close to my home in New York City, State Police Peekskill (SP stands for "state police" and denotes a state police barracks.). There, I rode with an experienced trooper who was to observe my performance and decide whether I had learned the skills taught at the academy. During the first two days, he said little to me, and he was visibly annoyed that he had to be in the car with me. Finally, on our third day together, after doing a property check on a house whose owners were out of town. Rather than put the car in gear, the trooper stared at me uncomfortably and said, "I hope you're not going to be like the other one they assigned to Peekskill." A little taken aback, I said I didn't know the trooper about whom he was talking. "I just hope you're not going to go around town screwing all the White women like that other Latino trooper."

I didn't know what to say. The anger and hatred in his voice were palpable. His question offended and angered me, so I considered my answer carefully. At first, I wanted to tell him to pound salt, but I wondered whether this might be a test to see how I would manage racist comments in demanding situations.

I scanned his demeanor, and any notion of a test left my mind. This guy was not trying to train me to deal with difficult circumstances, but he was giving me a chance to practice dealing with the many bigots I would meet as a trooper of Color working in mostly White communities. He was dead serious in his concern that I would try to have sex with White women, an idea he seemed to fear and hate. What should I tell him? I wanted to say to him he was a jerk. I thought of telling him that if he treated women with love and kindness, they wouldn't flee his presence and seek out other men and that ethnicity had nothing to do with it. But saying all that would have lowered me to his level, and he oversaw my training. If he authored a critical report about me, it could result in my termination. I knew no one I could trust to report this incident to if it came to that, so instead, I said, "I am a happily married man, and I only want to get through the training. Nothing more."

"Good," he said.

Was this how it would be for the rest of my time in the state police? Was I sacrificing my integrity for a paycheck? Did all White troopers feel the same way? I prayed they didn't and hoped I would meet troopers who were not so biased and prejudicial in their relationships with people of Color. I felt anger, shame, and frustration as we pulled out of the driveway. I was angry at him, obviously, and I was angry at myself because I didn't tell him off (but I knew discretion was the better part of valor in this case). My anger grew to cover the state police, and finally, I sat there enraged at America's racism in general. It was a familiar rage that hardened into determination. I knew I had to change things, and I knew the only way to make changes was to succeed in the state police, seek promotions, and change policies from within. We didn't talk much on the ride back to SP Peekskill.

When I got home that snowy evening, I replayed the conversation. I concluded that this trooper's assumptions regarding racist myths about the sexual power of African American and Latino men. The kidnapping, torture, and murder of Emmett Till in Mississippi were motivated by the same myths. Eldridge Cleaver addressed the issue in his book Soul on Ice.[97] As did C. Vann Woodward in The Strange Career of Jim Crow. Both authors explored the psychosexual pathology of White men's fears about Black and Brown men having sex with White women.[98]

Some years later, I met the Latino trooper the training officer had been talking about. We worked together as undercover narcotics investigators, and I told him the story of my encounter at SP Peekskill. He said he had dated many women in that area and knew it upset some White troopers. We both laughed at their fear and insecurity, but a hint of sadness was underlying our laughter.

The more I learned about the history of policing in this nation and the more I experienced its racism firsthand, the louder the voices of my friends from the Lower East Side grew in my mind. I continued to question whether I could do this work honorably and equitably. Paulo Freire wrote in The Pedagogy of the Oppressed that dehumanization is "the result of an unjust order that engenders violence in the oppressors, which in turn dehumanizes the oppressed."[99] The dehumanization and oppression of marginalized groups, especially Black, Brown, and Indigenous people, began long before the start of this nation. The European settlers of the so-called New World massacred the Indigenous people they found living here and then enslaved Africans, bringing them here to do all the physical labor that fueled the economy. They thought of the people of Color in these oppressed communities as less than human.[100] The concept of "Whiteness" was so rigidly defined by many White people that even newly arrived Irish immigrants experienced exclusion. In Harper's Weekly, anti-Irish cartoons featured cartoons by Thomas Nast and depicted Irish immigrants as ape-like barbarians prone to lawlessness, laziness, and drunkenness.[101] Gradually, these bigoted cartoons subsided, and the

Irish were admitted into the ever-expanding definition of Whiteness, as were other immigrants from Europe. Yet, then as now, people emigrating from the Southern Hemisphere have not been granted the same level of acceptance.

Since its inception, this country's laws and regulations have had the systematic oppression of marginalized groups built right in. Vigilantes and the slave patrols from which modern police agencies grew and enforced this inequitable structure. I vowed to do all I would not to rely on stereotypes as a police officer. I would fight the shackles of oppression by being a just and compassionate officer.[102]

At the academy, I learned there were significant differences in the training requirements and enforcement duties of police officers and peace officers, two terms I thought were interchangeable. In New York, police officers receive at least 700 hours of training before they are authorized to carry firearms. Peace officers usually receive less than 180 hours of training and are not automatically authorized to carry firearms. If their agency requires them to be armed, peace officers must undergo an additional 47-hour firearms course and requalify annually. Peace officers required to carry guns include corrections officers, sheriffs, and court officers, among others.

I focused on the notion of a peace officer while exercising my duties as a policeman because I understood my role more holistically. My role was to try to bring peace to a crime victim by solving the case and bringing the perpetrator to justice. I was there to help resolve any situation that disturbed my community's tranquility. Moreover, like many other officers, I believed every arrest should be carried out as peacefully as possible. I knew that would not always be possible, but even when I had to use force to execute an arrest, I made sure to use the least amount of force necessary. I was neither judge, jury, nor executioner.

As my academy training was reaching its final days, I learned about the recruits' graduation party, and I chose not to go. Lieutenant Cook, the affirmative action officer for the NYSP, heard I did not want to go to the party and summoned me to his office. He asked why I didn't want to go to the party, so I told him I saw no reason to celebrate with people who resented my presence, believed I did not deserve to be there and, in some cases, did everything they could to ensure I failed and never became a trooper. Cook heard me out and then offered this warning: "When you are a trooper, you won't have a choice. You are going to work side by side with them, and if you don't learn to get along with your fellow troopers, who will watch your back?" He said, "If you don't make friends, you will not survive this job." Now worried but still angry, I argued a little more before saying that I would go if ordered. "Otherwise, sir," I said as respectfully as I could, "I am not going."

Cook did not order me to go; he told me it was my decision, but he encouraged me to reconsider. He reminded me that I would soon be collaborating with troopers like these young recruits, and he said there would probably be senior troopers who might be even more determined to see me fail when I went into the Field. He told me I had better learn to work with them and socialize with them because it was best for my career.

The lieutenant didn't convince me, and I did not go to the graduation party. However, he was right, to a point. I did end up working side by side with many White troopers like the ones I met at the academy. Some were even less tolerant, and working with them was difficult. I couldn't shake off the lieutenant's comment that I wouldn't survive this job. Had he meant my career wouldn't survive? Or did he mean I would not survive physically? Not to be overly dramatic, but that comment made me think of the movie Serpico. Frank Serpico was a New York City patrolman who blew the whistle on police officers accepting bribes. He was shot in the face by a drug dealer after being set up by his fellow officers. Years later, he and I played drums together for the KUUMBA Caribbean Dance and Drum Group in Hudson, New York.[103]

Lieutenant Cook was right; I eventually learned to work and socialize with all kinds of troopers, but I only really had a good relationship with the troopers who were not biased against people of Color. Some troopers' discriminatory attitudes grew from a lack of exposure to other cultures and ethnicities. I'm not trying to excuse those troopers but felt their prejudice grew out of ignorance. I worked to educate them rather than remain angry at them and that helped me have a better relationship with them. Our disagreement about the party aside, Technical Lieutenant Cook was a great help to me and became a career-long mentor and dear friend. He offered the same support and guidance to hundreds of troopers from Judge Foley's protected-class women and people of Color. Years later, after I had risen in rank, he worked for me, but he was always my mentor. Lieutenant Cook cared more about the job and the troopers under his watch than his health. He died of complications from diabetes, and we mourned his too-early union with the Great Beyond. His guidance and support significantly contributed to my success as a trooper. The many conversations I had with Ted inspired me to author this book. He once told me if he authored a book about his experience. He would title it "A Darker Shade of Gray."[104]

A few months after I skipped the graduation party, I was at SP Allegany, my first assigned post. I worked with some incredible troopers, like my Field training officer, Dick Fisher, and Zone Sergeant Charles McCole. Yet sadly, some of the troopers at SP Allegany had already made up their minds based on their implicit biases. They assumed I would be five feet two, speak English with a heavy Spanish accent, and be named Juan. The joke was on them. I am five feet ten, I have a New York accent, and well, okay, they were partly right about the name. My middle name is Juan.

When I was at SP Allegany, one of the troopers' dispatching calls to me used the sound of my middle name to replace the number one. "Car Juan zero two seven, please respond," the dispatcher would call over the air. It was mildly clever but annoying and unprofessional at the same time. But as every person of Color knows, I would have gone crazy if I had responded to every microaggression. However, the trooper's dispatches went not just to the other police officers and first responders; the general public also heard these dispatches since many of the area's residents had police scanners. This would let them know when I was out on patrol, which was a little disconcerting. I told Dick the dispatch calls made me uncomfortable. He told me to ignore them, saying that the other troopers were having fun and meant nothing by it. "Right now, you need to focus on getting through the next thirty days of Field training and probation."

"Why should I let that lazy, out-of-shape trooper get away with it?" I asked.

"You have bigger fish to fry," he said.

I knew on one level that Dick was right. Making a big deal out of it could provoke more harassment. I suspect he spoke to the offending trooper because the "fun" stopped; Dick was a righteous and honorable man. I vowed to attain rank and change this kind of behavior. Dick helped me focus on completing my Field training successfully by reminding me I couldn't change anything if I did not hang onto the job.

Years later, when I had become a supervisor, a young trooper who had been a civilian dispatcher returned from patrol and decided to, in his words, "share some laughs." He then had the temerity to say to me, "All you people carry knives," echoing the recruit I almost fought at the academy, "so can cut your way out of the womb faster than most."

He chuckled until he saw the look on my face. "Sorry. Bad joke," he said.

"Worse," I told him. "I could bring you brought up on charges for using a racial slur."

I was bluffing about the charges and didn't intend to write him an official reprimand. Still, he now had a long way to go to regain my respect, and the first step was for him to make an authentic apology, not just dismissing it as a bad joke. I spent the next few months helping him do his job without insulting people who did not look like him. Other troopers at the station heard about what he had said, and they also chastised him. I never heard him utter another slur in my presence, and I never had a complaint about him making racist remarks.

For part of my career, I was part of the state's permanent SWAT team, the Mobile Response Team (MRT). Many members of the MRT were from my academy class. The team members were my brothers, and like any set of brothers, we loved each other, but sometimes we saw things differently. This brotherhood felt especially meaningful because my brother had died just two years before I joined the MRT. And like I did with him, I occasionally argued with some of the other MRT members. Most of these arguments ranged from sports to food to other things brothers fuss over. The most troubling disagreements were over the varying degrees of prejudice toward people of Color we saw on display in the people we served, in our bosses, and each other. Some teammates had an enlightened perspective on race. Some resented the affirmative action policies imposed on the state police. I understood their concerns about "reverse discrimination" but strongly disagreed. While regrettably ignorant of the historical need for affirmative action, those who held this view were still my brothers, and we knew we would protect each other with our lives. Given the dangerous nature of our assignments, we knew that during any mission, we had to perform with exacting precision and perfect timing to protect each other and the people we were serving. "There are no atheists in foxholes?" It was like that; we all answered to something bigger than ourselves because we had some of the riskiest duties police officers face. Our lives were often on the line, and this truth made our disagreements about affirmative action more painful. Some of my colleagues argued affirmative action gave unqualified candidates access to privileges they had not earned.

I said affirmative action is about equity, which is different from equality. For instance, if the state police gave us all work boots, we would have been treated equally; equity is when they give us the shoes, and these boots fit our feet. The state police, for decades, had barred African American men, Latinos, and all women from becoming troopers. Affirmative action tore down the barriers the state police had explicitly created to prevent diversity and inclusion in the organization.[105] Before the state police could be "the premier law enforcement agency of its kind," as it often claimed to be, it had to become more representative of the population it served. This meant the Division had to hire people of Color and women of all races and ethnicities in equal proportion to the population at large to correct for a history of hiring only White men.

We argued over this and other issues related to race. Team members taking racist positions in these debates often claimed they had not personally discriminated against anyone of Color, so they shouldn't "suffer the consequences" of affirmative action, which, after all, corrected for acts of racism they hadn't committed. They called the policy "reverse discrimination" because it meant fewer White men would become troopers even though they might be more qualified than "protected class" recruits. I argued they were overlooking all the advantages and opportunities they experienced as members of this nation's majority ethnicity. There was an advantage if you were born White in America. I understood this early on, as did many people of Color I knew. This privilege went unnoticed and unexplored by these critics of affirmative action. They had what Peggy McIntosh, author of "On Privilege, Fraudulence, and Teaching As Learning: Selected Essays 1981-2019," 'has called "an invisible package of unearned assets…about which… [they were] 'meant' to remain oblivious."[106] My MRT colleagues argued that meritocracy was the only way to achieve success. "You get only what you earn, they said, 'and anyone who works hard enough will succeed."

Their assertions showed no awareness of the help they received from the Constitution, which, for the first eighty years of its existence, disenfranchised everyone but White men. Like the discrimination they "didn't participate in," they weren't present for the signing of the Constitution either. Still, they benefited from the political and economic structures built around it. They disregarded that they did not have to have a federal lawsuit to gain access to a career in the New York State Police. They also did not understand the impact of their microaggressions. In their attempts to be humorous, they offered jokes about race and ethnicity I did not always find funny, and I would usually let them know. Sometimes, they said they made racist remarks that they thought were welcoming and kind, and in these cases, the sting was even worse. They would say that I was different from the other members of my ethnicity, more intelligent and willing to work harder. These statements were difficult to swallow because they were incorrect and belittled my entire community, including my family. If I was the intelligent, hardworking exception, what were they? Stupid and lazy? Thanks a lot for the compliment.

I experienced these attitudes throughout my career with the state police. Most of the troopers I worked with focused on the areas where we agreed. We found common ground in our commitment to being excellent troopers and serving people victimized by criminals.

Like the trooper who used the "you people carry knives" stereotype for a cheap laugh, there were some who used straightforward racial slurs in ugly attempts to be funny. One morning, as I entered the classroom at the academy, some of my White colleagues were laughing, and I asked them what was so funny. One guy, who was genuinely skilled at making us laugh, walked to the chalkboard and began writing as he said, "We were listing all the various names we can call you." He wrote beaner, wetback, and pepper-belly. These were slurs I had rarely heard before, as a Nuyorican. I was offended by the racist nature of these phrases.[107] Some of them continued laughing. I walked up to the board, erased the words, then turned and glared at them. The comedian said, "We're just joking with you, don't get mad."

Sometimes, my fellow troopers would also comment on the differences between various races and ethnicities related to criminality, drug use, birth rates, etc. Their opinions were almost always mistaken and hurtful. When offended, I sometimes responded with expletives, but I never lowered myself by countering with racial slurs. They often told me I should have thicker skin, that they were having fun and didn't mean any of it. While I appreciated their willingness to discuss these issues openly (regardless of the uninformed nature of their arguments), I refused to accept their casual racism as "brotherly love" or esprit de corps. Some understood and stopped; others just agreed to disagree.

When people express distorted and stereotypical views, I challenge them with facts. Some argued they were not personally alive during slavery or the Jim Crow era, so they should bear no responsibility for those crimes or the psychic scars they left on the soul and body of this nation. Unfortunately for everyone, this abdication of responsibility did not negate its history or its present-day consequences. Instead, it highlighted the men's ignorance of how dominant-group privilege and the institutionalized discrimination of public entities like the New York State Police had helped them before Judge Foley's decree. My unwillingness to surrender to frustration and despair drove me to debate these issues and call out microaggressions repeatedly, and it was worth the effort. Some of my peers became ardent advocates for affirmative action, diversity, and inclusion, and I feel like I had some influence there. Others of my peers and plenty of sergeants and commissioned officers I met along the way stayed on the continuum from cultural incompetence to outright prejudice and bigotry. That challenged me continuously as I balanced my need to find a successful career path against my commitment to effecting change within the agency. I knew future incidents would test my patience and tolerance repeatedly; nevertheless, I forged ahead, more determined than ever.

The biased remarks of sergeants and commissioned officers were incredibly disappointing. I had hoped the people with rank and the responsibility to lead might have more evolved views than some of my rank-and-file colleagues. Some of them did, but others did not. One afternoon in the mid-1980s, I overheard a captain who worked at the academy complaining loudly that the state police was no longer as good as they had been. He blamed the judicial decree that forced the state police to hire "minorities." He had not seen me coming around the corner, but once he did, he said, "Oh, but he's one of the good ones," and walked away before I could respond.

Years later, we were both lieutenant colonels and were sitting in a meeting on drug trafficking called by the superintendent. The guy who called me "one of the good ones" said he believed "minorities" engaged in the drug trade because it was inherent to their culture. "That's bullshit," I said loudly enough that everyone in the meeting heard it. The superintendent asked what was wrong. I stood up and said, "I am tired of hearing these racist comments from this man, and it needs to stop now."

"Calm down," the superintendent said, but I was seething with anger. After the meeting, the superintendent ordered us into his office and dressed us both down. He chastised me for letting my emotions get the better of me. Then, he ordered the other colonel to apologize for his offensive remarks. He apologized begrudgingly, and the superintendent instructed us to shake hands.

It was a small victory. I hadn't changed any hearts or minds, but if the colonel would think twice next time before espousing racist views, I would count it as a win.

While on the surface, this incident was merely a disagreement between two individuals, on a deeper level, it was a missed opportunity for the state police leadership to engage in dialogue about race and racism. They could have addressed microaggressions in the workplace. They could have illustrated to troopers that affirmative action restored equity rather than created inequity. They could have done more; but the superintendent only told me to calm down and return to work. And that's what I did, secure in my belief that I could defy expectations, disprove stereotypes, and make changes in the NYSP with hard work and integrity.

Chapter 5 - Dancing in the Parking Lot

At the state police academy, as our training to become state troopers began, my fellow recruits and I reported to our academy counselor, Trp. Furney. She would be our counselor for the next six months. She told us our room numbers and who our quad mates were and said we would receive our recruit uniforms once we passed the first exam. She ordered us to find our designated rooms, unpack our clothing, and pick up our linens from the quartermaster's office. Our counselor had instructed us to do this quickly, and in less than fifteen minutes, we retrieved all our linens, unpacked our clothing, and made our beds as required. We then heard over the loudspeaker something we would dread for the next six months: the voice of the desk officer summoning us back to the auditorium. We all ran back to the meeting hall and searched for our assigned seats, some of us finding them quickly while others searched and searched. Because some recruits did not find their assigned seats right away, they ordered us to the gymnasium and used calisthenics to punish the whole class for the mistakes of a few.

The announcement we all dreaded, "All Recruits, all recruits, back parking lot, PT clothes, five minutes," meant punitive physical training. Sometimes, as I learned later, it wasn't even punitive; sometimes, the extra exercise was just for the amusement of the counselors, making us dance in the back parking lot. Some counselors even used it as an opportunity to try to force out recruits from Judge Foley's protected classes by using punitive exercise sessions. On a positive note, they trained us on standing, marching, parade formation, the proper way to salute, and everything we needed to develop correct paramilitary formation and discipline. The militaristic approach of the NYSP dates back to 1917. In that year, the first superintendent of the NYSP, George Fletcher Chandler, a former Army surgeon, used an Army Field manual as the basis for the newly formed police agency's rules and regulations manual.[108]

Initially, the state police force consisted of four troop areas. Troop A covered western New York, Troop D patrolled central New York, Troop G handled the state's capital region, and Troop K patrolled southeastern New York. Today, twelve troops break down into zones; each zone controls a group of patrol areas. For example, SP Peekskill, now SP Cortlandt, where I did my initial Field training, was a patrol area in Troop K, Zone 3.

At the start of the New York State Police, Chandler used the military word barracks for patrol stations. The nature of rural policing at that time was that New York State Troopers, another of Chandler's military terms, rode horses on their patrols. That meant the patrol stations had to include stables for the horses, and they had sleeping quarters to house the patrolmen stationed there. At first, almost all the troopers were single men, and they either lived in the barracks or at local hotels or boarding houses when out on patrol.[109]

The counselors and instructors at the academy believed they would make us good troopers while weeding the bad ones out. Most of the academy staff focused on the ability to perform the duties required by the agency's values of safety, integrity, leadership, and service. Some staff members, however, believed only White troopers could be good troopers. These views were expressed in the form of microaggressions from some, while others made explicitly racist remarks. Sometimes, the marching drills went on all evening until dinner. Each day during the ensuing months, I reexamined my decisions given the challenges of the structural and interpersonal racism I faced. I considered myself part of the Civil Rights Movement and participated in protests as a young adult. In 1968, many Haaren High School students and I took to the New York City streets to mourn Martin Luther King's assassination. Our spontaneous protest was one of many urban demonstrations for civil rights that came together in response to the horrific murder of Dr. King. Our foray into civil disobedience was tame compared to the events happening in Harlem, Bedford-Stuyvesant, and the Lower Eastside. These neighborhoods were burning, people were looting stores, and police and civilians clashed in what some would call riots, and others would say were necessary revolts.[110]

The year 1968 was a tumultuous year for many of the nation's cities. Civil rights protests were frequent, as were labor strikes. Sporadic protests often became violent and destructive in Black and Brown communities. On the Lower East Side in Manhattan, I watched the police respond, sometimes acting more violently than the demonstrators. All these memories danced in my mind as I continued my journey of becoming a trooper.

As the resentment and bigotry shown by some of my peers and academy staff became more perceptible, I grew more determined to succeed and rise through the ranks. I would make the state police more inclusive no matter what it took. I also grew angrier, but I found healthy ways of venting my anger that, while sometimes risky, served me well. For example, every morning, we ran three miles around the campus. During those runs, I often chanted in Spanish, paraphrasing an improvised Santeria chant. This chant was my way of challenging the troopers and recruits who were against diversifying the state police:

> Agua que va caere - Water is going to fall.
> Agua que va caere - Water is going to fall.
> Que va caere – It's gonna fall
> Que va caere – It's gonna fall
> Venga Chango, Obatala, Elegua - Come, God of
>   Thunder, Sky-Father, Lord of the Crossroads.

The Afro-Caribbean religion, Santeria (Way of the Saints), is based on Yoruba beliefs and traditions. The religion is also called La Regla Lucumi and the Rule of Osha. Santeria is a syncretic religion that grew in response to the dehumanizing experience of slavery. It originated in West Africa and became a vital survival practice throughout Cuba and the Americas. This belief system comes from the religious traditions of the Yoruba people of West Africa. It helped preserve the culture and dignity of the people experiencing slavery. The people from West Africa in Cuba used it to practice their faith secretly by hiding it under a veneer of Catholic practices. Many Catholic saints have attributes like Santeria's Orishas (Saints).

For instance, Chango has characteristics that are also associated with Saint Barbara.[111]

Some fellow recruits who spoke Spanish and knew about Santería thought I was nuts. They would say, "Oye, Papi, what the fuck are you doing?"

"All they can do is make me do push-ups."

"No, brother, you're putting a bull's-eye on your back and maybe ours too."

"We already have a target on our backs," I said. "Or haven't you been listening?"

The worst they could do was ask me to explain what it meant, and I wasn't worried about that. Their fear made me more determined than ever to rise through the ranks and ensure people of Color who joined the NYSP wouldn't worry about being themselves. I was determined to change the agency while remembering my heritage and on my terms. Finding the middle path was critical to my success as a change agent. The cover of the vehicle and traffic law study guide featured an illustration of a White trooper, and I darkened his face to remind myself of my determination. I then added the captain's rank insignia to the collar of his shirt. Some of my White colleagues noticed this and laughed, saying I'd never make it out of the academy, let alone become a captain. I took their comments as a challenge. "Watch me," I told them.

I began researching which troops gave me the best chances for promotion. I surmised that the troop with the oldest troopers and sergeants would be the region with the most openings for non-commissioned officers. I knew sergeant was the first rank I had to reach on my journey upward. I conducted an informal survey of the troopers at the academy, asking them which one of the troops had the oldest officers and sergeants. They told me that troops A, C, D, and E had the most members near retirement age. They also told me these troops were tough to get into. Trp. Furney and Lieutenant Cook confirmed my analysis. They also agreed that those troops were the hardest to get into as newly graduated troopers since there was usually a long list of more seasoned troopers who wanted assignments closer to home. When you graduate from the academy, you go where there are trooper vacancies. Your first patrol station could be on the opposite side of the state from where you grew up. Troopers had to request transfers back to their home regions. The catch is that seniority determines who's transfer request list gets priority.

Toward the end of the academy training, each recruit received a "dream sheet" onto which we could write down the regions where we would prefer to work. To have the best chance of getting the troop you wanted, your academic standing and overall performance at the academy needed to be in the top 10 percent of the class. I had worked hard and met that criterion. I wrote troops A, C, and E on my dream sheet. The cities of Buffalo, Rochester, and Binghamton were within these troops' jurisdiction. Buffalo and Rochester had sizable communities of Color, including Latinx populations. Buffalo had the most diverse population outside of New York City, so it was reasonable to assume they would send me to the Buffalo area, which was under the jurisdiction of Troop A. I did get assigned to Troop A, but I ended up at a trooper's barracks nowhere near Buffalo, eighty miles south on the Pennsylvania border. This region of the state was nearly completely devoid of people of Color, and that included the Troop A personnel; I was floored but not deterred.

Chapter 6 - The Road of Shame

After graduating from the academy, I had five days to report to my Troop A training station, SP Allegany. I would receive field training from my "senior man," an arcane but official title for training officers used in those days, even if the training officer was a female. I was to train at SP Allegany for thirty days. If I completed all the assignments and proved to the satisfaction of my senior man that I had developed enough skills and knowledge to patrol alone, I could then report to my permanent station, SP Wellsville. In the five-day window after graduation, I went to settle my business in New York City and ensured my family was okay. An eight-hour drive from New York City, as far as my family and I were concerned, SP Wellsville might as well have been on Mars. I hoped this trip would improve my family's life on every level. It was also the next step in my plan to make the state police a diverse, inclusive, and racially equitable organization.

I didn't know whether my family and I could adjust to rural life. I was afraid that while I could endure the challenges, Pamela would miss her mother, sister, and brother, who stayed in the city. I worried about how being around all the White people in Allegany County would affect our lives. I thought we were likely to face biased attitudes or worse. How would Pamela and my children navigate this? Did I have the fortitude to be there for my family and rise through the ranks to make the NYSP more diverse and welcoming? Yes, I told myself. In for a penny, in for a pound.

I had never been to the Southern Tier of New York State, which is the part that borders Pennsylvania. I knew nothing about its people and culture. Given my experience in the academy and at SP Peekskill, I was excited and a little frightened. Would all the troopers and sergeants be racists, or only a few of them? Would the inevitable hazing happen because I was new or because I was a man of Color and, in the eyes of some, only on the job because of affirmative action? How would the community react? I had learned well how to perform as a trooper, but would that be enough?

I also worried about whether I could afford to live near SP Allegany while training. As mentioned, I took a significant pay cut to join the NYSP, praying the risk would pay off. I sent most of the money I made while I was training to my family in NYC, and for the first few years of my policing career, we were living paycheck to paycheck.

Full of excitement and apprehension, I drove the Death Trap out of New York City, praying it would last another year. On the way to SP Allegany, I passed through villages and cities I had never heard of, like Middletown and Monticello. I continued westward, feeling greater anticipation for what I hoped would be a life-changing career. I passed more towns I had never heard of, such as Elmira, Horseheads, Angelica, and Cuba. Those last two names seemed to affirm my decision to join the NYSP. Given the Spanish names of these cities in Upstate New York, I thought, wow, there must be a lot of Puerto Ricans and other Latinx people here; I soon learned how wrong I was. I also drove through Olean, New York (pronounced O-lee-Ann), from the Latin word for oil - oleum. In the 1920s and 1930s, Olean's nickname was "Little Chicago" because the Chicago mafia, including Al Capone, used the town for illegal liquor operations during Prohibition. It was also a center for illegal gambling and prostitution for the entire Northeast.[112]

After a daylong drive from the Lower East Side, I arrived at my training station, SP Allegany, in Zone Four of Troop A. My senior man, Richard Fisher, seemed stern yet welcoming. He was very professional and seemed eager to teach me how to be a good trooper. When I called him sir, as was mandatory in the academy, he put me at ease. He said, "Call me by my nickname, Dick." This welcoming gesture was dramatically different from my training at SP Peekskill, where the trooper who trained me was more concerned that I would sleep with White women than with offering advice and guidance.

Trooper Fisher and I worked the midnight shift during the first week, 11:00 p.m. to 7:00 a.m. At 7:00 a.m., I was exhausted as I filled out the blotter recording the previous night's activities. Fortunately, this state police barracks was in a refurbished residential house, and it still had bedrooms upstairs. These accommodations were not unusual; most state police stations served as barracks from the organization's beginning. This was what Chandler, the first superintendent who had a zeal for the military, dubbed the patrol stations back when most troopers were single and lived in the barracks. As more married men joined the division, fewer and fewer men lived in the barracks. In the modern era, the barracks often house troopers who have been transferred from another region and need a place to stay as they "work their way back home," always looking for transfer opportunities that will take them back to their region. It was comforting to know that I could work my way back home if I were assigned away from home.

Each day after breakfast, I went to my assigned room and tried to sleep, which was almost impossible because this was an active patrol station, and daily activities went on as usual. The dispatch radio blared out calls, and all the noise of processing arrestees echoed throughout the barracks as I tried to rest. This struggle for rest continued for several days until Fisher realized I wasn't getting enough sleep and took pity on me. He invited me to stay with him in his trailer. I was reluctant to accept this generous offer, but I knew I could not perform at my best without sleep. I agreed on the condition that I would occasionally cook Creole food for us, and he said okay. I introduced him to arroz con pollo (the poor man's paella, a fabulous Spanish dish), adobo seasoning, and other flavors from Puerto Rico. He introduced me to drinking a couple of Genesee Cream Ales right after the overnight shift to help with sleep. Dick was a generous man of integrity; I sensed no bigotry, just genuine curiosity about my culture. Lieutenant Heritage, then Troop A's Zone Four commander, and Zone Sergeant Charles McCole respected Trooper Fisher and told me I would learn much from him. When we were on patrol during the occasional day shift, community members said I was lucky he was training me. They weren't wrong.

One day, Dick and I received a call to respond to a shooting death in the town of Allegany. It was my first potential homicide investigation, and we were five minutes away in the city of Olean;

I looked at Dick as he turned on the siren and told me, "Move it." We raced to the scene, siren blaring and lights flashing. This case was a chance to see serious police work. I was thrilled, although I also realized this was someone's tragedy. My heart pounded as we arrived at the scene, just as other patrols and the local first responders did. Our job was to protect the area for the BCI, who would carry out the actual investigation. We helped as needed. The lead BCI investigator instructed us to follow the victim's body to the hospital, where the forensic pathologist would perform the postmortem examination.

The man suspected in the shooting said he was on the south bank of the Allegany River teaching his son how to hunt. The father spotted what he thought was a woodchuck, fired, and brought it down. He had no idea he had killed a young woman lying on the bank of the river. She had brown hair the hunter mistook for fur. It was a powerful lesson on many levels. I learned not to prejudge investigations; criminal cases are not always what they first appear to be. It would help if you let the case facts drive your questions and conclusions. This case changed from a murder investigation to a tragic hunting accident. This lesson served me well throughout my career.

As we drove away from the scene, Dick told me he thought I was a terrible driver, particularly on these winding country roads you don't find in New York City. But he praised my driving through Olean earlier as we raced to the scene. There was hope for me yet, he said. My Field training with this first-class senior trooper gave me the sense that I could and would survive in this organization. Yet I wondered, were there enough open-minded state police members like him to create the possibility of changing the intolerant culture of the NYSP? Dick, who had Army experience, had worked with people from diverse backgrounds. I might not have survived my first few months in the Field without him. He certified that I could work alone, a key factor for getting through probation. The certification was about understanding the procedures and my judgment and ability to engage people professionally, fairly, and firmly. Dick felt I could, and I was grateful for his guidance.

He also told our supervisors I needed more experience driving on backcountry roads. He was right! I had driven mainly in New

York City on streets that were well-lit and usually had signs showing the street names and block numbers. The roads in the rural Southern Tier often did not. When responding to complaints, I sometimes got directions like, "Take the second left past the old Ford farm with the big oak tree in the yard." An oak tree? There were Sycamores, but only a few, in the courtyard of the housing project where I grew up. I didn't know what oak trees looked like, but I learned.

To be a competent trooper, I had to learn about the culture of Allegany County. I could only do my job if I understood, for instance, that dairy farmers get up at three in the morning to milk the cows. I learned some local lore, like "if the corn is knee-high by the fourth of July, the harvest would be good." I developed a taste for ham and leek dinners and learned to like funky-smelling salt-rising bread, which does not use salt as a leavening agent but a naturally occurring bacterium. Once I finished my thirty days with Trooper Fisher, I could tell he was proud of me, yet he was stoic. He knew I had more of the probationary period to complete before I'd be a full-fledged trooper, so we shook hands as he wished me luck. There was no celebration or ceremony on this leg of the journey, just more work to prove myself.

For seven months, I had only seen my young family on weekends. I constantly missed them and worried about them because the neighborhood I had to move them into was tough. There was a lot of crime, drug dealing, and other issues in this neighborhood. In November of 1981, a month after entering the NYSP academy, we left our apartment in Brooklyn to save money. Pamela, the kids, and I moved into her mother's run-down fifth-floor railroad apartment in a five-story tenement building with no elevator. I was sometimes distraught because she was pregnant and would need help as she entered her last trimester. I fought the feeling of guilt; I prayed our sacrifice, in the end, would be worth the pain this journey had already caused us. I also suspected this would not be the last hardship we would endure as I pursued this career. I drove back to New York City from Allegany, rented a U-Haul truck, and packed up our household goods in just two days. We started this journey in October 1981, now May 1982; we headed to our new home and my first official assignment, SP Wellsville.

I felt like we were on another planet when we got to Wellsville. This community was even smaller than Olean. My family and I felt out of place, isolated, and disconnected from what we knew. The radio stations did not play R&B or salsa. I couldn't find the foods I used to buy to make my meals. There were no plantains to make mofongo, no adobo to season my dishes, and very few other ingredients to make the Afro-Caribbean dishes I loved. Rural life and culture gave my wife and me much to adjust to. Yet we felt blessed to have this opportunity to improve our lives. For starters, our new home in Wellsville had a backyard, something we would probably never have if we stayed in the city.

We arrived in the Village of Wellsville in the evening. I had packed the mattresses last so that they would be the first thing we unloaded when we arrived, knowing we would be exhausted. We brought them in and put them down on the living room floor. I ordered New York-style pizza from the Pizza King pizzeria. We fed our children their baby food as we wolfed down our slices. That night, we slept soundly. A few days after unpacking and settling into the house, we had a small picnic in the front yard. My daughter was about eighteen months old, and each time I tried to set her down on the grass, she would scream and pull her feet up toward her belly. I laughed, upsetting her even more. I did not understand why she was so afraid until I realized she had never been up close to the grass. I looked through her eyes and realized the grass looked like a bunch of sharp green spikes. I went in and got a blanket to sit on. She lost her fear of the grass, but it made me realize I had so much to learn in this strange new land, both on the job and off.

Allegany County was very rural, with more deer and cattle than people. The primary occupation in Allegany County was farming. Only a few industries were there during the 1980s; Turbodyne and Dresser-Rand manufactured turbines in their operations in the Village of Wellsville, the county's largest community. If you were a tenured trooper and achieved seniority, you were one of the county's better-paid and highly thought-of citizens. Although I was a rookie and my salary put just a few thousand dollars above the federal poverty line of $9,862 for a family of four in 1982.[113] I was still better off than many of Allegany's residents.

The local oil industry was far from what it had been in the late 1800s and early 1900s. Still, pumpjacks continued pulling oil out of the wells in Allegany County, the adjoining Cattaraugus County, and the Northern Tier of Pennsylvania.[114] I learned about the county's history of oil production while driving around on patrol to know the county roads better. I drove past a marker for the Seneca Oil Springs Reservation and thought, Native American territories in New York state? This was surprising news. As an Indigenous person, I knew Indigenous people lived in New York City, but I had not known there were Native American territories in New York State. The Seneca call themselves Onödowá'ga,' the "Great Hill People."[115] Their traditional medicinal practices used the oil oozing out of the ground in Cuba Lake. I drove my patrol car onto the Seneca land. I walked around the site where French Jesuit missionaries had learned about the medicinal use of petroleum from the Senecas as early as the seventeenth century. A historical marker on the site read: "1627, first petroleum discovered in America."[116] In the New York City public schools, my history and social studies teachers had not taught about my people's culture and history. Those who did cover African American culture and history focused primarily on slavery and how President Lincoln "freed the slaves," forcing those enslaved people not only to represent all Black culture in the United States at the time. Which they didn't, but to have their story wrapped up in the falsehood that formerly enslaved people lived happily ever after in their newfound freedom. When they spoke about Native American culture and history, they covered Thanksgiving briefly and moved on.

The historical marker, a commemorative stone with a metal plaque, made me think that as an Indigenous person myself, I should learn more about the Indigenous community and history in my new home. As I did know more, I came to see that marker's seemingly benign attribution, "first petroleum discovered in America," as an example of the way Indigenous people's roles in history are downplayed and outright ignored. The oil bubbling up in the region was not "discovered" in 1627; this merely marked the year when the Senecas showed the Franciscan monk the site of the oil spring. The inscription on the plaque reminded me of another myth of discovery that Christopher Columbus had "discovered" America. Neither tale respects Indigenous people nor represents their roles accurately. I returned to my patrol car and drove around the rest of the territory, but there was not much to see there then.

Some years later, the Seneca opened smoke shops selling cigarettes and gasoline on their land. These shops and similar enterprises on the larger Seneca territories, the Allegany and Cattaraugus territories, struck the match that lit the Thruway tire fires during the 1992 and 1997 tax protests. Driving around on the Oil Springs Reservation after finding that marker, I could not have predicted the impact the Seneca would have on my career in the years to come. I knew, however, that I needed to understand the relationship between the Seneca Nation of Indians, the United States, and New York State. This was how my complex relationship with my cousins, the Seneca, began for better or worse.

The oil industry in Allegany, Cattaraugus, and the Northern Tier of Pennsylvania has a storied history.[117] One of the towns in Allegany County, Bolivar, was pivotal to the industry. Bolivar was also one of those towns with Spanish names I had imagined meant there would be a lot of diversity in the county. In its heyday, Bolivar was a prosperous village. When I arrived, it was in decline, with little industry having sprung up to support the population after the oil boom subsided.[118] One consequence of the regional oil industry, and one of the legacies of its decline, was the transfer of Southern White racist culture into the county. I saw many pickup trucks with Confederate flags in their rear windows.[119] The local music of choice, country-western, also had a Southern sensibility. I believe the country music and confederate flags were present in part because when the oil business began to die in western New York, the oil workers moved south to Oklahoma and Texas. When they returned to Allegany County, they brought the Southern states' viewpoints on race relations with them. Unfortunately, the racist elements of that viewpoint dovetailed all too easily with the racist and prejudicial attitudes already present in this region of New York.

Figure 6. Tpr. Perez on Yeager Hill, 1982.[120]

During my first few months in Allegany County, the station commander of SP Wellsville, a sergeant born and raised in the county, gave me a trifold Allegany County map. He said I was useless to him because this was not New York City, and the grid system of streets I had always used to orient myself did not exist here. Many roads were unmarked. There were few streetlights outside the villages, and technically, Allegany County didn't even have anything large enough to call a "city" within its borders. The station commander told me to learn the roads so I could start responding to "complaints," the NYSP jargon for calls for service. Once, I got lost while trying to learn my way around the county. I was on an unmarked seasonal road and eventually realized that I was seeing only Pennsylvania registration plates. I turned around and drove several miles until I was out of neighboring Pennsylvania and back in New York State. One day, while I was out learning the names of the county's rural roads, I traveled onto another unmarked seasonal road in the Town of Wirt. When I looked at my trifold map, to my horror, I saw that this route was called Nigger Hill Road. This road of shame made me furious. I sped back to SP Wellsville.

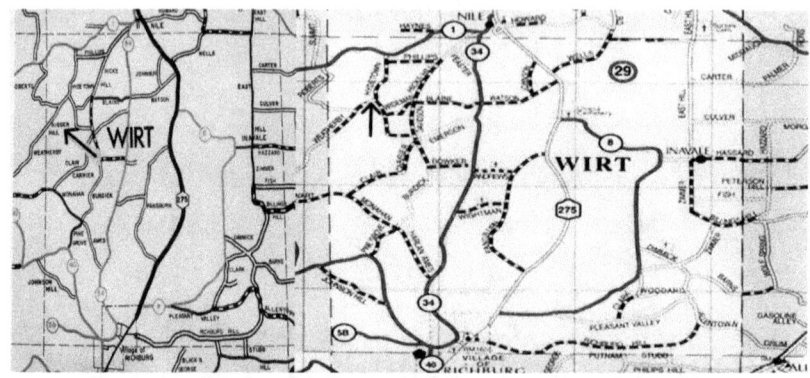

Figure 7. Comparison of Allegany County map with
the road of shame and the revised map with it.

Allegany County had been part of the Underground Railroad, and its citizens had helped African Americans escape slavery and settle in Canada.[121]

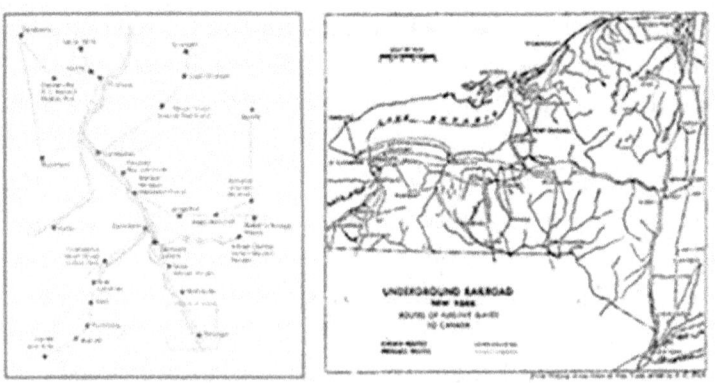

Figure 8. Allegany County Underground Railroad map
and a Map of NYS Underground Railroads Map.[122]

New York State's significant support for the Underground Railroad was well-documented, but many Allegany County residents, the sergeant among them, seemed ignorant of this. When I told him how upset I was about the road name and asked how a road could be called that in the 1980s, he responded dismissively. "That's where they lived," he said.

That made me even angrier. I wanted to scream at him about his insensitivity and racist attitude. I told him he was wrong, turned around, and left his office. It was unbelievable; I thought that hateful word was shouted at me and my childhood friend on Grand Street by a White man. How could it be on official maps of Allegany County? I sat in my patrol car, thinking about reporting the sergeant to the Affirmative Action office for being so dismissive, but I decided not to. To succeed as a trooper of Color, I had to manage these incidents without running to Lieutenant Cook for help. What he and Dick Fisher told me still held. I had to learn to work with all troopers and supervisors. Plus, I was still on probation. Instead of taking out my anger on the sergeant, I took the road's name as a lesson in changing the organization. I reread my police manuals and found a section about a trooper's responsibilities in the Field that instructed us to meet with community leaders, legislators, police officials, and others. In a flash, I knew what I would do.

In small counties like Allegany, the legislators are usually local business owners and other stakeholders who work only part-time in the government. I found out who they were, and the companies they owned or ran, and I spent the next several months meeting with them.

When they met with me, they would often say something like, "I knew we had some minority troopers in the county." I would let that pass and open the trifold map, explaining to them that I was considering raising my family in Allegany County but didn't think it would be possible. They would ask why, and I would point out Nigger Hill Road on the map and tell them I wanted the name changed. The most common response was that they had nothing to do with naming the road, and that had been its name long before they were born. "That may be so, but the funding used to print this map was approved on your watch," I would say, and add that all my friends and colleagues in New York City would be shocked to hear about this travesty. As I researched this, I found that other place across New York used similar shameful names for some locations within the state.[123] In fact the US has used racist terms and names to name road, lakes and other places for centuries.[124]

My campaign must have worked because, a few months into it, I received a call from a county legislator who said they had decided on a new name. Because the road was near Wirt, they had decided to change the name to Wigger Hill Road. I nearly pissed my pants laughing. The legislator on the phone asked why I was laughing so hard, and when I explained that *wigger* was a slang term for a White adoptee of Black culture that was short for "White n****r," there was a deafening silence. The said he would get back to me. They eventually changed the name to Hydetown Road.

Chapter 7 - Deer Jacking-Unseen Poverty

I grew up poor and had experienced urban poverty, but the depth of poverty in rural Allegany County was startling. I had never seen so many White people living in poverty. In the projects I grew up in, there were some White and Asian families, but most of the poor tenants were African American and Hispanic. When I began working as a trooper and was assigned to answer calls for police service, I would go into homes with dirt floors, homes with outhouses instead of indoor toilets, and homes with other features I had not experienced growing up. Getting and keeping jobs was difficult for people in Allegany because of a lack of industry and other job opportunities. Transportation and adequate childcare were lacking, and education and employment skills training were inaccessible to many. Many residents of Allegany County experienced the same issues I had experienced growing up in New York City, for instance, hunger and discrimination. In Allegany County, social class was the primary target of discrimination. In some ways, the lack of access to employment opportunities, education, and training was a more significant barrier in Allegany County than in New York City, where I could use the public transit system despite its considerable problems.

I also had to adjust to Allegany County's gun, hunting, and fishing culture. When I arrived in the spring of 1982, it was near the "Tom season" opening day, which I discovered was the harvest season for male turkeys. Hunters looked to bag the birds as trophies and for eating, and wild turkeys are delicious when perfectly cooked. As I began patrolling the county's roads, many cars and trucks I pulled over had a shotgun or rifle in a rack in the rear window or stowed in the back seat or trunk, whether the vehicle's driver was a man or a woman. I learned that hunting was essential to survival for people experiencing poverty in Allegany County. Wild game was such a critical part of their diet that some people in Allegany County would hunt illegally, out of season, at night, or over the limit on how many animals they could take. One of these practices is called "deer jacking," it happens when a hunter illegally shines a light on the deer at night, causing the feeding deer to freeze, making them easy to shoot.[125] Hunting was just a sport for the hunters who were only visiting out of the cities; hunters only wanted trophy stags with large racks of antlers. Some poor families, on the other hand, were hunting for food. When I caught them, I would warn them, allow them to keep the deer for food, and tell them that they would get arrested if they engaged in the activity again. The trophy hunters breaking the law were not so lucky; I usually charge them. All this was new and strange to me. In New York City, I only thought about two kinds of people who owned firearms: police and criminals.

One of the many car-deer accidents I investigated occurred during the opening hours of the overnight shift soon after I arrived in Allegany. I investigated a crash on State Route 248A in the town of Independence. While handling this crash, I saw the flashing lights of a police vehicle coming over the hill. I had not called for backup or heard SP Wellsville dispatch a patrol car. I was surprised when it was a New York State Environmental Conservation Patrol (EnCon) car. The arrival of the EnCon officer was unusual; as I said, I had not asked for help nor heard on the radio that this case needed an EnCon officer's response. The EnCon vehicle came to a stop, and the officer jumped out of his patrol car, smiling. He asked, "Are you Perez?" When I said yes, he replied, "I heard there was a new minority trooper, a Puerto Rican, and I wanted to meet you."

I was both offended and amused. I was offended because was I a creature in a zoo? Had he just said, "I wanted to meet the new trooper," I would have been okay with that. What myths about my ethnic background filled his thoughts? Yet, his curiosity seemed genuine, and I tried not to let my anger show on my face. It was funny, too, after all. He told me he had never met anyone like me.

As we stood looking at the steaming carcass, he asked me, "Have you ever tasted deer meat?" I said no, and the EnCon officer took a knife from his belt, stabbed the fresh roadkill in the back of the neck, and pulled his knife down along the spine. He cut out the "backstrap," which I knew was the tenderloin from my days as a butcher. He wrapped the bloody slab of venison in a gauze bandage he pulled from his first-aid kit. As he handed it to me, he told me I should cut it into medallions and fry it with garlic and fiddlehead ferns, which he called "fiddler ferns," that I could get at the local market. I thanked him for the cut of meat and the advice. Having finished his observation of the new "minority" trooper, my EnCon colleague got in his patrol car and drove away. I chuckled to myself, shrugging off the unintentional microaggression just like always, and completed the accident report and sent the motorist on her way. I returned home and placed the deer meat in the refrigerator before joining my partner back at work for our midnight patrol. At the end of my shift, I stopped at the grocery store to pick up the fiddlehead ferns.

As I walked into the house at 8:00 a.m., my wife began yelling at me about the bloody hunk of meat in the refrigerator. She told me she had heard me come in the night before and put something in the fridge. She had come down and looked, expecting to find a sandwich, but when she opened the package, she screamed at the sight of the bloody, steaming venison. I did all I could not to howl with laughter, which would have made her angrier. Later, I cooked the venison with garlic and the fiddlehead ferns. It was delicious.

This incident was one of many cases involving animals I investigated. I was assigned several cases regarding animals. One case illustrated the unseen poverty many people in Allegany County experienced. I had worked in a butcher shop for many years and could debone the forequarter of a cow's carcass in minutes, but I had not been near a living cow. One day, I was standing in a farmer's barn to support an Allegany Animal Control officer whom the farmer had threatened with a shotgun. She was investigating allegations that the farmer was starving his cows. The stench of manure, urine, and rotting hay filled my nostrils. I looked at the cow; its ribs were visible under the tight, emaciated cow's skin. I was standing behind the cow when it raised its tail. I saw the farmer and the officer standing alongside the cow move back slightly as they stared at me and then at the cow. Suddenly, the cow released a torrent of urine that arched toward me.

I backpedaled as quickly as possible, only having my boots and pant cuffs spattered with urine. Both the farmer and the officer were laughing uncontrollably at the city slicker. I glared back at them but laughed and said they should have warned me. I invited them to join me on the NYC's A train, where I would return the favor of not warning them about the panhandlers and others that might piss on them. They declined my kind offer. Later, I learned the farmer was a penniless widower with no one to help him. That was the real reason his cows were starving and so was he. I convinced the animal control officer not to charge him and to seek a way to help him.

Chapter 8 - A Uniform without a Shield

As I adjusted to life in the state police and the culture of Allegany County, I got constant reminders of my fellow state police officers' generosity and kindness. One of the White troopers I worked with would dress up as Santa during Christmas, stop by my house to bring cookies his wife baked, and give my children small gifts. Yet this same trooper, a guy with whom I had worked many night shifts, often made micro-aggressive comments he thought were funny. After I had gotten to know him for a few weeks, it became clear he also believed a lot of these "jokes." He said to me, "If I had a daughter, I would not let her marry you or any other minority." His regional manner of speaking, layered with racially derogatory terms and phrases, was the cause of many intense arguments. He called Brazil nuts "n****r toes," for example. This was the first time I had heard the nuts called that.

When I heard him say things like that, I would tell him not to use these racial slurs in my presence or with any of the troopers of Color. In that instance with the Brazil nuts, he laughed, saying that's what he'd always called them and that it was funny. He ultimately stopped after several more intense arguments. Despite his opinions on race, affirmative action, and other similar topics, I grew to accept him. He always had my back during encounters with alleged offenders and interactions with the community. While I worked with him, I did not see him act prejudicially toward people of Color. Very few of us were in the county, and I can only attest to the times I was with him. I also suspect my presence was another factor that helped keep him in line. He was an excellent trooper, racist attitude notwithstanding. I would always warn the new troopers of Color about him, saying that while he was flawed, he was an excellent trooper and would watch their backs when on patrol. I told them to push back when he made offensive jokes and comments. The advice of both Cook and Fisher rang in my head. I needed to learn how to work with all the troopers, whether I liked them or not because I had bigger fish to fry. Yet, learning to accept all troopers was complicated, especially when they were racist. But I could not let that keep me from my larger goal of changing the agency from within by attaining rank and wielding influence.

Still, the threat of deep-seated racism and the hateful attitudes held by other troopers and some of my neighbors never left my mind. I worried for my family because there was an active White supremacist survivalist training camp in Ulysses, Pennsylvania, less than twenty miles from my home in Wellsville.[126] I was one of only a handful of troopers of Color in the county. It would not have been hard to find out where I lived and when I was on patrol, away from my house.

"You're famous," my father said to me in Spanish when he came for a visit. "I didn't see you at the bus stop, so I asked the store clerk if he knew Trooper Perez. The clerk said yes and told me where you lived." I laughed and helped with his bags, explaining that since I was the only trooper like me in the village or the county, everyone in the village knew who I was and where I lived. My father asked how I dealt with such a different culture and all the White people. He had experienced plenty of racism and its painful consequences, and as a young man, he had self-medicated with alcohol. However, when I invited him to meet his grandchildren, he had been sober for years. I told him that there were enough good neighbors and troopers that my anxiety about my family's safety didn't get out of control. Fortunately, I said, I had met some kind and generous people, and I knew local police officers who performed their duties justly, competently, and with compassion.

One such officer was Walter Mackney. I first met Officer Mackney in the fall of 1982. I was assigned to back up a Village of Cuba police officer answering a domestic violence call. I drove through this small village and met Walt at the residence. He entered and spoke to the abused wife and the husband. Suddenly, the husband became enraged. I moved to help Walt restrain the man but stopped, seeing that Walter had quickly gained control and subdued him without injuring or being injured. I realized Walt knew Jujutsu. I helped Walt handcuff the man, placed him in Walt's patrol car, and followed them back to police headquarters in Cuba.

After that first encounter, Walt and I began discussing martial arts, jobs, and families. He and I became close friends, and Walt honored me when he asked me to be his children's godfather. He was and is one of the best and most committed police officers I have ever met. Walt self-identified as a man of Scottish and Polish descent. He had grown up in poverty as I had, but in Allentown Hamlet, Allegany County. I had thought I was poor when I lived in New York City; some of Walt's stories of rural poverty struck a nerve, and his family had been better off than some of their neighbors. For me, learning about rural poverty was both enlightening and disturbing.[127] Some years later, Walt successfully became a trooper, and after years of performing excellently, his troop commander recommended him for assignment to BCI as an investigator. As the BCI lieutenant colonel, I had the honor of adding him to the list of troopers from across the state for reassignment to BCI investigator and submitting it to the superintendent.

I invited Walt and his wife to join me for dinner in a Puerto Rican restaurant in the city of Rochester called El Taíno. While there, I noticed he was uncomfortable. "Walt, what's up," I asked. He thought the other patrons were staring at and talking about him. He and his wife were the only White people in the restaurant. I told him the initial stares were no different than at any other place when new customers walked in. After that, no one was staring at or talking about him. The other people were enjoying dinner with their families like we were. After a moment, he said, "Now I realize how you must feel; this is the first time I have been in a place where I was the minority."

Another example of the generosity of some troopers was a seasoned investigator at SP Wellsville, William K. Goetschius, who helped my family find a house to rent by referring us to a realtor he trusted even after I had mispronounced his name, Goatshit. Luckily for me, he had a sense of humor. I thought he had forgiven me until payback came along. The NYSP didn't use civilian dispatchers back then. Troopers answered calls and dispatched state police, local police, and other first responders on calls for service. On one occasion, as I "sat the desk," I received a call from a woman screaming that someone was raping her chickens.

I didn't know what to do. I put her on hold and asked the senior troopers and the sergeant what to do. They said to follow the procedures and take down the information. I took the woman off hold and asked for her name, address, and more details about what she alleged happened to her chickens. These questions infuriated her. She continued screaming. I knew it was against New York State law to have sex with animals, so I had to send someone to investigate. I put her on hold again, went to the investigators' office, and asked them what to do. They said I had to find out what the alleged acts were. I began questioning her again, and her voice cracked and deepened as she gave her answers. I then heard laughter on the other end of the line. The troopers and investigators at the station gathered, laughing loudly as well. Goetschius had often pulled this prank on rookie troopers, and I was the latest victim. He appeared from the locker room and congratulated me on surviving my christening as a Wellsville trooper. The joke was on me, I laughed and felt a sense of pride as a member of SP Wellsville.

This feeling, however, did not last long. One afternoon, when I was on dispatch, I called my wife and spoke to her in Spanish about our plans for that evening. A senior investigator with a rank equivalent to sergeant overheard me speaking Spanish and told me that if it were up to him, I would not be on the job. He would never have allowed me to fill out the job application, he said, and if I had managed to complete the form, he would have shredded it because neither men of Color nor women belonged in the state police. He retired a few years later after his son became a trooper. Thankfully, the son did not share his father's opinions on race and gender in the NYSP. He worked for me years later when I was the lieutenant of the BCI in Troop A. He was worried I might punish him for his father's sins and was relieved when he found out I would not hold him responsible for them.

I persuaded my mother to visit her grandchildren during my first year at SP Wellsville. While staying with us, she saw on the news that my brother had died. I was working the night shift, and she called me at work crying hysterically and told me what she had just seen. Initially, I worried whether the police had shot him or been murdered by someone involved in the drug trade. My brother led a troubled life. We each dealt with the trauma of our early childhoods, poverty, hunger, and a violent father in different ways. I was fortunate to have found the book *What Is Karate*, which led me to the discipline of martial arts. My brother was not as lucky as I was, and he began to use and sell drugs instead of finding a healthier way of coping. I called the NYPD precinct that patrolled that area and asked about the news report that my brother had died. They confirmed his death and said they suspected he had died in a drunken stupor or possibly committed suicide. However, there were no typical suicide notes or calls to our mother indicating he intended to kill himself.

My brother and I had fought over his behavior because he had repeatedly broken my mother's heart. Sadly, it got to the point where we had minimal contact. Our separation and disagreements grew more intense once I joined the NYSP, and I explained to him that his behavior jeopardized my ability to support my family. I told him I would see him at my mother's house to celebrate the holidays, but only if I was sure he was sober. I often told him I would be there for him if he wanted to change his life, but he always refused my help.

My mother thought I was too hard on my brother. For many years, she blamed me for his death and for the fact that she was not in NYC because I had invited her to visit. Tragically, she believed she might have been able to save him had she been there. I knew my mother, and I knew my brother, and we could not have stopped his self-destructive behavior. It took my mother years to reconcile her feelings about this, and we forgave each other before she lost her cognitive abilities in the fog of dementia. I knew I was doing the right thing by not enabling his behavior, but I still felt terrible. I wondered what my life would have been like if I had not joined the NYSP. A kind of survivor's guilt made me question whether I even deserved the chance to escape poverty. Building a bridge to a better life sometimes means stepping away from people who try to stop you. Unfortunately, that may include family members. My brother's death made me worry about whether I should be in the state police at all.

I needed to drive to New York City with my mother to identify my brother's remains and arrange his funeral, but the Gremlin would not have made it that far. Goetschius, who had helped me find a house to rent, helped again. He convinced a local car dealer to lease me a station wagon for the trip.

It also took me several months to resolve my feelings of responsibility for his death; I couldn't shake the feeling that I could have done more. I could have been more forgiving. I could have been more compassionate. I slowly forgave myself and pledged to do all I could to prevent other families from experiencing similar trauma. Moreover, I realized my family and I deserved the life we were building. The state police was the ticket to that, and I should not feel guilty about it because we had sacrificed and worked hard to get where we were. I would continue as a law enforcement officer, remembering to focus on the definition of "peace officer" I had adopted as my guiding light to act as an agent for social justice.

After my brother's death, on one of my regular visits to my mom's condominium in Brooklyn Heights, I sat staring out her window, satisfied that she had made it into the middle class. I watched the ships in New York Harbor sail past the Statue of Liberty. I thought to myself that my mother was one of the people Lady Liberty beckoned to these shores. Like many people from around the world, she felt welcomed by Emma Lazarus's poem "The New Colossus," which hangs on a plaque in the statue's base:

> Give me your tired, your poor,
> Your huddled masses yearning to breathe free,
> The wretched refuse of your teeming shore.
> Send these, the homeless, tempest-tost to me,
> I lift my lamp beside the golden door!

Like the state police, the United States is imperfect, but I am grateful for what they both provided me: freedom and opportunity. Holding my son on my mother's balcony, I turned to her and said,

"Mami, think about moving to Wellsville." At first, she said no. Before we left, she said, "Mijo, I will think about it." My mother had no immediate family members left in New York City, but it still took me a year to convince her to move to Wellsville to be closer to her grandchildren. I had already convinced Pamela's grandmother, mother, and sister, with her children, to move to Wellsville. Each of them stayed with us until they found affordable apartments. When my mother finally arrived, she followed suit and moved in with us until she found a house.

We were all better off living in Wellsville. Pamela's grandmother, mother, and sister struggled to make ends meet in the city. In Wellsville, we had a chance to thrive together. Moreover, as Pamela's chronic illness got worse, she would have family around her to support her. And finally, I knew my mother being near her grandchildren would help her manage her grief over the loss of my brother; at least, I hoped it would. Despite my own experience with that same grief and loss, I was unprepared for my first investigation of a fatal motor vehicle accident. When I arrived on Beechnut Hill Road that morning, I saw a man sitting on the back bumper of a tanker truck, his head in his hands. Exiting my vehicle, I saw a woman with three little children around her. She was crying, as was the truck driver. I reached him first and asked what happened. "I killed a little girl," he said through his sobbing. Shocked, I asked him to repeat what he had just said. He was inconsolable and cried even more intensely, unable to respond.

With her three children in tow, the mother approached the back of the truck. She was shouting and pointing at the truck's rear tires. "My baby is in there! My baby's in there!" I squatted and saw a little girl's body wedged between the dual tires, crushed and lifeless. I fought back tears. I had a job to do. I clenched my jaw and kept my composure. I too had a little girl around the same age. She was safe at home. Still, it was all I could do not to lose control. "I'll call an ambulance," I told the mother. The ambulance would take her daughter to the emergency room were the official declaration of death would occur, but I didn't say that part aloud. I went to my car and radioed for the ambulance. Then I returned to the driver and asked him gently what had happened. He told me the four children were running across the road as he crested the hill, and he couldn't stop in time to avoid hitting the youngest and slowest child. I then went to the mother and asked her what she had seen. She had sent her eight-year-old boy across the street to get the mail. She hadn't known all her other children, including her two-year-old girl, had followed him. She did not see the accident but heard the screeching brakes and a thud. I asked her if I could talk to her son, and she agreed. He confirmed the details.

I took the necessary measurements, photographs, and statements. Then, I helped the ambulance crew carefully remove the toddler's body from between the tires. We placed the tiny body in the ambulance and helped the mother get in. Her daughter's death had been instantaneous, I told her, and she hadn't suffered. I then drove to my house, called for my little girl, and hugged her for a long time as tears flowed from my eyes. My wife, startled, asked what had happened. In a whisper, I explained, and she, too, started crying. After a while, we regained our composure and assured our daughter everything was all right.

Several days later, the little girl's mother called and asked to meet me at the barracks. She arrived with her significant other, who came along as moral support. I brought them to the interview room and asked her how I could help. Her eyes red and swollen from crying, she demanded an explanation of how her baby had died. Her request surprised me, and I didn't respond right away. She had been there, after all, and while she didn't see the accident, she did hear what the driver said, and I had already told her that her child had died painlessly. I had tried to spare her the horrible details and didn't want to go over them now. I wondered later, Was that because I did not want to relive it myself? The mother cried and shouted, "I need to know what happened!" I hesitated, and her boyfriend began yelling at me, too, saying that she had a right to know. I told him to calm down, or I would ask him to leave. Hearing the commotion, the station sergeant opened the door and asked whether everything was okay. I told him yes and said the mother's friend was leaving, which he did, albeit unhappily, muttering expletives out the door.

I asked the mother to stay behind and cautioned her again that the facts would be harrowing. I asked myself, Should I tell her she could have prevented this tragedy by getting the mail herself? Instead, I explained how the accident happened and why the driver could not have prevented it. It was not what she wanted to hear. She blamed herself and wanted to shift the blame to the driver. Eventually, she stormed out of the room and left.

To this day, the horror of that accident stays wedged in my psyche. I tear up each time I think of this incident. I was a rookie, and I had not yet learned that the need to know precisely how and why someone you love died tragically is a natural reaction. It tries to fill the hole left by grief with answers. My mother and I knew this all too well. It took me only a few months to come to grips with my brother's death, but my mother's grief and search for the reasons took years to subside. Ultimately, we both learned to accept that sometimes there are no answers, just heartache that never goes away. After living in Wellsville for about two years, my wife and I decided to stay. We felt it would be a safe place to raise our children, even though we knew there would be challenges. I was concerned about my family dealing with racist attitudes in the community, yet most people were welcoming. New York City had 1,832 homicides in 1981, which made Wellsville a safer choice.[128] Some violent crimes did happen in Wellsville, but it wasn't as serious a problem as it was in the city.

Another benefit of staying in Wellsville was that we could now do something we would never have thought possible in New York City. We could afford to pursue the American dream of owning our home. Given the history of "redlining" and its continued impact even after it became illegal, I also doubted I would have qualified for a mortgage in the city.[129] I was privileged with the community support I garnered as a trooper in Wellsville. I faced an opportunity to create generational wealth, so I talked to that same realtor who helped us find our rental on Scott Avenue and asked her to help me find a home.

We found a modest three-bedroom place on Pleasant Street in the Village of Wellsville. However, I had no savings. The realtor told me I could go to the Farmers Home Administration (FmHA) for a loan. The FmHA provided direct and guaranteed loans that farmers, low-income families, and seniors in rural areas could access.[130] There I was, suddenly on the verge of achieving the American dream I never thought I would reach. But the reality of America's bigotry said not so fast. There were barriers to overcome before I could buy this house, and they started at the FmHA.

As a new trooper, I made only $13,606 a year, which was $3,744 above the poverty line during the 1980s, and placed our family firmly within the low-income tax bracket. We quickly qualified for FmHA loans under the guidelines. I found the local FmHA representative scheduled a meeting with him. He handed me the application at the meeting but said he thought I would not qualify. I asked why, and the look on his face led me to believe what he said was not based on any regulation. My gut told me the reason was my ethnicity. He then told me to complete the application anyway and that he would look it over. I filled out the form, returned it the next day, and asked him to look it over while waiting. He refused, saying he had to be thorough and it would take him some time. He told me to return in a week. I left, concerned he would deny me the loan based on his perceptible bias.

I called a week later, but he had yet to decide. A few days later, I returned to his office for the third time. He still had not made up his mind. As I left, I stopped to read a poster on his wall outlining the FmHA lending process. It included a line that said the FmHA was an equal opportunity lender. I ran my finger across that line several times and read it aloud. Then I turned to look at the agent. His face turned the color of a cooked lobster. Gotcha, I thought to myself. I asked if I could return next week to discuss the loan further. The fourth time I visited his office, the loan officer told me my application was approved, and I got the $33,000 loan. With it, I bought my first home.

The house's previous owner was a widow who had raised her family there. It was a two-story Federal-style house with gray siding and a detached garage. Its three bedrooms would give my family plenty of space. Every other year, I would dress up as a scarecrow for Halloween, wearing overalls, boots, and a straw hat, all stuffed with straw. I would sit motionless on the big front porch, waiting for older trick-or-treaters to ring the bell looking for their treat. That's when I served up the trick. I would say in a low voice, "Hello," and stand up very slowly. This would scare some of them and usually delighted the parents. Once, a kid reacted by kicking me in the leg! I leaped up and laughed as he ran down the street. On the off years, I would put a dummy in the overalls and watch from inside as the children approached the door cautiously and the parents waited for the jump scare. Some kids would kick the dummy to see if it would move as they quickly stepped off the porch. My children loved these antics and told me the neighborhood kids did, too. My family and I lived in that house for eighteen years, leaving for Albany when my son graduated high school.

Chapter 9 - Doors Open

I had decided during my training at the state police academy that I needed to advance as quickly as possible through the ranks. As a result, I went after every opportunity the state police offered. I knew I was an outsider who would not have been allowed to enter the NYSP ranks before Judge Foley's decree. And even though I'd gained entry and become a trooper, I suspected I would face the same racism as I moved closer to the inner circles of power and privilege in the state police. Indeed, some of the power brokers within the state police did all they could to ensure those doors stayed hard to open in hopes no members of marginalized groups would enter these halls of power and try to change the discriminatory policies and culture. Author Malcolm Gladwell gave a talk on pariahs, tokens, and pioneers.[131] I was already a pariah as far as the state police were concerned. I did not want to be a token, someone singularly different from the group that allowed them in, but once admitted, the door closed behind them. I wanted to be a pioneer who got into the state police's upper echelon and kept the doors open. I wanted to ensure the path upward was well-lit so others could follow.[132]

The New York State Police formed a special weapons and tactics (SWAT) team called the Olympic Team for the 1980 Winter Olympics in Lake Placid, New York. State police officials were concerned that a terrorist attack could occur during the 1980 Winter Games like the one that had happened during the 1972 Munich Olympics. At that time, it had only been eight years since the Munich Olympics, where the eight members of the Palestinian terrorist group known as the Black September killed two Israeli Olympic team members and took nine other Israelis hostage. The leaders of Black September demanded the release of Palestinian prisoners held by the Israeli government. The terrorists also requested a safe passage flight to Cairo, Egypt. At Fürstenfeldbruck, a NATO airbase, the West German police, in a failed attempt to stop the terrorists, ended up killing five of the eight Black September members, all the hostages, and a West German police officer.[133] The Olympic team disbanded soon after the 1980 game. But a few years later, the state police realized it needed a permanent SWAT team, given the ongoing potential acts of terrorism because of the Iranian revolution that included the taking of American hostages.[134]

My first opportunity occurred in the wake of the Iran hostage crisis. Division formed a new squad with stricter qualifying standards and a broader mission in 1984. The first name they settled on for this new SWAT team was the New York State Police Emergency Response Module. The acronym, "NYSPERM," makes me laugh to this day. Sure, maybe it was fitting, given all the testosterone involved in the conception of SWAT teams across the nation, but I was glad when they finally considered the acronym and changed their minds. The New York State Mobile Response Team (NYSMRT) was a better choice, and while it might prompt a few jokes, they'd be nothing compared to the alternative.

To be an MRT member, you needed recommendations from all your local commanders, starting with your sergeant, then the zone commander, and ending with your troop commander. I sent my request to compete for a slot in the MRT and did not receive an immediate reply because the troop commander sent a trooper with greater seniority, which I respected. Seniority was a standard part of contract negotiations between the state and the Police Benevolent Association regarding higher salaries, increased time off, job security, and other benefits. Once I gained more seniority, I hoped I would have more opportunities for assignments to specialized units.

I also understood there were disadvantages to the seniority system. For instance, since most troopers of Color had only a few years of service under their belts, if a budget crisis arose, the last hired would be the first fired based on seniority. It could also prevent individuals with superior performance to more senior employees from being selected for advancement. Senior troopers applying for promotions were given additional points on the test based on their time on the job, which also disadvantaged newer troopers. But in this instance, the good outweighed the bad, and my patience paid off. I got my shot when the more senior trooper, already trained as a K9 handler and a police sniper, failed the demanding physical examination needed to join the MRT. Although I had only a few weeks to prepare, I passed the grueling test. On February 24, 1984, I began training with twenty-four other troopers to become a member of the NYSMRT.

The training for the team lasted six months and took place primarily at the state police academy. Once on the team, members had to pass a challenging physical examination annually. These tests did not reflect the job skills you would need as an MRT member. The tests created by NYSP self-defense instructors, all of whom were powerlifters, were for strength and endurance. These were the requirements:

- Bench press: body weight ten times, 130 percent body weight once.
- Squat press: body weight ten times, 150 percent body weight once.
- Deadlift: body weight ten times, 200 percent body weight once.
- Military press: 50 percent body weight ten times, 75 percent body weight once.
- Run: 1.5 miles in less than eleven minutes.

MRT members had to complete each phase of this qualification process in a single day. This battery of tests weeded out those at a lower fitness level. This was the stage in the process that eliminated the first candidate from Troop A, which allowed me to take my shot. I had been a martial artist since my boyhood, and I knew that while strength and endurance were necessary, they were not as important as kinetic intelligence. That is, being agile and quick to assess obstacles. Some years later, the NYSP changed the qualifying exam, but on that day, I easily completed the weightlifting and running requirements.

After all that work, the weekend before reporting, I nearly ruined my opportunity to participate in the first training session. I started teaching Karate in a newly opened fitness center on Main Street. I rented floor space and put the word out, and adults, children, and several local police officers, including Walt Mackney, joined the class. A few months later, another martial artist invited me to give a demonstration in a neighboring town.

I had practiced tameshiwari, breaking wooden boards and bricks, for decades. As I placed the two bricks one atop the other and raised my hand, I thought this would be an easy demonstration of skill, concentration, and speed. I struck the bricks with my palm's edge. They did not break. Embarrassed, I quickly hit them again because I had allowed myself to be distracted. This time, they broke, but so did my hand. The audience applauded as I thanked them for their interest and hid the pain. I wrapped my right hand, drove to Jones Memorial Hospital, and walked out with a fiberglass cast on the hand I used to draw my service revolver. I reported to the academy that following Monday.

When I arrived, the officer overseeing the training session asked what had happened. I told them, and they said, well, you're here. Let's start your training. Great, I thought, relieved I wouldn't miss my chance for assignment to the MRT. At lunch, I entered the cafeteria and stood in line with my tray, not noticing the uniformed colonel sitting at the commissioned officers' table at the front of the room. I enjoyed my lunch and returned to the classroom. When I got there, the zone sergeant in charge of the MRT training pulled me aside and asked, "What the fuck did you do? The colonel wants to see you now." I marched to another building on the campus that served as the NYSP headquarters and asked the sergeant at the front desk what floor the colonel was on. The colonel's office had a waiting room, and his assistant sat down and waited. I sat there, nervous, for what seemed like forever, but it was only five minutes. When the assistant said, "Trooper Perez, he will see you now," I walked into the office and stood at attention.

"Reported as ordered, sir."

"Relax, let me see your hands," he said and glared over his reading glasses. "What the fuck is with the cast?" I told him it was a minor injury. I said the cast was coming off tomorrow, leaving off the fact that I'd be removing it myself several weeks early.

"Can you draw your weapon?" he asked sternly.

"Yes, sir."

I turned, faced sideways, drew the 357 Smith & Wesson, and holstered, all the while hiding the pain as best I could. I turned back toward him. He glared at me but finally said, "Okay, be careful. dismissed." Relieved once again that I would not be leaving the MRT training that day, I saluted the colonel and turned to walk out when suddenly he said, "Stop! What is that knife doing on your belt? You are out of uniform." He then ordered me not to let him see me out of uniform again. I saluted and walked out. Luck was with me that day. That evening, I split the fiberglass cast in half. I got some athletic tape to use during the training day, and at night, I would place my hand back in the cast and wrap it with the tape to keep it in place as I slept. My hand healed, though maybe not as well as it could have. To this day, it hurts during inclement weather.

During the arduous training, our team spirit arose organically. We trained from February through June 1984, starting with the three weeks of defensive tactics. Once this phase was over, we trained one week every month for the next few years. Between training sessions, we responded to critical incidents whenever the team's special skills could improve the outcome. The training forged our strong kinship, and the dangerous missions over the years only strengthened it.

Figure 9. The Original Mobile Response—The
Defensive Tactics Course Instructors[135]

For the first three weeks of the training, the self-defense instructors had created requirements based on their defensive tactics instructors' qualification criteria, but for the MRT, they made the requirements much more demanding. They believed this would mean only the best and most committed candidates would make it through. On one level, the change was appropriate; they needed to create a team, and the members who succeeded would believe they were part of the best team ever. The more rigorous the entry criteria, the more likely those who made it would think of themselves as worthy of membership in an exclusive group; still, the overly rigorous process was not the right fit for the MRT and what it needed from its members.

Figure 10. Firearms and Tactical Raid Training-
Troopers Perez, Wall, and Vitale (July 1984)[136]

The MRT would be an exclusive and prestigious team; I was one of only two candidates of Color and a White woman who hoped to earn a position on the team. We joined the others for defensive tactics instructor training. To the chagrin of some instructors and supervisory staff, we three passed and became the first defensive tactics instructors certified with Foley's label "protected class" of troopers. Soon after, the other Latino trooper left to join the FBI, and the woman left the Division for personal reasons. I continued and earned my position on the team. At the time, I was already a seasoned martial artist with more than twenty years of experience, and I can tell you that this self-defense training was far harsher than it needed to be. It was also technically flawed because many instructors had minimal martial arts experience. Their self-defense training had come mainly from the NYSP and relied on strength, not skill. I offered to share my skills during the training sessions, but the instructors expressed no interest. I even told them I had competed in the New York State Police Olympics and had won gold and silver medals. Of course, this didn't matter to them because the harsh discipline's real purpose was weeding out the "weakest" candidates.

Figure 11. Photo of the medals I won in the
1983 New York Police Olympics.[137]

With the instructors ignoring me, I decided to soldier on and prove I could become an MRT member. It also matched my larger goal of changing the NYSP from within. No affirmative action quotas would help me qualify for the MRT. When asked how I became a team member, fellow troopers and MRT members acknowledged that. This helped change the perspective of my brothers on the team and their colleagues, and I counted that as a small victory in my mission to effect change from within. When I became certified as a defensive tactics instructor (DTI), I was periodically assigned to teach defensive tactics to recruits. Being a DTI allowed me to talk to recruits about the power of diversity and inclusion. I was glad recruits of Color got to see someone like them who was a member of the division's elite specialized unit. Many of these recruits had grown up captivated by SWAT teams in movies and TV shows. They had fun learning from the defensive tactics instructor from the MRT. They discovered I was a black belt in several forms of Karate and Jujutsu.

After the three weeks of DTI training, we underwent extensive firearms training on multiple weapons platforms. We fired thousands of rounds of ammunition and developed higher levels of expertise in using .357 caliber revolvers, 12-gauge shotguns, .270 caliber sniper rifles, and .9 mm submachine guns. We earned emergency medical technician (EMT) certification, gained skills in wilderness rescue operations, and became a formidable team, training once a month after the initial training concluded. But just weeks before the end of the training period, this mission tested the newly formed MRT's readiness.

On May 22, 1984, James J. Swan, thirty-five, escaped from the Cattaraugus County courthouse. Swan had been on trial for the slaying of a New York State Trooper, Gary Kubasiak, a nine-year veteran of the NYSP who had died in a shoot-out at the Swan family home. I have attended many funerals of police officers killed in the line of duty. I mourn their deaths, and the grief of the families they leave behind is lasting. I am also proud of them. Trooper Kubasiak and the 162 other New York State Police troopers who have died in the line of duty gave their "last full measure of devotion," as Lincoln put it in his Gettysburg Address. As the guards led Swan into the courtroom, Swan broke away from sheriff's deputies and escaped through an emergency exit.[138]

Captain Gregory Sitler, now the leader of the MRT, briefed us on the mission's details and informed us that NYSP headquarters had approved the MRT to aid in capturing the escapee. Sitler ordered us to gather our gear and prepare for several days of searching. When the captain left, the sergeant asked me to lead the way to the sheriff's office in Cattaraugus County because I was from that part of the state. We all met in the back parking lot of the academy, the site of the punishing physical training sessions I had endured as a recruit a few years before. We got in our vehicles and began the six-hour drive to western New York.

Our caravan arrived, and we reported to the quartermaster to register for lodging and travel expenses. The area commander briefed us and assigned our team to search wooded areas, rail lines, and other areas in and around Little Valley, Cattaraugus County. We broke up into units of two and searched for a couple of days. Swan was captured on May 24, just two days after he escaped, in an abandoned cabin in an adjoining township just five miles away. He was convicted and sentenced to life in prison. We were excited about the mission but disappointed we had not been the ones to catch Swan. The search had covered a wide area of western New York and involved hundreds of officers. It was our first real mission, proving we were a cohesive team ready for deployment. We returned to the academy to complete our final month of training and prepare for graduation ceremonies, which seemed anticlimactic after the mission. I had finally learned the lesson both Cook and Fisher had imparted, and this time, I attended the graduation party held by my comrades and our supervisors. Some of these guys occasionally made stupid jokes, but I had gained their respect, and they had gained mine.

I remained a member of the Mobile Response Team for more than five years. Despite the occasional conflicts with my colleagues, it was one of my best experiences in the state police. Once I earned my sergeant's chevrons, Captain Sitler appointed me team leader for half of the MRT. The MRT had two teams: the West Team responded to any crisis west of State Route 81, which included twenty-eight counties, and the East Team covered the rest of the state, including Long Island. This appointment to leader of the West Team was an incredible honor. All my brothers on the team congratulated me, and they all knew affirmative action had nothing to do with it. My MRT comrades and I genuinely cared for each other. This closeness developed because it was built into our training and deliberately cultivated by the supervisors and training instructors. Our commitment to excellence and each other led to a deep and genuine esprit de corps that starkly contrasted the weak one the initial academy tried to create by making us hate the instructors. The MRT training and our unexpected first mission turned us into a band of brothers.[139]

Chapter 10 - Santa Claus

By 1987, I had been on the MRT for three years, and the first promotional examination I qualified for was the permanent rank of sergeant, approaching in the summer of 1988. My family and I were still living in Wellsville, and though they endured my not being home often and missing some celebrations and family events. Pamela, my daughter, and my son were proud of me and very supportive. My daughter was six and a half years old; my son was five, and they enjoyed bragging rights with their friends and within the family. I explained to them that when I passed the exam, I would only get positions as sergeant that stationed me away from home again, but I would work my way back home as quickly as possible.

Passing the sergeant's examination was critical to me on two fronts. First, my salary would increase, strengthening my family's social mobility and economic security. Second, it would enhance my role as a change agent in the NYSP and move me closer to my goal of being a policymaker. If my fellow troopers of Color and I diversified the leadership of the state police, we could do more than hope; we would work to serve the communities of New York State more equitably, particularly communities of Color and other marginalized communities.

I asked lots of questions about the sergeants' promotional exam. Everyone I spoke to said it was incredibly challenging. Some even hinted that this upcoming round of promotional exams would be made more difficult by the exam writers unit because it was the first time Judge Foley's protected class troopers were eligible to participate in the promotional process. Given all this chatter, I began preparing in the winter of 1986. I ensured my police manuals, New York penal and criminal procedure laws, and other books were up-to-date. I also asked about the open secret within the state police: copies of earlier promotional examinations. While security to prevent leaks about upcoming exam questions was highly robust, the old exams were not so closely guarded. The old exams did not give the answers to the questions of future exams. They did reveal the style and direction of the exam writers, who didn't often change since the unit overseeing the exam's preparation and publication also stayed relatively constant. I had heard these exam copies circulated among the "good old boys" network within the state police. Sharing these exam copies was an exclusive form of social capital I hoped I could access. Possessing these older exams could result in disciplinary action, but that rarely happened. While most supervisors in the NYSP would deny ever having a set of these old exams, most Division members knew these existed and would acquire them during exam cycles. The problem with using these old exams was that the structure of the test questions did not comport with the new sentence structure. The questions on the old exams appeared straightforward and used only two or three sentences. However, once I took the sergeants' test, I saw that the questions were a paragraph long and more complex in their structure.

In the winter of 1986, Lieutenant Cook pulled me aside while I was back at the academy for some in-service MRT training. "I finally convinced the bosses I needed more help if they wanted the Affirmative Action Office of the New York State Police to work," he said. "Would you consider becoming a technical sergeant and coming work for me in the Affirmative Action Office?" I thanked him and told him I needed to consider it and speak to my family first. The offer meant I would have to work in Albany. I didn't want to uproot my family and move there because once I passed the promotional exams that summer, I would almost certainly have to move somewhere else within the state to take a position as a sergeant. I talked with my family about this career path, and we decided I would move wherever I needed to as I rose through the ranks. Rather than being uprooted with every promotion, my family would stay in Wellsville until our youngest child graduated high school. This decision changed the career timeline I had laid out, and the idea of being apart from my family for long stretches gave me a pit in my stomach.

Pamela was the strong one. She said, "I got this. I love you. We will support you one hundred percent." We were working toward her goal, too, she said. She never wanted us to experience poverty again, and if my being away from home periodically was what we had to endure, so be it. "Our babies deserve to be free from hunger and want," she said. Both kids hugged me and said they would miss me. I told them I would be home on the weekends and play with them even more during my time at home. That news made them laugh and shout, "Yay!" I could never have succeeded without my family's support. We all made sacrifices to gain a stronger foothold in the middle class. If I stayed in the NYSP, my salary would increase, our financial stability would become more durable, and we would climb the socioeconomic ladder. All this moved us further away from our days in poverty.

I told Lieutenant Cook I would accept the position if he made the offer official, but I also took a significant risk. I said I had worked so hard to be a member of the MRT, and I reminded Cook that I was the only person of Color on the team. I told him I felt I needed to remain on the team for the sake of diversity, illustrating we could do any assignment in the Division when given a fair chance. The position was also personally meaningful because of the work I had put in and the friendships I had built with my team members. Cook said, "Pedro, what a set of balls! I offer you a promotion, but that's not enough. You have the nerve to ask me for more."

I thought, well, if he says no, I can stay on the MRT and continue studying for the sergeant's exam. He glared at me momentarily, then a mischievous smile crept across his face, and he said, "Okay." "Thank you. I will give you 150 percent," I said.

In January 1987, I became a technical sergeant in the Affirmative Action Office of the New York State Police. As I had done before, I packed up and moved into the dorms at the academy in Albany. Recruits and tenured troopers there for in-service training sleep two to a room with one bathroom for every two rooms. There were also a small number of single occupancy rooms for visiting instructors, sergeants, and commissioned officers who had official business in Albany. You needed the approval of the major in charge of the academy to stay in the single rooms, and I counted myself lucky to get one. Along with Lieutenant Cook, I joined an African American man and a White woman, both technical sergeants. My new colleagues were all members of Judge Foley's protected class of troopers who helped the credibility of the Affirmative Action Office and, in many ways, qualified us for the positions. Lieutenant Cook was ahead of his time in that respect. He understood that to be taken seriously by the protected-class troopers, the office was supposed to advocate for, and the office staff would need to include protected-class troopers. No White men were working in the Affirmative Action Office. I suspect he recruited me because of my frankness with him during my time at the academy and my success as a member of the division's elite MRT. No one could argue that affirmative action or special consideration was involved in that achievement.

The Division offered no formal training in affirmative action to the other sergeants or me. It was a missed opportunity. Inside the state police, we had individuals who opposed affirmative action, and we had recruits admitted to the NYSP through its affirmative action program who needed help managing the bigotry they encountered from within and outside the division. I was unaware of diversity training, cultural sensitivity, or policy review procedures Lieutenant Cook may have had associated with his position. I saw this as a failure on the part of the state police. Despite these concerns, I accepted the position, hoping to effect change by helping men of Color and women succeed within the state police.

Lieutenant Cook needed additional staff to carry out the office's mission. He devoted most of his time to investigating accusations of discrimination and helping protected-class troopers across the state. He focused on ensuring these troopers transitioned successfully into the state police job and its culture. Soon after I arrived in Albany, Cook recruited Arthur Taggart, an African American senior investigator from Troop A, the westernmost of all the troops. Taggart was assigned to the Affirmative Action Office to help investigate allegations of discrimination and violations of the affirmative action policy. Cook's staff now included three technical sergeants and one senior investigator, each of us from a protected-class cohort. We gave the appearance that the state police were committed to diversity and inclusion; however, that commitment had yet to permeate the culture of the state police in meaningful ways. Many of the organization's members had not bought into it. The question remained: Would they ever?

At first, my job was researching and compiling relevant data on affirmative action. I read social science journals, newspapers, and magazines to flesh out any comments about the state police's affirmative action program. I helped develop in-service educational programs about affirmative action for all employees. I was part of developing the mechanism for resolving incidents of discrimination in ways consistent with the rules and regulations of the state police and the governor's executive orders. I also investigated alleged acts of discrimination against any state police employee. During this period, the governor and the legislature increased the NYSP's authorized strength by adding several hundred new trooper positions, and the state police rapidly expanded its workforce. This increase required the addition of a second state police academy at Brockport College, a few miles west of Rochester, New York. This academy was closer to Wellsville, where my family still lived.

I went to Lieutenant Cook and asked for an assignment to that post. "I was there last year as one of the defensive tactics instructors," I told him, "so I'm familiar with the setup and the officers commanding the academy there." Unfortunately, Cook had someone else in mind for that post and said no. A physical altercation occurred at the NYSP Summer Youth Camp in Albany. One technical sergeant, a Black man, had slapped another technical sergeant, a White woman because she allegedly made a snide remark about his hamburger grilling skills. Lieutenant Cook moved the man to the temporary police academy at Brockport to calm things down. Cook's formal disciplinary investigation led to the technical sergeants settling their differences, and the man was allowed to return home to Albany.

That created a vacancy for an affirmative action officer at the Brockport Academy, and Cook let me transfer so I could be closer to my family. Brockport was only eighty-six miles north of Wellsville, and I could commute home most nights. It made things easier for the six months I was there since Pamela fell seriously ill and was diagnosed with lupus and interstitial cystitis during this period. I am sure the cause of the cystitis was a botched emergency C-section in 1980. When my daughter was born, she went into fetal distress. The doctor lacerated my wife's bladder during the caesarian procedure. It also caused my newborn daughter's admittance to the neonatal intensive care unit (NICU). She received an antibiotic injection while in the NICU, and the injection site became infected, leaving a significant scar. She remained in the NICU for a week before I could take her home. Pamela's hospital stay lasted several months. Luckily, we were still in Brooklyn then, and because my mother worked the night shift, she could watch my daughter during the day while I was working. Pamela recovered enough to leave the hospital. As she slowly recuperated, we raised our daughter and son, focusing on our journey.

I told Lieutenant Cook about my wife's diagnosis and requested a transfer back to SP Wellsville. Cook ensured I understood that meant I would return to Wellsville as a trooper, not as a sergeant. Undaunted, I told him it was the best course of action. I also told him I had begun studying for the examination for the permanent rank of sergeant. He suggested I remain in the Affirmative Action Office while I prepared for the test, and once I passed the exam, he would approve my transfer. As always, I told him it was a family decision. I would speak with my wife and children and do what they wished. Pamela said the doctors believed they could help her manage the initial stages of the illness but that it would likely become debilitating in the future. Pamela and I sobbed but agreed to forge ahead. We decided I would stay at the Affirmative Action Office until I got my permanent sergeant's rank. With the children, we would get through this together. She said to me, and only half-jokingly, "You better pass that exam." I told Lieutenant Cook what we had decided, and he reaffirmed that he would honor my transfer request once I passed the exam. Using a combination of family sick leave and vacation days, I took time off work for a few weeks to care for Pamela until she was stable and could manage more independently with the help of her mother, mine, and her sister also helped during this period. Once I was back at the Affirmative Action office in Albany, I continued studying but adjusted my schedule. Many troopers there frequented Ralph's Italian Restaurant, which had great Buffalo wings and decent prices. Along with Ralph's, there were Chinese, Japanese, and Indian restaurants within a couple of miles of the academy. I rotated through these restaurants, eating at a different one each night. I took my study materials, picked an out-of-the-way corner, ordered a small pitcher of beer, and spent a couple of hours eating dinner and studying the manuals. I kept to this schedule from January through June 1987, just before the sergeant's exam. The only interruptions to my studying schedule were when my family needed me and Mobile Response Team assignments.

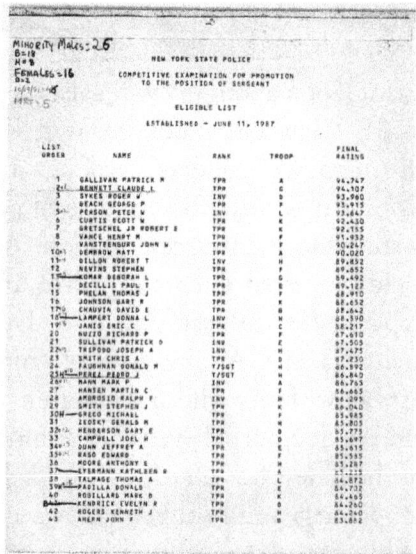

Figure 12. 1987 NYSP Promotional List for
Permanent Rank of Sergeant[140]

The sergeant's promotional exam occurs every four years. The score on the written exam, plus points added for seniority and excellent on-the-job performance, are added to establish the final grade and your position on the promotional list. Once set up, the list remains in effect until the Division announces a new list four years later. As sergeants' vacancies occur, individuals on the promotional exam list are selected to fill those vacancies. As a rule, there may be scores of vacancies during the life of the list, but not hundreds. This limited vacancy rate meant it was in the best interest of those seeking to be a sergeant to score as high as possible; otherwise, they may have to wait for the next exam. Several hundred troopers took the sergeant's exam every time it was available. Some studied diligently, and others used it as a day off. The highest score in my exam cohort was 94.747, and the lowest passing score was 63.455. I initially scored 86.84 and was ranked twenty-fifth out of 201 troopers who passed the test that year. My grade increased to 87 after an appeal showed an error made by the graders, but the increase did not change my position on the list.

Forty-two protected-class troopers were on this list, and all of us achieved this without affirmative action points or considerations. Still, throughout my career, I heard those who opposed affirmative action mutter that our presence on the job was because of Judge Foley's decree. Therefore, we didn't deserve any promotions or commendations we earned. The forty-two included sixteen women (including two Black women) and twenty-six men of Color (eighteen Black and eight Hispanic). Additionally, forty-six of the men and women on this list were from my recruit class, and five of the men were on the Mobile Response Team with me.

On January 7, 1988, I received my sergeant's permanent rank, and as I had discussed with Lieutenant Cook a year before, I requested a transfer back to SP Wellsville as a station sergeant. Lieutenant Cook kept his word. He approved and sent my request for a transfer up the command chain. Once transferred back to the Wellsville barracks, I would supervise some of my old colleagues, which might have been challenging, but it was not a problem. Most troopers were proud that one of their own was on the MRT. The station sergeants were supportive, but they were uncertain about assignment MRT missions that would take me away from Wellsville; from their perspective, while it was terrific to have bragging rights, they needed me present to help with enforcement efforts and schedule patrol coverage. It took several months before the Colonels approved the transfer. While I waited, I remained in the Affirmative Action Office and continued living at the academy. I was now the team leader for the West Team of the MRT, which oversaw calls in the western part of New York

State. Sometimes, when a case was significant enough, the entire MRT was called to respond. One such case occurred in June 1988. Several weeks before moving back to Wellsville, while still working at the Affirmative Action Office, I received a call from Captain Sitler, the MRT's commanding officer. He said, "I just spoke to your boss, Lieutenant Cook, and told him we need to deploy you to help execute a dangerous search and arrest warrant on the Mohawk territory tomorrow morning."

The Haudenosaunee in New York had often tried to exercise what they considered was their full sovereignty. Haudenosaunee is the name six of the Indigenous nations chose for themselves. While it is also known as the Iroquois Confederacy, the origins of the term Iroquois are unclear. Some scholars say it refers to a language, not a people; others claim the Algonquins dubbed their rivals Iroquois, meaning rattlesnake, because their rivals were fierce warriors and skilled hunters.[141] Finally, upon encountering these people for the first time during the colonial era, some historians believe that the French coined the phrase.[142] In the years between my learning about the Oil Springs Seneca territory and the date of this assignment various Indigenous nations began opening what at the time considered illegal gambling operations and casinos. The St. Regis Mohawk nation had bought slot machines and installed them at casinos in their Akwesasne, New York territory. Interestingly, Akwesasne, the "Land Where the Partridge Drums," is the only American Indian territory that sits on the border of two separate countries, Canada and the United States.[143] Before the colonization of this hemisphere by the European nations, there existed "the Iroquois [Haudenosaunee; 'People of the Longhouse' Confederacy of upper New York state and southeastern Canada. The Iroquois Confederacy is often characterized as one of the world's oldest participatory democracies."[144] Six eastern U.S. and Canadian Indian nations were members of this confederacy.

Once the Revolutionary War broke out, members of this confederacy chose sides. The Mohawks and Seneca fought on the British Empire's side, and the others chose the fledgling United States. Those divisions morphed several times and continued through the

War of 1812, narrowly won by the United States.[145] That formally decided where the border between these nations would be, leaving the Mohawks on Indian land divided by the international dividing line they had no part in determining. The Jay Treaty granted the Mohawks on either side of this border the right to cross freely.[146] It also conceded several layers of protection to those Mohawks living on their territory's Canadian side. Irrespective of these considerations, some members of the Haudenosaunee nations felt and still feel that it weakened the confederacy and each nation's sovereignty.[147] These events led to strengthening, in the United States and specifically in New York state, greater oversight of Native American affairs on Indigenous land. This compact gave rise to the NYSP's authorization to enforce New York State criminal laws and to help federal agencies enforce federal laws on the territory, as in this instance. That day, we helped enforce federal gambling statutes, which I would do as I headed to St. Regis. I donned my MRT fatigues, gathered my equipment and enough clothing and personal toiletries to last several days, checked my firearms, and loaded everything into my patrol car. I met the captain and the other MRT members in the state police academy's rear parking lot. It would take approximately four hours to get to the rallying point at Massena state police barracks.

Once we arrived at SP Massena, Troop Commander and his BCI officers briefed us on the situation. They told us several Mohawk casinos were using illegal slot machines. My team was assigned to secure the Bear's Den casino. The commander gave the other squad a different casino. Both teams asked for a floor plan, the approximate number of people in the casinos, and more details to ensure a reasonably safe operation. We executed the warrants with little resistance since we entered at 5:30 a.m. We seized two hundred slot machines as evidence and arrested four individuals. A couple of weeks later, on July 21, 1989, over two hundred state troopers and FBI agents, including the entire MRT team, returned and executed a second raid of the other casinos. Tensions mounted between the elected Mohawk Governmental Council and the traditionalist Mohawk Council, who requested the removal of slot machines. The Mohawk business community and their supporters who had installed the slot machines in their privately owned casinos were also part of the dispute.[148] The National Indian Gaming Commission (NIGC) of the Department of the Interior, created after the passage of the Indian Gaming Regulatory Act of 1988, would allow Gaming on Indian lands; the local states with these Indian lands had to develop a compact with Aboriginal nations seeking to establish casinos. At that time, New York had not agreed, and slot machines were illegal in New York.[149]

Some Mohawks agreed with casino operators that these casinos were not illegal and that they were supplying jobs and enhancing economic opportunities. This faction began protests. Mohawks who thought allowing the casinos would corrupt their nation and destroy the Mohawk culture also planned to protest. Doug George, the editor of The Akwesasne Notes, a Mohawk newspaper, said, "The general reaction here is a great sense of relief." Because of the "removal of 293 slot machines and 30 other gambling devices." This police action exacerbated an already volatile factional dispute within the territory. My team remained in Troop B for several months that summer and the team would rotate back several times between 1989 and 1990. Because of these two factions' violent disputes in the past and the potential for this violence to happen again, state police set roadblocks to protect all local citizens. The Mohawk security forces also set up roadblocks, but their goals went beyond safeguarding their citizens. They were also there to block law enforcement from entering the territory. These roadblocks were in place for months.

Then, in May 1990, two Mohawks on the Canadian side of the Mohawk territory were shot and killed as the dispute escalated into a shooting civil war; one Mohawk was from the anti-gambling faction, and the other was from the pro-gambling side.[150] Doug George, an editor and anti-gaming proponent, was charged with the second-degree murder of Harold Edwards, a pro-gaming advocate. Doug George pled innocent. The deaths occurred during a shootout at George's residence."[151] Many Mohawks wanted then-Governor Mario Cuomo to send in the National Guard to quell the violence. Governor Cuomo told reporters, "We will not send military force because of the risk of bloodshed, because of what it would provoke."[152] The slaying of the two Mohawks prompted hundreds of

New York State Police to enter the U.S. side of Akwesasne territory. Ultimately, New York State and the Saint Regis Mohawks negotiated a compact allowing Class III Vegas-style slot machines.[153] Little did I know then how much of my career would involve many challenging encounters with my Aboriginal cousins.

I interacted the most with the Seneca Nation of Indians, the Tonawanda Seneca Nation, and the Tuscaroran nation, three Haudenosaunee nations. I understood the need for economic development for the Indigenous families living within New York State. As I drove through these territories, it was impossible not to notice the depth of economic deprivation. Many traditional older houses needed repair, tar-paper shacks, rundown trailers, and other signs of communal poverty. On the other hand, the owners of gas stations, cigarette shops, and those who managed the casinos were doing very well. I wondered about communal property and sharing, which seemed to be evolving in some Indigenous nations and, in some instances, potentially becoming a cultural imperative.[154] The solutions they devised because of the constraints imposed by interpretations of United States policies vis-à-vis their sovereignty were exceedingly complicated. They often ran afoul of New York state law according to these interpretations and constraints. Meanwhile, the poverty of the people of these territories was improving slightly but persisted. This wealth gap is still the lived reality for many Mohawks today. On the US side of St. Regis Indian land, 11.1 percent of households live below the Federal poverty line of $27,750 (family of four). On the three Seneca Nation of Indians' lands, the poverty rates on the Allegany territory, 25.5 percent of its families live below the poverty line. In Seneca Cattaraugus territory, 32.4 percent live in poverty.[155]

I learned more about "Indian Lands," its people, its culture, and the United States' role in the theft and impoverishment of my cousins' lands and community. According to the American Community Survey, "1 in 3 Native Americans are living in poverty, with a median income of $23,000 a year."[156] I could not help but reflect on what had happened to my people on the island of Borinquén. We, too, faced the same income inequality Indigenous people faced and continue to confront. I pondered New York State's role, its policing agencies, and my role as a state police member in causing or sustaining these inequities. How could I ensure I would be a change agent for the Black, Brown, and other marginalized communities the troopers serve? How could I be a change agent for how we interacted with the Haudenosaunee within New York State? I was not sure. I did know I could control how I acted when engaging with the "First People" by my professional and fair performance of my duties. In every interaction with the people I served, I would try to ensure my actions did not foster these inequities. It was clear one potential solution to these injustices was closing the achievement gap among Native American children by improving educational outcomes. Families would also benefit through enhanced entrepreneurial and socio-economic opportunities.[157] I understood the need to access these opportunities as I had. I hoped I could find a way to demonstrate my respect for their sovereignty and express authentic empathy regarding the painful history of Native Americans so that, at a minimum, I would follow the Hippocratic oath - do no harm.

Once back at Wellsville, my former colleagues accepted me as their supervisor without any trouble. The transition back to SP Wellsville was smoother than expected, although some troopers and the community still had cultural competency issues. I had two superb supervisors, Station Commander Noel Herberger, who oversaw SP Wellsville's operations, and Zone Sergeant Charles McCole, who managed state police operations in Zone Four of Troop A. Both vastly differed from the first station commander I met during my first year at SP Wellsville, who was dismissive of my concerns about the Allegany County map with its infamously named road. Both already knew me; I had worked with Sergeant Herberger when he was a trooper at Wellsville, and Z/Sergeant McCole was there when I first arrived. He had helped transport me for a week to and from SP Allegany when my Gremlin finally died in the summer of 1982. I purchased another more reliable car the following week. During those trips, I learned that Z/Sergeant McCole was from Long Island and knew he had no issues with my ethnicity. His reaction and acceptance were refreshing. It gave me hope that what I had initially set out to do, which was to help the state police accept men and women of "Color" could happen.

Now that I was a permanently ranked sergeant back home, I set my plans for the next promotional opportunity, NYSP lieutenant. Again, I analyzed what the best options for moving forward would be. I realized that seeking an assignment to the BCI would be helpful. It would nearly double the number of positions I could qualify for within a 100-mile radius, a commutable distance from my house. If I stayed on the uniformed side of the division, nine positions were available; if I had BCI experience, that number went up to sixteen.

On February 23, 1989, I sent my memorandum requesting an assignment to the BCI. My supervisors all approved the memo. The BCI captain scheduled an interview. On the day of the meeting, the captain asked me into his office and inquired about any felony cases I had investigated. I told him about a serial burglar my partner and I had arrested. And how we gathered all the evidence to ensure a conviction. He then asked, "Do you speak Dominican?" I had to bite my tongue to keep from laughing. There is no such language. Dominicans speak Spanish. I knew what he meant. Did I understand the slang terms and jargon unique to the Spanish spoken by people from the Dominican Republic? The difference would be like the differences between US English and British English. In his report, the captain wrote, "Perez speaks fluent Spanish, also Dominican…" He added, "He previously lived in New York City and had an excellent understanding of different societal cultures." How did this qualify me for the BCI? I did not know. Yes, my fluency in Spanish did, as it related to this assignment, given that many of the targets of drug investigators at the time were Latino. His queries had been what I feared when considering a BCI appointment years earlier. My ethnicity, language skills, and having grown up in a marginalized neighborhood of Manhattan seemed more important than my other abilities. Yes, drug dealers and associated crimes were in that community, but I was not involved. That was why I did not initially apply for BCI; I had to consider it for a chance to achieve a bigger prize: becoming a lieutenant. While this was opportunistic, I believed I could also prevent ethnic biases from corrupting the narcotics investigations.

I could also watch and speak out if I saw these biases playing out in other cases I became aware of while in the BCI.

In September 1989, I accepted reassignment to the BCI. A position I had turned down a few years earlier when a narcotics unit senior investigator asked me to seek this assignment. He had been one of an increasing number of Black and Latino troopers appointed and assigned to the BCI narcotics units. This push for more troopers of Color in the BCI resulted from the crack cocaine epidemic sweeping across New York State. The state police appointment to the BCI as an investigator is a promotion by assignment rather than through a promotional examination process. Usually, the designation was performance-based, although figuring out whether the level of your performance merited consideration was very subjective depending on which region of the state you were a trooper in. I was of two minds concerning accepting the offer of assignment to the BCI. First, I enjoyed being on the prestigious Mobile Response Team. There were only eighteen troopers on this team for the entire state. At the time, I was the only member of Color on it. On the other hand, I wanted the position based on my investigative abilities, not solely because of my ethnicity, language skills, and urban upbringing. However, my larger goal of becoming a change agent within the state police settled my internal questions.

The first time I turned down a BCI assignment, I had not reached the rank of sergeant, and I did not see any real advantage to leaving the MRT. I also was enjoying the hell out of being on the team. This time, there were clear advantages to accepting the position. It would increase my knowledge about criminal investigation and open more doors when I achieved the rank of lieutenant. The Division has two major sections: the Uniformed Force and the Bureau of Criminal Investigation. Successful passage of the lieutenant's exam earns the sergeant, as mentioned, the position of the permanent rank of lieutenant in the uniformed force. As I had done when considering which troops to request when at the training academy, I researched how many uniformed lieutenants' positions were available within one hundred miles of Wellsville once I passed the test. At the time, uniformed lieutenants were Zone commanders.

There were eight; plus another five BCI lieutenants posts with that radius. This time, I sought and accepted the assignment as an investigator to enhance the possibility of not traveling more than one hundred miles, forcing me to live once again away from my family.

For the NYSP, there were positive and unforeseen consequences of Judge Foley's mandate; the state police's diversification allowed it to respond more effectively to this drug enforcement effort. The crack epidemic in New York State and the lack of diversity within the state's local police agencies outside of NYC allowed the state police to significantly promote protected-class troopers to narcotics units to address this crisis. But the downside for the individual members of Color was their assignment to other, more traditional major case squads within the state police was rare. Moreover, they could only rise to policymaking positions if they took the promotional exams. My dream of diversifying the commissioned officers' ranks and the upper echelon of the NYSP would take more work to achieve. I weighed the factors in play, thinking about the direction I wanted my career to take within the state police. I considered the past practices and the internal culture of the state police, with its bias against the uniformed trooper positions versus the BCI. I concluded that once I passed the lieutenant's examination and achieved the permanent rank of uniform lieutenant, I could more easily get an appointment as a BCI lieutenant if I had BCI experience. Just as important, I was suffering from severe arthritis in my left hip from all the martial arts and MRT training. I had lost a step; I could not move with the agility and speed needed. I did not want to cause injury to my comrades on the MRT. These factors made my decision easier.

As I began to work as an undercover narcotics investigator, I stuck to my plan to continue studying to earn the lieutenant's permanent rank. When I sat on wiretap cases, as many Latino investigators had to do, they acquired the position for the same reasons I served in the Affirmative Action Office and was admitted into the ranks of the BCI: ethnicity and language skills. I access more insidious reasons linked to pervasive and racist stereotyping of troopers of Color recruited from the cities of NYS cities with open-air drug markets where crack cocaine had become endemic and the ugly opinion that because we may have lived in these communities, we understood the drug culture and could more easily infiltrate drug gangs. There were small kernels of truth here (i.e., if the drug gangs and their suppliers were composed of Spanish-speaking individuals and used their language to negotiate their drug deals, then the ability to speak Spanish was essential). Yet, to presume troopers with Spanish surnames spoke Spanish is flawed. The rate at which the children of Latino immigrants born here, or Puerto Ricans who are US citizens who chose to live on the mainland, speak Spanish decreases with each generation.[158] The reasons for this are relatively straightforward. One, the American ethos of the melting pot, is that every immigrant group experiences this same phenomenon of assimilation. Yet, in grade school, I experienced racial slurs and comments about returning to where I came from and told my mother. She insisted I respond by saying I was born on the island of Manhattan, not Puerto Rico, and that I only speak English. Although bilingualism is valued today, language-immersion public schools did not exist back then.

Moreover, to be successful in getting a good education and, after that, a good job requires fluency in English. The other flaw in this approach was that it ignored the systemic racism of the US drug policies from its start. During the turn of the nineteenth century, after a large influx of Chinese immigrants who had helped to build the transcontinental railroads and who took part in the California Goldrush were no longer needed or welcomed. Their use of opium, which was not illegal then, began to attract White women and then became illegal because of the fear of their potential rape and murder in these Chinese-owned and operated Opium dens. These anti-Chinese propaganda images are illustrative of this fear. It led to several pieces of racist legislation:

- the Chinese Exclusion Act in 1882
- the Pure Food and Drug Act of 1906
- the Opium Exclusion Act of 1909
- the 1914 Harrison Act

What was also ignored, particularly during the illegal drug trade of the 1980s and today, is that the marginalized communities where most of the drug sales occurred could not sustain these markets without all the White customers from the surrounding communities and suburbs. These customers would return to their homes where there was little violence connected directly to drug trafficking. Consider what the first commissioner of the Federal Bureau of Narcotics said:

> "In 1937, Harry Anslinger, the first director of the Bureau of Narcotics and Dangerous Drugs (BNDD, the predecessor of the DEA) and a blatant racist, spread wild tales about the effect of cannabis. He said cannabis, or marihuana as he called it, was used by "Negros, Mexicans, Puerto Ricans, jazz musicians and other social undesirables."[159]

Once again, I struggled with being a part of enforcement efforts that were discriminatory in many ways. One fact often overlooked is that people of Color and White folks use drugs at nearly the same rates; Black and Brown people are investigated and incarcerated at much higher rates.[160] At the same time, open-air drug markets, "crack houses," and illegal drug trafficking in general in the United States would not be sustainable if Americans did not desire and consume these illicit drugs. Yes, these unlawful drug markets are often in marginalized urban neighborhoods that could not support this illegal trade without White suburbanite buyers. Why? A recent Netflix documentary, Crack: Cocaine, Corruption & Conspiracy, provides some answers.[161] The Netflix documentary highlighted the tragic effect of an emerging highly addictive drug during the economic decline of the Reagan era. Cocaine destroyed lives, families, and communities. In the 1980 Republican National Convention, Ronald Reagan accepted the nomination for the president of the United States. He promised to improve the economy and American lives, especially for disenchanted White voters. He told voters, "For those without opportunities, we'll stimulate new opportunities, particularly in the inner cities where they live. For those who've abandoned hope, we'll restore hope, and we'll welcome them into a great national crusade to make America great again."[162]

Historian Elizabeth Hinton said, "Reagan's administration created a proliferation of wealth for a few at the expense of the many. The Reagan administration eliminated half a million people from the welfare rolls, one million people from food stamps, and 2.6 million American children from lunch programs." The result was extreme poverty among inner-city residents. In 1982, America had one of the highest rates of unemployment. Due to our country's history of racial disparities, the Black and Brown communities' unemployment rate was always twice that of the White neighborhoods. Cocaine entering the United States increased by 50 percent between 1982 and 1994; 63 tons of cocaine came into the US. It entered using multiple routes and modes (such as airplanes and boats) from Central America and the Bahamas, resulting in a drop in its cost. What had been an expensive drug affordable to the rich and famous turned into a drug available to many. In marginalized communities, particularly the Black and Brown communities, the creation of crack cocaine was an effort to escape the trauma of poverty. The stimulant sold at $5 or $10 a hit; it was a game changer for low-income communities. What was once the rich man's drug had become accessible to poor people.[163]

Unfortunately, some Black and Latino men began to build businesses through drugs to make money. They were making thousands of dollars a day. Many felt it was the most efficient way of supporting themselves and their families. The overwhelming profit led to gun violence in urban communities. Many young men obtained high-power weapons to protect their turf. According to the Netflix documentary – "Crack: Cocaine, Corruption & Conspiracy," "Crack gave more people guns. More people could afford guns. And more people started to settle their differences with guns."[164] The crack cocaine epidemic turned into a pandemic. Tragically, women and children got caught in the crossfire of rival drug dealers. The money corrupted everyone; drug dealers paid off many police officers. Some stole drugs and resold them. During this period, it was all about the money. The "Just Say No" to anti-drugs campaign by former First

Lady Nancy Reagan was very hypocritical.[165] During this time, "the US government was turning a blind eye to cocaine smuggling into the United States," according to the documentary. The US government supported a dictatorship in Nicaragua, and in 1979, it fell. Reagan's administration financially supported insurrectionary bands to take on Nicaragua's Marxist government. However, Congress did not want to condone the war in Central America. So what did the former administration do? They started looking for alternative sources of funding. The government sold arms to Iran and took the profits (about $30 million) to fund an illegal war in Central America. It led to our government disregarding the cocaine smuggling by the Nicaraguan Contras. While political leaders were fueling the drug epidemic, our justice system punished marginalized communities and victims of their corruption. Instead of supplying resources to combat the issue of poverty, the government criminalized the oppressed.[166]

After Reagan's administration, former Presidents Bush and Clinton strove to be hard on crime. Law enforcement targeted low-income communities and became more militarized. Police departments transformed investigative teams into elite, well-funded units with unique resources and powers. In 1994, the federal anti-drug budget was up to $12 billion, six times what it was during Reagan's inauguration. Millions of dollars went into expanding the private and public prison system, leading to mass incarceration in America. Toward the film's end, journalist Brian Barger asks two thought-provoking questions: "If you got a war on drugs, is it not a war on the people supplying the drugs? Or is it only a war on the victims of the drug war?" Regrettably, the war was on the victims of the drug war. The crack epidemic compromised the safety and well-being of poverty-stricken communities. Since then, the US government has taken a health approach to address the issue of drug abuse instead of criminalizing the users. That should have been their strategy all along. The US government enabled drugs to erode America's inner cities and has yet to make amends for the devastation of communities of Color. The government called this a war on drugs; no, it was a war on marginalized communities.[167] Given this tragic history and the more significant societal issues of systematic racism, there remained the fact the narco-traffickers engaged in ruthless violence. That meant in the neighborhoods where these dealers plied their trade. Grandmothers could not sit outside with their grandchildren for fear a stray bullet might strike them or the child. I could bring peace to those communities by joining the narcotics unit. I reconciled that I could focus on reducing the violence by disrupting the open-air drug markets and stemming the tide of illegal drug sales in the communities with the greatest need.

I would bring my manuals and the other books necessary for studying when assigned to eavesdropping cases. Sitting in on an eavesdropping case could be incredibly mind-numbing. These cases required long hours of sitting by eavesdropping and recording equipment, listening to upper-level drug dealers' conversations. They discussed the criminal enterprise and their personal affairs, but the eavesdropping had to stop when we heard discussions unrelated to their illegal activities. We had to follow court-sanctioned minimization rules.[168] Therefore, we were ordered not to listen to any part of a target's conversation that did not pertain to the felony investigation approved by the judge. For instance, upon hearing the target talking about a baseball game, we had to turn off the recording and jot down the time/date and tape-recording number. After a few minutes, we could listen again to the conversation and record if it was related to a crime or crimes listed on the warrant. The difficulty was deciding what was or was not pertinent to the case. Some suspects spoke openly about their criminal enterprises; others used cryptic language that needed deciphering. For instance, baseball teams could be code for drugs: "the White Socks" could mean cocaine or "the Brown Socks" heroin. The number of balls could stand for grams, strikes for ounces, and home runs for kilograms; thus, you had to listen carefully to decide on the evidentiary nature of the coded dialogue.

While the BCI captain who initially interviewed me was wrong about a different Dominican language, he was correct from the following perspective. Regional jargon, slang, and accents within any language differ. These differences can constitute a local language variant as a dialect. One instance illustrating the nuanced differences in local language usage happened during an eavesdropping case. An investigator of Mexican descent sat in on a wiretap involving Puerto Rican and Dominican suspects in a drug trafficking case. During the wiretap, the drug suspects began using "Spanglish" and Nuyorican slang.[169] Nuyorican is a term to describe Puerto Ricans and their descendants living in and around metropolitan New York City. It combines New York (Nuyo) and Puerto Rican (Rican).[170]

On the phone, one suspect asked his partner whether he was going out in the cold properly attired in Spanglish (con coat o sin coat, meaning with or without an outer jacket). During another part of the conversation, they spoke about how many Chinas one suspect would get. The word china in Puerto Rico is slang for the orange fruit and is used instead of the European Spanish word for orange, Naranja. This investigator was unfamiliar with Puerto Rican, Dominican Spanish, and Nuyorican Spanglish jargon and slang. He interpreted these phrases to mean the dealer was going to get cocaine ("coat") and "China" as China white heroin. He set off a chain of events because of that misinterpretation. He alerted our superiors that the case had reached a critical turning point and could conclude because the dealers were receiving a significant illegal drug shipment. The captain called everyone in to plan the search-and-arrest raid for these suspects. Fortunately, another investigator well-versed in the jargon of these targets listened to the taped dialog and, realizing the correct interpretation, stopped the raid. The case concluded with the arrest of the suspects in possession of actual cocaine and not oranges weeks later. All the Puerto Rican investigators laughed but defended him to the captain, explaining that this was an honest mistake. The problem was that the captain had told our colonels. They then briefed the head of the state police, who was not very tolerant of errors, especially by his commissioned officers. The investigator could not be saved and was removed from our case and not assigned to other wiretap investigations.

Monitoring wiretaps had humorous interludes, and completing these cases with these upper-level drug dealers' arrests was satisfying. But it involved hours of boredom. Few of us enjoyed this work. I used those hours constructively, studying my manuals, creating acronyms and mnemonics, and other methods to memorize the volumes of information needed to pass the lieutenant's examination. I recorded hours of audio tapes to help me learn and remember essential manual sections. Also, I asked my young daughter and son to record words of encouragement on these tapes. I listened to the tapes while driving the four hours to and from the wiretap room's location in the Buffalo area. I loved hearing my son and daughter on these tapes. It inspired me to study harder and reminded me, not that I needed reminding, why we had and were sacrificing so much. It also lessened the guilt about being away so much. I saved money to afford a hotel room I would rent during the last few weeks of the case. I did this so I would not lose the four hours of study time by driving to and from the office. Finally, I saved two weeks of vacation and took it just before the exam to study from dawn to dusk. I took and passed the promotional examination for the permanent rank of lieutenant in the uniformed force. Soon after I passed the exam, I heard a new narcotics task force was forming in the southern tier of New York and asked that the state police join it. I convinced the Troop A BCI captain to transfer me there as its office was within thirty miles of my home.

Moreover, I knew it would be a while before I would get the lauded and hard-earned promotion because of statewide budget cuts forcing a freeze in hiring and promotions within state agencies.[171] The Division kept the promotional list before mine active, and once they lifted the budget freeze, they promoted a few candidates from that list to fill the existing vacancies. They reached the candidate who had been fortieth on that list. Then the NYSP closed that list and activated the list I was on in the seventh slot, which was fair to do, although they would have reached me, granting me the benefit of seniority at that rank level sooner. I had to wait nearly a year.

My time at the Southern Tier Regional Drug Task Force (SRDTF) was interesting. I investigated illegal drug and untaxed alcohol trafficking in the Seneca Nation of Indians' Allegany and Cattaraugus territories.[172] The Seneca Nation had requested help from the SRDTF with drug trafficking in their region from both Senecan and non-Indian drug dealers. The SRDTF agreed to help but did not specify how or who would be assigned. The supervisor of the task force selected me for several reasons. First, my ethnicity would make it easier for me to frequent nightclubs, bars, and other Seneca locations without drawing much attention. I could not pretend to be a Seneca Indian, but they would accept me if I said I was a Mohawk/Puerto Rican from Akwesasne, the "Land Where the Partridge Drums," visiting friends. I got the assignment also because I had the most knowledge about their culture and customs among the investigators assigned to the SRDTF. So I spent several weeks moving between Cattaraugus and Allegany territories and had moderate success finding drug dealers and investigating and closing cases on their land. In the southern tier communities, there were no open-air drug markets. Drug dealers did not stand on the streets hawking their drugs. They sold drugs mostly in bars and dance halls. We set up drug dealers using confidential informants (CI) who would introduce undercover operatives to a local dealer. Most informants agreed to work for the police after reaching a plea deal with a prosecutor for a lighter sentence after an arrest on a criminal charge. They usually snitched on the people they knew, including, in some instances, friends and, on rare occasions, family members.

I also worked undercover in the southern tier's small cities, towns, and villages, like Alfred, Jamestown, and Olean. In one case, a CI agreed to call a drug dealer selling LSD in Fredonia, a small town in Chautauqua County. The CI told the dealer to meet him at a McDonald's on Main Street. I was dressed in plain clothes and was part of the surveillance/arrest team. The dealer arrives, and the CI confirms he has drugs. The CI signaled us. We quickly raced into the parking lot. Jumping out of the passenger's side of the undercover vehicle, I ran to the driver, pulled him out, placed him on the ground, and was about to handcuff him. Suddenly, I heard the wailing sound of a police siren and the shrieking noise of the local police car coming to a stop just behind me. I had my revolver drawn and was about to holster it. When the local police officer screamed at me to drop the gun with his weapon pointed at me, I froze and yelled, "I'm a trooper, I shouted with dread!" "Drop the fucking gun!" shouted the officer. I slowly lowered my sidearm while holding the drug dealer as a uniformed trooper screamed at the local patrolman, "He is with us. He's a trooper." The officer holstered his weapon. I got up, my heart pounding in my chest. I turned toward the officer and started to laugh because of fear and seeing the officer dressed in a Santa Claus costume. He had been at an elementary school celebrating the holiday season with the children. I thought, Shit, how would I explain this to my family? I just got shot by Santa Claus. Luckily, that explanation was unnecessary; it was just a change in underwear.

This assignment was riskier in some respects because of how close it was to Wellsville, particularly Alfred and Olean, New York. Many people shopped at Olean and enjoyed an evening in the restaurant and movie theater. Olean had more amenities than Wellsville, so my undercover identity was very vulnerable, and someone from Wellsville could have recognized me and blown my cover.

Finally, after passing the lieutenant's exam, scoring high enough to be seventh on the list, and waiting for the budget freeze to end, the day came to reap my well-earned promotion. Being on the promotional list affords the sergeants on the list the opportunity to fill a lieutenant's vacancy. While there had been a small number of Latinx sergeants before me, none had become a commissioned officer. I was fortunate to achieve a double first. I became the first Nuyorican commissioned officer and first man of Color assigned to the BCI as a lieutenant. There were only a few African American commissioned officers and no Latinos. I was glad the affirmative action program was not involved in this milestone. The state police did not lower the standards for passing the exam; on the contrary, they made the exams even harder. But still, some White officers argued that it played a role. I was only the fourth person of Color to have earned the permanent rank of lieutenant and the first Nuyorican to do so in the New York State Police's history. I ask. Why?

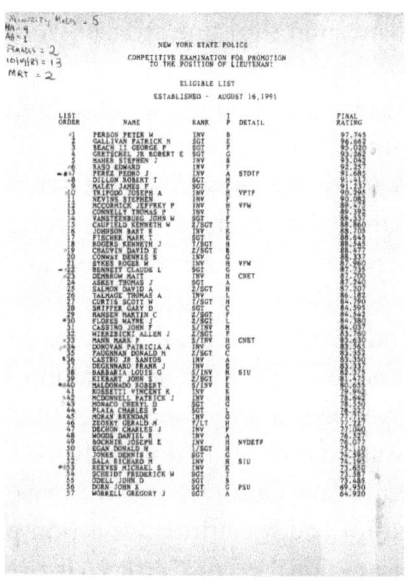

Figure 13. Lieutenant Promotional List.[173]

This lack of appreciation for the underlying reasons for the need for affirmative action would crop up repeatedly. The diversity in the state police commissioned officer corps was still negligible and would remain so for years. A June 1, 2021, article by Jim Mustian and Camille Fassett of the Associated Press, titled - "NY State Police Struggle to Diversify amid National Reckoning." Check our database. They confirmed my warning about the lack of diversity. They wrote:

> "Those percentages of minorities, who are also underrepresented in senior leadership positions, are "as good as almost nothing," said Michael Jenkins, a policing expert who teaches criminal justice at the University of Scranton. "The agency is in a tough position to argue otherwise. Bruen, who assumed command of the state police last year, agrees the agency's minority recruitment program needs work."[174]

I agreed and said so in the same article:

> "Pedro Perez, a former New York State Police deputy superintendent who retired in 2010, said the consent decree was dissolved without any inquiry into "whether the attitudes of the officers and leadership was sufficiently changed."[175]

This racial and gender discrimination caused Judge Foley to require affirmative action policy implementation in the first place. Some officers and troopers never let me forget that affirmative action opened the door I walked through to disqualify my achievement. They ignored what they knew to be accurate, that the two promotional exams they and I qualified for had no affirmative action privileges or added points. That the promotional exams "protected class" troopers would become eligible to take were made more difficult, not less. These officers also did not see the years of privilege they had received because of their ethnicity. In her article "White Privilege and Male Privilege" (1995), Peggy McIntosh writes about "White privilege and the myth of meritocracy."[176] In another article, "White Privilege: Unpacking the Invisible Knapsack," McIntosh writes, "I was taught to see racism only in individual acts of meanness, not in invisible systems conferring dominance on my group."[177] It was not invisible in the outcomes of the criminal justice system. We need only to look at who gets stopped and arrested by police, who gets prosecuted and convicted, and how sentencing is inequitably applied, those in poverty and Black and Brown folks! It was not invisible to John Heritage when he sued. It was not invisible to Judge Foley. It was not invisible to me as I sat in Rules and Regulations class as some White recruit troopers expressed their disdain for affirmative action. It was visible when I was a sergeant, when a young White trooper said, "All you people carry knives, so it must be easy to cut your way out the womb faster than most." It was not invisible or funny. Yet changes were happening. I was the fourth, and I was determined not to be the last person of Color to reach the rank of lieutenant. Moreover, the commitment of my mentors to diversity and inclusion proved that I would not be.

Chapter 11 - Operation Crackdown

Starting in 1992, Operation Crackdown was a narcotics investigation that began in Buffalo, New York, and then was deployed statewide to other New York State cities under different names. I headed the initial Buffalo operation for the New York State Police. I dubbed it "Operation Crackdown." I played on the words of this narcotics investigation's operational goal involving "crack cocaine" and taking down the dealers of these drugs. This investigation was in response to the crack cocaine epidemic that had spread out of New York City into upstate New York cities, including Buffalo. The violent crime and homicide rates in Buffalo because of narcotics gang violence had skyrocketed.[178] Buffalo happened to be the hometown of Superintendent Thomas Constantine; therefore, for him, this was a personal as well as a professional matter.

It was emotional for me, too; my brother's involvement with illegal drugs caused his death. He managed his adverse childhood experiences through self-medication. During his teenage years, we were still relatively poor. He chose what he saw as an easy way to heal himself and make money to support "his medications." Once involved in the trade, he could not find his way out, and the easy cash cost him more than he bargained for: his life. This personal tragedy continues in many communities across this nation. Today, we have learned addiction is a health problem and treat it as such. During this crack-cocaine scourge and other periods when illegal drugs ran rampant in poor communities, it was viewed only as a crime problem, not a public health problem. We can resolve law enforcement problems through drug investigations, followed by arrests, prosecutions, and then incarcerations on a massive scale, yet this is not always the equitable and most effective solution.[179] This failure to recognize addiction as a healthcare dilemma instead of a criminal justice problem led inextricably to the prison population in the United States skyrocketing from 250,000 in the 1970s to 2,400,000 in 2020, an increase of 800 percent.[180] This failure has been worsened by the creation of private prisons whose stocks trade on the stock market, making billions of dollars for the shareholders. Political leaders, local clergy, some community activists, and law enforcement officials, like me, tragically did not see this coming. We all heard the cries of mothers losing their children to the violence of drug gangs and their demand for action from politicians and the police. Many of these people approach to drug abuse have evolved because the opioid epidemic has hit White communities with greater intensity than communities of Color. Many of America's politicians and people in the criminal justice system now see it as a health crisis. This political evolution, of course, does not diminish the damage already inflicted on the poor and communities of Color; America has the highest incarceration rate per population of any developed country.[181]

Operation Crackdown became the model for the New York State Police narcotics program across upstate New York. For this operation to work, it had to involve a multi-disciplinary approach that included the city of Buffalo and Erie County governments following up with investments into the neighborhoods where these open-air illegal drug markets existed.[182] We knew marginalized people dealt with significant disparities in every aspect of their lives, such as healthcare, employment, legal rights, housing, and access to other essential services. These communities often suffer abuse, exploitation, and mistreatment by caregivers, family, neighbors, friends, acquaintances, and professionals. They are often silenced and made invisible victims of discrimination, violence, social isolation, and assault. They live in fear of drug gangs, criminality, and violence. Most disturbing and horrible, they also fear the police because of how they over-police their community. The community needed access to resources as simple as getting the sanitation department to clean the streets and as complex as creating economic and educational opportunities. It also needs to enhance public and private cooperation to achieve the community's goals if the government hopes to achieve safer, drug-free streets. The plan also included getting the Buffalo City officials to work more closely with local civic and faith-based institutions, for example, Buffalo's Macedonia Baptist Church, Crisis Services, Community Action Organization, African American

Cultural Center, and Hispanos Unidos de Buffalo. I understood that drug enforcement alone will not deliver a long-term solution to the underlying problems that plagued cities like Buffalo if we accept the intersectionality of poverty, structural racism, lack of access to resources, and other inequities that contribute to criminal behavior. Law enforcement alone cannot solve this crisis.[183] Some believe crime causes poverty; others think poverty causes crime; this is a chicken-or-egg argument in many ways.[184] As far as I was concerned then and now, regardless of the criminal justice and political debate, we needed, and need, to take steps to enhance the safety of our communities so that a grandmother and her grandchild can sit outside their home without the fear of a stray bullet from a gang member's gun injuring or worse killing her or her grandchild.[185]

We also needed the Erie County Sheriff's Office, the Buffalo Police Department, New York State Police Troop A Narcotic's Unit, and the recently formed New York State Police "Community Narcotics Enforcement Teams" (CNET) to collaborate in this endeavor. The strategy was to infiltrate the neighborhoods where open-air markets for the purchase of crack cocaine existed.[186] The Buffalo News reported:

> "Provoked by the violence and by complaints
> from residents living near drug houses, the police
> began a four-month investigation in April."[187]

These neighborhoods were poor communities on the east and west sides of Buffalo. The Fruit-belt on the east side was a primarily African American community with some Hispanics. The other was the west side of Buffalo, a Hispanic neighborhood with some African Americans and other ethnic groups living there.[188] A significant part of the investigation was to send CNET undercover investigators to buy narcotics from the street dealers. NYSP Troop A's narcotics unit had worked on narcotics cases in Buffalo for some years. We tasked the narcotics team with finding the street-level dealers and developing a database of who they were. From this database, we could find, arrest, and prosecute as many street dealers as possible to target upper-level drug traffickers. The goal was to investigate, apprehend, charge, and prosecute at least one hundred street-level dealers. Then, bring in a large cohort of state police officers, Drug Enforcement Agency agents, the city of Buffalo PD, and Erie County Sheriff deputies to round up these drug dealers in one day. None of the police departments in upstate New York had ever done this.

This assignment was dangerous for the police officers working on the streets. I had been an undercover narc on those very streets some years earlier. I knew the area very well. I had successfully investigated, arrested, and helped in the prosecution of multiple upper-echelon drug traffickers as well as scores of street-level dealers. Many of my colleagues and I risked our lives in working drug cases. For example, I had entered a crack house on Virginia Street on Buffalo's west side. We did not have undercover surveillance devices, like discreet transmitters, which would allow your backup team to hear what was happening inside the apartment building.

We were also not issued clandestine firearms that matched our undercover persona. We had to use our official police sidearm, go in unarmed, or use personal weapons; the former choices were too dangerous. I used my Jennings .22-caliber pistol, which was small enough to fit in my front pocket. I entered the building's foyer with the confidential informant (CI), who introduced me to an upper-level cocaine dealer, and I was to pose as a customer who could buy kilos of cocaine. Two lookouts greeted him and me; one held a shotgun, and the other a machete. The shotgun-wielding lookout barked at the CI, "Who the fuck is this guy," referring to me as he pointed the gun at my chest. I stood my ground, hiding the fact I was scared shitless, my right hand on the little pistol in my pocket. I hid my fear and glared at the CI and the dealer's accomplices. The CI yelled; he had permission from his cousin.

His "cousin" was a significant local drug dealer. To fulfill his deal with the local district attorney, the CI was "snitching" to get a lighter sentence. Unconvinced, the lookout looked at me and asked, "What the fuck do you want?" I stared back at him unflinchingly; on the outside, gripping the pistol tighter, I said. "I am here to 'cop.' Your man knows that. If you want to piss him off, don't let me in and see what the fuck happens!" The seconds ticked by; it felt longer, and he relented. I bought the ounce, got the beeper number of the dealer, and left the apartment. That case led to a significant eavesdropping case that resulted in a multi-kilo dealer and his gang getting arrested and successfully prosecuted. Yet, like trying to block a flood, we could not fill enough sandbags to stop the influx of crack and the violence that came with it. We produced this innovative approach, hoping it would put a dent in the illegal and violent drug trade in Buffalo and other upstate New York cities.

My career as a commissioned officer in the state police hinged on this immensely complex undertaking and its successful conclusion. There were no more promotional tests. Everyone understood performance determined advancement in the Division once you reached the rank of lieutenant and whether your superior officers acknowledged that, most of all, the superintendent. This high-profile case had the full attention of Superintendent Constantine. That thought would periodically surface, yet I knew the best way to unburden myself from the weight of this was to focus on the work itself. If I get that right, what happens after that? The investigation took months to finish. During those months, I negotiated and developed collaborative efforts with the Erie County sheriff's office, the Buffalo police chief, and the special agent in charge of the DEA office in Buffalo. I worked out all the arrangements and managed this significant and first-of-its-kind investigation. During this case, I had little sleep, worrying about the undercover investigators we deployed because of the danger of gang violence. The politics between the state police, Erie County Sheriff's Office, and Buffalo's City Police Department was also a significant concern.

My concerns were proven valid. During the first phases of this investigation, the Erie County Sheriff's Office and the Buffalo Police Department city experienced significant public pressure given the unprecedented rise of homicides occurring in Buffalo. Under this pressure, they revealed that the state police had sent dozens of undercover officers to investigate narcotics trafficking in the city. By making this announcement, they jeopardized the lives of every single undercover officer engaged in this case, and it placed a target on the backs of any new face that showed up on the streets. Once that happened, I had to withdraw the investigators and stop the investigation. I spoke to Major Roloff and told him what happened and my decision, considering the circumstances. I explained I requested a meeting between all the stakeholders of this initiative. I tried and failed to get their cooperation; he immediately said you need to speak with the superintendent. He called Superintendent Constantine as I sat in the major's office. He explained the situation. Major Roloff switched on the speaker, and the superintendent asked me what I needed. I asked Superintendent Constantine, "Sir, I need you to speak directly to the sheriff, the mayor, and the police chief of Buffalo." He understood the gravity of the error they had just made. He knew he had to get them to agree to stay silent about the investigation once we restarted the undercover operations. The superintendent asked me how long we needed to wait before resuming the initiative. I told him we needed at least a month.

During that time, I would send undercover agents and work with our informants to figure out whether it was safe to recommence the investigation. I also needed to determine whether the street-level dealers were again openly selling to anyone in the open-air markets. Both Major Roloff and Superintendent Constantine said I had made the right decision. Superintendent Constantine ended the call by saying he would travel to Buffalo and meet the sheriff, mayor, and police chief to get them back on board. Major Roloff dismissed me and said, "Nice fucking job, go home, get some rest." After the meeting with the Major and driving the eighty miles back to my family that evening, I arrived home. As I walked through the door, my wife told me that Troop A headquarters had called, asking me to contact the Major's office. I called the dispatcher, who informed me that tax protesters had blocked the New York State (NYS) Thruway. I had to go to SP Dunkirk, the Patrol station next to the Thruway, where the demonstrators had gathered, to meet Major Bruce A. Roloff. New York State's Appellate Court had decided for New York on the case concerning the collection of excise tax on the sale of cigarettes and gasoline on the Seneca and other Native American territories on July 9, 1992.

On July 16, 1992, over two hundred Seneca, Tuscaroras, Mohawks, and non-Native American protesters blocked the New York Thruway in Erie County. Seneca protesters also blocked State Route 17, Southern Tier Expressway, in the City of Salamanca, Cattaraugus County, and the Tuscarora demonstrators also blocked State 31 in Niagara County. In each instance, the protesters blocked portions of NY State roads as these roads traversed their territories. They set fires to piles of tires by the Thruway and rolled these burning tires and other debris onto the Thruway's driving lanes, endangering innocent motorists and Thruway workers. I empathized with the Native Americans' distrust and frustration with the New York State and the US governments. The United States and Native American nations had negotiated many treaties that the US often broke. For instance, "Under the Treaty of 1794 and Well-Settled Case Law, the Nation Retains the Rights to Self-Government and Exclusive Jurisdiction Over its Internal Affairs."[189]

Figure 14. Burning tire fire on the NYS Thruway.[190]

The Seneca's view was that this was another treaty broken by New York State, which they considered had no authority since NYS was not a nation. The history of broken treaties by the federal and state governments, in this case, Pennsylvania and New York, is long and painful for the Indigenous people of America. For instance, in 1936, a historic flood submerged much of metropolitan Pittsburgh in the Allegheny River because of unusual spring rain and snow melts. It became known as the Great St. Patrick's Day flood. This flood, at its height, reached forty-six feet. The US government built a dam to prevent a similar catastrophe, creating the Allegheny Reservoir. Construction did not begin until 1960. When completed in 1965, the Seneca Nation of Indians lost one-third of the territory granted them by the Canandaigua Treaty signed by President George Washington. The Seneca vehemently opposed its construction. They sought President Kennedy's help to stop its construction, but he refused, displacing nearly seven hundred Seneca and the destruction of their houses. It also buried their sacred sites and cemeteries underwater. Johnny Cash wrote a song about this tragedy: "As long as the grass shall grow."[191]

Seneca leaders often said they had little trust in the United States. They had less trust in the government of New York with its continuous history of treaty violations. They would only negotiate with the federal government because they were a sovereign nation.[192] I understood and respected their assertion. Still, I disagreed that it meant they did not have to obey New York State law. Nor did it mean the New York State Police could not enforce those laws on Native American land. New York State police agencies had the right to administer NYS criminal laws allegedly violated by or against members of their nation on Indian land.[193] As an aboriginal person, after reading the various treaties between the Seneca, New York State, and the United States, it did appear that New York's imposition and collection of taxes on Seneca lands was still undecided.[194] The Seneca Nation had a valid argument. But endangering innocent people's lives and committing crimes to make a political statement was unacceptable. All this deeply saddened me because, as an Indigenous person, I knew how it felt. Puerto Ricans have and continue to suffer under the indignity of colonization and governmental policies that limit our self-determination. I saw how my father suffered. Consider former President Trump's "let them eat cake" moment when he was in Puerto Rico in the aftermath of Hurricane Maria.[195]

I was very conflicted about my role as a police officer. I had sworn to protect and serve; I pledged to be an officer committed to restoring peace and social justice. I was then part of a long line of government officials engaged from their perspective in the oppression of their rights. I did not want to behave like the Alabama State troopers during the march on Selma. Ultimately, we did not because the difference here was that the protest in 1964 for voting rights was peaceful. It was the police in Selma, Alabama, who turned to violence.[196] The New York State police response I was leading was responding to a peaceful march that turned into a violent and destructive riot. I nevertheless felt terrible about the situation but found some solace in the fact that we were protecting innocent motorists and other civilians using the highways and were very restrained in our use of force when attacked by the rioters. I grabbed a change of clothes and other gear I needed and said goodbye to my family, telling them I was not sure when I would get back but would be back. Pamela and my children understood, having seen me respond to missions while on the MRT. They were frightened each time but learned to accept that this was my job and theirs was to, in the words of a famous World War I, "keep the home fires burning."[197]

When I arrived at SP Dunkirk, the situation was very chaotic. Troopers from across Troop A and adjoining troops, along with sergeants and commissioned officers, were racing in. The cacophony of these officers shouting orders and patrol car radios in the background added to the urgency of the moment as the officers organized the troopers into response squads. Lieutenant Michael McManus and I met with Major Roloff, the troop commander of Troop A. He said, "You were on the Mobile Response Team (MRT)?" I said yes. It was clear he assumed that my stint on the MRT gave me the knowledge and skills to conduct the tasks ahead. He gave us our marching orders. "You and Mike take a squad of troopers to the overpass of State Route 438; free it of protesters and keep it cleared so we can open the NY State Thruway." This point of the NYS Thruway, State Route 438, an 11.7-mile road in Irving, NY, crossed over it and was within the Seneca's Cattaraugus land. This state highway was the major thoroughfare on the Seneca Indians' Cattaraugus Territory. We closed several roads and created detours around the demonstrators to gain control of the Thruway and ensure it was safe.

Mike and I looked at each other, then saluted and went outside. I told Mike this was going to be tough, and he nodded. We found the sergeants and told them to gather their squads. We then quickly briefed the gathered troopers and then marched to the bridge. There were dozens of protesters on the overpass, and they had been throwing debris onto the roadway, endangering motorists. Other protesters lit tire fires on the hill beside the bridge and along the NYS Thruway shoulder. The smoke was acrid and irritating, burning our throats and eyes; I worried about the carcinogens as we moved through the smoke.

We arrived at the bridge's foot, and I saw a protester illegally parked on the shoulder of the road, blocking access to the path leading up to the overpass. I heard the trooper tell him to move the truck, and the man refused. The young trooper turned to me for help. I walked over to the motorist and said he risked an arrest for obstructing governmental administration if he did not move his truck. He shouted, "Fuck you and your governmental, whatever!" I warned him again. He then began to roll his window up. I told the trooper to arrest him and remove the vehicle. As the trooper opened the door, the man resisted. The man was much larger than the young officer. I stepped in to help. I grabbed the man's hand, which he had clenched on the steering wheel, and applied a wrist bend to gain control. He continued resisting and now tried to punch me with his other hand. I prevented him from striking me by placing him on the ground and applying a Jujutsu wrist-bend technique. He finally stopped fighting. He was arrested, handcuffed, and escorted back to the command post for processing. Another trooper moved the vehicle out of the way.

Some protesters on the overpass began throwing rocks and other things at us as we marched up to the roadway. We formed a skirmish line and began moving the demonstrators off the bridge. They resisted by throwing more objects and attacking us with sticks, fists, and even homemade pepper spray. This part of the protest lasted for what felt like hours but was only fifteen or so minutes. Our orders were to keep the overpass unobstructed by protesters until they were relieved. We were there for hours. During this period, the protesters changed tactics and began using their cars to drive through our formation on the overpass. They moved toward the line of troopers at high speeds and slammed on their brakes, narrowly missing us. I requested the command post send us patrol cars to protect us from the protesters' vehicles. The command post radioed it would take some time for those cars to arrive. We managed to stop and extract some protesters, who were driving toward us, from their vehicles. We arrested them for Reckless Endangerment and seized control of their cars. We created a barrier with the seized vehicles to protect ourselves from other protesters, who continued to drive their cars toward us. When the demonstration ended, we returned the vehicles to their owners.

Once again, the demonstrators changed their tactics. Some now drove slowly toward us, claiming they lived on the other side of the bridge and needed to get home. Lieutenant McManus and I discussed what we would do and decided to let them pass if their identification supported their claim. This response went well until one set of protesters tried to gain access to the other side of the bridge. We requested they show their driver's licenses to prove that their addresses were, in fact, on the other side of the bridge. They refused. I was standing on the driver's side of the vehicle, wedged between it and another car we had used as part of the barrier. He suddenly drove his truck through the line, narrowly missing the troopers standing in front. The vehicle pinned and spun me like a pencil between two hands as the car raced by me. Startled, I regained my balance. Miraculously, I was unharmed. Then I heard a loud thud and saw a sergeant lying on the ground. The truck had hit him, and the suspect was racing away. We ran to the sergeant, who was severely injured but was still alive.

We radioed the command post and requested a Medevac helicopter at once. We provided first aid to the sergeant as we waited for the chopper's arrival. Suddenly, I heard the roar of a state police helicopter as it flew quickly over the bridge, leaning sideways. Then, the pilot stopped the ship, leveled off, and landed the chopper on the two-lane overpass. We could feel the rush of air as the pilot kept the rotors turning. The EMTs ran to the sergeant to assess his condition and give critical, stabilizing medical aid. They placed him on a backboard, put it on the gurney, and loaded him onto the Huey chopper. The engine roared, and the helicopter lifted off just as quickly as it had landed, tilted to the left, and swiftly peeled away toward the hospital. Happily, the sergeant recovered from his injuries. We found the person who drove the car, arrested him, and prosecuted him successfully.

Once we gained control of the overpass, Major Roloff took several squads of troopers to another bridge east of our position, the Miles Strip Road overpass, to clear it of protesters. Major Roloff met the same kind of resistance, as I was told later by troopers with him. He led them up onto the overpass, fending off the rioters attacking them. When one of the rioters struck Major Roloff before they made it to the top of the knoll, he sustained a severe head injury because the unknown protester struck him in the head with a two-by-four, knocking him out. The troopers described how, once again, the courageous copter pilot expertly maneuvered his craft, deftly landed on the overpass, and medevac the major to the hospital. It took him months to recover from this blow, which caused a concussion and other problems. We opened the Thruway at about 6:15 a.m. the following morning. The protesters stayed on the east side of the Thruway, tending the tire fires and chanting.

An order came across the police radio to return to the command post once my relief arrived. Exhausted, I returned to SP Dunkirk; I briefed the captain, who was now the acting troop commander due to Major Roloff's injury. He told me I had to respond to SP Allegany to help reopen State Route 17, and I was to join Captain Edward Haag and begin the negotiation with the Tribal government to open State Route 17 the next day. I went to the hotel, showered, and slept for a few hours.

I wore a civilian suit the following day and drove to SP Allegany. When I met with the captain, I quickly briefed him on what I had come to understand about the Seneca culture and their unwavering belief in their sovereignty. He said we would meet with the Seneca

Nation's council and discuss opening the Southern Tier expressway. The captain and I entered the Seneca Nation's administrative building in Salamanca. We faced young men armed with assault rifles and the elders holding ceremonial feathers and walking sticks. The young men ordered us to disarm. I was about to refuse when Captain Haag, in full uniform, said he would not remove his weapon. He said, "This is an official part of my uniform, no different than the ceremonial items you hold. I would not ask you to remove those items." I stood there, staring at the young men, readying myself for whatever came next. One of the Seneca council elders began yelling at us, saying we were on their land and had to obey their laws. The captain and I held our ground. I thought what a clever response, the captain suggesting the uniform was just as sacred as were their ceremonial grab and paraphernalia. Nevertheless, I felt the same fear I felt when confronted by a shotgun-wielding guard at the "crack house" in Buffalo. I feared, if disarmed, they might try to hold us as hostages and not be able to defend ourselves. I was in plain clothes, and while my sidearm was not visible, they would try to search me if he surrendered his weapon. I knew I would refuse, which would have probably gotten the captain, some of them, and me injured, if not worse. All this ran through my head for only seconds but felt like an eternity. Luckily, none of that happened.

Another elder stepped forward, shouting back at the council. "This negotiation is the fastest way to get all these invaders off our land." They finally agreed and let us into the council room, and we had not disarmed. A different elder, still fuming, walked over to where we were seated and slammed his ceremonial walking stick on the table. He continued his tirade about their sovereignty and our disrespectful attitudes. This display lasted for twenty minutes, but it felt like hours because the young men stood between the captain and me, menacingly holding the rifles leveled at us. Finally, one of the other council leaders spoke and set out a list of demands. I was to support the captain, but he would do the negotiations. For more than an hour, the debate about their demands continued. They insisted we remove all the troopers from their territories and not enter their lands without their permission. The captain said troopers from outside Troop A would leave, but troopers assigned to Troop A would remain. They demanded we not support any excise tax collectors. Captain Haag said we were not tax collectors; the issue was above our pay grade. They, their lawyers, and the governor's attorneys had hammered out an agreement they were already aware of and that we were there to work out a deal to reopen the highways and restore the peace. This last comment infuriated several of the councilors. Who accused us of violence and breaking treaty after treaty for centuries. I disagreed with the comment we were the ones causing the violence. But I agreed that while the captain and I had not broken any treaties, the government we represented had.

I was conflicted by that reality. My role as a police officer, given my ethnicity, and every other time confronted with this fact. Was I acting as an oppressor? Was I betraying my Indigenous cousins and my conviction to be a defender of social justice? All this felt like a burning dagger stabbing me in the soul. I did not resolve those feelings then and still wonder now. All I could do was rest on the fact that I followed the law and never abused my authority when enforcing it during the preceding days when responding to the riotous situation. I would face this dilemma many times. I also realized on one level that they could not bark at the government directly, so this was their chance to express their years of pain, frustration, and anger to us as governor representatives. So we had to endure it, like it or not. After several hours of yelling and berating by some councilors, we left the meeting, agreeing to meet the next day.

In the interim, the Seneca Nation's attorneys had petitioned a New York State Appeals Court judge for an injunction, which the judge granted. This ruling barred the state from collecting the excise tax on cigarettes and gasoline. The Seneca councilors met with us the next day and worked out reasonable procedures for reopening the highways they had blocked. We also agreed to reassign troopers from outside Troop A, who used to patrol the territories during these protests, back to their original duties and regions. The tax protests ended on July 19, 1992, and we opened all the highways affected by the protests. I was relieved that the confrontation ended but feared we would be back because the underlying issues of broken treaties, marginalization of this community, and the state's need to fill its coffers would continue. I also knew that the Seneca's struggle for equity and justice would not stop, and I thought they should, albeit peacefully.

I returned to Buffalo on July 20 and continued overseeing Operation Crackdown. The superintendent had scheduled a meeting with the mayor, police chief, and sheriff that week. The superintendent met with each of them privately and convinced them to keep the Operation Crackdown investigation quiet until the day of the round-up. They agreed. He called me and said to restart Operation Crackdown once I thought it was safe. After several weeks of waiting to see if the rumors of narcs on the streets had subsided, my senior investigators and I walked around several neighborhoods of Buffalo where the open-air drug markets and "crack houses" were. One of these communities was known as the Fruit Belt because, during the 19th Century, German immigrants planted fruit trees in large orchards. Eventually, many of the streets had fruit names.[198] I parked my unmark car at the Masten Avenue Armory, dressed in "street" clothes, walked down Lemon Street, turned left on High street, strolled passed Peach Street, and headed back north to the Armory, walking up Grape Street. The street dealers were hawking their drugs, and a couple whispered to me as I passed them, "I got the good 'black rock.' These 'nuggets' are the bomb." Upon hearing and seeing that, I knew we could start the investigation back up. I told the acting troop commander, who let the superintendent know. I told the senior investigators to relaunch the operation. For the next several weeks, undercover investigators from Troop A's narcotics unit and CNET hit the streets to identify and buy drugs from all the dealers they could.

I decided the National Guard Armory on Masten Avenue was the perfect location for operational headquarters. It was near the neighborhoods where we conducted most of our undercover operations. We could deploy the arrest teams from the Armory and process over one hundred expected arrestees we would apprehend. I surveyed it, and chose the armory areas for processing and securing the prisoners until the county judge could arraign them. I then went from the Masten Avenue Armory to each neighborhood where we believed the drug dealers lived. I clocked the mileage and the travel time to and from these spots. I noted any geographical obstacles that might hinder arrest teams, emergency medical technicians, and other officers who needed to respond. We were nearing the end of this initiative, and I had to begin orchestrating the arrest procedures and other associated planning to end the operation successfully. For the next several weeks, I continued planning for the end of the investigation. I met with representatives from the Erie County Sheriff's Department, the Buffalo Police Department, the Erie County District Attorney's Office, and the various NY state police units assigned to the investigation.

The investigation required a minimum of two purchases of "crack cocaine" by an undercover Investigator from each drug dealer. Then, each dealer's identity and address had to be verified to ensure we apprehended the correct suspect. While it was dangerous for the undercovers to buy drugs from these drug dealers, finding them was even more perilous in many instances. Some had no prior arrests, some were from other parts of New York State, and some had no permanent address. All this made this task extremely difficult and time-consuming. We were eventually successful in finding nearly all the suspects.

It was a cool late summer morning on August 19, 1992. The Masten Avenue Armory was bustling with hundreds of police officers and their supervisors from several regional police departments, EMT squads, and Erie County District Attorney's office members. They gathered to hear the New York State Police superintendent, Thomas Constantine, give his pre-raid briefing and comments from the Erie County District Attorney's office and city of Buffalo officials. Although he was technically still on sick leave because of the injury sustained during the tax protests earlier that year, Major Roloff was there too. The day before, I had briefed the Troop A and CNET narcotics operatives, the NYSP Mobile Response members, and other units from the state police who would take part in the next morning's raid.

The speeches ended; the arrest teams left the armory to apprehend suspects and execute search warrants, as did the other units to support this operation. The armory was again quiet and nearly empty as I left to see the operation firsthand and to ensure direct supervision as needed. I drove to the Fruit Belt and Westside neighborhoods of Buffalo, where the operations were focused. I saw citizens of those communities standing on their porches or outside their apartment buildings, applauding and encouraging the police. One patrol car after another slowly began returning to the armory to process, secure, and charge their prisoners.[199] The officers and the media also reported that Buffalo citizens who live in and around these neighborhoods began applauding as the police rounded up and removed the drug dealers.[200] This illustrates communities suffering from high crimes and violence welcome fair policing practices. These communities deserve to live in neighborhoods where their children play on the street without stepping on used crack cocaine vials or fear stray bullets injuring or killing them.

The defendants were processed and arraigned at the armory without incident. Patrol units slowly returned to their original assignments. The judge and the Erie County assistant district attorneys returned to their offices. The media left. The commanders, too, went back to their offices. I walked the now quiet and dimly lit armory, wondering about the months of work it took to conduct this operation and whether it would make any difference overall. I was not sure then and still ponder that now. I was satisfied with orchestrating the massive operation that enhanced the families' safety and their children in Buffalo. But I could not forget a mother's comments in a community meeting on a different drug case I had attended months earlier. "You should be ashamed of yourself; you are arresting your own people and children," she cried. I responded that my job was to make her block safe so she could sit on her stoop without fearing a stray bullet would strike her or her grandchild. I did not convince her; her comment shook me because she was not wholly wrong. No explanation I could offer her or myself would have fully addressed her legitimate concerns about law enforcement, often negatively affecting the Black and Brown communities then and now. Her concerns were reasonable. How do we justify the inequitable enforcement of laws designed to oppress the poor, the marginalized, and communities of Color.

During the 1990s, politicians, religious leaders, and community activists wanted greater police enforcement of drug laws, particularly in communities with "open-air" drug markets, increased violence, and murders.[201] No one could have predicted the consequences of intense drug enforcement strategies in the communities needing police intervention to end violent drug gang crimes. These communities and their leaders wanted safe and vibrant communities free of illegal drugs and the ensuing violence. Understandably, many community activists, religious leaders, politicians, and I have changed our minds about the efficacy of traditional drug enforcement policies. Back then, few considered drug addiction a disease, nor did we use health interventions. Instead, we used arrests and prosecutions of drug users and dealers, with unprecedentedly adverse outcomes for Black and Brown people, to curtail drug trafficking, resulting in what critics now call "mass incarceration."[202] This enforcement strategy, especially with numerous mandatory minimum sentencing laws, compels judges to impose more and longer jail terms. We did not adopt the healthcare strategy accepted today with the advent of the opioid addiction crisis occurring in White neighborhoods, a balanced approach to community safety, creating sensible drug enforcement policies, and fair policing strategies based on verifiable crime data and community trust.[203] Policies and practices buttressed by equity and social justice. Public confidence in the police has severely diminished over the decades, and in the community of Color, it never really existed. Our citizens demand changes to policing once again. "Change happens at the speed of trust, according to Steven R. Covey."[204] It will take time and authentic engagement to regain the trust of communities we have failed.

The current police reform initiatives are hardly new and repeat the earlier commissions' recommendations to investigate police behavior and practices. The National Commission on Law Observance and Enforcement (also known unofficially as the Wickersham Commission) was a committee set up by President Herbert Hoover on May 20, 1929.[205] In 1968, the Kerner Commission provided a comprehensive report. It addressed the racial inequities creating the circumstances leading to violent unrest in the inner cities and the need to professionalize police.[206] The report issued a dire warning: "White society," the panel reported, "is deeply implicated in the ghetto. White institutions created it, white institutions maintain it, and white society condones it." The nation, the Kerner Commission warned, was so divided that the United States was poised to fracture into two radically unequal societies, "one black, one white." Fifty-three years later, that is as true today as it was then.

In 2014, President Obama's Task Force on Twenty-First-Century Policing made similar observations and recommendations regarding building trust and changing this tale of two Americas.[207] And yet again, with the nationwide Black Lives Matter protests and the police killing of George Floyd that led up to it. We face another call for much-needed change in law enforcement practices and policies. I hope my grandson does not hear about another commission looking to improve policing and address America's systemic racial and economic oppression.

Chapter 12 - A Bridge toward Change

The year 1992 was very eventful. It had been a little over ten years since I joined the state police, after shading the trooper icon image and drawing Captain's bars on the V&T study guide, reflecting my ambition not only to advance but also to increase the diversity of this agency. I had reached the bridge out of poverty and crossed it. My children did not have to rummage through garbage cans for deposit bottles or the occasional edible food scraps to sustain themselves. Their mother did not have to go hungry so that they could eat. The journey began on Covent Avenue in NYC when I took the troopers' entrance exam. It continued on January 8, 1987, with my appointment to technical sergeant in the Affirmative Action office, followed by passing and earning the sergeant's permanent rank on April 11, 1987. Then, I got assigned as an investigator in the BCI on September 1, 1989. On August 16, 1991, I passed the Lieutenant's promotional exam and earned the Uniform Lieutenant's permanent rank.

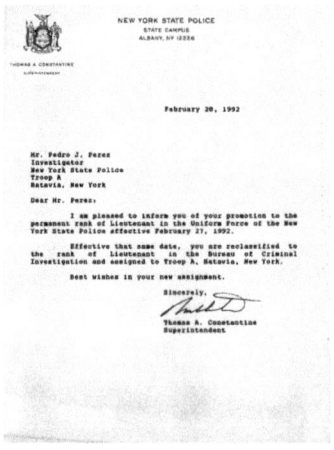

Figure 15. The special letter was issued to newly promoted and reassigned lieutenants and other officers using the purple font. In the state police folklore, Purple was the color chosen by Colonel Chandler's wife for the NYSP Uniform tie and hat headband modeled

after the ancient Rome's Praetorian Guard, under the belief Purple was part of their uniform, signifying their alliance to the Emperor.[208]

On February 20, 1992, my decision to seek an assignment to the narcotics unit as an investigator paid off. I earned the chance to serve as a BCI lieutenant in Troop A, my original troop. I would oversee major crimes like homicides, robberies, and narcotics investigations. I would work directly for Captain Bruce Roloff. He took me under his wing and helped me learn how to be a competent BCI-LT. He also taught me about the "good ole boys' network" within the state police.[209] He was an excellent BCI captain and had Superintendent Constantine's ear. I credit him for helping me cross the bridge to change my circumstances and the NYSP. I walked into Troop A headquarters and stepped into Captain Roloff's office. I stood at the threshold, saluted, shook hands, and sat down.

He said, "Pedro, congratulations. Are you ready to get on the train, the inside team?"

"Thank you, Captain, the train, the team?" I said, slightly confused as to which train and which team. There was a smarter-than-the-average bear attitude in the BCI commissioned officers' club and the BCI. Many uniformed troopers resented this but also coveted a position in the BCI. Did he mean the Troop A Officer Corps or some other team?

"Pedro," he replied laughingly, "my team and the train that I and only a few others can ride."

"Of course, Captain."

"Well then, call me Bruce."

"Okay, Captain, I mean Bruce."

Captain Roloff then sternly clarified his meaning, "You work for me. If the major asks you to do anything or asks about what is going on in the BCI, let me know ASAP." Even before I could understand Troop A's Officer Corps' internal politics, the captain had just given me the loyalty test warning. He yelled, "Scott, come join us in my office!" Scott Brown was the other BCI lieutenant assigned to Troop A. We would be partners again; he and I had trained together during the defensive tactics course to qualify for the MRT. Scott and I shook hands and agreed to meet after I met with the major. He went on, explaining what he expected from me. He then said the major was waiting to greet me formally, which the major did. I intuitively understood what the captain meant by warning me to be careful about my interactions with the major. The captain was telling me to be loyal to him. He did not trust the major; only they knew why. That was my first bitter taste of internal state police politics. Managing organizational politics became more challenging as I moved up the chain of command, as did dealing with politicians.

Figure 16. Troop A's Commissioned Officers' Corps. [210]

The state police during that era rewarded sergeants who earned the top ten rankings on the lieutenant's promotion list with two options: a master's degree fully paid for by the Division or being selected to attend the FBI National Police Academy (FBINPA). I chose the latter because it was a prestigious achievement, and once again, I would be the first trooper of Color to attend FBINPA.[211] I also knew I could financially afford my continuing education because of the pay raise the promotion granted me. So, I delayed trying to earn my bachelor's degree and a master's degree until I returned from FBINPA. I would then fulfill my dream of following in my mother's footsteps. Once I began working on my degrees, I knew I would have to wake up at four and study until six each morning, seven days a week, until I achieved that goal. I was ready, but first things first.

Figure 17. Members of the 173rd FBI-NA session. Pictured in the first row to third from the left is Akira Oyaizu; I am standing in the third row (fourth from the left).[212]

I had packed my bag and loaded my gear, readying myself for the seven-hour trip from Wellsville, New York, to the FBI Academy in Quantico, Virginia. I would travel back and forth on the weekends for the next ten weeks.

"Yasmine and Aramis, come down and give Papi a kiss," I called.

My daughter was ten, and my son was eight. They came running down the stairs from their bedrooms, cackling. "Daddy, are you becoming an FBI agent?" my daughter asked.

"No, Babi, I am attending a training course to become a better lieutenant."

My son asked, "When are you coming home?"

"Friday, Papo, Friday," I answered.

I kissed them and my wife as I said my goodbyes. I drove south, thinking about this trip and the journey that brought my family to this point. I used the most direct route from Wellsville, New York, to Quantico, Virginia. As I drove south on US Route 15, I thought of my mother and how hard she worked to pull us out of poverty. I remembered her resting on the couch on Sundays in our apartment because of her exhaustion from caring for her children as a single mom, working a full-time job, and then going to night school as she sought her college degrees.

My stream-of-consciousness voyage down memory lane was suddenly interrupted by another road sign near Pennsylvania and Maryland's border just south of Gettysburg. I had not realized how close the Mason-Dixon Line was to New York State. As I had done when I saw the Seneca Indian Territory Oil Spring informational marker, I pulled my car over to the side of the highway and carefully backed up to be sure I had read it correctly. This marker and my memories of my mother refocused my commitment to changing the state police. It was a sad epiphany. I recalled the Confederate Battle flags I saw in Allegany County. I had feared for my family because of the White Supremacist survivalist training camp in Ulysses, Pennsylvania. Some people believed that while the Southern states had lost the civil war they had won the peace because of the legislative power they now had in the US congress and senate. This marker, created to settle a land dispute, became a symbol that outlined the differences between where Slavery was culturally and economically acceptable. A practice many died to preserve, and those states of the union slowly came to oppose Slavery.[213] To be clear, before 1865, slavery existed in many northern states. These states benefited as much as the South economically from this horrendous and inhuman practice throughout its existence. New York City was a major financier of much of the slave trade. The cities of Bristol and Newport in Rhode Island were major slave ports.[214] Slavery largely buttressed America's economy.[215] Given the bigotry I experienced as a man of Color, both before joining the state police and during my tenure as a trooper. Given the state police's racist history, as shown by the DOJ 1979 investigation that led to Judge Foley's decree, the racist comments made by some of my fellow recruits and seasoned troopers, and the academy's Captain's retort, "Oh, but he's one of the good ones." I knew the amount of work that lay before me if I was to make a difference in mitigating and maybe even eradicating systemic racism within the state police.

I hoped my assignment to the FBI National Academy would be a bridge toward changing my career as a commissioned officer and in the state police. Was I now engaging in "Respectability Politics?" Would it reduce affirmation action's stigma on my achievements to this point in my journey from poverty to a state police commander? Was I naive and on a "fool's errand?" I said no. But maybe I was; that did not matter. What was important was my promise to my family that they would be proud and lifted out of poverty. I arrived at the FBI National Academy 173rd session on April 4, 1993. I returned home every weekend until I graduated on June 18, 1993.

The special agent in-charge welcomed the 257 law enforcement professionals from federal, state, and local agencies. My cohort included twenty police officers from across the globe. On the first day of my arrival, my FBI counselor mentioned the coveted "Yellow Brick," which we could earn by running the Yellow Brick obstacle course. I told him I had to replace my hip and could not run the obstacle course. He mentioned another physical fitness challenge I could participate in, although it did not come with the Yellow Brick award. I could swim a mile every day and earn a shirt, and I accepted and swam every day at noon. The counselor also told us that they had preselected roommates to ensure members from the same department or region did not share the same room. My roommate was Akira Oyaizu, a lieutenant with the Japan National Police. "Kon'nichiwa," I said as I introduced myself to Akira. I knew a little Japanese because of my years of studying Karate. "Good afternoon," Akira replied. "You have a good Japanese accent. Do you know a lot of Japanese?" Akira asked.

"No, just a few words, Akira. Your English is excellent," I told him.

We spent many evenings in the "Boardroom" of the FBINA, drinking pitchers of beer and eating pizzas and wings.

One evening, Akira asked, "Do you like sushi?"

"Yes, I love sushi," I replied. "Have you heard of Uni?"

"No," I said.

His embassy had sent him a package with some needed supplies and a wooden box of "Uni," sea urchin. He opened the box, and the salty ocean scent filled my nostrils. It was orange, thick, and buttery in texture and tasted briny. We ate the entire box, washing it down with some sake they had also sent. We were both young and ambitious. We talked about our families and what we wanted to achieve in our careers. We were both interested in learning about each other's countries and cultures. He tried to understand why, in the world's leading democracy, people of Color were subject to discrimination. These frank and challenging conversations made our bond even stronger. In those discussions, he acknowledged the same pattern of discrimination existed for certain groups in Japan, specifically Ainu. The Ainu are Japan's Indigenous Aboriginal people.[216]

While we drank beer one evening, I asked, "Akira, can I be a cop in Japan?"

"No," he replied. "Why?" He told me I could not be a police officer in Japan because I was not Japanese. "What if I married a Japanese woman and we had a child? Could my child be a cop," I asked. "No," again, he replied. "What, why?" I asked. "Because he would not be 100 percent Japanese. You see, you must be 100 percent Japanese to be in the National Police," he sternly replied. I told him he or his kids could be cops in America once he and they became citizens. We both took a long swallow of the ice-cold beer in our glasses and laughed. This new friendship was incredible, a once-in-a-lifetime experience. But I still wondered why only Japanese nationals were allowed to join their police force. I remembered learning more about Japan after reading about Masutatsu Oyama when I found his first book. As I pursued the discipline of Karate, I read more about Japan and its culture. I realized early on how xenophobic Japanese culture was. I had read a quote from Ethel Payne, considered "the First Lady of the Black Press," describing the treatment of children of Black soldiers in Japan during World War II. During the occupation, some American soldiers, including men of Color, had sex with Japanese women; the children of these relationships were called "occupation babies" by U.S. military officials. The soldiers abandoned many of these children, and the U.S. government did nothing to prevent that from happening.[217] The Japanese hated these babies and treated them with disdain because they considered them racially inferior.[218] The US government was frankly no better in how it regarded these babies and the mixed-race babies born in Germany and England because, in that era, the ban on interracial marriages was still the law of the land in the US.[219] The Supreme Court finally overturned anti-miscegenation laws in Lovings v. Virginia.[220]

I have been to Japan, and he visited me when he came to New York City. In 2003, I went to Japan to continue my martial arts training in Shotokan Karate and Hakko Ryu Jujutsu. Akira met my colleagues from Albany's Karate dojo and me at the Japan Karate Association (JKA) headquarters.

He said, "Do you still love sushi?"

"Yes, even more so," I said happily.

"Good, I made a reservation at a famous Sushi restaurant where you can catch your fish," he told the other American martial artists and me. We all walked to the closest Sobu Line subway station and rode the train to the Shinjuku stop. I stared at the large boat-shaped dining area in the center of the large open aquarium in the middle of the Zauo restaurant. Zauo in English means "sit" and "fish."

I felt the moist air, smelled the cooking fish, and listened to the laughter of the diners as they caught their fish. Akira had reserved a private room for us. The host escorted us to the room, explained how to use the fishing rods in the room, and then opened the room's sliding window, giving us access to the aquarium. I dropped my line into the water and quickly caught a large silver-skinned fish. The waitperson came back into the room. She asked, "How do you want it prepared?"

"Sashimi, Onegaishimasu, arigatō," I replied.

Some of my dojo friends gagged when the waiter brought back my plate of sliced and still-twitching raw fish.

"How can you eat that?" one of them said.

"Like this," I said as I picked up my chopsticks, grabbed a fish slice, and ate it.

It was delicious. We all laughed, sat down, and drank too much Sake. I spent two weeks in Japan.

I was surprised to see homeless men and women living in tents as I walked through Shinjuku Central Park. Like in the United States, the public often ignores people experiencing homelessness. While the problem is not as grave as in the USA, it was nonetheless disturbing. When I asked Akira, he seemed embarrassed and said, "It is shameful, and we move them away from most tourist areas. No different from what you guys do in the States." I asked why there were homeless people in Japan. He answered he was unsure but blamed drugs, alcoholism, poverty, mental illness, and individual choice. I wanted to know more precisely and learned there were many reasons, like in the USA. The causes mentioned earlier were factors, but Akira added the bombing during WWII that leveled Tokyo, the 1990s global economic collapse, and the deinstitutionalization of the mentally ill.[221] I remembered Jim Kelly's line in the movie "Enter the Dragon;" "poverty is the same all over the globe… It stinks."[222] I could not put it out of my mind for the rest of my time in Japan. Akira and I have been friends ever since. We continue to correspond via emails and letters.

Once I completed the FBI Academy stint, I returned to resume my duties as a BCI lieutenant in Troop A, supervising major crimes. I spent the next six months focused on investigating these cases. On January 13, 1994, Superintendent Constantine promoted me to lead the statewide Community Narcotics Enforcement Teams as BCI captain and CNET Detail Commander. Once again, I was the first Nuyorican to earn and reach this rank in the New York State Police. I knew the work I had done during "Operation Crackdown" and handling the tax protests in Troop A were factors in promoting me to captain. Several senior officers close to the superintendent quietly mentioned it to me during subsequent meetings I had with these colonels.

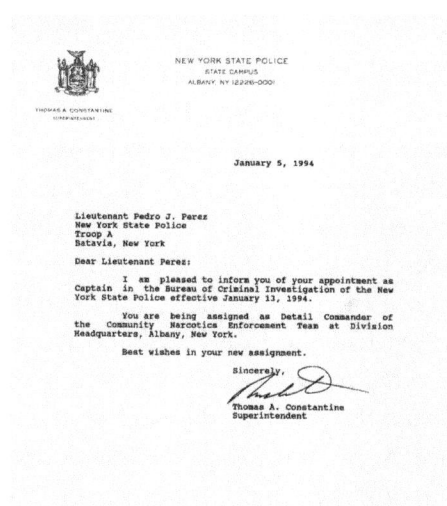

Figure 18. Letter of appointment to CNET Detail Commander. [223]

This promotion meant I had to move again to Albany, New York, where the CNET headquarters was. However, no rooms were available at the NYSP academy this time. Instead, I, fortunately, found a room slightly bigger than a broom closet at Troop T barracks near Albany for four months until a space opened up at the Academy.

This detail was established in 1990 by Superintendent Constantine in response to the surging crack cocaine epidemic in upstate New York cities. The five regional Community Narcotics Enforcement Teams (Capital, Hudson Valley, Central, Southern Tier, Western) deployed across the State provide trained state police undercover narcotics investigators to local law enforcement authorities upon request. CNET was critical for many rural, suburban, and small city police departments that typically lack the personnel or resources to maintain trained undercover narcotics units. CNET investigators also target illegal gun dealing.[224] The crack cocaine epidemic had spread from New York to other major metropolitan areas of the state. It then infected suburban and rural parts of New York. The illegal drug epidemic ironically followed the same route all goods and services used to cross the state. The National Interstate Highway system was supported and created following President Dwight D. Eisenhower's National Interstate Defense Act.[225] Those highways were the New York State Thruway and the Southern Tier Expressway in New York. And in a twist of fate, both motorways were paths used by American Indians centuries before. The NYS Thruway route, for example, has been used by New York State's Indigenous nations to move themselves and their commerce across the state. Governor DeWitt Clinton used the same pathway for the same reasons when he planned and then had the Erie Canal constructed.[226] Railroads, automobiles, and cyber network cables follow this ancient trail.

I traveled across the state for the next several months, visiting each CNET office. I met with each lieutenant and their teams. I asked questions about their local enforcement efforts, what they needed to execute these operations successfully, and any issues interfering with these cases. I had them arrange meetings with the local district attorneys, county sheriffs, elected officials, and police chiefs. I asked these officials the same questions and reaffirmed the NYSP's pledge to provide the undercover narcotics operatives and their expertise in narcotics enforcement investigations. Most of these officials welcomed CNET and expressed their commitment to cooperate in multi-agency regional investigations that arose out of their local cases.

A few officials, especially in smaller cities and rural regions, seemed taken aback by my ethnicity. This reaction was particularly true in some areas where Black and Latino migrants worked harvesting crops. My presence and rank challenged their view of the occupations people of Color in this region had. My commanding a New York State Police operation was not among those jobs. These were primarily White communities. Many of the users of illegal drugs in these communities were White, as were their street-level dealers. The mid to major drug traffickers were often African American or Hispanic from larger cities like New York, and cartels from Columbia, Mexico, Panama, and Venezuela usually supplied Syracuse, Rochester, and Buffalo. Over time, these criminal justice officials came to accept, out of necessity, my role. What often helped change their minds was learning I was the architect of one of the most successful major drug investigations, "Operation Crackdown."[227]

Each of the CNET offices assisted many small cities' police departments in closing down their open-air drug markets. These undercover operations sometimes took months, resulting in smaller round-ups like those held in Buffalo on August 19, 1992. The Division continues to aid smaller municipalities with their significant crime enforcement efforts, including narcotics cases. A new initiative called "Operation IMPACT" (Integrated Municipal Police Anti-Crime Teams).[228] Operation Impact, established in 2004, morphed into the "Gun Involved Violence Elimination (GIVE) initiative in 2014. The focus of the GIVE Initiative was to help local police agencies reduce gun violence.

Superintendent Constantine retired to become the administrator of the federal Drug Enforcement Administration. This created an upward shift for ranks below superintendent. Colonel James F. McMahon became the eleventh superintendent of the New York State Police on April 4, 1994.[229]

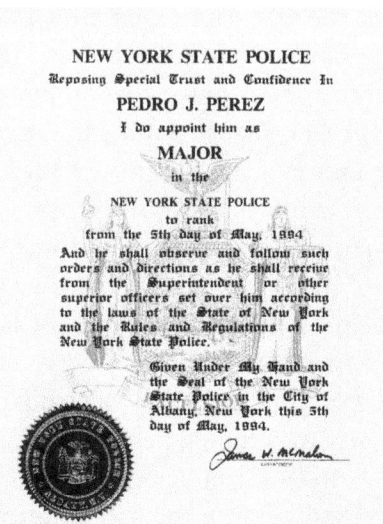

Figure 19. Promotional Certificate for Major. [230]

I was the third person of Color to earn the rank of Major in NYSP history. Major John Heritage, whom I first met in 1982, taught Rules and Regulations at the state police academy. I met him again when I worked for him in Troop A, where he served as Zone Commander. Major Heritage was the first person of Color to earn the rank of major. After successfully petitioning the U.S. Justice to address the discrimination, he and his fellow plaintiffs in the United States V. State of NY No. 77-CV-343 case. He continued to forge a path for other troopers of Color to follow as he rose through the ranks of the state police. Harry J. Corbitt, in 1993, was the second African American to earn this prestigious rank.

In 1988, Governor Mario Cuomo appointed Major Heritage to head the Bureau for Municipal Police at the Division of Criminal Justice Services. I followed John Heritage's inspiring rise in the state police; he unknowingly served as my role model as a courageous change agent. Heritage confronted racism, broke down barriers, and charted a path many troopers of Color followed. The first step on his journey to change the NYSP from within was the lawsuit he filed against the state police's discriminatory promotional practices, ultimately leading to the US Justice Department's investigation and Judge Foley's finding against New York State and the NYSP. I wanted to mirror his achievements, if not surpass them. I was determined to continue the legacy of change John Heritage, Theodore Cook III, Harry Corbitt, and Pamela Sharpe had forged. Like Heritage, Cook, and Corbitt, Sharpe was a pioneer. Pamela Sharpe became the first Black woman to earn the commissioned officer rank. As a technical lieutenant, she supervised the human resources section of the Division. There, she helped author a publication on the history of the state police, which was well-received by many, but not all in the organization. To continue the legacy of changing the NYSP from within, a couple of newly promoted persons of Color and I spent the ensuing years of our career encouraging troopers of Color to pursue higher ranks within the Division. We had significant moral support but limited success at getting enough troopers of Color to take the promotional exam because of the progressive difficulty of written tests and the ongoing concerns that passing the test would mean they have to accept assignments to regions far from their homes and spend months if not years trying to get back to their families.

Chapter 13 - Red Beans and Rice

September 6, 1979, Chief Judge James T. Foley ruled the New York State Police was guilty of "a 'pattern or practice' of discriminatory employment practices with respect to blacks, Spanish-surnamed Americans, and women in deprivation of the full enjoyment of rights secured by Title VII of the Civil Rights Act of 1964..., and the Fourteenth Amendment to the Constitution of the United States."[231] Judge Foley added:

> It is to be remembered that the more a Nation is favorable in affording equal treatment to all its members—especially through the relinquishment of past evils—the more secure will be its government and greater will be the general welfare of its people. A young, vigorous and courageous President speaking in the troubled Sixties in a stirring National Address, June 11, 1963 said: This Nation... was founded on the principle that all men were created equal, and that the rights of every man are diminished when the rights of one man are threatened. 1963 Public Papers of the President of the United States—John F. Kennedy (1964)[232]

The judge's order provided some guidance on the solutions vis-à vis the NYSP's hiring practices:

> "The state defendants are ordered to continue their efforts in the area of minority recruitment. Such efforts should be in the guise of an ongoing affirmative action program to attract members of the minority community."[233]

Judge Foley understood lasting changes to organizational cultures happen from within, so he imposed the affirmative action hiring mandate with hiring goals of "50-40-10;" 50 percent White males, 40 percent men of Color, and 10 percent females regardless of ethnicity. He gave limited guidance on how the agency would address its culture of systemic racism nor on the interpersonal racism of some of its members. He imposed a solution to mitigate part of the NYSP's systemic racism as expressed in its hiring practices when he required the agency to change its entrance exam questions to include only those that were "job-related or validated examination for the entry-level position of trooper." He also required. "All other procedures or policies entering into the selection or rejection of applicants including background investigation and need not be centered on any one particular method or validation strategy."[234]

He provided no specific remedies, nor could he for instances of interpersonal racism such as when an academy captain said as I walked past him, "Oh, but he's one of the good ones," or when the training trooper out of SP Peekskill disgustingly hoped I would not "fuck white women."

Thus, in an understandable attempt to encourage military bearing and discipline, our instructions pertained to how to line up for your meals and the proper sequencing of entering the dining room when we reported to the dining hall. The counselors showed us how to gather our trays, plates, and utensils. Then, find a seat in the dining room. All this was bearable, but what ensued was a flawed attempt to create inclusion and a feeble try at the acceptance of diversity by the academy staff. This was a superficial and insulting application of Judge Foley's edict for diversity within the state police. As we moved later into the academy training session, I became more incensed by the counselors' insistence that minorities were not to sit together at the same meal tables. If I or other recruits of Color were seated together, an incumbent trooper would order us to move to another table to create the appearance of an integrated academy.

This seating rearrangement forced superficial integration. Moreover, the counselors never asked White recruits to change to a table full of recruits of Color; they always asked the males of Color and the females to move. Over time, this created deep resentment among the recruits of Color, including me, worsening racial tension. No one officially discussed this policy with recruits, but we talked about this with each other, both protected-class and non-protected. These discussions often became heated, particularly with some of the White recruits who believed I did not deserve to be allowed in the academy in the first place, so I should not complain. The problem with this forced integration via seating arrangements would surface when incumbent troopers would come to a table full of recruit troopers of Color and force them to move to a White recruits' table. None of the counselors or other incumbents took the time to articulate what they were trying to do. In this way, they failed the entire recruit class: White, Black, Latino, and female. It appeared that neither the counselors, the academy officers, nor any other incumbent troopers were trained in nor understood issues of diversity and inclusion enough to hold an intelligent conversation about them. Diversity and inclusion are related concepts often used in tandem but are not interchangeable. Diversity is about an organization's representation or make-up, and inclusion is how different people's contributions, perspectives, and presence are valued and integrated into an environment. Given Judge Foley's mandate, the Division clumsily worked at diversity; it had no choice. They were nowhere near accepting, valuing, and integrating our contributions, perspectives, or presence. Even years later, when having a diverse workforce allowed the state police to respond to the crack cocaine pandemic of the 1980s, there still was reluctance to acknowledge that women and men of Color made the Division much more effective police department.

If this table seating arrangement's goal was to help us learn to work together as a team, it failed dismally. Judge Foley disagreed with my reaction then, but I am unsure how he would feel now. New Times reporter Michael Oreskes wrote in his 1984 article: "Judge Foley rejected each contention. He said the breaking up of groups of Black Recruit troopers at meals was part of academy's policy against cliques, and was, in fact, a decision that shows a realization that racial tensions will lessen if the recruits get to know each other."[235] In the same New York Times article, he went on to say:

> "Racial and ethnic jokes,' he said, were told at every level of society. 'Many give humor and many are offensive," he wrote. "I find that the alleged jokes included ethnic jokes other than those relating to blacks and Hispanics. The stated purpose was to ease tension and to break the monotony of the classroom. I found those purposes acceptable."[236]

As to the policy against cliques, there was a cafeteria section just for the academy's command staff. Incumbent troopers attending in-service training sessions sat together. The academy did not enforce the division's policy of preventing cliques on the command staff; they could sit together. Troopers attending in-service training could sit with other in-service colleagues. So much for avoiding cliques. How did having some of my most trusted colleagues on the MRT call me Beaner and the other slurs or the awful and offensive attempt at humor by the young trooper who said, "All you people carry knives," ease racial tensions? It did not! In this same New York Times article, Judge Foley cites that the 1981 NYSP academy recruit troopers class started with 192 recruit troopers, ninety-four White males, and eighty-eight of them, or 93.6 percent; seventy-six male recruit troopers of Color; thirty-nine, or 51.3 percent, graduated. Regardless of ethnicity, female recruit troopers were not part of the lawsuit. Judge Foley noted that the disparity between the graduation rates of White recruit troopers and recruit troopers of Color shrank subsequent academy sessions. In the recruit training session of the March 1983 class, for example, 77 percent of Black and 96 percent of White recruit troopers graduated, according to statistics provided by the state police.

Most recruits resented this, particularly troopers of Color because we were the only ones targeted to move from one table to another. As mentioned, I remember only one formal discussion about affirmative action in the "Rules and Regulations" course Lieutenant John Heritage taught. The forced integration was ineffective because the New York state police needed to train the academy's counselors and the executive staff on diversity and inclusion. Suppose they had conducted this training for the incumbent troopers and supervisory staff or brought in a consultant group to discuss these issues. They would have gone a long way in creating a smooth transition for the young recruits of Color, the female and White recruits. It would also have helped the entire organization overcome its unfortunate legacy and move more quickly, effectively, and with a more significant potential for successfully transitioning into a truly diverse and inclusive police force. Moreover, it would have allowed the New York State Police to be the first or at least one of the first police forces in the US to have an in-depth and meaningful discussion about diversity and inclusion on race, ethnicity, gender, and socioeconomic status. The NYSP was not the only organization to miss this opportunity to engage in a meaningful and positive conversation about bigotry, gender discrimination, colorism, poverty, and their effects on American culture. Our nation missed the opportunity and continues to ignore it, a tragic failure whose consequences do great harm every day. As I described earlier, I had drawn the captain's tracks on the cartooned trooper's collar on the front flap of the vehicle and traffic law study guide. I showed it to my colleagues of Color and told them we should all resolve to take the first promotional exams for which we were eligible. It is one way we could change the state police for the better.

We could become policymakers and thereby create mechanisms to change its culture. Some of the recruits of Color expressed no interest in my dream. Others thought it was laudable but wanted to get through the academy without considering promotions. I fully understood these sentiments; many of these recruits of Color were younger than I was and were more concerned about avoiding the troop assignments far from their neighborhoods. Given New York State's demographic distribution of people of Color, most African Americans and Latinos lived in the major cities of New York State: Buffalo, New York, Rochester, and Syracuse. NYSP troops encompassed each of these cities; for instance, Buffalo falls within Troop

A's region, and Troops M, E, and D covered the other large urban centers, respectively. As a recruit, it was possible to get favorable consideration, but the likelihood was slim. Accepting your assignment to Troops where the opening was more realistic, and those could be far from your home city.

Years later, only a few of the recruits I spoke to at the academy pursued promotions. Some did not graduate, others preferred being patrol troopers, and others took the exams but needed higher scores to make the cut or failed outright. I worked closely with several of them and developed a deep and lasting friendship with Anthony Ellis III. We did not know each other at the academy, but we served together in different areas of the organization over the years. Finally, we worked together in Troop A and then at Division headquarters. Anthony always spoke truth to power and helped me navigate the difficulty of my first year as a major. We also worked closely to create greater diversity in supervisory ranks by encouraging those we felt could help the agency become more inclusive and fairer. While our focus was troopers of Color and female troopers, anyone committed to diversity and inclusion would get our help and encouragement. When he and I were together in Troop A, it was one of the most rewarding experiences I had as a member of the commissioned officer corps within the state police. Together, we changed for the better how the policing community in Western New York viewed diversity, at least while we were there. We did this in several ways; our presence at Western New York's Chief of Police Association meetings gave them our unique perspective. They began recognizing that they needed to diversify their workforce but had yet to succeed. Part of the reason these smaller police departments did not recruit persons from the Black, Brown, and Native American communities was the local residency provision of the hiring policy. They required an applicant to live in the village before being eligible to apply. The current hiring policy for Erie County, New York:

> "Candidates must have been legal residents of
> Erie County for at least one month immediately
> preceding the date of the written test and must

be legal residents of Erie County at the time of appointment."[237]

Ellis and I explained that they could not do what the division had done: recruit from the communities in the cities with large populations of people of Color. We alerted them to the risks a person of Color took if they moved to small cities, towns, and villages. The costs of relocating, finding somewhere to live, and the fear of exposing their children to racism and ostracization because of their unique ethnicity. Moreover, what would happen if these candidates were not successful in completing the hiring process? All the expenses of relocating would have been for naught. We suggested they change their policy to only require residency upon appointment, meaning the candidate would have a job before moving. The chiefs did not advocate for this policy or change their approach, as recommended above. The lack of diversity in police departments is still challenging for many of these agencies.

Having successfully survived and graduated from the training academy, I nervously chanted to myself as I drove on the Southern Tier Expressway west into the Catskill Mountains, which looked like broccoli tops. At first, I had not noticed the Native American head logo on the road sign for State Route 17, which would take me from just north of New York City to SP Allegany. I initially took this image as a positive omen, a sign from my ancestors. As a child, I played the kids' game of "Cowboys and Indians." I always played the Indian. When watching the TV show "The Lone Ranger," I identified with "Tonto." "Tonto" was the name the Lone Ranger would use when talking to his sidekick, and Tonto would reply with the name; he called the Lone Ranger "Kee-mo-sah'-bee." There are multiple versions and definitions for these names. As I grew older, I realized the names were from Indigenous languages. Kee-mo-sah'-bee could mean "he/she looks out in secret," and Tonto could mean the "wild one."[238] But as a child, I heard "tonto," which in Spanish meant a fool, and Kee-mo-sah'-bee; I heard it as "Quien no sabe," "he does not know." I thought the characters were insulting each other as "frenemies."[239] I could not have known how prophetic and impactful this image would be in my life and career.

Moreover, in the years ahead, I understood this sign demonstrated my naiveté regarding the insulting and racist appropriation of Indigenous culture, symbols, religion, and images. This was not my ancestors reaching out as a sign of hope but an omen and a demand that I learn more about my Native American cousins. I needed to understand the message I sent to them when dressed in the uniform of the state police, even as I tried to serve them equitably. This lesson would be particularly poignant and painful to my whole being as the Haudenosaunee fought to gain greater control of their territories, economies, and civil rights during my tenure as a trooper. I learned the depth of the trauma they and Puerto Ricans experienced then and now because systemic racism was and is the same. Furthermore, I understood that the prejudice I was experiencing and seeing on some levels was startling, especially when I was in uniform but woefully familiar. Often, some of it resulted from ignorance and unfamiliarity with people of other ethnicities and cultures. I saw it in the reactions of some people I met on and off the job, in uniform or not. It taught me my uniform did not shield me from racism or simple curiosity.

Superintendent Chandler selected the gray cloth for the uniform he designed. In a Google book by Albert S. Kureka, Here Come the Troopers: New York State Police 1917–1943, the author cites the Superintendent's reason. Chandler chose the gray cloth; "He [Chandler] felt there had to be a reason for the color of the uniform and came to the conclusion that white was usually employed to depict right, while black was the symbol of evil."[240] Learning this was shocking. For nearly thirty years, I wore a uniform whose fabric color symbolized racism. This was a hidden example of structural racism. Some might suggest I am overstating, overthinking, and ascribing a racist attitude where there was none. However, this denies the body of research on this matter, such as that of Douglas Longshore, the University of California, in a Sage Publications article, "Color Connotations and Racial Attitudes:" "The colors black and white have long carried opposite connotations. Black has connoted evil and disgrace, while white has connoted decency and purity (Gergen,

1967; Isaacs, 1963; Jordan, 1968; Podair, 1970)."[241] It may very well be that "implicit bias" unknowingly influenced Chandler, given his stated belief that the color white stood for right and black represented evil.

Whether racism or curiosity, it did not initially feel any different. I learned to wait before passing judgment, and some may see this as wrong, but I would sometimes take the opportunity to entertain myself instead of getting angry. For instance, when meeting some complainants, they sometimes asked in a roundabout way about my origins. "So where do you come from?" Knowing the real question, I would answer that I came from the state police barracks. My frustration with questions about my ethnicity grew. What did that have to do with the performance of my duty? Sometimes, my answer would not satisfy them, but they did not have the nerve to ask the real question, so they would rephrase it by asking, "Where do you live?" I would answer, "I live in Wellsville." Some, unsure I had understood their question, would finally ask about my family's origins. "What are you?" Since they now more plainly asked what they wanted to know, I would answer that I was from New York City and an Afro-Caribbean Taíno Indian with a Spanish surname. That would confuse them even more.

Ultimately, I would say I was of Puerto Rican descent, a Nuyorican. With great glee, many exclaimed, "Aha, I knew it." What they meant was that they knew I was not White. These queries were annoying and strangely entertaining when they were about me and not my family. I also noticed that store detectives followed me when I was shopping in department stores in Allegany County and the nearby city of Olean in Cattaraugus County. Once I spotted one, I would stop, turn around, and ask them if they worked there. Then, I would ask them to help me find what I came to buy. Recognizing their function and why they followed me would embarrass them, and I would feel glee tinged with anger. I would often return to those stores the next day or soon after that, but this time in uniform. I would seek out the same individual, meet with them and the store manager, and converse with them about what had occurred.

One manifestation of racism that was indeed heart-wrenching for me was that I had to go to my children's schools several times because their classmates would use racial slurs, upsetting my children and their cousins. One crisp afternoon in October 1986, after working the overnight shift, I awakened to a call from my sister in-law that my niece was crying. I asked why? She told me.

"Kids at school teased her about her name and complexion." I drove to their house and hugged my niece.

"What did they say," I asked.

Shaking, she told me they had said her name meant her back was wet. I am sure you just heard the slur echo in your head. I knew at once the slur they had used, "wetback."[242]

"What did the teacher say?" I asked.

"She didn't say anything," she replied.

I went to the school and met with the principal. I told him, "You are responsible for the safety of my children, not just physically but emotionally, psychologically, and educationally." I demanded that the school do something about the bigotry that was occurring.

The principal told me that he could not control the children's biases, that the teachers were not teaching intolerance, and that it was the parents' fault. My response was that between 7:30 a.m. and 3:30 p.m., they were loco parentis, so they were 100 percent responsible for these children.[243] I told him my next visit would be to an attorney if they did not do something about this. My action at the school did not stop all instances of bigotry my children and nieces had to endure. However, it did help to reduce the number of incidents that occurred over the years I lived in Allegany County. One might wonder: should the fact that I was a trooper and my uniform have shielded my family and me from the incidents described? It could not, did not, and would not. I was wrong to think that would have given me the status troopers had in the rural parts of New York State. White officers built that status for sixty-five years; apparently, it remained theirs. I had not earned it yet and maybe could not, given I was not White.

Additionally, the uniform's status would not trump the deep-seated bigotry in some of the people I met. As systemic racism remained alive and well, I could do nothing to stop it; in some communities, I was an enforcer of systemic racism. Indeed, segments of the Black, Brown, and Indigenous communities viewed me as such. I walked a razor's edge for thirty years with my feet in both camps. Some people of Color saw me as a sellout because I chose to work in a police force seen as the enforcement arm of systemic racism and experiencing racism both in and out of uniform. An interesting contradiction is that the state police do not wear shields (badges) on their uniforms, as many other police departments do. Superintendent Chandler considered it when he first designed the trooper's uniform and then decided not to; instead, he used other insignia on the collar of the uniform shirt. Some of the older troopers told me the practice stemmed from the fact they rode horses, and their shields could get caught on a low branch, pulling the trooper off his horse. I do not know if this was true, but it seemed plausible. Nevertheless, I found it ironic that my uniform did not include a shield or shield my family and me from racism.

I had many arguments with some of the troopers at SP Wellsville about their belief that people of Color were innately criminal. Some troopers argued that African Americans and Latinos were more likely to commit crimes than White people because they were intellectually inferior and lazy. I reminded them that most of the people we arrested in and around Wellsville were not Black or Hispanic but were their cousins, friends, and neighbors, "White folks." To this, their only retorts were, "Fuck you, Perez," or "Okay, there are a few minorities smart like you, but only a few." Unfortunately, this would not be the last time I would hear these arguments while I worked in the state police. This acknowledgment of my intelligence being unique but uncommon among nonwhites was insulting. Did they believe my mother was ignorant or my children were not bright? It enraged me, and I knew if I did nothing, it would make me sick or lead me down the same road my father took. Instead, I once again followed my mother's strategy. I worked hard, pursued higher learning opportunities, and sought advancement within the system to change it. Moreover, behave as a peace officer working for justice, acting well within the color of law as required by Title 18, United State Code, Section 242.[244]

They would also comment that I "pulled myself up by my bootstraps" to pursue the "American Dream." Bootstrapping, an idea and phrase I loathe, is the notion that we can achieve success without any help from others. The argument is that hard work and only hard work will determine whether you are successful. These troopers discounted the impact of systematic discrimination, implicit bias, and overt bigotry. They ignored the benefits of networking, ethnic privilege, well-funded schools, and the other advantages afforded to the current dominant ethnic and socioeconomic groups of the United States. Did these self-made success stories arrive on these shores self-conceived without parents? Did they create the infrastructure they used to become successful, and did they not see the help others provided? I do not discount the need for hard work. I have worked hard, but I also know that "hard work" is no guarantee. I became angrier when I researched the meaning of "bootstrapping" and discovered its origins. The source of the "rags to riches" story of individual success without aid from anyone came from the perverse mythology of Horatio Alger. The tale of the rugged individualist who started with nothing and, without help from others, ended up successful did not ring true to me. Alger did not lift himself out of poverty; his story is more lurid than most people realize.[245]

These heated debates reinforced my awareness that the New York State Police had racist and sexist members. These individuals had not examined their prejudice or, as we now say, their implicit biases. Because of this failure of self-critical examination, once they became leaders, they tainted the organization with their policy and enforcement decisions. I wondered how I could survive working within that organization without losing my integrity, without losing my soul, and without destroying the hope that I could make a difference. I resolved to enhance my influence by speaking truth to power and ensuring that I rose through the ranks to become a policymaker focused on equity and social justice, not merely law and order.

In my career, I had several opportunities to speak the truth, specifically about affirmative action and the bigotry within the Division.

One occasion that reveals this most clearly occurred while I was the troop commander during the 1997 tax protest. The colonel suggested I use water tankers and K9s to control protesters. I refused and told the superintendent I would not behave as the chief of the Birmingham Police Department did during the 1963 civil rights protests in Birmingham, Alabama. Another occasion that lay bare these efforts was for all the years I was a member of the state police, and for decades before I joined, troopers marched in the St. Patrick's Day parade in NYC. I suspected the reason was the American Irish community's history and influence on policing in America, particularly in New York and Boston cities.[246] At every police or fire department funeral, you can hear the mournful wailing of bagpipes. At nearly every funeral I attended as a trooper, I often listened to the shrieking and mournful cries of the bagpipes. I respect their journey out of poverty. They went from being a hated ethnic minority to a strong community with an enormous impact on politics and policing. Harry Corbitt, Theodore Cook III, and others, including myself, asked Superintendent McMahon sometime in 1995 if he would consider also marching in the African American Day and Puerto Rican Day parades. "Why," he asked. "Because it would demonstrate the Division's and your commitment to diversity and inclusion," I replied. He said he would think about it. Within a year of our conversation with Superintendent McMahon, we marched in all three parades. The superintendent asked me to speak that same year during the Division's first Hispanic Heritage Month celebration. I decided to talk about the increasing support for English becoming the United States' official language. Some White troopers and senior officers within the state police were for this to happen. I perceived it was a reaction to the increasing number of Latinos in the country and the Division.[247] I asked if "we" were ready to change all the foreign and Native American names of thousands of communities and other words we had adopted. Were "we" prepared to change Florida's "Boca Raton" to the "Mouth of the Rat" or New York's mountain range from "Catskill" to the "Cat's River." "Kill" means river in Dutch, a West German dialect. Did we want to stop using "honcho," an Americanization "hancho," the Japanese word for a boss?[248] Would we seek to change all the Native American names used to name counties and other communities in New York State, like Manhattan, which come from the language of the Native American Lenape people? The silence of most of the senior officers was deafening. Still, many others in the audience applauded loudly. One young Latino lieutenant approached me and said, "You walked that tightrope without a net. Aren't you afraid it's going to mess up your career?" I said no; I had already gotten higher in the organization than I had ever dreamt. Moreover, I told him it was the truth and needed to be said.

Meanwhile, I enforced the law, remembering that social justice was one of my core values. I treated people fairly as I applied the state's laws. When I arrested someone alleged to have committed a crime, I would do my best to treat them as I would have my mother processed if she became subject to arrest, that is, with as much dignity as that undignified moment would allow. Years later, when I became a supervisor, I would share my enforcement philosophy and practice with the troopers I commanded. I would remind them that their safety and the safety of the individuals arrested were paramount. I also remember arguing with my peers at SP Wellsville during scheduled safety road checks and issuing traffic violation citations for faulty motor vehicle equipment. Ostensibly, the enforcement of various regulatory statutes of the New York State Vehicle and Traffic Law is to ensure mechanically sound vehicles and thereby protect the lives and limbs of drivers and other users of the NYS roads. Some troopers referred to poor people they stopped at these road checks as "welfare rats." This term incensed me because I had been on welfare as a child, although my mother never admitted we were. As I recall, as a little boy, she would send me to a neighboring building in the low-income housing projects I grew up in to get "government cheese" and other food items. These troopers did not know or did not care that most of these poor folks had not chosen to be impoverished. Jobs, workforce training, and entrepreneurial opportunities were all lacking in this county. Moreover, this was and continues to be an example of the "criminalization of poverty."[249] I asked my colleagues not to use terms like "welfare rat," at least not around me. They did not see issuing these tickets as the problem, saying it was okay because they also issued a "notice of correction," which would void the ticket once the vehicle owner repaired the faulty part and could prove it. This would make the car safer, but I argued it also meant the owner sometimes had to choose between food for their child or tires for the vehicle. I suggested issuing only one ticket and warning the owner about the other equipment needing repair.

The New York State Police did not have a quota system for the number of traffic citations each trooper had to issue. Instead, local supervisors would figure out the average number of tickets issued by the troopers they supervised. The supervisors used that average as an aspect of the performance evaluation system for the troopers. A trooper issuing more than the average, all else being equal, would get a rating higher than those writing less than the average. The Division did not use traffic enforcement tickets as a revenue enhancement strategy like some police agencies. In these instances, traffic enforcement has become a municipality funding scheme. These tactics are inherently regressive, making poor people suffer and worsening poverty. Regrettably, this practice has been part of municipal budget funding schemes for decades. When coupled with racism, it occasionally ends in tragedies; an example is a tragic case detailed in the United States Attorney General's Report: Investigation of the Ferguson Police Department. The singling out of low-income African American drivers for defective vehicle citations had been a significant source of funding for the municipality of Ferguson, Missouri, for decades until a Ferguson police officer killed an unarmed Black man, which triggered mass demonstrations and gave birth to the Black Lives Matter movement. I continued to argue that we should do our jobs justly and treat people fairly and equitably. Some of my peers agreed, and they tried to balance enforcement and fair treatment of the people we served. Others just kept doing what they had always done, only worrying about how many tickets they issued to keep their supervisors at bay. The Ferguson Police learned this the hard way.[250]

I focused on being a "peace" officer, performing my job justly, and it did not stop me from earning every promotion. So did the sharing of social capital by some of my commanding officers and the goodwill of superintendents Constantine, McMahon, and

Corbitt, without whose approvals I would not have gotten promoted. However, internal and racial politics also regrettably played a role as they had before the 1980s. The "good ole boys' network" was an exclusive form of social capital shared with only those in the network, a network made up of White males at the time. This network's recommendations for advancement continued to carry enormous weight, and "Who you knew" was still a crucial factor. Racial politics, or more accurately, the unspoken reality of "colorism" and ethnic biases, had not died. Colorism generally occurs within ethnicities of Color. In contrast, it also happens when a dominant majority seeks opportunities for an individual within a group of people of Color.[251] It still affected the promotability of those labeled "protected class" individuals. Some argued the reverse had happened, that promotional opportunities leaned toward men of Color and females regardless of ethnicity.

Even now, the scarcity of commissioned officers of Color means that argument does not stand up to more than superficial scrutiny. Admittedly, I rose to the rank of major quickly. Whether that rise was due to a combination of my hard work, my ethnicity, the social capital my mentors shared (the "good ole boys' network"), and serendipity, I do not know. Why the agency leaders decided to promote me is for them to explain. I know there were many White troopers who, like me, rose quickly, and no one seems to ask whether their Whiteness was a factor in their promotion. I endured another painful microaggression cut, adding to the scars on my psyche. Once again, I was angered but more determined than ever to change the agency so other troopers of Color would not have to suffer having their achievements tarnished by racism embedded in the assumptions that their ethnicity, not their performance and character, earned them a promotion. I had to live with that feeling of being judged by my ethnicity and not by paraphrasing what Dr. King hoped would happen by the content of my character.

Nevertheless, as mentioned earlier, I wanted to take the sergeant's and lieutenant's exams before affirmative action became institutionally embedded in the promotional process. The state police did not institute an affirmative action policy for promotion like the

NYPD. However, it could have been because of the lack of diversity in the sergeants' and officers' corps. Given that some members of the state police were still resentful of the imposition of affirmative action, I could not avoid the implicit and, on occasion, explicit belief that without affirmative action, I would not have achieved the permanent rank of lieutenant.

I knew my performance was equal to any other Lieutenant's and, in some cases, better. The possibility that my ethnicity played a role was unavoidable. I would have been a fool not to recognize this and more of a fool not to accept promotions because I felt ethnic politics might have tainted these promotions in some people's eyes. My job at each stage was to perform so flawlessly that no one would deny my earning the rank. That placed tremendous stress on my family and me. My family and friends felt I had already worked too much in a job, a 24-7 commitment. My family sacrificed so much as I pursued advancement in the state police. It is not just the missed birthdays, holidays, and other traditional family events; I could have missed the little moments like my daughter's reaction to the lawn grass or my son's preschool reaction. While understanding these dynamics, I still urged my colleagues of Color to seek advancement to higher ranks as quickly as possible. It was my earnest attempt to help diversify the agency to create an organization that genuinely valued inclusion. I also wanted to end the notion that "affirmative action troopers" were unqualified to be in the state police by encouraging a desire within my brothers and sisters of Color to reach higher ranks.

I proposed that we gain high-level supervisory positions. We would disperse throughout the organization's hierarchy as we became supervisors, leaders, and policymakers at every tier of the organization. We should not allow ourselves to be content with only diversifying the lower echelons of the NYSP. Instead, we would look to become the organization's leaders. I would say, "Imagine having red beans and rice or hearing Salsa and Rhythm & Blues music at every troop headquarters." Regrettably, I must acknowledge that this was one of my greatest disappointments: not convincing enough troopers of Color to achieve that. I had this desire at the start of my career. I reminded some of my peers of what I did at the academy as a recruit.

I had darkened the skin on the drawing of a trooper on the V&T law study guide pamphlet and penciled in the captain's bars on the drawing's shirt collar. I shared my aspirations with other men and women of Color, imploring them to join me in achieving that goal. I continued that mission throughout my career. For instance, at every state police gathering, I sought out troopers of Color and White troopers who had expressed interest in being allies in this endeavor, whether at a parade or any other event, to meet and discuss this strategy.[252] I always hoped that we could actualize permanent change vis-à vis diversity and inclusion within the state police by becoming its leaders. The problem was that many of the troopers I spoke to had not understood when they first joined the NYSP that the promotional process required them to fill vacancies wherever they existed. These vacancies were often far from their homes since many of the Black and Latino troopers I spoke with came from the major cities around New York State. Moreover, there were only a few openings in patrol stations near those cities; it often took years to return home. Like mine, their assigned barracks were in very rural areas of the state. When I arrived at SP Wellsville, my family and I significantly increased the number of people of Color in Allegany County. I could not get my culture's food, produce, or other items like Café Bustelo or plantains.

My mother or father would occasionally send me what I called care packages of the ethnic foods I enjoyed. Otherwise, I traveled eighty miles north to either Buffalo or Rochester to get these items. This reality was tough on my peers' families and mine. Access to services and goods, or other things we were accustomed to and relevant to our culture and ethnicity, was an issue. These problems may seem trivial, but when coupled with racist attitudes, comments, and other indignities we confronted, it made living and working in these areas complicated. These colleagues did not want to risk another assignment away from their homes again. They were right. I understood.

Moreover, the promotional tests were already challenging, even more so for the "protected class," as troopers of Color became eligible for the next rank. I mentioned a "black market" for copies of old promotional exams. When looking at tests before 1985 and those after 1985, one could easily discern the change in the words, sentences, and paragraphs used as questions. The earlier exam questions were straightforward and used short sentences. The questions after 1985 became increasingly longer and more complex. Some could be paragraphs long, and the vocabulary was at the graduate school level. The lengthening and increasing complexity might have been coincidental, and I might have been paranoid. However, I think not. Either way, I was not going to stop. Frankly, I had no problem with their constructing the promotional exams to reflect the intellectual skills needed to perform in these supervisory roles; it was the timing and motives I resented. I just studied harder and longer. Even if unintended, the more demanding examinations, the potential of moving again, and the stress this process placed on families deterred many of my brothers and sisters of Color from taking the promotional exams. Instead, many chose to seek appointments in the investigator ranks, severely limiting their ability to reach policy-making positions. I understood why many of my colleagues refused to pursue the promotion process.

Yes, the process was and still is grueling. The reward of reaching higher rank and prestige, plus the increased salary that came with it, made enduring the ordeal worth it. True, it came with the actual probability of assignment anywhere in New York and dealing with cultural isolation again. This achievement did not feel like a reward to my colleagues, but to me, it did. Each step I took up the career ladder made my family financially secure. We could afford a middle-class lifestyle, own our home, pay for our children's college, and the rest of the benefits a middle-class family received. It also got me closer to a point where I could influence statewide state police policing policies and tactics, ensuring they were socially just and fair.

Chapter 14 - The Fires Burned

I had crossed the bridge from poverty to the middle class by achieving the rank of state police Major and designated Troop A commander; my family was now firmly in the middle class, but it came with a hefty price tag. I knew what it had cost, the sacrifices my family made for us to cross the bridge, though I did not realize how much more we would pay. How many more birthdays, holidays, and other important family events would I miss? My wife's lupus illness was slowly becoming more debilitating. We wondered how long she could continue working. My children were becoming teenagers, bringing the usual family tensions as they pushed the envelope of what was permissible in our household. I knew I would not have to routinely place my life on the line as I did many times as a patrol trooper and as a member of the MRT. Drug gangs threatened my life when I was an undercover investigator. I nearly suffered a severe injury or, worse yet, died when a truck full of tax protesters spun me like a top of the State Route 438 overpass in 1992. It was an election year, and I worried there would be more violent tax protests. There were rumors that the state would again try to collect the excise tax charged on the sales of cigarettes and gasoline in Indian territories. The United States Supreme Court ruled that year that New York State could collect these taxes from non-Native American purchasers.[253]

During the gubernatorial campaign between incumbent Governor Mario Cuomo and George Pataki, Pataki indicated he would begin, if elected, to enforce the Supreme Court's decision in July 1995. Pataki won, becoming the fifty-third governor of New York. If he did try to collect these taxes, most of the Aboriginal nations, especially Senecas, would vehemently and possibly violently oppose those taxes. I feared I would soon see the fires burned. I wondered what I would endure as I pondered whether this new governor would journey down this dangerous road. Amid all the struggles my family and I lived through in reaching this next step of our journey, surprises and the challenges we were sure to meet were waiting.

Some of those surprises were wonderful. One happened in 1996, in the weeks before the Atlanta Olympics. The global journey of the "Olympic Flame" arrived in western New York. I remember reading that the 1996 Atlanta Committee for the Olympic Games (ACOG) sought 5,500 community hero torchbearers to help carry the torch throughout communities across the U.S. from April 27 to July 19, 1996. The torchbearer did not have to be an athlete to carry the Olympic flame. The ACOG announced it sought people who make meaningful contributions to others to carry the 3.5-pound torch up to one kilometer. It suggested all community heroes should have one or more of these core values and ideals:

- Outstanding volunteer work, leadership role model, or mentor
- Acts of generosity or kindness
- Extraordinary feats or accomplishments locally or nationally.

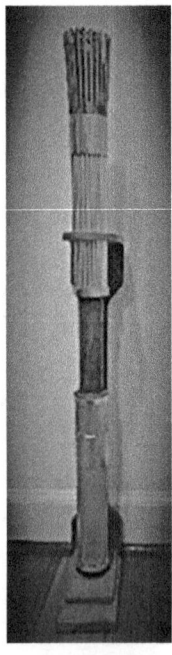

Figure 20. 1996 Atlanta, USA Olympic Torch. [254]

I do not know who submitted my name, but I had the privilege and honor to carry it on one of its legs through that region.[255] There was a long caravan of support vehicles and motorhomes where the runners of each leg would ride until their leg of the relay came up. Along the route, hundreds of people gather to cheer the runners on and get a glimpse of the torch. It was a fantastic experience I never believed I would have. My heart swelled with pride as I slowly jogged with the torch. I thought of my family and our journey. The fires burned across the globe, the torches lighting the skies with hope for peace. I hoped to pass down the torch to future generations of the Perez family.

Figure 21. Perez carrying the 1996 Atlanta, USA Olympic Torch. [256]

I had another tremendous opportunity during this period when President Clinton's second presidential campaign came to western New York.

Figure 22. President William J. Clinton visits Chautauqua Institute.[257]

Although I sensed his perfunctory engagement, which I suspected came from meeting hundreds of people and shaking all those hands, I was honored to have briefly met President Clinton. Yet it seemed so inauthentic, and I felt something odd about him. After he passed, I quietly looked at my hand disconcertingly. I was slightly amused and, at the same time, upset with myself for thinking that way. Years later, I had a completely different experience with President Bush when I met him.

To Pedro Perez
With best wishes

Figure 23. President George W. Bush in Rochester, New York.[258]

He had a genuine smile on his face as he approached me. He reached, shook my hand, and said, "Hola Colonel Pérez, ¿cómo estás?" I was stunned for a microsecond because he unexpectedly greeted me, speaking Spanish. I replied, "Bien, ¿y usted Presidente?" He seemed like a man with whom you could have a beer and chat. He was down-to-earth and relaxed.

I also had the good fortune to meet President Obama when he visited the Hudson Valley Community College. Once again, for many reasons, it was a completely different experience than meeting President Clinton. He strutted toward me with a slight bop in his step and a broad smile. As we shook hands, he said, "It's good to meet you." I replied, "I am honored!" He was authentic, relaxed, and seemed to genuinely enjoyed being there. I cried joyfully when he was elected the first man of Color to hold this high office. I never believed it would happen in my lifetime. I pray he is not the last.

To Pedro Perez
With best wishes,

Figure 24. President Barack Obama, - Troy, New York.[259]

Meeting three presidents was unbelievable and far beyond anything I could have imagined when my family and I began this trek to a better life. Who I met next still amazes me to this day.

Figure 25. Mrs. Coretta Scott King, - Albany, New York.[260]

As a YMCA Black and Latino Achievers Committee member, I met this powerful and inspiring woman at the Capital District YMCA's Black and Latino Achievers Awards ceremony. The YMCA leadership selected Mrs. Coretta Scott King as this event's first keynote speaker. I organized a New York State Police Detail to protect her during her stay in Albany. She was so gracious and calm. Her speech was inspirational. She urged the achievers to pursue excellence and to engage in preserving the hard-earned civil rights she, her husband, and thousands had fought, bled, and died for with a sense of unwavering joy. After the speech, she agreed to meet me, the other organizers, and the security team.

She asked, "Colonel, why are all your troopers whispering when they speak to me?"

Amused, I replied in a whisper. "You are so calm. No one wants to disturb your peace."

She grinned and said, "You too?"

"Yes," I whispered.

We laughed. Years later, I was honored to stand at the same podium as a keynote speaker for that year's Black and Latino Achiever event. Meeting and speaking with Mrs. King was the most important of all the people I was honored to meet. Without her, Dr. King, and the thousands of people who fought for "Civil Rights," Barack Hussein Obama would not have been president. Moreover, the Justice Department may not have filed a lawsuit against the NYSP. Judge Foley would not have heard the case and decided that the Division had been using discriminatory practices to prevent Black and Brown males and females regardless of ethnicity. Which, in turn, would have allowed the NYSP not to hire me.

Chapter 15 - Major Perez Off the Rez

It was the summer of 1994; a few months earlier, I had attained the rank of major, troop commander of Troop A. I went to the village of Cuba with my family to buy some cheese and other items sold at the Cuba Cheese Shoppe. I decided to take the scenic route using the back roads. I remembered my first time in this area as we drove around Cuba Lake when, as a new trooper, I traveled throughout Allegany County to learn about my patrol area. It had been another bright, sunny summer day. But not just the road system. I knew then, and more so during that period, that as a major, I had to learn and understand this community's people and culture to perform equitably and justly. It was all strangely intriguing and frightening at the same time. I was determined not to fail. Back then, I felt very vulnerable because of the racist attitudes of other troopers I met along the way. I heard that severe harassment of some troopers of Color caused them to resign or get fired for mistakes for which White troopers would instead receive leniency. Let me be clear; some troopers, including those of Color, were not suited for police work and deserved termination from the ranks. These may have been exaggerated stories, but I knew there was still significant resentment about our presence in this organization. In comparison, I had successfully not merely survived but had thrived and earned the coveted rank of troop commander. As I remembered those early days of affirmative action, I also recalled promising myself I would not resign or make any mistakes that would get me fired. Strangely, seeing the commemorative stone marking the Seneca Nation of Indians' Oil Spring reservation again did not lessen my anxiety as it had when I first saw it.[261] It had only been two years since the violent excise tax protest that I survived without being seriously injured or dying.

As the major of Troop A, encompassing the eight westernmost counties of New York, I oversaw all state police operations within Troop A, which had several hundred state police members. Most were troopers; others were investigators, senior investigators, sergeants, lieutenants, captains, and a dozen civilians serving in various positions. The Western Satellite Crime Laboratory (WSCL) was also within Troop A in Olean, New York. The troop also policed more Indian territories than any other troop. These Indigenous territories had several forms of government, including traditional Indian chieftain governments and constitutional republics, like the Seneca Nation of Indians.[262] There are five Indigenous territories within Troop A's patrol area; three were part of the Seneca Nation, the Cattaraugus Territory, the Allegany Territory, and the Oil Springs Territory. The Seneca are one of the original Five Nations (later six) of the Haudenosaunee or Iroquois Confederacy. Their people speak the Seneca language, an Iroquoian language. The Seneca and all the Iroquois peoples had a matriarchal system in which decisions and property passed through the maternal line. Children born into the mother's clan received their membership status from her. The Seneca Indians of the Cattaraugus and Allegany territories decided to form a constitutional republic in 1848 and began holding democratic votes for their leaders.[263] They also decided to rotate the presidential elections biannually between the Cattaraugus and Allegany territories.

The Tuscarora Indians and the Tonawanda Seneca Nation were the other two. The Tuscarora is a federally recognized Indian nation and the Sixth Nation of the Haudenosaunee. The Tuscarora nation migrated south to the Carolinas centuries earlier before returning to New York in 1722. The US government granted the Tuscarora a reservation in Niagara County in 1803. The Tonawanda Band of Seneca Indians is also recognized federally. The Tonawanda Senecas seceded from the central Seneca Nation in New York. The Tonawanda Band of Seneca Indians secured federal recognition as a separate nation in 1857 under the "Treaty with the Seneca, Tonawanda Band." They bought back most of their territory with their share of proceeds from the earlier land sale.[264] Both nations wanted to continue using their traditional chieftain government, led by hereditary Seneca chiefs (sachems - primary chiefs) selected by clan mothers. They reorganized their traditional government with a council of chiefs representing their eight family clans. They forged their democracy by a majority vote of leaders of the clans, which formed the basis of the band.

Traditionally, clan mothers selected hereditary chiefs who ruled for life (unless one displeased his clan mother).

The other federally recognized Indian lands within New York are:

> Cayuga Nation
> Oneida Nation of New York
> Onondaga Nation
> Saint Regis Mohawk (formerly the St. Regis Band
>   of Mohawk Indians of New York)
> Shinnecock Indian Nation [265]

The Cayuga situation and their land claims are exceedingly complicated. The national registry recognizes them but holds their land in "Trust" in the center of New York. There have been several trials and court decisions on their land claims, which remain unresolved.[266] Located on the Poospatuck ("Where The Waters Meet") territory, Long Island, is where the Unkechaug Nation ("People from Beyond The Hill"), live. The federal government does not currently recognize this nation, but New York does recognize it as a Native American nation.[267]

I needed to learn more than ever about these nations within the Troop A region, their history, and the treaties between them and the United States. So, I took a deeper dive into the nature of their sovereignty and our authority to enforce New York's criminal statutes on Indian Land. The people living on the Indian Lands in Troop A deserved our best service, as did all the Troop A citizens. For me, the struggle for social justice and the urgency of serving all people equally, equitably, and professionally within my jurisdiction was vital. Protecting poor people, marginalized communities, and communities of Color was paramount to me. As the troop commander, I faced the dilemma of trying to serve equitable and just police services to aboriginal communities within Troop A. How could I reconcile the centuries of genocidal practices, both physical and cultural, broken treaties, racial discrimination, and systemic oppression on the part of the United States, the state of New York, troopers as the enforcement arm of the state, and my actions in 1992 during the tax protest. One of the most destructive and horrendous examples of their trauma and pain was the forced removal of children from their parents and their placement in various Native American boarding schools.[268] One of these schools was in Troop A within the Cattaraugus Seneca territory at Irving, NY. It was the Thomas Asylum for Orphan and Destitute Indian Children.[269] An ugly and racist phrase grew out of this horrendous endeavor. "Kill the Indian to save the man" represented the belief system behind these schools. These schools sought to erase Native American culture, an explicit act of cultural genocide.[270] An activity that is still happening within our borders.[271]

I would have to face all these honestly and compassionately, recognizing it may have been enough that the trust was too broken to achieve any meaningful dialog. I knew I could get past my emotions regarding nearly being run over by a truck during the protest, but could the leaders of the Indian nations and the people themselves accept a gesture of reconciliation? I knew that achieving credibility in pursuing an accord of mutual respect and cooperation. I had to acknowledge the suffering caused by the United States, New York State, and its police. I had to explain my role during the tax protest and what I meant by fair policing. I had to show genuine regret for the harm caused by the government and any perceived injury I may have caused. Would they be ready to accept this authentic gesture of peace? I had to sincerely show that I would seek to address past grievances to find common ground. This work would have been a complex process at any time, but 1994 proved even more challenging because it was an election year for the Seneca Nation of Indians. It was a tumultuously disputed election year, with several incidents of violence adding to what would be an arduous attempt to establish a cooperative and collaborative relationship between two critical factors. First, federal and state governments interpret the sovereignty of Indian nations differently. The sad and racist history of the nature and extent of Indian sovereignty is complex and covers the length of existence of the United States. I was not and am not a scholar on these issues.

Nevertheless, I had to try and understand if I wanted to provide law enforcement services on Indian land. It tormented me as I tried to fulfill my pledge to provide fair and impartial policing, yet Indigenous leaders and individual people challenged me at every attempt. Frequently, they told me they were a sovereign nation, and the state had no jurisdiction. Only the federal government had the right to enforce federal law; the state and its police could not enforce state laws. Independent nations have "absolute sovereignty;" these nations can control all the affairs within their borders without interference from other countries.[272] The US has absolute sovereignty. The other political divisions within its border, such as states, counties, cities, towns, commonwealths (Puerto Rico, Northern Marianas Islands, territories (Guam, American Samoa, and US Virgin Islands), and Indian territories have what is called "divided sovereignty."[273] These political entities can regulate their affairs within the borders of their state, town, or, for this treatise, Indian lands but cannot forge treaties or declare war on other foreign nations. New York state cannot sign a treaty with England nor declare war on it. The Seneca Nation of Indians is limited in the same manner.[274]

Learning all this was overwhelming, but I believed I had no choice. The lives of the Indigenous people, the communities surrounding the lands, Troop A members, and mine depended on my assiduous understanding and application of the law. During this period, I had many sleepless nights. I then learned that New York state and its police agencies could enforce criminal laws on Indian land under the concept of concurrent jurisdiction if granted by Congress, which it had granted to some states, including New York.[275] Aboriginal nations and the territories mentioned above, did Congress have the right to do so, or was this a continuation of colonial power, oppression, and cultural genocide? Some Indian leaders knew we had jurisdiction and understood its import but would resist our enforcement unless critically needed. Like when I worked undercover investigations into illegal drug trafficking on their lands. There was hope, and I again engaged the Indigenous leaders to elicit cooperation. I resisted bringing this up unless I had to because the situation demanded action to resolve a criminal justice matter on their lands. I would cite this section of federal and state laws and judicial decisions allowing our concurrent jurisdiction to enforce New York's criminal statutes.

§232. Jurisdiction of New York State over offenses committed on reservations within State: The State of New York shall have jurisdiction over offenses committed by or against Indians on Indian reservations within the State of New York to the same extent as the courts of the State have jurisdiction over offenses committed elsewhere within the State as defined by the laws of the State: Provided, That nothing contained in this section shall be construed to deprive any Indian tribe, band, or community, or members thereof, hunting and fishing rights as guaranteed them by agreement, treaty, or custom, nor require them to obtain State fish and game licenses for the exercise of such rights.[276]

These leaders rarely accepted my assertion concerning state police jurisdiction. Some would insultingly ask if I was an "Apple?" that is, red outside and white on the inside, because they recognized my Taíno Indian heritage. Nevertheless, they considered me a traitor to the Native American cause. These comments were painful and reminded me of what some of my friends in NYC said when I first told them I was joining the state police ranks. For the decades I was in the Division, I faced these accusations about my loyalties. I know many police officers of Color experienced the same anguish.[277] I felt the sting of these kinds of racist comments related to whose side I was on. People from different ethnicities questioned which group I belonged to, from my Nuyorican friends and African American, White troopers, people I engaged with, whether I was performing my law enforcement duties, and now from my Indigenous cousin. I was in the middle of an emotional hurricane of reproach and, at times, hate. Any answer I gave, I felt, would increase the intensity of the whirlwind of emotions and those accusing me of betrayal. So, I was careful about when to answer, to whom, and why I would reply. My loyalties were to my core values, spiritual faith, family, and justice. In this instance, I ignored those painful ethnic slurs as understandable but unproductive remarks. I understood why; my uniform stood for the structure that historically had caused much disruption in their lives and the ensuing trauma; the title of Trooper is also a source of pain for many of my Indigenous cousins. Consider the generational trauma they experienced when the US Army, from the mid-nineteenth century to just before the start of the twentieth century, sent its troopers to fulfill the country's manifest destiny. That resulted in the displacement and deaths of many Indian nations. I would acknowledge those facts while asking them to consider developing a mutually beneficial relationship. Some leaders reluctantly considered the offer, cautioning me that they could not control all the people's sentiments on their territories; others refused to engage.

I had the privilege of talking with Robert Porter, Esq. He was one of the leaders willing to dialogue; even when those talks ended with our understanding, we only agreed to disagree.[278] At the time, he was the attorney general for the Seneca Nation of Indians. Robert Porter said the plain meaning of the nation's 1842 Treaty of Buffalo, which states, in part, that the US "will protect such lands of the Seneca Indians, within the State of New York, as may from time to time remain in their possession from all taxes, and assessments for roads, highways, or any other purpose."[279] His informed opinion was the fundamental point of contention between NYS and the Seneca Nation of Indians. Troop A and I found we were in a centuries-old dispute.

This Harvard-trained lawyer made one of the most salient observations during our talks about US Code 232, the excise tax dispute, and the apparent wealth gaps between the Seneca owners of gas stations and cigarette shops and the ordinary citizens living within the territory's borders. "Major, our economic journey is at the same stage as that of the United States during the 'Robber Baron' era of the late nineteenth and early twentieth centuries. We are working on growing our nation's economy and ensuring it is fairer to all our members." I have never forgotten his superb analysis. They were in what we call the Gilded Age. He said they were facing the same disparities and would resolve these in their own way. He argued that the attempted imposition of the excise tax violated their sovereignty and was another example of New York breaking historical treaties. He and many other Native American leaders I met in western New York constantly affirmed that the Buffalo Creek Treaty of 1842 prohibited the imposition of property, excise, and sales taxes from either the federal or New York State governments.[280]

"I am not a tax collector, and I just want to offer professional, expert, and equitable law enforcement services to the people on your lands," I often reply. Moreover, I would add that troopers can only enforce NYS criminal statutes, and the excise tax issue was a regulatory situation. My comments often bristled many leaders, who would retort that they did not accept state police criminal jurisdiction on their land. I still wondered how the Seneca would navigate through, as Porter described it, their "Robber Baron" era.

This era occurred in the late nineteenth and early twentieth centuries in the United States. Carl Schurz coined the phrase in 1882. He "used in his Phi Beta Kapa Oration at Harvard University to describe certain big businessmen whose highly individualistic practices seemed to him suggestive of the war-like pillaging of the feudal nobility of the Middle Ages."[281] Presidents Glover Cleveland, William McKinley, and Theodore Roosevelt worked to bring these "robber barons" under heel by breaking up monopolies to reduce corruption and create fair opportunities for workers and consumers.[282]

The Sherman Act marked the beginning of a new era in which the federal government was starting to become more involved in the economy. It also marked the beginning of a very influential political movement, Progressivism, which spanned the presidencies of Teddy Roosevelt (1901–1909), William Howard Taft (1909–1913), and Woodrow Wilson (1913-1921).[283] The Seneca's legislature recognized they had to bring under control some of their business leaders because of their self-enriching exuberance. These men engaged in entrepreneurial ventures that filled their pockets without regard to the tradition of shared wealth. The Seneca government embarked on passing legislation that tried to force these individuals to contribute to the general welfare of all Seneca. Moreover, they passed laws to force the booming tobacco and gasoline business owners to give back to their people but did not enforce these adequately. The statutes they devised included:

- Indian Cigarette Retailer Tax (1987): A tax of 10 cents applied to every carton of cigarettes sold by Indian merchants. (Passed by tribal council.)
- Automotive Fuel and Cigarette Tax Agreement (1989): In a deal with the state, the nation agreed to a tribal tax on gasoline and Tobacco sales. The tax could generate $5 million to $10 million annually for the tribe. (Passed by Tribal council.)
- Wholesale Distribution Law (1994): Created Seneca wholesaling company to collect a markup of 8 cents a gallon on gasoline, 13 cents a gallon on diesel, and $2.90 on a carton of cigarettes. (Passed by tribal council.)
- Motor Fuel Regulatory Law (1997): Imposed taxes of 5 cents a gallon on gasoline and 13 cents on diesel. (Passed by council.)
- Trade and Commerce Law (1997): Imposed taxes of 5 cents a gallon on gasoline and $1.50 per cigarette carton. (Passed by council.)
- Motor Fuel & Cigarette Products Regulatory Law (1997): Imposed taxes of 4 cents per gallon on gasoline, 8 cents per gallon on diesel, and $5.50 per carton of cigarettes. (Passed by council.)[284]

Porter was confident in carefully acknowledging the state's concurrent narrow criminal jurisdiction with the federal government while asserting US 232 was probably unconstitutional. These attempts proved ineffective. Later, they led to a violent and deadly clash on the reservation a few months after Dennis Bowen's election as president in 1994.[285] I was entirely out of my depth. I was neither a historian nor a constitutional lawyer and had not received a briefing or training about these extraordinarily complex issues. At the same time, I was not sure of the statute's constitutionality. It frustrated me because I just wanted to provide reasonable and fair police services, according to him and other Seneca, which they had not gotten before. I agreed with that assertion. I was partially correct, as outlined in a recent Supreme Court decision that has not only stated that police can and should provide police services on Indian land. That delivering local police service was constitutional; the determination expanded the issue of concurrent criminal jurisdiction.[286] The United States Supreme Court ruled, in Oklahoma v. Castro-Huerta, in a 5-4 decision that the federal and state governments have concurrent jurisdiction to prosecute non-Indians who commit crimes against Indians on Indian lands. I continued to study why New York State sought concurrent jurisdiction. What I learned were the underlying reasons. First, since the actual and complete extermination of the Indigenous people of the Americas did not happen, continued cultural genocide was the central motivation for assimilating the Indigenous people, using the ongoing process of seizing Indian land.[287] I focused on affording the kind of police services to which they were entitled. They were Americans, New Yorkers, essentially paying my salary through the taxes they were paying, just like their neighbors in the villages and cities surrounding their nation.

Moreover, major crimes, from drug trafficking to homicides, need professional and expert investigative entities, which did not exist within the Seneca Nation of Indians at the time. So I continued to walk the razor's edge, trying to balance legitimate policing without bias or malice. Doing so was often tricky, but the troopers and I remained committed to that cause. Nevertheless, I felt the tables had turned on me, and my friends' comments when I decided to join the state police rang out. Was I now the "New Man," supporting structural racism by my mere presence?[288] In other words, had the uniform corrupted the system of justice I was enforcing and the actions I had taken as a trooper? Had I gone from oppressed to oppressor? Given the circumstances I was confronting, how could I consider myself a "peace" officer?

Paolo Freire described this in his profound treatise The Pedagogy of the Oppressed:

> "In this situation the oppressed do not see the 'new man' as the person to be born from the resolution of this contradiction, as oppression gives way to liberation. For them, the new man or woman themselves become oppressors. Their vision of the new man or woman is individualistic; because of their identification with the oppressor, they have no consciousness of themselves as persons or as members of an oppressed class."[289]

I had a fierce internal debate about my journey out of poverty. Had it followed the pattern laid out by Freire, did I adopt an attitude of adhesion? Was I identifying with the oppressor? All these self-recriminating questions agonizingly raced through my head and heart. No, my inner voice screamed. Again, with deep conviction and keenly aware of what others might say then and now, was I merely fooling myself to justify my role under these circumstances? I rested on the knowledge that my behavior as a law enforcement officer was evidence that I had not succumbed to the syndrome described in Freire's astute analysis.[290] The fact remained that I was a New York State Trooper. I could not escape the NYSP's history nor avoid what they considered as continuing the historical oppression this community suffered. During the 1992 excise tax protests, my performance and leadership ensured we only took action to quell the violence, stop criminal behavior, and prevent indiscriminate police action against Indigenous people protesting peacefully. I assured the troopers under my command would only use the minimum force to protect innocent motorists using the Thruway and those protesting peacefully. We did not stop Senecas from trying to get home using the Street 438 overpass. Captain Haag and I listened carefully to the demands of the Seneca Nation's leaders, and where we could find common ground, we did.

There was no question that many Senecas, as well as members of the other Indian Nations within Troop A, saw us as invaders, an occupying army neither needed nor welcomed. In my naivete, I thought they would see past my uniform and recognize my commitment to justice and fairness. I understood what it was like to be the other. Ironically, I was now "the other" for entirely different reasons, given the circumstances. I expressed my regret for the centuries of oppression and disenfranchisement they and I experienced. The skepticism and disdain they felt were palpable. I acknowledged that words were not enough. I told them to hold me accountable and that they could call Division headquarters to report their dissatisfaction with my performance. I promised to hold the troopers who responded to calls for service within the Seneca Nation accountable for their behavior and gave them my office number. I left many of these meetings as frustrated as they were.

However, the meetings with Robert Porter, sometimes contentious, would leave me hopeful. The depth of his commitment to his people was powerful and inspiring. His perspectives on and analysis of Native American law, history, and sovereignty issues were humbling. They forced me to learn more about Native American culture and the different forms of government that existed among the Indigenous groups and sometimes within a single Native American nation in Troop A. To successfully serve this community, I had to build trust. To do that, I knew I had to do what I did when I first arrived at the Wellsville state police barracks. I needed to ask questions, listen to the answers, and learn more about Haudenosaunee within Troop A. I also had to work to ensure they knew I respected their sovereignty and culture while doing my job. I had walked a fine line as a member of the state police since 1981. I had challenged bigotry within the ranks, called out my fellow officers when they acted inequitably or worse, and behaved with authentic compassion, especially when enforcing the law. I often felt like Sisyphus, forever pushing a boulder up a hill in Hell. Was I too clever by half? Again, no, I hoped. Despite these feelings of futility, I needed to be intensely self-critical. I had been entrusted with immense power by the people. I, and all police officers, make life-and-death split-second decisions rightfully scrutinized for years afterward. Nevertheless, the boulder rolled back down the hill in November 1994 during the presidential elections held by the Seneca, as a result of the election's disputed result that showed Dennis Bowen winning the presidency. I hoped to prove my commitment to serving equitably.[291] The Seneca constitution calls for elections to rotate between residents of the Cattaraugus and Allegany territories every two years. President Bowen, from the Allegany territory, expressed his commitment to proving his lawful election and bringing his nation together.

The Seneca Nation of Indians government's struggle to control their "Gilded Age" would take time. During that struggle, they had to endure the violent reaction to their attempts to control their nation's economy, and elections foreshadowed our recent equally violent and deadly electoral crisis. In both cases, an ensuing violent attempted coup occurred.[292] In both instances, it was about retaining political power and the access to benefits that power provides. This internal dispute between different factions within the Seneca Nation became increasingly violent. On the one side was the incumbent Seneca Party, which refused to relinquish the presidency to newly elected President Dennis Bowen; on the other were Bowen and his supporters. In response, I deployed more troopers to staff heightened patrols and roadblocks on the territory around the clock. While initially objectionable to the Senecas, as the violence increased after the disputed election, they reluctantly accepted my decision.[293]

In early 1995, after the election dispute became more violent, I met with Erie County's Sheriff Thomas Higgins and Cattaraugus County's Sheriff Jerry Burrell to help coordinate our response to this crisis. I explained that I was redeploying troopers to increase patrols and staff roadblocks to Seneca's land to help keep the peace and ensure all the region's citizens could safely travel through these territories. To do this, I would need their support by having their deputies oversee some calls for police response typically assigned to state police patrols, and they both agreed. I also told them I was setting up a meeting with the Seneca leaders on both sides of the dispute. They chuckled as they wished me luck. Sheriff Burrell pulled me aside and handed me another dilemma as if this crisis on the

Seneca Nation's territory was not enough. Sheriff Burrell said he was under tremendous pressure from Kevin King's family because of his unsolved murder. Kevin King died from injuries he suffered in a gang assault in October 1994.

"Sheriff, you know we offered to help you investigate this back in October, and your detectives declined our assistance," I said.

"Yeah," he replied. I told him, "Captain George Brown, my BCI captain, and I have been following this case and are still ready to help."

He thanked me, adding Randy King, a successful local business owner, and Kevin King's brother had hired two Buffalo attorneys and a private investigator. He lamented their comments that his department had "botched" the investigation. The King family sought state-level law enforcement involvement and considered filing a wrongful death lawsuit. I reiterated that we would help with the case's reinvestigation; all he had to do was ask. Until then, although there were clear suspects, only one person was in cuffs for Kevin King's murder. It took a couple of months before we got involved. Immediately after speaking with the Sheriff, I called Superintendent McMahon and told him about the request. The superintendent empathetically commented that I had my hands full, but he believed my team and I could handle it. "Yes, sir. I will keep you posted." I now had no choice but to address what both factions of the Seneca election dispute called a potential "civil war."[294] And this major reinvestigation of King's homicide. It was unusual to have two significant incidents on one level, but on another level, as a troop commander, you were expected to manage multiple crises. My team and I put on brave faces and said to each other, "We got this."

The New York Times put it this way:

> "After the shootings, both factions declared in almost identical statements that the reservation was "on the brink of civil war."[295]

The Los Angeles Times reported:

> "We're on the verge of a civil war,' said Rose
> Patterson, a Bowen aide. 'If people allow the
> violence to continue, it's going to be a long time
> before police leave the reservation."[296]

In an interview with the New York Times reporter John Kifner,
I put it this way:

> "This is like a very large-scale domestic," Maj.
> Pedro J. Perez, the commander of Troop A,
> said with a sigh at his headquarters trailer by a
> Thruway toll booth the other day. He spoke with
> an experienced police officer's knowledge that
> domestic disputes can be among the most vola-
> tile, dangerous situations an officer can face."[297]

That said, I asked Captain Brown to prepare a team of his top
investigators to open our investigation of this case. Soon after, the
attorney general called a meeting at his Buffalo office to discuss this
case and the steps he needed us to take. We already knew the original
autopsy's conclusions were not exact because the forensic pathologist had not received all the necessary information to determine the
"manner and cause" of Kevin King's death.[298] Captain Brown and his
BCI investigators described the circumstances surrounding the beating death of Kevin King. At the same time, I listened at the temporary command post at SP Dunkirk just outside of the Seneca Nation
of Indians territory.

"Here is the background on the King case," said Captain
Brown. On October 23, 1994, a calm autumn night outside the
Eastside Pizzeria and Coffee shop in Olean, New York. Kevin King
died in this pizzeria's parking lot after ten individuals assaulted him
and his two friends, and it was a fight he had not started, according
to witnesses.

"He was laying on the ground, and they kicked him over and over and over again, in the back, in the ribs, in the legs, in the hips, and one girl kicked him in the head," said one witness, Pamela Brochu of Weston Mills.[299]

There were many witnesses, including the alleged perpetrators and Kevin King's two friends who, although injured, survived the beatings. There was plenty of evidence strewn about the crime scene, including beer bottles, pepper shakers, and saltshakers allegedly used as weapons. The Sheriff's investigative team failed to recover some evidence, including hair and skin tissue possibly from one of the victims. The arrest of the person who bludgeoned another person that night with a beer bottle had occurred, but others allegedly involved in King's murder remained at large for months. It took Randy King's relentless campaign and public protests to get the Cattaraugus County Legislature to petition Attorney General Dennis C. Vacco's involvement on March 8, 1995. The Attorney General accepted the case on March 24, 1995.[300]

I kept Superintendent McMahon informed on this case and the ongoing and increasingly violent dispute in the Seneca Nation of Indians throughout this period. So I was not surprised when he called and said we were to help the attorney general conduct the investigation and aid with the prosecution. There had been mistakes in the investigation despite Sheriff Burrell's understandable yet flawed assertions that his investigators left no stone unturned. The court granted our request for an exhumation and second autopsy on March 28, 1995. We asked Dr. Michael Baden to perform the autopsy. Dr. Baden, director of the Forensic Sciences Unit of the state police, said he would conduct the second forensic examination of King's body to establish the manner and cause of his death.

Dr. Baden was New York City's chief medical examiner and was co-director of the NYS Police Medico-Legal Investigations Unit. In the 1970s, he served as the chair of the Forensic Pathology Panel of the United States Congress Select Committee on Assassinations, which re-examined the assassinations of John F. Kennedy and

Martin Luther King. For thirteen years, Dr. Baden hosted the HBO "Autopsy" series, and this series showed how the forensic sciences helped police solve crimes. He authored over eighty professional articles and books on aspects of forensic medicine and two nonfiction books.[301]

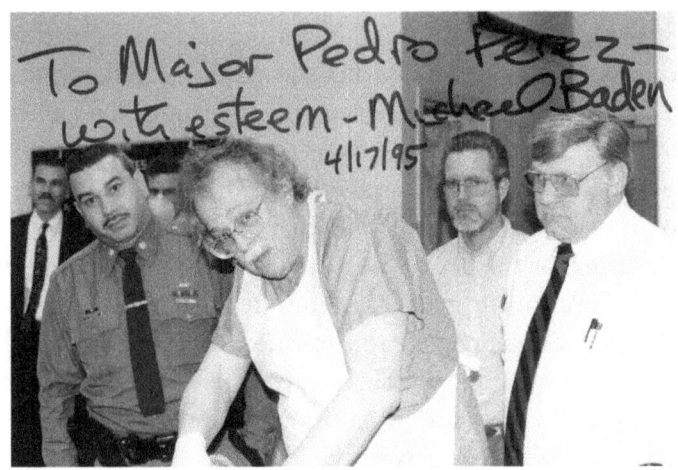

Figure 26. This is a photo of the day of Kevin King's exhumation. Forensic Pathologist Dr. Michael Baden performed the second autopsy. Present in the back row are BCI Captain George Brown, an unknown state police Investigator, Cattaraugus County Sheriff's Deputy Ernest Travis, and Sheriff Burrell.[302]

To protect the chain of custody, we had to personally see the exhumation and transport of King's body to the site we had secured for Dr. Baden to perform. Dr. Baden opened the chest cavity and, with a surgical saw, began removing the ribs one by one to confirm what we had seen in the original X-rays we had secured as evidence. These X-rays revealed there were possible fractures in King's ribs. The stench wafting up from the body cavity filled our nostrils. The surgical saw buzzed as it cut through the bones and embalmed sinews; bone and tissue fragments became airborne. Because Dr. Baden had placed his head nearly inside the chest cavity, Baden's hair had some of these pieces logged within his already wild-looking locks. Each time he successfully dislodged a rib, he would hold it up for all to see the fracture. Understandingly, some observers became nauseous and left the room to void their breakfasts. Dr. Baden concluded that the cause of death was blunt force injuries to the head and chest with fractures of ribs and fatal cardiac arrhythmia. Dr. Baden declared the manner of death was Homicide. I would work with Dr. Baden again when I served as Lieutenant Colonel in charge of the BCI and oversaw the annual Colonel Williams International Homicide Seminar.

Ten suspects were indicted and arrested in November 1995. Two years later, eight of these individuals were found guilty and brought to justice for the beating death of Kevin King.[303]

The Buffalo News reported:

- Shawn Appleby, twenty-nine, of Eldred, Pennsylvania, who admitted the most serious charge, second-degree manslaughter. He will receive a prison term of two and one-third to seven years.

- Shane Appleby of Germany, criminally negligent homicide, one and one-third to four years

- Cory Shea, twenty-eight, of Longwood, Florida., criminally negligent homicide, one year in the county jail and/or probation.

- Brian E. Mooney, twenty-three, of Liverpool, criminally negligent homicide, one year in the county jail and/or probation.

- Karrie L. Haggerty, twenty-three, of Liverpool, third-degree assault, one year in the county jail and/or probation.

- Sandra S. Haggerty, twenty-eight, of North Tonawanda, Karrie's sister, who admitted to a third-degree assault charge.

- John L. Reynolds, considered the mastermind in the fatal beating of Kevin King, was sentenced to four to twelve years in prison on his second-degree manslaughter conviction.

- A seventh defendant, Troy A. Fusco, thirty-one, of East Aurora, is expected to plead to a charge of third-degree assault, which carries a one-year jail sentence.[304]

While Captain Brown oversaw this investigation, the situation on Seneca lands worsened. Newly elected President Bowen faced fierce opposition from the rival political party, the Seneca Party, and it tried to impeach him and installed Karen Bucktooth as its presidential appointee. Both parties sued each other in New York State court. A court-ordered injunction held sway until the US Justice Department reviewed the dangerous political quagmire and ruled on the election results' legitimacy. Several violent incidents, beatings, and a nonfatal shooting occurred weeks before on the Allegany territory as the factions moved closer to a civil war and as people of the reservation waited for a decision from the courts and justice department. My command staff and I also waited for the court decision while at the Mobile Command Post at the SP Dunkirk of the NYSP Troop T (Thruway). Before the court decided on March 25, 1995, what everyone feared happened, a deadly shootout occurred on the Cattaraugus territory. Karen Bucktooth, who has been declared president by her supporters in the business faction, the Seneca Party, was just down the road from the administrative building and was barricaded inside a recreation center, where a sentry swept the area with binoculars. Karen Bucktooth told the Buffalo News. "We're here protecting our constitution, which can't be changed, can't be altered," she insisted. "That's what really burns me up, violating the constitution."[305]

Rose Patterson, an aide to Mr. Bowen, said five of Karen Bucktooth's supporters tried to enter the William Seneca Administrative building. Seneca Nation of Indians officials identified the men as Myron Kettle, sixty-two, Sam Powliss, and Charles Thompson; both men were about thirty years of age. Both men sustained bullet wounds in the back and one in the head. A fourth man, Daniel Rice, a supporter of Mr. Bowen, was shot in the leg and hand and was in stable condition at the Erie County Medical Center in Buffalo. Mr. Bowen, in a telephone interview with a news reporter, said that twelve carloads of Bucktooth supporters had been at a birthday party for Mr. Kettle Friday night at five gallons of vodka were drunk. Mr. Bowen told reporters that Mr. Kettle was given a rifle for his birthday. Kettle and some friends attacked the administrative building from cars at 4:20 a.m. and 5:00 a.m. Fatal shoot-ings occurred at about 6:00 a.m. at the William Seneca Building, a tribal government office that Mr. Bowen's supporters have occupied since January. Mr. Bowen said five men tried to storm the Seneca Building; some got inside and began spraying halls and rooms with shotgun and rifle fire. Mr. Rice was wounded; Bowen said, "Our people returned defensive fire." He did not concede his rivals' accu-sations that his supporters shot the slain men. Mr. Tim Clark, Ms. Bucktooth's spokesperson, said those men died attempting to enter the building after Bowen supporters shot out their tires. As these men ran, leaving the building, Bowen's supporters returned fire.[306]

Like the American Civil War, this internal feud divided families: a Bowen supporter allegedly shot and killed a family member who had been a Seneca Party supporter, who was among the men who entered the building. Erie County Sheriff's deputies and EMTs had cleared the scene when I arrived later that morning and entered the building. Several young men stood at the entrance foyer and pointed their AK-47s at me. I was in full uniform and told them to lower their weapons, as I was there to help. Ultimately, one of the senior leaders of Bowen's group stepped in between us. They lowered their rifles. I quietly exhaled as he led me to President Bowen's office. It was not the first time I had a firearm pointed at me; I feared for my life each time. Each time it happened, I hid that fear. After some war-ranted emotional outbursts, he said he needed a safe escort out of the building. I was impressed with his commitment to saving his nation from what he believed were corrupt individuals trying to make them-selves rich while many other Seneca remained in poverty. I suspected his intense emotions grew directly out of efforts to save the soul of the Seneca Nation of Indians. I did not know if what he was saying was true. Frankly, my only concern was restoring the peace.

I radioed for an unmarked cargo van to pull up alongside the building and led President Bowen to the van. I instructed the plain-clothes Investigator to drive the President to a safer location. As I was about to leave, Ross John confronted me. He was a wealthy Seneca business entrepreneur who may have been one of the "Barons" Robert Porter had alluded to in our conversations. John played a pivotal role in the election dispute. President Bowen sought an injunction from the United States District Court for Western New York. Ross John Bowen claimed John had been improperly appointed to the Nation's Tribal Council. The newly elected President wanted to prevent Ross John from acting or sitting as a member of the Council.[307]

I left, knowing I would be back. I returned to the Command Post and saw a sign at a convenience store. It read "MAJOR PEREZ OFF THE REZ." I could not stop laughing. It was a very clever message. It was clear that only some of the Senecas shared that sentiment. It was also apparent that no one would have admitted wanting the state police involved in their internal conflict. It was the middle of the afternoon, and I did not want to agitate the Senecas further. I did not stop and take a picture of the sign, but I still wish I had. As mentioned, I knew I would be back later that day and for many more days afterward. Because of the shooting deaths over the election dispute and the national coverage that it received, the federal departments of Justice and Indian Affairs had taken notice. The superintendent told me that the US Justice Department assigned a mediation team. I was to meet with and escort the US Justice Department's representative, Michael Hernandez, leader of the federal Justice Department's four-person mediating team, to meet with the disputing parties. Eventually, Mr. Hernandez calmed the factions and assured each side that all the armed individuals had left the occupied government buildings on the two Seneca territories. In April 1995, a court decision certified the election results.[308]

According to Michael Anderson, special assistant to Ada Deer, assistant secretary of Indian affairs in the Department of the Interior, it was to take effect at once. President Bowen was the duly elected president of the Seneca Nation of Indians. The regional leaders of the Bureau of Indian Affairs (BIA) confirmed the decision. The BIA sharply criticized the Seneca Party's tribal councilors for their improper impeachment of Dennis Bowen. Franklin Keel put it this way: "The impeachment was rife with error,' Keel said. 'Dennis Bowen was not safely removed from his position as president. The appointment of Karen Bucktooth is a nullity. All business conducted by the council after the attempted removal of President Bowen is unconstitutionally void."[309]

President Bowen said, "With this decision, we will do everything we can to bring our nation back together."[310] When President Bowen refused to accept his impeachment, the Seneca Party and his other political opponent sued him in New York's State Supreme Court. Bowen countered by suing the court in the US District Court, Western District of New York. In November 1997, US District Court Judge Richard J. Arcara cited: "Issues of tribal self-governance are recognized by the Treaty of 1794 and the Supremacy Clause of the United States Constitution" and ruled that the state court had no jurisdiction.[311]

For the next year, things remained relatively calm. We slowly returned our operational posture to where it had been before the internal dispute. Seneca businesspeople and the Seneca Nation knew this was financially lucrative. The Seneca government and some Seneca entrepreneurs worked to get the profits of selling untaxed cigarettes and gasoline to enrich themselves and improve their nation.[312]

I worried about the ongoing dispute over excise taxes that loomed large for the next few years. Governor Cuomo tried in 1992 and had to pull back because of the tax protest that turned into a violent riot. Governor Pataki, just elected to office, and one of the issues he ran on was resolving the excise tax dispute, sought to negotiate with the Haudenosaunee. If he pushed too aggressively, I had no doubts the protests would begin again, and I could only hope there would be no violence. I continued meeting with leaders of the Indigenous nations within Troop A, and we agreed to disagree about jurisdiction. As I drove through the territories, I looked for the sign "MAJOR PEREZ OFF THE REZ," but by then, it was gone. That would all change in 1997.

Chapter 16 - My Cousins - History, Identity, Sovereignty, what did I learn?

I understood the challenge of being the "Other," navigating intercultural ignorance and defending against racist attitudes and actions. I knew that for all the Indigenous peoples of the Americas, preventing genocide and preserving their cultures has been a struggle for 532 years. African Americans, who have since 1619 also fought for more than 405 years to free themselves, survived the brutality of slavery and lynchings; it has also been an ordeal. We, people of Color, struggle to fully realize the promise outlined in our flawed but aspirational founding documents. We have turned hope into a verb. The actions of thousands of people working to create a "more perfect union" today prove hope can be a verb; consider the passage of the Thirteenth, Fourteenth, Fifteenth, and Nineteenth Amendments. Nevertheless, I also realize we all go through acculturation as children, and the bombardment of racist stereotypes becomes embedded in our hearts and minds because of our upbringing.

Moreover, the educational system's failure to address this type of acculturation reinforces these awful attitudes and negative beliefs of people of Color, females, and Indigenous people. The lack of education regarding the ugly truth about the attempted genocide of people, slavery, systemic racism, interpersonal racism, and misogyny continues to injure all the people of the United States. A relatively innocuous example of the latter was when a White trooper from my recruit class, who also had qualified for the MRT, asked me during the team's training, "How did you get into the state police? Are you a US citizen?" He did not know that, as a Puerto Rican, I was a US citizen.

This trooper was from Johnstown in Montgomery County, New York. It is a small city surrounded primarily by the Adirondack Mountains, forests, and farmlands, with very few minorities, if any, living in or around the region. He admitted that he had never seen or met a Puerto Rican and had only seen a few African Americans and Indigenous people. I was annoyed, but I also found this humorous. Since he was not asking the question insultingly, I tried to educate him about US/Puerto Rican politics. At the end of the Spanish-American war, I explained, the United States got Puerto Rico, the Philippines, Guam, and other captured territories. I added that in 1917, the US Congress granted Puerto Ricans and other peoples from the captured territories a limited form of citizenship.[313] They were also subject to the limitations of "divided sovereignty." For instance, the territorial status of Puerto Rico as a US territory means the US citizenship of Puerto Ricans born and who live on the island falls under the control of Congress. The Constitution does not necessarily guarantee it. Therefore, the citizenship of Puerto Ricans is subject to the political capriciousness of Congress and the president, which constantly changes depending on the ideology of new partisan majorities and presidents. The same limitation exists for the peoples of Guam, the other US territories, and the Indian lands designated as "nations within a nation."[314] That the US Congress essentially controlled that colonial relationship. I hoped knowing my story would encourage him to show greater empathy and equity when meeting people like me.

I prayed he would not assume they were noncitizens or migrant workers as some folks I met in Allegany County had thought my family and I were, or worse, during that era, drug traffickers. I explained that the US versus PR relationship on a constitutional and a lived-experience basis was exceedingly complicated. As such, it embedded limitations in the island's constitutional status and its people. The US Congress essentially controlled that colonial relationship.[315] Given the ugly racist historical perspective of many in Congress, the debate regarding whether Puerto Ricans were worthy enough to join the "Union" still exists. I explained how these racist attitudes and the pseudo-science of eugenics led to forced sterilizations of Puerto Rican women, especially darker-hued Boricuas.[316] I also explained how full constitutional protections and privileges would apply only when Puerto Ricans moved to or were born on the mainland. Finally, I said, "I was born here. I am a citizen and grew up on the island of Manhattan. So, I enjoyed the full protections and rights of citizenship just like you." Finally, I explained that Puerto Ricans and other Indigenous peoples fought in every US War, starting with the American Revolution, and have continued to serve this nation with honor.[317] This history lesson created an even greater sense of urgency regarding what I needed to learn about the Indigenous people in Troop A for my professional and personal growth.

Seneca President Bowen sought an injunction from the United States District Court for Western New York. Bowen claimed Ross John's appointment to the Nation's Tribal Council was improper. I had not known the deep distrust and animosity between the Seneca and the state police. I tried to respectfully develop a relationship with my cousins, researching their history, identity, and sovereignty; what did I learn? I knew then that understanding the complex definition of sovereignty would be crucial for me as the commander of this troop. Indigenous nations vehemently disagreed that New York State and its police, which included troopers, local sheriffs, and other municipal law enforcement, had the right to enforce New York State criminal statutes on their land under US Code 232. Furthermore, they disputed New York's right to impose and collect State taxes on their land, which, based on my reading of the treaties from the 1700s, forbidding taxing Indians seemed accurate. What was also true was that New York State courts and the US Supreme affirmed that these treaties did not prohibit taxing sales to non-Indians on Indian lands.

Based on these assertions, some years later, they acted on their conviction and opened "smoke shops," selling cigarettes, other tobacco products, and gasoline on their lands. These shops and similar enterprises on their territories struck the match that lit the fires on the Thruway years later during the 1992 protest over New York State's attempts to impose excise taxes on Tobacco and gasoline. The Seneca believed this violated several treaties between their nation and the United States.[318] Those treaties, when signed, were between separate and sovereign nations. The complex and nuanced definition of Tribal sovereignty has been evolving since the eighteenth century.[319] This evolving definition and later rulings were sometimes arrived at without input from Native Americans or their representatives.

Understanding the nuanced definition of sovereignty was critical for me. As I stated, state police responded to the initially peaceful protests over taxation when they became disruptive and violent on various Indigenous territories within New York. Of course, not every American Indian in New York State lived within the designated areas. According to US Census population estimates, as of July 1, 2019, about 194,000 New Yorkers self-identify as American Indian or Alaska Native. This count is a low estimate, given undercounting issues. Over half of this State's urban Native American population lives in New York City, and it may be the most significant urban Native American population in the country.[320] Often, these First People of this land we call the United States live in urban centers where they are invisible, as have been their centuries of suffering. I understood I had to speak for those who could not speak for themselves and those affected by structural inequities. The Indigenous people were the first to suffer the injustice and brutality imposed upon them by the United States, even before it was a nation.

The nearly completed Aboriginal genocide in this hemisphere and slavery are the original sins of the United States. Native Americans did not become citizens of this country until June 2, 1924, when the US Congress granted citizenship to all Native Americans born in the US. The Indian Citizenship Act did not fully solve that inequity because some Indians were not allowed to vote as individual states governed the implementation of their right to vote. This tragedy did not end until 1957 when each state accepted and implemented, however reluctantly, the Act.[321] Sadly, although the passage of the Fifteenth Amendment (1870) granted African American males the right to vote, it did not extend that right to Black women. Nor did the passage of the Nineteenth Amendment because many states set up laws preventing African Americans from exercising their franchise.[322] Black and Brown communities had to wait decades before they would rightfully be granted their franchise in 1965, a hundred years after the passage of the Fifteenth Amendment.[323] This 1868 amendment overturned the infamous Dred Scott Supreme Court decision.[324] Women had to wait until 1920 and the passage of the Nineteenth Amendment to gain their rightful franchise. These amendments were the steps the United States needed to take to continue its journey toward a "more perfect Union." The lived experience of Native Americans, African Americans, the Latinx community, poor people, women, and other marginalized Americans was far from perfect then or now. The current attacks on voting rights prove this vulnerability of America's voting system.[325] In 2021, the US Supreme Court upheld a pair of Arizona voting restrictions that dealt a severe blow to the 1965 Voting Rights Act. In a 6-3 ruling, the justices upheld Arizona statutes prohibiting anyone other than a close family member or caregiver from collecting mail-in ballots. The court also allowed a regulation requiring officials to reject votes from people who showed up to cast a ballot in the wrong precinct, even if the person is otherwise entitled to vote in the state.[326]

As I began grappling with these complex issues and communicating with Native American leaders, I emphasized that they deserved the same level of professional and fair law enforcement services that every other community within Troop A's jurisdiction received. Once again, the issues of their sovereignty and the state's authority to enforce criminal law arose.

Chapter 17 - The Thruway Again, a Bridge to Nowhere

It was a frigid day on January 6, 1997. I had driven eighty miles from Wellsville, New York, to Troop A headquarters in Batavia, New York. Driving north during the winter months was always harrowing. I would often go through Lake-effect snow squalls. These storms come off the Great Lakes, Lake Erie on the west side, and Lake Ontario on the northern border of New York like the outstretched fingers of a frozen hand. That morning, I drove through blizzard-like conditions for several miles, in regions with clear skies with no snow falling and again through areas with blizzard conditions. While I had done this for years, I was still amazed at how much snow I could see falling in one spot and finding no snow just a short distance away.

I gave my "7:00 a.m." briefing to the Field Commander, Colonel Robert Leu, head of state police uniform and BCI operations. These calls were a required ritual done by every troop commander. After hearing from all the troop commanders, he would brief the superintendent. This morning, our talk turned to the potential tax protest that might happen if Governor Pataki forced the excise tax collection so fiercely opposed by the Seneca and the other members of the Haudenosaunee in 1992. It was yet to be determined whether the Indigenous nations' governments would even consider the proposal, let alone agree. All the information we gathered in Troop A indicated the Haudenosaunee would use the same tactics they employed in 1992, burning tires and throwing debris onto the roadway of the major state highways crossing their land.

"Are you working on a response plan?"

"Yes, Colonel. As you know, I was here when they injured Major Roloff the last time they protested," I replied.

He said, "Good because the superintendent will want a briefing from you soon."

"When does he want the briefing?" I asked.

He said, "Soon, I'll let you know."

My officer corps and I had reviewed the 1992 "After Action Report" and the associated photos and videos of the protests. We suspected the protesters were likewise analyzing our earlier response. We wanted to anticipate their tactics and counter them to prevent or at least minimize injuries that could occur to both the protesters and our troopers. We had begun a series of meetings with local Police Chiefs, Sheriffs, and Fire/EMS departments to elicit their cooperation. Several of these departments were reluctant to get involved, saying they had many Senecas in their ranks. They feared retaliations, work stoppages, and other disruptions to their operations. One of their significant concerns was that they would still respond to calls for service on Seneca territory once we left, and the state police would not be there to protect them from retribution. Some said they supported the Senecas and their fight for respect and protection of their sovereignty. While I understood, I was disappointed but kept asking them for help. We all knew how dangerous this had been during the 1992 tax protests for all involved, protesters and first responders alike. We were all trying to understand the new enforcement scheme and whether it would prevent a large-scale protest that could result in injuries and even deaths.

We did know that NYS governors, from Mario Cuomo to George Pataki, had tried various schemes to induce cooperation. The loss to New York State in tax revenue, depending on who was counting, was between $90 million and $200 million a year. This loss would grow as New York State continued to impose excise taxes on cigarette sales. These losses impacted all areas of New York State, including New York City, because of its proximity to the Unkechaug and Shinnecock territories on Long Island, New York. Whatever the collection scheme was, we had to plan a proper police action to quell new protests if the Native American nations violently resisted tax collection as they had in 1992. In 1996, Governor Pataki's office tried to collect excise and sales taxes from sales of gasoline and tobacco products to non-Native Americans on their territories. The foundation of this new approach was the years of court cases, including the

1994 U.S. Supreme Court Decision in Department of Taxation and Finance of New York versus Milhelm Attea & Bros. Inc.:

> "Enrolled tribal members purchasing cigarettes on Indian reservations are exempt from a New York cigarette tax, but non-Indians making such purchases are not. Licensed agents pre-collect the tax by purchasing stamps and affixing them to cigarette packs in advance of their first sale."[327]

The Supreme Court held: "New York's regulations do not, on their face, violate the Indian Trader Statutes [pp. 6 - 16]."[328] This U.S. Supreme Court decision gave Governor Pataki legal authority from the federal and state governments' perspectives, but setting up a reasonable plan implementation remained elusive. Nearly all the Haudenosaunee Nations' traditional governments and elected governments still vehemently refused to collect excise and sales taxes from sales made on their land to non-Native American customers or do anything they perceived impinged on their sovereignty. Everyone on both sides wanted to prevent the recurrence of the 1992 violent tax protests. The years of failed negotiations did not resolve the complexities of collecting the taxes allegedly owed to New York state. The solution proposed was a compromise between the interests of the state and the Haudenosaunee. The state wanted to ensure these taxes were levied on non-Native Americans when they bought tobacco products from stores on Indian lands. The Haudenosaunee traditional governments wanted to protect their sovereignty and economic interests.

The interim agreement had four key stipulations:

- "No state taxes would be collected on sales of cigarettes at stores on Haudenosaunee territories."
- "The state recognized the eighteenth-century treaties between the Haudenosaunee and the United States government."
- "The sovereignty of the Haudenosaunee was recognized and reaffirmed by the state."

- "The state recognized the traditional Haudenosaunee traditional governments' right to regulate trade and commerce on its territories."[329]

The agreement created a formula for counting the number of cigarette cartons sold to non-Native Americans. This formula also tried to create parity between cigarette prices on Native American land and those sold by non-Native American convenience stores near the Haudenosaunee lands. The compromise solution called for all Indian-owned gas stations and convenience stores on Indian land to acquire a license issued by the Indian government, which required business owners to pay the fee. These fees would finance the Haudenosaunee traditional governments. Nearly all the traditional governments of the Haudenosaunee considered the proposal offered by the governor. However, the Mohawk and Seneca elected governments, often controlled by Native American business owners, refused to negotiate. Some convenience store owners may have rightly believed sovereignty applied to them as individuals and not just to their nations. This belief created a problem for the Indian Nations and the state of New York. In that, these individuals obeyed the laws when it was in their self-interest and disobeyed laws when they were not.[330]

When the Haudenosaunee traditional governments tried to negotiate with their businesspeople, many of these owners fought against their governments.[331] These business owners sometimes allegedly supported the violent attack against leaders and other members of their nation who agreed with internal policies designed to create a fee structure to share some of the incredible wealth garnered by these businessmen. Some scholars and others debate whether sharing resources as part of the Native American ethos is a recent phenomenon, and others believe that it was a historical tradition within the Indigenous culture.[332] In any case, the Haudenosaunee traditional governments believe in it. In contrast, the Native American entrepreneurs focused on enriching themselves and not necessarily their Native American governments, the definition of a robber baron.[333] In the spring of 1997, the warrior faction of the Indian Businessman Association allegedly threatened that any Native American leader who negotiated with the state would be considered a traitor and face violence. The homes of two traditional chiefs considering the governor's offered solution experienced fires soon after, allegedly set ablaze by opponents of the proposed solution, making good on their threats.[334]

My officer corps and I needed to know which Haudenosaunee Nations would accept and which would reject the settlement. It was clear to us that the elected government of the Seneca Nation of Indians would not. They had protested in 1992, blocked the State highways that traversed their lands, set tires on fire, and resorted to violence.[335] The State highways that were blocked in 1992 by the demonstrators were:

- State routes 31 and 104, which cross Tuscaroran Territory;
- NYS Thruway (Interstate 90) and SR-438 on the Seneca-Cattaraugus Territory;
- SR 17 (now Interstate 86) crosses the entire Seneca-Allegany Territory's length.

The Seneca-Allegany Territory is unique because it is the only Native American land encompassing an entire US city, Salamanca

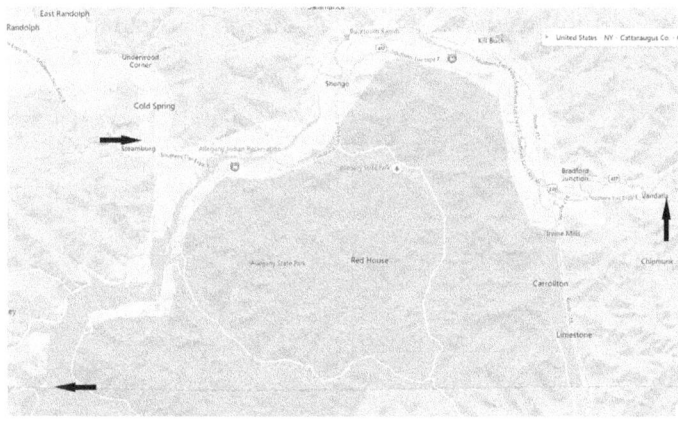

Figure 27. The Black arrows mark the eastern, western, and southern boundaries of the Seneca-Allegany Territory. The Southern Tier Expressway (ST-R-86) traverses the length of the Seneca-Allegany Territory and through the city of Salamanca, starting on the eastern

side at lower Birch Road, Vandalia, New York, and ends at the West Perimeter Road, Steamburg, New York, on the western side before turning south ending at the Pennsylvania state line.[336]

Because the local fire departments were reluctant to send their members and equipment to suppress tire fires set and used by protesters, especially on the Thruway, I had to rely on troopers to do that. Our plan included training troopers to drive payloaders, water tank trucks, and other equipment that we would use to put the tire fires out. We all inhaled the toxic and carcinogenic fumes from tire fires in 1992. We did get Troop T and the Thruway Authority permission to use their equipment and training on using this equipment. We employed our undercover investigators and their confidential informants to gather intelligence on the protesters' planned response within Troop A. We also knew they were gathering intelligence on our response. They would drive through hotel parking lots next to the state roads we needed to keep open to count the number of marked police cars. We used several hotels just east and west of the Seneca territory to house troopers from different troops across the state to support our tax protest response.

Keeping the state highways open and safe for the motoring public was critical to that response, and it was particularly true of the New York State Thruway.

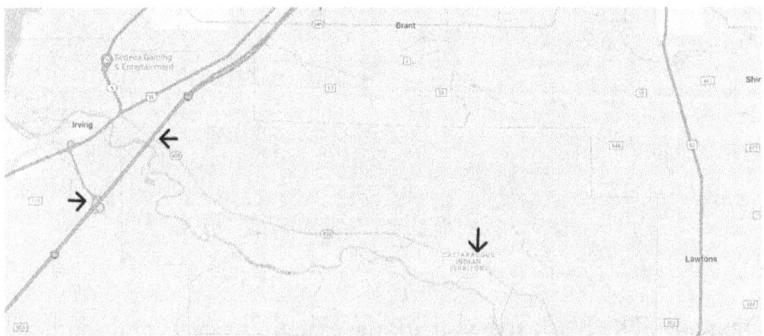

Figure 28. Moving from left to right, the lower arrow points to the temporary NYSP command post's location for the tax protest just off the Seneca territory. The top arrow shows where State Route 438

highway overpass is located and was used by tax protestors to throw debris onto the highway. It also points out the general area on the east side of the Thruway where protestors lit tire fires on a grassy knoll to roll them onto the eastbound lanes of the Thruway. The arrow above the above the "Cattaraugus Indian Territory points to Seneca Nation of Indians governmental complex for the Cattaraugus territory.[337]

The New York State Thruway is part of the Interstate and Defense Highway system. President Eisenhower appointed General Lucius D. Clay to head the committee proposing an interstate highway system plan in 1954. General Clay summarized the motivations for the construction of such a system:

> "It was evident we needed better highways. We needed them for safety, to accommodate more automobiles. We needed them for defense purposes if that should ever be necessary. And we needed them for the economy. Not just as a public works measure, but for future growth."[338]

The NYS Thruway is economically crucial and, from a national security perspective, was without question an essential transshipment route for people, goods, and, during a national emergency, the military. The last thing I wanted to do was go to the Thruway again and the ST-438 overpass, a bridge to nowhere. Yet I would have no choice if the protests began.

A month and a half had passed since my phone call to the colonel. He summoned me to Albany. I met with the superintendent and colonels at Division headquarters to brief them on my tax protester response plan. The first thing I discussed was the incident commander issue and my belief that naming me was a prudent and practical step. I explained how I had seen the failure to do so in 1992 and the resulting operational chaos and inefficiency that it caused. In 1992, the state police response and coordination was divided between two different troops, Troop A and Troop T, resulted in an unnecessary complexity as neither major supervising these troops became the incident commander (IC). In turn, this failure to appoint an IC confused not just the members of the state police responding but also the local authorities. I would ask to be the designated incident commander. Although the Thruway crossed the western edge of the Seneca's Cattaraugus Territory, the rest of the Seneca lands and Tonawanda and Tuscarora territories were wholly within Troop A's jurisdiction. As I heard myself say this, I thought, be careful what you wish for; it might come true, along with all the blame if the plan fails and little credit if it succeeded. The superintendent grinned as he and the colonels considered it; the superintendent said, "Okay, you got it. What else do you suggest we do?"

I informed the superintendent that I had troopers within my command with construction experience. I told them I had begun retraining these troopers on heavy equipment, such as payloaders, water tankers, and other equipment. We might need to use the equipment to remove barriers and extinguish tire fires used by the protesters to block the Thruway and the other state roads I needed to keep open. The superintendent nodded approvingly. But one colonel suggested using the water tankers to hose down the protesters and deploy K9 officers. I said, "No, I will not do that." The colonel sternly and disapprovingly asked why. I thought I was not employing practices that violated my values and, just as significantly, tactics stained with the legacy of racism and police abuse of their authority. I wondered whether this would resonate with these men. Looking at the superintendent, I focused on what I knew would catch their attention.

I said, "I do not want the state police or myself on the cover of major media outlets." I looked at the colonel and added, "Sir, do you remember Birmingham, Alabama, and Bull Connor during the Civil Rights movement?"[339] I reminded them that Birmingham authorities spray powerful jets of water through fire hoses and the K9s against children. I also called to their attention that in 1992, women and children protested on the Thruway.[340] The nature of our response in 1997 was even more important to me than in 1992 because I was now the major of Troop A.

The superintendent pushed back his chair and said, "He has a point." The colonel never let me forget that, in his eyes, I had embarrassed him. I knew he would look to even the score, but I would worry about that later. I went on with my briefing and suggested I needed several hundred more troopers and their supervisors to keep the two major state highways open: the Thruway and the Southern Tier Expressway. I explained that I had sought the cooperation of the Cattaraugus and Erie Counties Sheriffs to help answer calls for police service during the protests so that my troopers could staff checkpoints and other tasks needed to manage the demonstrations. I showed them the detours I planned to set up, one for passenger cars and another for commercial tractor-trailer big rigs. The detours for the big rigs had to avoid train trestles as the trestles' clearance height was too low for them. We discussed several other logistical details, and ultimately, the superintendent approved my plan. I returned to Troop A and told my team, "Okay, we own this monster."

We spent the next several months preparing, training, and watching the negotiations. By March 1997, there was no compromise between the Governor's office and the Seneca Nation's elected government. It was also clear that while the Tuscarora and Tonawanda Seneca's traditional governments negotiated with the state, many of their members supported the Seneca and would likely hold sympathetic protests as they had done in 1992. The state's "Interim Trade and Commerce Agreement," scheduled to take effect on April 1, 1997, would set another series of protests across New York in motion.[341]

Some business owners had struck self-enriching arrangements with New York State in direct opposition to their nation's government. The internal political dilemma for the Tuscarora traditional Indian government was the relationship, or rather the lack of it, between themselves and Joseph Anderson, a Tuscaroran entrepreneur. He owned cigarette stores and gas stations within Tuscarora Nation's territory.[342] Rather than bow to the terms of the negotiated compromise, he accepted New York state's jurisdiction about selling gas and tobacco products to non-Native Americans. He paid the state excise tax to receive gasoline and cigarettes at his enterprises. I met with Joe Anderson during this period. He gave me a tour of his cigarette manufacturing operation. He bought cigarette rollers, "the same kind used to make Marlboro cigarettes," he bragged. During our conversation, he hoped to continue to run his business without the state's interference. He had paid the excise tax on the oil he was importing from the Middle East and tobacco leaves from some southern states for his gasohol blending facility and cigarette manufacturing plant, respectively. His acceptance of the state's jurisdiction and payment of taxes did not spare him from the first efforts to stop what the state considered illegal distribution of untaxed gasoline and cigarettes to Native American lands.

The agreement between the state and the Haudenosaunee traditional governments obliged Joe Anderson and other members of the various Indian nations to register. They also had to pay the traditional Indian governments' fees or else have their supplies of gas and cigarettes seized by the New York State Department of Taxation; this did happen to Anderson and the other Indian businesspeople because they had not followed their governments' regulations. Only those Indian Nations that signed the thirty-day interim agreement and the businesses running within the territories that followed the rules of the Indian nation could receive these products. All signatories of this agreement tried to work out a long-term deal. Those Indigenous nations opposing the solution would confront this issue in two venues: the courts and the streets. The latter efforts were more concerning to me because of the possibility of violence. The former had already taken years and would take many more years without solving the street-level problem. Anderson's position was that New York State had received all the taxes it was due and should not intervene on behalf of Haudenosaunee traditional governments to enforce their tax collection. Anderson's shipments were ultimately allowed by the courts.

The relationship between New York State, the imposition of the excise tax on gasoline and cigarettes, and the traditional governments' authority to levy fees on the Indigenous business owners remained unsettled.[343] New York state's enforcement of the interim agreement began on April 1, 1997; within a week or two, most of the cigarette shops and gas stations within the Seneca Nation's territory closed, and many of the workers, both Native American and non-Native American, were furloughed because they ran out of gasoline. Three weeks before the enforcement began. The demonstrations and tire fires started. Protest signs and flags hung from the Thruway over-passes. I deployed troopers to check traffic and the protests at each demonstration location to ensure the safety of the motorists, protest-ers, and first responders.

During the first few days of April 1997, to "put teeth" in the interim agreement's enforcement provisions, New York State's Department of Tax and Finance (NYSDTFD) seized several ship-ments of gasoline. Peace officers of the NYSDTFD impounded a tractor and tanker trailer leased to respondent Queensway Tank Lines Inc., driven by William A. Bramhall. Bramhall did not pro-duce the documentation required by tax law. His documents showed that 8,506 gallons of unleaded motor fuel were going to Mohawk Petroleum Wholesale of St. Regis Mohawk Nation for Triple J's, a gasoline retailer. NYSDTFD took possession of another tractor and tanker trailer, then leased to Queensway driven by Bruce Kenneth Faddies, and Faddies also failed to produce the required documents. The NYSDTFD agents determined he was transporting about 8,538 gallons of unleaded motor fuel to Seneca Hawk, another gasoline retailer located in the Cattaraugus Territory of the Seneca Nation.[344] These actions poured gasoline, pun intended, on an already volatile situation. Simultaneously, this instance and the more outstanding issues would take months and sometimes years before the courts' lit-igations occurred. Their judicial resolution would do little to quell the unrest at protest locations. The demonstrators increased in num-bers, tire fires grew hotter, and the potential for violence at the pro-test sites intensified.

April 8, 1997, was a calm, clear, dry spring morning in western New York. I was at the temporary NYSP command post at SP Dunkirk when a report came in that a fatal car crash occurred on the Southern Tier Expressway at that protest site. At times, dozens of protesters tended many large tire fires along that stretch of highway. As the demonstrators had done at the Thruway location, these protesters lit these fires and threw debris onto the main traveled part of the roadway. Sometimes, the fire smoke would significantly reduce visibility, particularly at night. I drove to the location and called Captain Kevin G. Molinari, the commander of this zone, to get some details about the incident. He said he had deployed troopers to this area over several days because of the ongoing protests and fires. He had traveled from SP Olean and met with Lieutenant Christopher Cummings and the squads of troopers to plan for that day's response. These experienced officers and competent professionals carefully and skillfully supervised our response to the intense protests within Seneca's Allegany Territory. Captain Molinari devised the plan, left Lieutenant Cummings in charge, and returned to SP Olean. As I continued driving to the scene, I called Colonel Leu and briefed him on what I knew then, saying I would supply more details once I had them. I arrived and walked to the site of the fatal crash and saw the burning wreckage of a Dodge pickup truck just slightly in front of a loaded dump truck along with a trailer at the rear of the dump truck. I did not see skid marks, which indicated the pickup truck driver may not have applied the brakes, or if he did, they failed. I did see skid marks revealing sideways movement after the crash. When I arrived, the driver's body had been removed and taken to the local hospital. Lieutenant Cummings reported on circumstances leading up to the crash.

Lieutenant Cummings said protesters had once again lit tire fires and that he and Captain Molinari arrived with a squad of troopers at the scene. The captain spoke with the small gathering of protesters and figured out they had not intended to engage in physical confrontations. He said he and Captain Molinari remained concerned that the lanes of traffic would become impassable because of smoke or fire endangering motorists. Based on these concerns, they decided to suppress the fires and remove the debris from the road's edge. He said the captain placed him in charge of debris removal and left the protest site. Lieutenant Cummings employed the plan we had devised to use payloaders on loan from the Department of Transportation during the protests to remove the burning materials from the edge of the road. A trooper drove the payloader rather than a DOT employee for safety reasons. The debris was then pushed down the adjacent embankment toward the south edge of the expressway property to make it more difficult for the protesters to build their fire on the road again. The use of that equipment required the eastbound lanes of traffic to stop. Two troopers drove their marked police vehicle up the eastbound entrance ramp at Exit 17 and positioned the car sideways with emergency lights activated. Lieutenant Cummings said this was to block the two eastbound lanes of traffic and any vehicle entering the expressway from Route 394.

At 8:31 a.m., the troopers blocked eastbound traffic. Most expressway motorists slowed, stopped, and waited for debris clearing, save one. At that juncture, the accident's cause was undetermined. Was it human error, mechanical malfunction, or the roadblock itself? Since all the other motorists who arrived at the roadblock location slowed and stopped successfully, I leaned strongly toward human or equipment failure.

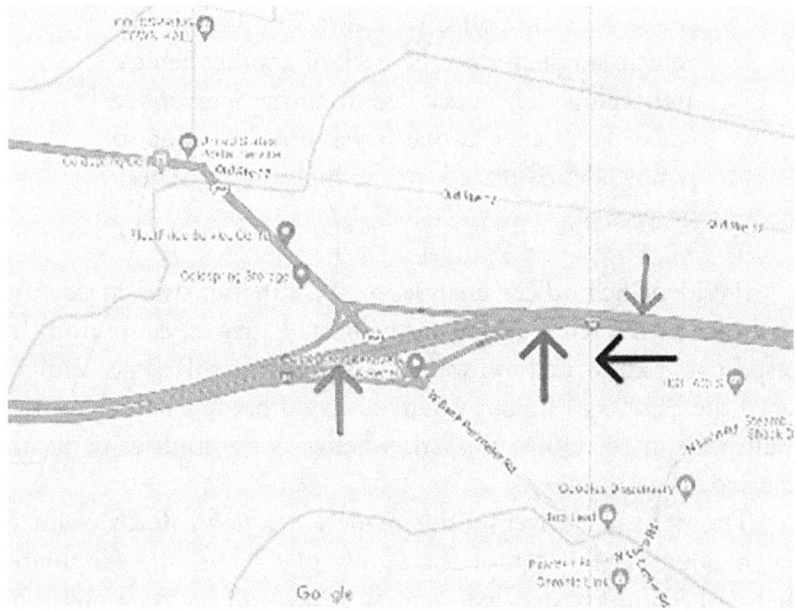

Figure 29. A map of the fatal crash at the Seneca Allegany
Territory tax protests. From left to right, the first arrow points to
the approximate location of the crash; the second arrow shows
where the police vehicle blocked the Eastbound on-ramp; the
third arrow points to the western border of the Seneca Nation of
Indians—Allegany Territory; the last arrow points tire fires.[345]

On April 27, 1997, the president of the Seneca Nation of Indians, Michael W. Schindler, wrote a letter to President Bill Clinton asking for federal intervention in the excise tax dispute.[346] In President Schindler's summary, he mentions the accident without having been at the scene and before the completion of the investigation:

> "April 1997: New York State Police stated they were 'attempting' to regulate traffic on Route 17 in Steamburg, New York. [Allegany Reservation] while amateur video shown on all local news stations show that Officers had their backs to traffic and were observing a tire fire. Meanwhile, a non-native gentleman from Forestville, New York, came around a corner at the speed limit where no state police were directing traffic. His vehicle smashed into the back of another vehicle and exploded; he was killed instantly. State police Major Perez alleged that it was due to having to remove debris placed on the highway by Seneca protesters."[347]

President Schindler's analysis of the situation was inaccurate. Nevertheless, the letter asking for help made perfect sense from his perspective. I know we both want this situation resolved peacefully. I hoped the Bureau of Indian Affairs or any other federal department would step in to resolve this crisis before more injuries or deaths occurred.

The deceased driver's sister made a wrongful death claim in March 2004. The Judge of the Court of Claims, the Honorable Michael E. Hudson, decided the case in favor of the state police on January 10, 2005, in Buffalo, New York. In his decision, he settled the question, was it human error, mechanical failure, or the roadblock that caused the fatal crash?[348]

> "On the proof presented I find that the sole legal cause of the accident was Mr. Spoon's failure to

respond to the readily apparent conditions he faced, and that the traffic stoppage simply provided the condition or occasion, rather than a cause, for that tragic incident. Highway traffic can be expected to slow or stop at times for any number of reasons. Drivers are expected to "maintain safe distances between their cars and cars in front of them (Vehicle and Traffic Law §1129 [a...])."

President Schindler's statements trying to assert that protesters' tactics of setting tire fires and resulting debris were not the primary factors in this fatal crash; Judge Hudson's conclusion refuted that assertion:

"Further, I conclude that in responding to the protest, and in blocking traffic while they removed burning debris from the edge of the expressway, the state police were performing a function that must be characterized as governmental rather than proprietary. The activities clearly involved traffic regulation along Route 17. Moreover, the size and organization involved in the police response, as well as the use of riot gear and investigation of the potential for an altercation with the protesters at the site, also evidence their performance of a crime prevention function."[349]

We had responded to these protests, tire fires, and other tactics on this highway and the other roadways mentioned earlier for several weeks. The judge allowed videotaped evidence of the protests and the tire fires from a witness who had seen these fires and recorded the demonstrations. From a videotape (Exhibit 9) filmed by witness Melody L. Peterson, who resided to the immediate north of the expressway, it is clear that, at times, those fires were rather large.[350]

While the fires on April 8 had not gotten large, Lieutenant Cummings ensured that they would not. Lieutenant Cummings confirmed that the fires and protests had been significant for several days before the accident. Nevertheless, the plan we had forged had proven effective, and he felt it would continue to be so long as we had the support of the added troopers and supervisors for the other troops. I agreed. He and his troopers finished clearing the roadway of debris after the "Accident Reconstructionist" gathered the evidence and data they needed to draft a report. I returned to the temporary command post at the Thruway near Seneca Cattaraugus territory and called the Field commander. I briefed him and said the report would take time to complete. Based on witness interviews and skid patterns on the roadway, I told the colonel it appeared that the deceased driver did not see the roadblock in time to stop. I asked if he had heard any new information on the governor's negotiations with the Seneca. He said nothing had changed, and I was to keep the roads open.

I grimly said, "Sir, I will do my best, but the situation is getting more dangerous."

He replied, "Indeed," and ended the call.

We had managed to keep the roads open for several weeks. The troopers kept putting out tire fires every night, removing the burning tires and other debris when the protesters threw them onto the highway. I had not had a day off since mid-March and would brief the colonels daily. I felt I had no choice because of the nature of these protests and what occurred in 1992. During the week of April 7, 1997, after informing the Field commander of our response status, the colonel in charge of Division administration called and thanked me for successfully executing my mission but said that he had unpleasant news.

"Your operation costs us a million dollars a day in overtime and other expenses. Do you need all those troopers from the other troops?"

Shocked, I replied, "What? I cannot guarantee we can keep the Thruway and the Southern Tier Expressway open and safe for travel."

"Well, figure it out because we are pulling them," he said sternly.

"Colonel, I am calling Colonel Leu." "Go ahead, these orders are from the superintendent, and the Governor's office instructed him," I said. "Yes, sir," I added and hung up.

I called the Field commander, who listened to my concerns and warnings. I said, "We cannot keep all the highways open without the additional troopers. Once the protesters see fewer troop cars." And the hotels' staff tell the families and friends the out-of-town troopers have left. The Seneca and their allies will intensify their unlawful and dangerous tactics. More people are going to get hurt and possibly killed." He had heard enough and ordered me to take the weekend off.

"Pedro, I am sending the Uniform Lieutenant Colonel to relieve you. He will arrive first thing Friday morning."

I ended the call and briefed my command staff; they all said this was ridiculous but agreed I needed time off. I told the lieutenant colonel about the status of our operation on April 11. Colonel, we have three major state highways. We have been keeping open State Route 31, which crosses the Tuscarora nation's land; Interstate Route 90 (NYS Thruway), which crosses the SNI's Cattaraugus' land; and the Southern Tier Expressway (St-17) that crosses the length of the SNI's Allegany land. Colonel, you should also be aware that Salamanca is inside their territory. I also told him it is the only US city inside Indian land. I told him which captains were in command of our response in each location and how many troopers were needed to staff the operation 24-7.

"Colonel, I know the orders are to reduce staffing levels, but I hope once you see what we are up against, you will go back to Albany to tell the boss not to reduce our numbers." He listened distractedly, clearly having decided that the superintendent was right. He thanked me and said, "Go home." During that weekend, the protesters changed their tactics, having seen how we had successfully kept the Thruway open by quickly removing the burning tires and other debris.

On Sunday, April 13, 1997, hundreds of protesters marched down the Thruway's embankment at the State Route 438 overpass and then onto the highway. They used their bodies to block traffic.

213

We already had a process to detour motorists by rerouting them several exits west and east of the Seneca territory. At the same time, we cleared the road of hazards. The command staff used the detour process, but moving people off the roadway took much longer. I learned this from the lieutenant colonel when I returned on Monday, April 14. He also said he had detained one of the march's leaders but ultimately let him go. The lieutenant colonel left and returned to Albany after briefing me. My command staff said it was lucky we still had troopers from the other troops present when that happened. They wondered whether we could keep the road open if the protesters tried marching onto the Thruway again now that the added troopers were returning to their home troops. I asked BCI Captain Brown to gather intelligence from our confidential informants and other sources to determine when the protesters would block the Thruway again. That Monday afternoon, several news reporters asked me about the previous Sunday's mass gathering of approximately two hundred protesters and their blockage of the Thruway. The media had been tracking this story during gubernatorial election season, and the reporters generally took a balanced approach. In a New York Times article by Raymond Hernandez titled "Pataki to Seek Some Taxes on Cigarettes Indians Sell," Mr. Hernandez's prescient opening paragraph lays out the core issue:

> "Setting the stage for a potentially bitter showdown, the Pataki administration announced today that it planned to start collecting taxes on some gasoline and cigarettes sales on Indian reservations despite persistent opposition from Indians who consider it an infringement of their sovereignty."[351]

The anti-excise tax protestors, the pro-excise tax convenience store owners, innocent motorists, the troopers, command staff, and I were all in that bitter showdown those past few weeks. I had to contain my frustration and anger about the situation because a resolution should have occurred decades ago and the system I was trying to change. At the time, I had to focus on keeping a lid on this boiling kettle. I provided the reporters with the facts as I knew them. I avoided rendering an opinion on the excise tax issue. I said, "We are just trying to keep the roads open and everyone as safe as possible." To their question about the previous Sunday, I told them the Thruway was now open; one protest leader was temporarily detained and then released, and there were no arrests.[352] That is all I knew concerning that incident. Finally, the most complicated question came. Did I think the protesters would try shutting down the Thruway? "We have been preventing that for weeks. We will continue trying to prevent it and respond appropriately should it happen." At least, I wished I had said that instead of my terse but honest reply, "I don't know," as I walked away from the interview.

The rest of that week, the protesters continued lighting tire fires and other tactics, trying to close the roadways on the Allegany and Cattaraugus territories. We kept all the routes open at each of the four protest sites, particularly and most importantly, the Thruway, by continuing to use the debris-clearing process and detouring traffic as needed. We avoided making arrests unless necessary because of the reduced number of troopers assigned to respond to the protests. The intelligence we gathered on the possibility of another mass gathering of protesters intent on closing the Thruway suggested they would try it again. We needed to find out when it would happen but could not.

On April 20, hundreds of protesters gathered on the State Route 438 overpass, walked down the embankment, and marched onto the Thruway. What I had feared and warned the colonels about happened. It appeared we were vastly outnumbered. I knew I could not force the protesters off the Thruway without using physical force.[353] The intelligence gathered suggested there might have been protesters armed with rifles hidden on the overpass. The intelligence also suggested protesters had homemade pepper spray and other toxic chemical sprays and also armed with bats, two-by-fours, and other bludgeons. These hundreds of protesters included women, children, and elderly war veterans. Also embedded among the protesters were news media reporters. Seneca President Schindler claimed in his letter to President Clinton that two thousand Seneca and non-Seneca had gathered to hold a peaceful rally. That is not what happened.[354] The reports we received revealed they would engage in a violent clash with us if we tried to remove them. I decided the best action was to talk to some protest leaders, hoping to negotiate a peaceful resolution and open the roadway. Three of my captains and I walked down to them and tried to talk with the protest leaders. I left instructions with the rest of my command staff and the thirty or so troopers clad in riot gear to remain behind unless they saw us getting attacked by the mob. Then, they were to drive down to help extricate us from the protests. This part of the highway was hilly and dipped below the State Route 438 overpass. We walked down the hill toward the protesters to identify a leader with whom I could negotiate. The captains and I were wearing our regular uniforms, not riot gear. The protesters could not seek the troopers gathered just over the knoll from where we met. Standing in front of the protesters, I approached and began speaking to one of the leaders.

Figure 30. Major Perez speaking with Seneca
Nation of Indians tax protests leaders.[355]

Suddenly, other protesters grabbed Captain Brown and began punching him. Someone sprayed Captain McManus directly in the face with homemade bear spray. He grabbed his face in pain. Captain O'Connor and I went to Captain Brown and McManus's aid. Captain O'Connor was knocked to the ground, injuring his knee. He courageously managed to help me get Captain Brown back to safety. The squad of troopers and their supervisors hurried to our location as the protest turned into a riotous mob. Protesters used homemade sprays, bludgeons, and their fists to attack us. An unknown protester punched my head; I ducked, only having my Stetson knocked off my head. I immediately grabbed off the pavement and held in my fist as I defended myself against the punches raining down. I ordered two troopers to take Captain McManus back to the command post for medical attention, and I quickly gave my hat for safekeeping. Because amid the cacophony of screams, I heard someone shouting, "Get the major's hat, get the fucking major's hat!" I did not want them to have a souvenir. It was unbelievable. I fought off protesters while trying to get the protest leaders to calm the situation.

Figure 31. Major Perez, after defending himself during the protest, attempting to get Seneca protest leaders to calm their followers.[356]

In all my years of policing, including my SWAT team experiences and during my time as an undercover narc, I had never been more frightened. The shotgun pointed at my head in the "crack" house, the AK-47s and young Seneca pointed at Captain Haag and me, nor the knife-wielding drunk I had to subdue during a bar fight when I was a brand-new trooper, none of these were as frightening as this situation. The intensity of their anger and hatred toward us was something I had never experienced. I also feared a trooper or protester would be gravely injured or killed. I was afraid one of my troopers might draw his firearm and shoot a protester out of fear for their lives. I was also genuinely concerned about the unconfirmed intelligence gathered from allies and confidential informants that some protesters on the overpass also had rifles and might shoot at us. The use of which could cause my troopers to return fire.

Figure 32. On April 20, 1997, New York State Police and Seneca Nation Indians and their non-Indian supporters clashed on the New York State Thruway on the Cattaraugus Indian Reservation. The Senecas protested New York state's attempt to collect taxes.[357]

The photo showed the moments after I had pulled a trooper back to his feet and when a protester had jumped on my back, dislocating my right shoulder. A second protester, seen on the top of the state police car, also jumped and tried to knock me to the ground but failed. I put my right hand in my pocket to protect my shoulder from further injury. After what felt like an eternity, I found the leader

I had spoken to earlier during a moment of calm as I summoned the troopers to regroup. I told him I would pull my troopers back if they stopped attacking us. He agreed. He turned and walked toward several other men, and together, they began telling the people in the front to fall back toward the State Route 438 overpass. I ordered a tactical retreat, withdrawing all the troopers and our vehicles back to the Thruway exit. Once I saw all the troopers and our cars gone, I walked over to the man I had spoken with and said I was leaving. Finally I said, "You know I will be back to talk soon." I limped back to my vehicle and drove to the command post. It was the longest walk I had ever taken. News reporters interviewed Seneca President Schindler the next day, and he acknowledged we had tried to negotiate peacefully. "They tried to come over to talk to us, but we're just way past that now," Art Schindler said. "I can't control anybody's reactions. Nobody wanted to hear them."[358] While I understood their frustration and anger toward the state's attempts to tax them and their belief their sovereignty was in jeopardy. I could not condone the violence and criminality. Yet, I was deeply saddened because now I was the trooper who was part of the system oppressing my Indigenous cousins. I felt I had betrayed my promise to be a "peace officer" as I drove to the command post.

The communication officer at the command post had called the Field commander to report what had happened. When he saw me, he told me Colonel Leu "wants you to call him ASAP." I called the Field commander and told him what had happened. I told him I would need the troopers from the other Troops to return to help open both the Thruway and Southern Tier Expressway. I did not have to say it, but his tone acknowledged I had been right. He said hundreds of troopers would be there by nightfall. I thanked him and did not mention that we both knew reducing the number of troopers was a costly mistake.

He then asked, "Were you injured?"

I told him I was okay, not wanting to be relieved.

"Pedro, go to the hospital and get checked out."

"No. I am okay," I muttered.

"Major, this is not a request."

I hung up and drove to the local hospital. They x-rayed my shoulder and knee injuries to determine the extent of the damage I sustained during the hand-to-hand combat with the protesters. I was relieved and ordered by the superintendent to go home. He said he would get the state police surgeon to arrange an examination and ensuing surgery at the New York Hospital of Special Surgery to repair my shoulder. The muscles and other connective tendons holding my shoulder joint got torn off the bone, and I could not raise my right arm. I also had a torn medial meniscus and sprained anterior cruciate ligament. The pain in my shoulder was excruciating, and the knee pain was tolerable. I would eventually need to have my knee repaired, but repairing the shoulder was critical if I wanted to keep working. Fixing my shoulder was crucial because if I could not draw my assigned weapon, I would have to resign for medical reasons. I could have a limp and still do my job.

That afternoon, as I drove home, I received a phone call from Arthur O. Eve, the deputy speaker of the New York State Assembly.[359] He asked me if I was all right.

"Yes," I answered.

He said, "Major Perez, I am so glad you were in charge of the state police response; otherwise, we may have had another Attica."[360]

Arthur O. Eve was the longest-serving assemblyman of the New York State Assembly, serving from 1967 until his retirement in 2002. He was the first Dominican American elected to public office in the United States. His father was born in the Dominican Republic and moved to Harlem, marrying a Black woman. Arthur Eve was born and raised in Harlem, NY. As deputy speaker of the Assembly from 1979 to 2002, Eve was the highest-ranking Black man the New York state legislature. He was the second most powerful person in the Assembly and the fourth in the line of succession for the governor's post. During the 1980s, Deputy Speaker Eve helped pass legislation to require affirmative action on state-funded projects, approved funding for the African American Institute of the State University of New York (SUNY), and helped get New York state to accept the Martin Luther King, Jr. Holiday Bill. Many historians believed Deputy Speaker Eve did more to initiate access to educational opportunities for minorities and economically disadvantaged people, undergraduate and graduate education, medical degrees, pre-natal, daycare, and infant care than any other state legislator.[361] I understood what he meant when he referenced Attica. He had been one of the negotiators trying to bring an end to this deadly prison riot. Auburn and Clinton prison protests of the 1920s and the Attica protest in 1971 were uprisings that turned into violent riots sparked by years of intolerable prison conditions. Tragically, Attica was the worst example of excessive use of deadly physical force by the state police. I was concerned that things could spiral out of control, so I tactically withdrew. I knew that to reduce the risk of excessive force, I would need more troopers to deal with the immediate situation, but a lasting peace had to come from the politicians on all sides of the excise tax issue.

The Thruway remained closed as the protesters set more tire fires and set fire to a vehicle they had driven onto the highway. Additionally, troopers came from across the state and arrived on April 21, 1997, and reopened the Thruway. All the other roads blocked by protesters reopened the following day. It was clear to my command staff and the colonels in Albany that my position was correct. To manage this situation, the sustaining staffing level of troopers across New York State was paramount. However, the protests did not end; they spread. The protesters continued to set tire fires and display banners and other protest signs. I feared for the safety of the troopers, the motorists using these highways, and the protesters. The possibility of either side overreacting and causing more injuries and deaths was increasing. Reaching a negotiated settlement to end these protests was paramount.

Figure 33. More tires being stack atop of the fire on the NYS Thruway.[362]

On April 22, 1997, while waiting at home for a call from the state police surgeon, Lieutenant Cummings called and told me, "Major, looks like there may be an agreement to end the protests. However, some kids from the Salamanca school were at the protest site and started tire fires. We did not respond, and luckily, their parents came to the site and stopped them." Lieutenant Cummings and I were relieved that the parents responded and stopped their children from getting in trouble with the police or, worse, being injured. That same day, the Seneca and Governor Pataki's delegation reached an agreement. The troopers brought in from the other troops returned to their original assignments. The Seneca Nation used its marshals alongside the state police to keep the peace. The demonstrations, tire fires, and road blockages ended. The Seneca Nation of Indians' leadership fulfilled their part of the agreement on their territory. They understood that the violence of the protests was not seen as reasonable by many in the surrounding communities. So, being seen as maintaining the peace alongside troopers gave them better press coverage.

The Haudenosaunee tax protests moved to the Onondaga Indian Territory. Initially, the protests had not been on State Route 81, in Onondaga County, where State Route 81 crosses the Onondaga Indian Territory in the center of New York. Now they were, and the outcome was different from what happened in Troop A.[363] As I sat home during those ensuing weeks recuperating from the shoulder surgery, I often received calls from my colleagues briefing me on the ongoing protests in Troop D. Two seemingly contradictory matters still troubled me. One, I was proud of how Troop A, its command staff, and troopers managed the protests for the weeks before April 22. We managed to keep all the demonstrations under control regarding their intended goal of shutting down the highways, particularly the two interstate highways. While there had been some injuries and one fatal car accident, while tragic, it could have been much worse, especially on April 20. My decision to withdraw that fateful day, I believed, saved lives. The second, and personally very troubling, was that for all my intentions to be a "peace" officer, serving all the people of Troop A with equitable and just policing. I felt I had not lived up to that ideal. We did not act as tax collectors and only enforced observed criminal violations that endangered lives. I was working for the system that was once again seemingly impinging on Indigenous sovereignty. I did not reach a balance between those two thoughts and wondered whether that was possible.

On May 18, 1997, I watched the news coverage of the tax protests in the Onondaga Territory and the state police response. I was horrified by what I saw. The scene appeared to be out of the control of the state police supervisors. The newscast showed videos of troopers charging into a line of protesters who were not blocking State Route 81. I saw several troopers using their riot batons to subdue a protester who, because of the police action, was actively resisting. While it is illegal to resist or try to resist an arrest.[364] The state police response was, in my opinion, an abuse of their authority. The Kerner Commission report's conclusions about police performance was what I feared was happening in Troop D:

> "The police are not merely a "spark" factor. To some Negroes police have come to symbolize white power, white racism and white repression. And the fact is that many police do reflect and express these white attitudes. The atmosphere of hostility and cynicism is reinforced by a widespread belief among Negroes in the existence of

police brutality and in a "double standard" of
justice and protection—one for Negroes and one
for whites."[365]

I cannot imagine the Indigenous protesters occupying the
shoulder embankment of State Route 81 not seeing the troopers
responding to their initially peaceful protest in any other way than
described above. During this engagement, the Troop D major was
dressed in civilian clothes, approached a news cinematographer, and
ripped the video camera out of the reporter's hands, breaking it. He
faced a lawsuit for this and the response to the protest; he and NYS
lost.[366] Reportedly, the major returned to Troop D's temporary command post and left his captain responsible for the response. On one
level, I understand why this major decided to lead from the command post instead of at the protest site. He knew what had happened
to Troop A majors, who led the response. Both Major Roloff and I
were severely injured. I suspect he did not want to be the third Troop
Commander hurt during the state police response to a tax protest.

Moreover, having broken a camera earlier, it was prudent not
to answer the media's inquiry about that reaction while leading the
response. While I can understand his motives, a major's job in those
kinds of incidents is to be at the scene to ensure his officers' proper
performance. Thus, I would not have given the order to arrest over
the radio, and I would have given the command in person. His
behavior was not in keeping with the highest traditions of the state
police; it was a failure to lead from the front. The major instructed
the captain not to negotiate but to disperse the protesters and arrest
whomever they believed had trespassed on the State Route 81 roadway.[367] The troopers crossed onto the private land to execute arrests.
However, they could not pick out which protesters had trespassed.
One trooper was ineffectively flailing her baton while holding her riot
helmet, which she had not appropriately secured on her head.[368] The
news video shows this trooper walking away, holding her baton and
helmet. It was not clear why or where she was going. The assigned

internal affairs officer, Inspector Valvo, was stopped from completing his internal investigation, and questions were left unanswered:

> "Why did the troopers remove their name tags from their uniforms, in violation of state police policy, before marching into the protesters? Did the troopers use excessive force on protesters who weren't fighting them? Why weren't the protesters given an order to disperse before troopers moved in? The officers in charge of the operation had seen firsthand how violent the Indian protests could become, because they'd witnessed a dozen troopers being assaulted in protests in Western New York a few weeks earlier. Retaliation seems to be the only explanation for why the officers would violate state police policy, make illegal arrests, use excessive force and "endanger the lives of the protesters and the troopers," Valvo said.[369]

As I watched, I could not help but remember what I told the superintendent when I briefed him on Troop A's response plan and admonition that how we responded was as crucial as the need to keep the highways open and safe for motorists, the protesters, and our troopers. It was apparent that the command staff of Troop D had not considered the manner of the response as crucial as the why, and they had not thought about the protesters' civil rights.

I agreed with New York State Police Internal Affairs Bureau's (IAB) Inspector Salvatore Valvo's opinion. I had worked for Inspector Valvo when he was the Major of Troop A, and his questioning during investigations was sometimes abrasive and difficult to accept. I also concurred with the NYSP's first deputy superintendent and the other IAB inspector. Not allowing the IAB investigation to proceed was another missed opportunity to make the state police a better, more equitable, and effective agency. The public saw this response as another incident where the public believed there were two tiers of justice, one for police and another for civilians, in this case, Native

Americans.[370] In this instance, although I had and would disagree with both these leaders in other matters during my career, I did not because given the gravity of the allegations of police abuse. It was unusual for an IAB Inspector to be summarily removed from concluding the investigation merely because the target of the investigation was offended by what Valvo said.

> "They were brutalized,"
> "Their rights were violated. Falsely arrested. What were these guys thinking?"[371]

I remembered what the deputy speaker of the New York State Assembly, Arthur O. Eve, was concerned about when he praised my discretion during my response to the tax protests. Deputy Speaker Eve worried about police abusing their power as they had done during the state police response to the Attica Uprising. The state police lost the lawsuit filed by ninety-eight people who claimed the Division violated their civil rights. Valvo's comments about the lawsuit were interesting.

> "If these guys did nothing wrong, why do we, the taxpayers, have to give the Indians $3 million?" he asked.[372]

Notwithstanding Valvo's comments concerning settling this lawsuit, governments and corporations often satisfy lawsuits because it is less costly on many levels than trying to litigate the case in the courts. In this instance, the video evidence and the disruption of the internal affairs inquiry might have ended in a decision unfavorable to New York State or the state police, costing the taxpayers even more money.[373] While listening to the news accounts of the situation while I recuperated, I was angered and frustrated by Governor Pataki's decision then and not before the protests in Troop A. Had he done so in March 1997, the motorist's death on the Southern Tier Expressway and the injuries we sustained during Troop A's response might not have happened.

I healed from my shoulder surgery and returned to duty. I was summoned to state police headquarters to participate in an after-action debriefing. During that session, the same colonel who suggested I use the water tankers or K9 unit in my response plan made a snide remark. "We cleaned up your mess." Some attendees laughed, and I replied, "You mean the government's mess." No one laughed. This situation was a centuries-old debacle, a failure to live up to treaties, a continuing violation of Indigenous civil rights, and the ongoing dispute over the interpretation of sovereignty, "divided sovereignty," and criminal jurisdiction on Indian lands. It was the inability to find common ground by the governors and some Haudenosaunee leaders, primarily the Seneca government. Soon after that, the superintendent made the call to me that no troop commander wanted. Superintendent McMahon called me and asked, "Pedro, are you ready to come in?" Was I ready to be promoted to Inspector and assigned to IAB? I said, "No!"

He replied that it was a rhetorical question and that October 1997 was likely the effective promotion date. For several reasons, most majors serving as troop commanders wanted to avoid getting promoted to inspector assigned to the Internal Affairs Bureau. First, as the troop commander, you are the head of the regional state police operations. With that came tremendous prestige; the second was that service as an inspector in the IAB felt like a demotion, not a promotion because you were no longer in command. Finally, while internal affairs is critical to ensuring the police are policed, serving in IAB brought much scorn from the rank and file. The nickname for IAB among the troopers was "Rat Squad," as a member, you were called a "Cheese Eater."

When these calls came from the superintendents, Majors had two choices: accept the position or retire. I was still too far from retirement and needed to complete my family's journey out of poverty. My children would soon graduate from high school and go to college, and I needed every nickel I could earn to pay for their continuing education. Did pure ambition blind me? I told myself it was for the family. Was it a heartfelt desire to change the troopers from within, or was it now mostly ego? It was all that and a bag of chips. All these questions echoed louder in my head and heart, particularly the sacrifices Pamela and the children made as I pursued this career. I always made these decisions with my family. I sat with Pamela, Yasmine, and Aramis and asked them what they thought about accepting another promotion that would force me to live in Albany during the weekdays. I told them we would continue to live in Wellsville until Aramis graduated from high school. Aramis was relieved, as was Yasmine. Pamela's chronic illness stabilized, although we both knew it would become more challenging to manage in the years ahead. We stayed up late for several nights, discussing our options. She knew this would move further away from the difficulties and worries of being poor. She also enjoyed how people treated her and the children because I had been the major of Troop A. She said, "We are at a place I never imagined we would reach. Together, we have accomplished a lot." She mentioned that we had a house, health insurance, good food, two cars, and, most importantly, we still had each other. We hugged, cried, and finally decided. She said you have more work to do if you want to have a bigger impact on policing. "Go for it!" she shouted as we drank coffee. I accepted the promotion, and this leg of my journey ended. A new path lay before me. For the next decade, I navigated the complex politics of the Division headquarters and then, as I rose in ranks, the internal and external politics of the state police.

Chapter 18 - The Puzzle Palace

Troopers, regional commanders, and I used various names to describe state police headquarters, like "the Ivory Tower" or "the Puzzle Palace." I often heard the officers assigned to the Division headquarters called "Perfumed Princes," regardless of gender. Because those of us in the "Field" felt they had forgotten the challenges and demands placed on troopers who now patrol the communities where they used to work. Now, I would be considered a "perfumed prince" by my colleagues in the "Field." Many saw these officers needing to be more in touch with the changes and complexities of frontline policing. I swore I would not become a "perfumed prince" by staying connected to troopers and supervisors still working in the "Field."

Nearly every major I knew wanted to avoid a promotion to internal affairs. Nevertheless, it is one of the most critical jobs in any police agency. I understood that, yet I also rue the day I received a phone call. I wondered whether this was a reward or political expediency because of how I handled the tax protests earlier that year. You go from having one of the most coveted jobs in the New York State Police to a job troopers begrudgingly respected, but they treated you differently. For instance, when I was a major, I traveled across the state and stopped at regional state police barracks to refuel, and some troopers would offer to gas my car up and do what they could to assist me. Then I became an Inspector, and when I arrived at those stations, some of the same troopers would not offer to help.

A falsifying fingerprint scandal in Troop C prompted the state police to create a new inspector's position to review all the NYSP fingerprint files; I got that assignment. Several state police investigators and lieutenants confessed to forging suspects' fingerprints in burglary and murder cases.[374] The corruption became known when, in 1991, former investigator David L. Harding bragged about having forged fingerprints during a CIA job interview.[375] All but one of these former officers were convicted and incarcerated.[376] A team of forensic investigators and I had to inspect every forensic unit in the

NYPS, review every fingerprint in the state police files, and rewrite the NYSP forensic manual to ensure sufficient safeguards to prevent this from happening again. We also had to inspect every narcotic unit, rewriting the NYSP narcotics manual with the same goal of avoiding corruption and the mishandling of evidence. This assignment was arduous. Captain Theodore Cook, my mentor, worked for me and was second-in-command of this detail in an interesting twist of fate. To complete this assignment meant the team and I had to schedule inspections every other week. One week, we conducted the review; the alternate week, we assessed the results and drafted the report. That meant not only was I away from my family each week, but It also meant that during the weeks of the inspections. I was away from the NYSP academy dorm where I stayed. The inspections would alternate between the narcotic and forensic units. Cook and I would also meet with local police chiefs, commissioners, and district attorneys.

Once again, in these meetings, I saw the same initial reactions of these local law enforcement officials as I had when I was the CNET commander. Those who remembered me were more at ease with seeing us. We were often the only police officers of Color that some of these officials had dealt with in their service area. Cook and I worked carefully to put these officials at ease. When we experienced micro-aggressions, we would gently defuse the situation by pointing out that without our investigators of Color, their local investigation may not have been as successful. We kept this pace up for eighteen months. During those months, Cook's health began to deteriorate. We had to admit him to a hospital because of his diabetes. He lost several toes and ultimately succumbed to the chronic disease. It broke my heart; he was an exceptional and generous mentor and friend.

After nearly two years of this assignment, we completed the inspections and revisions of both manuals. I learned so much more about the forensic sciences and the pseudo-forensic sciences.[377] For instance, I learned about the methods employed to compare latent (visible) fingerprints for identification. I discovered that each trained fingerprint examiner used a unique set of ridges and bifurcation to establish a match between the latent print and the alleged suspect.[378]

The international standard for individualized identification varies from country to country, and many countries used twelve points of minutia as the standard in the past. The United States and the United Kingdom opted out of using a numeric and began using a non-numeric, holistic approach.[379] As I questioned the more senior fingerprint examination experts, I realized there were subjective variations on what individual forensic investigators would use as the minimum among these fingerprint minutiae. I also more clearly understood how the validity of arrests, evidence collection, analysis, and prosecution depended on the character and integrity of everyone involved. Moreover, some accepted methods of identifying evidence, like bite or tool mark comparisons, handwriting analysis, and even fingerprint comparisons, could result in false identifications because there is no universal standard. This realization broadened my perspective on the complexity of providing peer-reviewed and valid forensic evidence in criminal investigations and the grievous errors made when using forensic techniques that have not undergone rigorous scientific analysis.[380]

In 1999, I was transferred from IAB to Field Command as the inspector overseeing all NYSP narcotics units. The move was a relief; I welcomed being out of the major's graveyard. Many in the organization call it that for several reasons; one is a simple hierarchical fact that there are fewer colonels than inspectors, so the competition for recognition and promotion is fiercer. Second, once in IAB, many former majors retired after being passed over for promotions. It was a sign that I could continue my journey to positions of more significant influence. As always, I recognized I had to do my job superbly and not be overly concerned about the next step. Based on my past successes and lady luck, I trusted I could do this new job expertly. It was in my wheelhouse based on my work in narcotics, my implementation of Operation Crackdown, and my time as the commander of CNET. Moreover, the previous two years provided significant experience and contacts across the state.

I traveled to every state police narcotics unit and local county drug task force situated in the major cities of New York. The focus of these visits was to ensure the state police investigators and resources were helping to accomplish the goals of these task forces of reducing, if not ending, illegal drug trafficking and related violence. The latter remains a very elusive goal for many reasons. Pursuing it led to "Mass Incarceration" because of the apparent inequity in enforcement tactics and inequitable legal statutes and sentencing guidelines. During my work to ensure drug enforcement units with assigned state police personnel were accomplishing their goals with unshakable integrity.

I also worked to help the state police, the associated state, and local emergency response entities coordinate their efforts to prepare for the Y2K scare. The scare was also known as the "Millennium Bug."[381] The "Bug" was a computer coding problem that nearly the whole world believed civilization as we knew it would end because computers run most of our modern infrastructures. Much of the work during the last days of 1999 and the first days of 2000 would happen at the State Emergency Management Offices (SEMO) on the NYSP headquarters' sub-basement floors. The building was designed in the 1970s to withstand a nuclear attack. It had several underground stories intended to support the collapse of the three floors above the ground on top of these subbasement floors to provide extra protection to the state government leadership and emergency response entities. It had two massive doors we had not used for some time and needed repair. It also had decades-old rations and other supplies needing replacement and updating. There were fears that terrorists and other criminal groups would take advantage of the chaos caused by the system failures.

We held several trial runs of our response plans and then went to our assigned posts on New Year's Eve. I worked the first shift at the SEMO center from 7:00 p.m. to 7:00 a.m. The evening was uneventful, except for a minor Canadian border incident involving a tourist detained for suspicious activity, which I resolved relatively quickly. I reported this to the superintendent. We received no reports of other significant incidents that night or in the following days. To add humor to the noneventful Y2K detail, the head of the SEMO and the superintendent awarded me a gag certificate of accomplishment for protecting our borders. We all laughed and were relieved the doomsday predictions did not materialize.

On May 25, 2000, the superintendent promoted me to assistant deputy superintendent with the rank of lieutenant colonel. Once again, I was the first person of my unique heritage to hold this title and rank within the state police. I remained in this post for seven years. I had the honor and daunting responsibility of supervising and overseeing the BCI. The BCI had over a thousand criminal investigators, senior investigators, and dozens of BCI commissioned officers. I managed the background investigations of all state police candidates and governmental appointees to state agencies, including members of the governor's office and other state entities. Authorized in 1935 by the state legislature, the BCI conducted complex investigations needed so that the uniform force could maintain patrols. It also provided investigative expertise and assistance to local departments. The same 1935 legislation authorized the creation of a crime laboratory, which I also administered. Then, in 1936, the Bureau of Investigation became the Bureau of Criminal Investigation, and the crime laboratory opened in Schenectady. I burst with pride, having achieved this highly lauded post. I knew I could do the job and rested in the knowledge that I would not have gained this critical position if the superintendent did not believe I was worthy.

In this new role, I was also responsible for ensuring the Colonel Henry F. Williams Homicide Seminar continued to succeed globally. Superintendent Constantine started the seminar in 1987 to honor the late Assistant Deputy Superintendent Williams, who oversaw the BCI and had been the BCI captain in Troop A and Constantine's mentor. Colonel Williams was instrumental in creating the forensic unit in the state police. The first seminar had 130 homicide investigators from across the nation attend, and the colloquium grew and expanded to accept homicide investigators and detectives from agencies around the world. I was among the longest-serving light colonels who oversaw this seminar. During my tour as the BCI colonel, I got to work with Dr. Michael Baden, the world-famous forensic pathologist who helped with the Kevin King homicide case and many more globally renowned death investigations.

One year during the seminar, the Russian delegation of homicide detectives invited me to share war stories, hearty Russian bread,

Salmon Caviar, and Russian Vodka. Every chance they got, they would shout "Colonel Perez, our good friend," as a toast and pour a shot of Vodka, not stirred or shaken, just straight Vodka, into our glasses. Their tribute started at 9:00 p.m. and lasted until 4:00 a.m.; when I left, I went to my room, showered, and reported back to the seminar. Luckily, I had eaten a big dinner. I ate more hearty bread and delicious Salmon roe and avoided drinking Vodka at every toast by switching to a glass of water. I was tired but not hung over. When these detectives finally strolled into the lecture hall, I had the podium and shouted, "Hello, my good Russian friends." I told the officers gathered in the lecture hall that they had tried to get me drunk but had not succeeded. The audience laughed, as did the Russian detectives. That night, I slept like a baby. These gatherings created contacts across the United States and the world, which helped the state police respond to unprecedented disasters, like September 11, 2001.

On that fateful day, I was on vacation mowing my lawn when I saw Pamela waving her arms frantically from a distance and beckoning me to stop. I ran toward the house, not knowing what had happened. I hugged her and asked what was wrong. She pulled me into the house and pointed to the TV. I turned and saw the second plane hit the World Trade Center. She and my children were crying, and I knew what to do. I quickly showered, dressed, and grabbed my "Go Bag." I kissed Pamela and my children. I began my thirty-mile trip to Division headquarters. On the way in, I started calling state police commanders in NYC to ascertain the situation there. I also called the Field commander and informed him I was coming to work. He said he would brief me once I arrived.

We spent the next seventy-two hours working around the clock to help provide personnel to assist NYPD and the other agencies responding to downtown Manhattan. We took turns going to the World Trade Center to ascertain what else was needed. We sent several hundred uniform troopers to limit crash site access and guard checkpoints with the NY State National Guard. Troopers also road subways and helped defend transportation hubs like Grand Central Station and Pennsylvania Station. We deployed BCI teams to assist Disaster Mortuary Operational Response Teams (DMORTs). The

DMORT team supported local mortuary services at the "Pile." They work quickly and accurately to identify and reunite victims and their remains with their families in a dignified and respectful manner.[382] Many members of the state police, the NYCPD, and the NYCFD helped search for victims during the rescue phase. The last person rescued from the collapsed rubble of the World Trade Center was Genelle Guzman-McMillan. She worked on the 64th floor and, after being buried for twenty seven hours, longer than any other person.[383]

The searchers then helped search for the victim's remains once there was no hope that anyone was still alive. There are still responders dying from the aftermath of the 9/11 terrorist attack. The list of victims is long:

- 2,977 people died (and countless more suffered severe injuries and long-term health issues).
- 2,753 died at the World Trade Center site.
- 184 people died when American Airlines Flight 77 crashed into the Pentagon.
- 40 died on United Airlines Flight 93, which crashed near Shanksville, Pennsylvania.
- About 343 of them were New York City firefighters.
- About 23 were NYPD officers.
- About 37 were police officers from the Port Authority of New York and New Jersey.[384]

Countless victims and first responders are still dying due to 9/11-related illnesses. The victims ranged in age from two to eighty-five years. Approximately 75 - 80 percent of the victims were men. The identity of the 1,649th victim, according to the New York City Medical Examiner's Office since September 2021, was determined.[385] NYSP personnel still suffer and are dying from grave illnesses caused by the carcinogenic and toxic air surrounding the fallen towers. Since 9/11, 24 state police members have died from illnesses related to their assignment to the World Trade Center detail.[386] Their families and many others across the globe also bear the emotional scars caused by the events of that tragic day. Some of the injured troopers are among my dearest friends.

In the months following the attack, NYSP created the Upstate New York Regional Intelligence Center (UNYRIC), modeled after similar information-sharing regional multi-agency central repositories for the numerous databases used by law enforcement agencies. Its goal was to provide "one-stop shopping" for data stored in many files maintained publicly and privately by the law enforcement community. For nearly seven years as the BCI lieutenant colonel, I administered hundreds of major criminal investigations, providing the investigative units with the resources they needed to close those cases successfully.

One of the most complex and tragic investigations involved Ralph "Bucky" Phillips.[387] This case started as an escaped prisoner investigation and became a multiple homicide investigation involving hundreds of federal, state, county, and municipal law enforcement officers. The BCI was primarily responsible for gathering evidence of the escape, homicides, aggravated felony assaults, burglaries, and intelligence on Phillips's whereabouts. The uniform force of the Division deployed hundreds of troopers, the MRT, K9, and other assets to staff checkpoints, searching areas where Phillips could have been spotted and capturing him.

On April 2, 2006, Ralph Phillips, who spent twenty out of the prior twenty-three years incarcerated, escaped the Alden Correctional Facility in Erie County. Phillips escaped by cutting through the kitchen ceiling with a can opener. Phillips dropped a note while transferring out of the Chautauqua County Jail, threatening to "splatter pig meat all over Chautauqua County." He used "pig," the derogatory slang word for a police officer. Phillips, a Seneca Indian, was raised in Chautauqua County and had friends in several Indian nations of western New York, as well as contacts from his time in jails and prison. Phillips stole numerous vehicles and broke into several cabins across Western New York, including Chautauqua, Warren, and McKean County, Pennsylvania. Clearly, he was getting lots of help during this time on the lam. Shortly after escaping, Phillips hid with the family of Joshua Rickard, whom he had served time with at Comstock Correctional Facility. Phillips had protected Rickard, twenty years his junior, in jail, Rickard's mother, Peggy Rickard, said later. In return, they took him in at the Tuscarora Indian Reservation in Niagara County.

On June 10, 2006, around 1:00 a.m., Troopers Sean Brown and Donald Will approached the Ford Mustang stolen by Phillips. Phillips, to avoid capture, shot Trooper Brown with a .38-caliber revolver in the abdomen on Parrott Road in the Chemung County town of Veteran just west of Elmira, New York. Phillips then drove away, leaving Trooper Brown with serious abdomen wounds. Brown's partner, Trooper Will, transported him to St. Joseph's Hospital in Elmira. Brown was released four days later. He returned to work in August 2006. While Trooper Brown was recovering, the hunt for Phillips intensified; numerous reports of stolen vehicles and break-ins had occurred. These reports led to the search of a cabin where an abandoned backpack containing evidence connecting Phillips to the attempted murders of Trooper Brown and Trooper Will.

Because of numerous tips and the awareness that family and friends were helping Phillips, members of the MRT had staked out the house of one of his relatives in Pomfret, Chautauqua County. On August 31, 2006, Phillips, who had secreted himself in a snip-er's nest, got the drop on Troopers Donald Baker Jr. and Joseph A. Longobardo. Phillips used a high-powered .308-caliber Hunting rifle he had stolen from a Gun shop to shoot the troopers. Although mortally wounded, Trooper Longobardo returned fire. The critically injured Trooper Baker radioed other MRT members, alerting them of the ambush.

We suspected eleven rounds were fired during the short but deadly gun battle. A bullet struck Trooper Baker on the right side and exited out of the left side of his body. A medevacked copter took him to Hamot Shock Trauma Center in Erie, Pennsylvania. Trooper Longobardo suffered a gunshot that severed an artery in his leg; another medevacked copter took him to Erie County Medical Center in Buffalo, New York. Trooper Longobardo succumbed to his wound on Sunday, September 3, 2006. Trooper Baker was transferred from Hamot Shock Center to Albany Medical Center on November

9, 2006, where he continued his recovery. Phillips remained at large until authorities located him just south of the New York border in Pennsylvania, and he surrendered on September 8, 2006.

On Wednesday, November 29, 2006, Phillips admitted to shooting trooper Sean M. Brown with a .38 revolver during a traffic stop outside Elmira on June 10 in Chemung County Court. Then 150 miles west, as part of a plea agreement, that afternoon in Chautauqua County Court, he admitted shooting troopers Joseph A. Longobardo and Donald Baker Jr. with a high-powered .308- caliber rifle in a wooded area outside his former companion's home in rural Chautauqua County on August 31. Prosecutors said Phillips would remain in prison for life without the possibility of parole.

Superintendent Wayne E. Bennett, who had been in overall command of the state police during the Phillips case, asked for the after-action report. Superintendent Bennett was a very demanding "old school trooper" who unwaveringly believed in the exceptional ability of the NY state police. He preferred complete control of state police operations during this case and allowed only limited input from other agencies.

This case was complex and controversial, mired by many challenges that led to errors that delayed the capture of Phillips. The most critical error was the failure to communicate effectively between the agencies involved. It had become clear that the family and friends of Phillips were listening to police radio frequencies and sharing what they heard with Phillips, helping him elude capture. To thwart this, state police leaders at the troop level decided to use cell phones to communicate with each other. Cell phone coverage in this part of New York was sketchy. In the woods, where the MRT and other police officers were, cell coverage was nearly nonexistent; thus, wherever information arose about Phillips's location, it was often not relayed to them.

Moreover, the other agencies often needed to be more clued in on these calls. Another cause for concern was the need for a mobile command vehicle to manage communications and dissemination of intelligence to all agencies involved. Furthermore, some agencies shared their frustration with the failure to share important information with officers up and down the chain of command. In the after-action report, many outside agencies were critical about its conclusion. The report found that "a majority"' of police agencies interviewed found the communication and cooperation between the state police and other agencies "in the range from effective to excellent."[388] Yet, Niagara County Sheriff Thomas A. Beilein said state police should have sought more help and expertise from other agencies. He went on to say:

> "I still feel strongly that our department and other agencies could have helped them," Beilein said. "They didn't want our bloodhound. They didn't want the Erie County sheriff's helicopter. That just doesn't make sense."

Chautauqua County Sheriff Joseph Gerace, whose county was the focal point of the search, agreed. He said,

> "From what I've read of the report, I don't think they addressed the issue of interagency cooperation enough," Gerace said. 'The state police declined help from us at times…, people from my department with a lot of expertise. I really believe it was a problem with egos, involving a few individuals."

Another criticism from several unnamed law enforcement officials said Buffalo FBI officials grew frustrated over the reluctance of state police commanders to accept federal help.

> "It was the first time I ever heard of the FBI having to negotiate with another police agency to put someone on the 10 Most Wanted," said one police official who is familiar with the situation.[389]

Even Phillips was critical of the state police operations. Phillips told the investigators that "using troopers in fixed post situations was stupid" because they could be targets, especially at night. "He states that first of all, at night, they have their lights on, and you can see them a mile away. Also, all you have to do, and he said he did it [on] more than one occasion to exit a perimeter, was to go between the cars and escape," according to the report.[390] Of course, confirming much of this was impossible because there were no witnesses, although the report does refer to instances when troopers spotted Phillips but did not pursue and capture him.

The report revealed several close encounters by troopers with Phillips. A K9 trooper failed to let his dog loose to chase after Phillips in a wooded area. "It is reasonable to believe the dog would have easily seized and detained Phillips," the report said. In another instance, the report shared, troopers saw Phillips run across a hill in Chautauqua County. They summoned a helicopter, but the troopers had no portable radios and could not direct the pilot where to look for Phillips. Perhaps most damaging was an August 19, 2006, incident where a trooper encountered Phillips motorcycling through the Town of Charlotte in Chautauqua County. The report says the trooper failed to pursue him into an apartment house, and Phillips eventually escaped into adjoining woods from a back window. The most damning language of the report, the unidentified trooper was faulted for not calling for backup from nearby patrols.

> "It is difficult to understand the actions of the trooper in this situation," the report concludes. "Unfortunately, this was a significant reason why Phillips had ample opportunity to flee the residence and evade capture."

Phillips is serving his sentence in Clinton Correctional Facility. There, prison officials accused Phillips of having "escape paraphernalia," a dummy made from clothing stuffed into a sweatshirt and other items. He remains a flight risk. The Phillips search was one of the largest in the nation.

As mentioned, Superintendent Bennett was an "old school trooper." So, I was not surprised Superintendent Bennett and I had an intense exchange about diversity and inclusion within the state police ranks a year before the Phillips case. It occurred during the periodic command staff meeting at the Division headquarters, and all the commanders of the various troops, details, and units were required to attend. In that forum, I was commending the troop commanders for their efforts to send me a diverse list of troop candidates for the BCI. I told them, "Thank you for doing your best in submitting a diverse BCI list. Adding troopers of Color is becoming more challenging because we are recruiting fewer than we had. I thank you."

Superintendent Bennett interrupted me and said, "Perez, I do not care about how diverse the list is. What I care about is. Are the candidates on the list qualified?"

I immediately replied, "Sir, every BCI list I gave you and every other superintendent I worked for only had highly qualified candidates. All the candidates, and I mean, all are qualified."

The superintendent glared at me and said, "Be that as it may, you heard me; submit lists with qualified candidates. Let's move on!" Another cut from a microaggression. I looked at First Deputy Superintendent Felton, hoping he would chime in and support my statement, but he kept his blank expression. When the meeting ended, I pulled Felton aside and asked why he had not said anything. He said, "Why waste my breath? He is old school, does not care about diversity, and does not believe in affirmative action and what it brought to the state police." Bennett retired on February 26, 2007, and First Deputy Superintendent Preston Felton became the acting superintendent. On March 8, 2007, acting superintendent Felton promoted me to "full-bird" colonel/chief inspector-IAB. In December 2007, he appointed me as Field Commander, the third highest rank in of the Division.

During Acting Superintendent Felton's tenure, I realized how much more complex it was to handle the external political impact on the state police command staff. At this tier of the state police, there were frequent interactions with the governor's office, the office of the state's attorney general, the heads of other agencies, and many legislators. At this point, I had had meetings with mayors, county legislators, and other politicians, and I effectively managed their expectations, requests, and complaints. They could not easily force policy changes, impact careers readily, or cause other actions. But the governor and the attorney general could, as could the State Senate and Assembly leaders.

I was shocked as the whirlwinds of political maneuvers designed to leverage state police resources from certain politicians pulled in Felton. In a report issued by the New York State Commission on Ethics and Lobbying in Government, dubbed by the media as "Troopergate."[391] The report said:

> "There is reasonable cause to believe based on the record evidence that, during 2007, senior officials in the Administration of Governor Eliot Spitzer engaged in a course of conduct that violated the Public Officers Law. The evidence also supports a reasonable belief that these Spitzer Administration officials caused the state police to serve the Governor's and their own non-governmental interests in a manner that compromised the state police...
>
> Finally, there is reasonable cause to believe that in doing so, these Spitzer Administration officials misused their official positions to cause the state police to engage in conduct that was wholly unrelated to the state police's statutory mandate of detect[ing] and prevent[ing] crime...
>
> Specifically, there is reasonable cause to believe that to advance the Governor's and their own non-governmental interests, these Spitzer Administration officials caused the state police (i) to gather information regarding Senator Joseph

Bruno's travel that the Police would not have gathered as part of the state police's official business; and (ii) to create purportedly 'official' documents reflecting Senator Bruno's confidential travel information, never before publicly released by the state police, that they caused to be disseminated to the press."

The report specifically stated:

"The governor's staff ordered the state police to keep special records of Senate majority leader Joseph L. Bruno's whereabouts when he traveled with police escorts in New York City and to recreate records if they did not exist. The report said that the acting superintendent of police, Preston Felton, took an unprecedented role in assisting requests from the governor's staff and the media for information related to the Senator's whereabouts."[392]

On July 24, 2007, New York Times News Service reporter Danny Hakim put it this way in the Boston Globe:

"The report said that the acting superintendent of police, Preston Felton, took an unprecedented role in assisting requests from the governor's staff and the media for information related to the senator's whereabouts. And the report concluded that there was an orchestrated campaign by the governor's office to obtain and provide information to the news media, with the help of the state police, to essentially discredit Bruno, the state's top Republican."[393]

Soon after the release of these investigations by the NYS attorney general's office, the Albany County District Attorney's office, and the Commission on Public Integrity, then Governor Eliot Spitzer apologized, stating this to the media:

> "As governor, I am accountable for what goes on in the executive branch and I accept responsibility for the actions of my office," he said at a press conference this morning, with many of his staff members looking on somber and staggered.
>
> "I apologized to Senator Bruno and I did so personally this morning," he added. "In addition, I apologized to the men and women of the state police, and to acting superintendent Preston Felton personally for allowing this esteemed institution to be drawn into this matter."[394]

A year after this humiliation, another scandal involving Governor Spitzer and the NYS Police became public. Spitzer said he was resigning on Wednesday, March 12, 2008, in his offices in New York City. He announced Lieutenant Governor David Paterson would succeed him effective Monday, March 17, 2008.[395] This debacle made history ingloriously; David Paterson became the state's first Black governor and, because he was legally blind, the first blind governor. The scandal began after federal law enforcement officials disclosed that a wiretap had caught Spitzer spending thousands of dollars on a call girl at an upscale Washington hotel the night before Valentine's Day. Investigators said he had arranged for a prostitute to take the train down from New York to testify before a congressional subcommittee about the bond industry while he was in the nation's capital. Federal law enforcement officials said Spitzer had hired prostitutes several times before and had spent tens of thousands of dollars, perhaps as much as $80,000, on the high-priced escort service Emperors Club VIP. The women from this escort service could charge as much as $5,500 an hour.[396] Is this another example of two-tiered justice: one for ordinary folks and another for celebrities, the wealthy, and the connected? Four people were charged and pled guilty to running the prostitution operation that led to Spitzer's political demise. The Department of Justice (DOJ) did not criminally charge Spitzer for violating the Mann Act. The Mann Act makes transporting women or girls for prostitution across state lines a federal crime.[397] According to the DOJ, clients, "Johns," at the federal level are often not charged.[398] DOJ prosecutor Michael Garcia said the investigation revealed no evidence that Spitzer misused public or campaign funds for prostitution and that he paid for sex with his private funds.[399] In a Ken Burns's documentary, he reported that some prosecutors oppressively enforced the Mann Act. Illustrating another example of a two-tiered criminal justice system, of using laws to selectively prosecute individuals with opposing political views?

> "Such an interpretation of the law in effect criminalized all premarital or extramarital sexual relationships that involved interstate travel. With behavior that was so commonplace now illegal, federal prosecutors had a weapon that could very easily be abused in order to prosecute "undesirables" who were otherwise law-abiding citizens. Jack Johnson's conviction in 1913 was ostensibly for transporting a white prostitute from Pittsburgh to Chicago, but was motivated by public outrage over his marriages to white women. In 1944, actor Charlie Chaplin was acquitted of a Mann Act indictment stemming from a paternity suit. In actuality, the case was motivated by Chaplin's left-of-center political views and was personally instigated by FBI Director J. Edgar Hoover, who had called Chaplin one of Hollywood's "parlor Bolsheviki." In 1959, black rock 'n roll star Chuck Berry was convicted of violating the Mann Act and served 20 months in prison for transporting across state

lines an underage Apache girl who was weeks
later arrested on a prostitution charge."[400]

Within a week of the revelations that shocked the Division that
Spitzer met call girls while his protective detail of troopers guarded
him, acting superintendent Felton announced he was retiring on
April 4, 2008. As part of the state police succession plan, I immediately became the Acting superintendent and would serve until a new
leader was appointed and confirmed.

During the weeks between Felton's leaving and Corbitt's
appointment, I received a call from Attorney General Andrew
Cuomo regarding his investigation into Troopergate. During that
call, the AG stated he needed his prosecutors and investigative team
to interview some troopers. I answered, of course, "I will arrange for
them to be available with their attorneys." His tone changed, and he
said brusquely, "As law enforcement officials, we understood that if
someone comes with an attorney, there is a presumption that they
have something to hide." I replied. "No, that is not, in fact, the case.
In our system, having an attorney present does not create a sense
of guilt. There's a right to an attorney." The conversation became
heated; he said to make the troopers available as he said that the first
counsel for the state police, Glen Valle, had just stood at my office's
open door. I waved him in and told AG Cuomo I would have Mr.
Valle contact the AG's office to make the appropriate arrangements.
The AG hung up, and I immediately told Mr. Valle about the call.
We were both stunned by the comment, and Mr. Valle said he would
call the AG.

April 16, 2008, the NYS Senate confirmed the appointment
of Harry Corbitt as the thirteenth superintendent and first African
American to serve in this lauded position.[401] Superintendent Corbitt
appointed me the First Deputy Superintendent, making me second
in command.

On December 30, 2008, Mr. Valle testified in the investigation of the state police by the AG's office Special Counsel Sharon L.
McCarthy. At the beginning of the interview, Mr. Valle asked to have
a few things placed on the record. He testified under oath.

"I believe prior to your becoming part of it, Ms. McCarthy, it was indicated to me, it was communicated to me that Andrew Cuomo indicated to at least one high-ranking member of the New York State Police that if a member or employee of the state police appeared with counsel, having apprised themselves of that right, that would be viewed with a negative inference. I was also told by another member of the Executive Committee that Mr. Cuomo said to this high-ranking official that if anyone from the state police showed up with counsel, he, being Mr. Cuomo, would figure that they had something to hide."

He ended this portion of his testimony by stating:

"But I want to place on the record the fact that I am represented by counsel and I have absolutely nothing to hide. And I object if there's any inference to the contrary because I have chosen to appear here today with counsel."[402]

The AG's office statement to the New York Times was:

"There had been a conversation with Mr. Perez, but disputed his recollection; it said Mr. Cuomo told Mr. Perez that Mr. Valle, the chief counsel, could not represent the agency because he would probably have to testify."[403]

There was nothing wrong with my memory then or now.[404] Be careful what you wish for, kept ringing in my head. I had risen to the second-highest rank in the agency, having witnessed all the political mayhem that left a scorched landscape of broken hearts, lives, families, and careers. How would Corbitt and I navigate this political ocean filled with hidden depth charges? "Con Cuidado," carefully, I heard my mother whisper in my head. She often said when I shared how things were going during my visits back to Wellsville. It did not take long for the multiheaded political serpent to appear.

Paterson, having seen the "Dirty Tricks" employed by his predecessor of using elements of the state police to keep tabs on political opponents. Immediately after appointing superintendent Corbitt, Paterson admitted that he had several extramarital affairs and used drugs because he believed there was a rogue element within the state police.[405] He is quoted in a New York Times article on the matter:

> "There was obviously an element in the police force - and it wasn't Republican or Democrat - it was just out-of-control people who had power that were clearly monitoring a lot of the elected officials," the governor said. "And I was kind of afraid of leaks of inaccurate information about myself."

He provided no evidence but added:

> "In the week that I was awaiting becoming governor, I was told by many elected officials that they were stopped for traffic violations and then had to read about it on blogs," Mr. Paterson told reporters. "At the same time, I'm hearing these kinds of outrageous rumors about myself. And so it wasn't the primary reason, but it was one of the reasons I decided I was going to tell my own story."[406]

Governor Paterson asked Attorney General Andrew Cuomo to open an investigation; the AG's office accepted. I did not believe such a unit existed within the state police. However, I also knew individuals within the state police could behave this way and, when caught, would be disciplined accordingly. Former Superintendent Bennett said in the same New York Times report:

> "I spent just shy of 39 years in the state police," said Wayne E. Bennett, a former state police superintendent who is now the commissioner of public safety for Schenectady, N.Y. "I can honestly tell you I had no knowledge of any situation that even remotely comes close to this kind of suggestion." But he said he could not rule it out entirely. "Is it possible that we had one or two or three people acting independently?" he said. "I can't dismiss that possibility."[407]

Superintendent Corbitt advised the media and the AG's office we would fully cooperate with the investigation. He told the Democrat and Chronicle newspaper on May 18, 2008:

> "During my tenure in the state police I have never heard of a rogue unit, never received any information and I talked to several superintendents and they have shared the same opinion," he said. Corbitt, who joined the department in 1978, continued, "I don't believe there's a rogue unit, but that's what investigations do. They uncover the truth. So I'm going to leave that to the AG's report."[408]

All these accusations and resulting investigations strained our relationship with the governor, and at times, it was very contentious. Corbitt and I had several meetings with the governor and his advisors to seek cooperation in their background investigations. Several of Governor Paterson's senior staff failed to answer investigators' questions or provide necessary documents as requested. This behavior was particularly true in the case of Charles J. O'Byrne, the governor's chief of staff. Mr. O'Byrne, a former Jesuit priest, long-time consultant, and advisor, had refused to answer questions and provide access to his financial records that were part of the background check. Superintendent Corbitt and I met directly with O'Byrne and the governor to request cooperation and explain that it was in the best interest of his administration.

Moreover, it had been the standard operating procedure of all previous administrations. In April 2008, the governor's office instructed us to investigate O'Byrne's failure to pay his taxes, and we found that he owed around three hundred thousand dollars to the IRS. Governor Paterson told the New York Times on October 22, 2008, "...that the investigation into the debts did not compromise his job..."[409] I have no recollection of Superintendent Corbitt or me making such an assertion. On October 24, 2008, O'Byrne resigned.[410] Our relationship with Governor Paterson's administration remained tumultuous for the next two years.

We nevertheless had an agency to run. We ushered in several innovative programs and equipment during the next two years. One of the critical issues we had to continue evaluating and determining the best course of action was enhancing the safety of Division members and the people we were serving. Criminals and terrorists were better armed than most police officers. Based on my suggestions, Superintendent Corbitt agreed we needed more advanced counter-terrorism programs.

We considered what the Division did when it formed the 1980 Olympic Special Weapons and Tactics team to protect the athletes and participants. New York State and its law enforcement authorities did not want that to happen. Yet once the Olympics ended, the NYSP Olympic SWAT team disbanded after it went off without a terrorist incident, not considering the ongoing terrorist threats that continued to exist.

Because of this and other terrorist attacks, the NYSP created the Mobile Response Team to protect New York citizens from potential terrorist attacks and other deadly criminal incidents. The Division also began making other changes because of the increasing threat of terrorism and ultra-violent criminal individuals and groups. Consider that three cities in the United States that experienced the most terrorist attacks between 2001 and 2011 were New York City, with twelve; Washington, DC, with nine; and Los Angeles, with eight.[411] There were twenty-one mass shootings during this same period, which caused the deaths of 192 US citizens and injured 153 persons. In 2009, in Binghamton, New York, fourteen people lost their lives, and four persons were injured when a lone gunman entered the American Civic Association, a nonprofit committed to helping immigrants.[412] Troopers responded to assist the Binghamton police and the Chemung County Sheriff's deputies. Governor Paterson expressed condolences to the victims of this mass shooting.

Sadly, to our utter surprise, in November 2009, Felton admitted breaking state law during Eliot Spitzer's scandalous use of the state police.[413] Felton, a good man, have been bamboozled into cooperating with the Spitzer administration in their unfortunate shenanigans. Superintendent Corbitt and I were determined not to fall into the same trap.

Then, October 31, 2009 happened. I had just finished a late dinner and was resting when my cell phone rang. On the other end of the call was Major Charles Day. We promoted him to major and assigned him to head the Executive Services Detail (ESD). ESD is the division's equivalent of the Secret Service; ESD protects Governor Paterson and the Lieutenant Governor.[414]

"Hello, Charles, what's up?" I asked.

He replied, "Sir, I tried calling the superintendent, but he did not answer his phone. I have a serious matter I need to discuss with him."

"Okay, tell me, and I will see if I can help. I will contact the Supt and let him know what's up."

"Okay," he replied.

He says, "I just got a from governor's aide, David Johnson. He asked me to help him with a domestic dispute between himself and his girlfriend. Johnson told me he visited his girlfriend at her apartment and saw her dressed in a "Baby doll" costume. That his girlfriend said she was going to the Halloween party."

Major Day said that Johnson told him he got upset when he told him not to go in that outfit, which she refused. The major said,

"Johnson told me he grabbed her, tore the costume off, and pushed her. She then tried calling 911; they scuffled again, and he left her apartment. Johnson then called me and asked me to call his girlfriend. What do I do?"

I told Major Day, "Do not call her for him. Call her to be sure she is okay and help her call the NYPD to report the incident. Help the NYPD as needed and stay in touch with them as they proceed with the case."

I had several concerns regarding this case. Major Day had some facts about what happened and only heard the Johnson version. Two, the governor is legally blind. Moreover, if Johnson's girlfriend retaliated while Johnson was with the governor, that could endanger the governor. Finally, if the NYPD sought to arrest Johnson while he was with the governor, and we were unaware of that, it could jeopardize the governor's safety. I then called Superintendent Corbitt and told him what had happened and the instructions I had given Major Day. He was only to contact the girlfriend to help her file charges with the NYSP, maintain contact with the NYPD to help them as needed, and keep abreast of their investigation to protect the governor's physical safety. I followed the chain of command by calling the superintendent, as I assumed the superintendent would do when he notified Governor Paterson. Superintendent Corbitt agreed with the instructions I had given Major Day, saying, "She is a victim of crime, and we need to act accordingly. Let me know when Day contacted the girlfriend, the status of her condition, and the investigation." I notified the superintendent that Major Day contacted the girlfriend and the NY City PD. This case roiled in the news, the executive chambers, and the Division for the next several months.

Despite this turmoil, Superintendent Corbitt and I continued to work to create a more diverse agency. We embarked on a campaign to introduce ourselves to leaders in communities of Color across the State. We asked these leaders what the state police could do to engender greater trust. What did they see as barriers to establishing better relationships with them? We talked frankly about "Driving while Black or Brown" because it was one the most significant concerns raised by these leaders, as was racism within the police departments, including the state police. We offer suggestions on not being targeted, like obeying traffic laws, ensuring the vehicle complies with regulatory safety measures, and what to do when stopped. We explained that we both had "The Talk" with our children.[415] We told them first, obey the law. If you get stopped, turn on the car's inside lights, roll down the window, keep your hands on the steering wheel, stay calm, listen carefully, and answer questions about who you are. But once the questions are about the law and allegations of you violating it, say nothing except you want to have a parent with you during questioning. Nearly every African American and Latino family has for decades explained to their children how to safely navigate White culture, particularly in the southern and western regions of the United States. Given the ethnic make-up of most police departments in New York State, particularly in the rural sections of the state, having the "Talk" was necessary.[416] We also discussed the benefits of joining the state police for individuals from their communities regarding a career. How having a more diverse police force could help reduce incidents of racism during police encounters.

All this came to a screeching halt in February 2010. Rumors about the governor's direct involvement in the Johnson case began surfacing in January. The story was that the governor called Johnson's girlfriend, asked two of his staffers to call her, and revealed his other top aide, Clemmie Harris, a retired trooper, had contacted the day after the domestic occurred. On February 24, 2010, the New York Times published a story about Johnson's alleged involvement in a violent domestic abuse case. Governor Paterson suspended Johnson and asked the Attorney General, Andrew Cuomo, to investigate the allegations of the case and the state police's alleged attempts to quash the NYPD's investigation into the matter.[417] I thought, here we go again. I was glad an independent counsel would handle the investigation, and the highly respected former Chief Judge of the New York State Court of Appeals, Judith S. Kaye, was appointed.[418] I did not know then that Independent Counsel Kaye was also investigating whether the Governor received free tickets for the 2009 World Series at Yankee Stadium. In that matter, he was fined $62,125 by the state's Commission on Public Integrity.[419]

Independent Counsel Kaye's report concluded:

> "Finds no evidence that the state police or the Executive Chamber interfered with the NYPD response to the October 31, 2009 domestic incident."[420]

Superintendent Corbitt retired on March 3, 2010, telling me the difficulty of working for this governor and relentless media scrutiny made the job unnecessarily stressful. Once again, I was the acting superintendent. During the next few days in March of 2010, I heard rumors that the governor sought another colonel to serve as acting superintendent and intended to replace me with another colonel. Colonel John Melville, showing organizational loyalty and adhering to the chain of command, told me. "Boss, I was called by the governor's office and asked if I would serve as the interim superintendent." "Thank you, John," I replied, hiding my anger and disappointment.

I felt this was in retaliation for my having pushed so earnestly for the governor's cooperation on background investigations of his executive chamber's staff during the first year of his administration that caused some of his aides to resign. I called the governor's office and asked why they had not simply asked me to step aside; the answer I got from his secretary was that they were under incredible pressure and had to move quickly.

"Do you think it has been easy working with the governor? You should have had the decency to speak directly to me."

I hung up and paced the office. I considered how they had behaved the last year and wondered what dirty tricks they might have tried to get me demoted to my permanent rank of lieutenant, which could have reduced my salary and subsequent pension. I chose instead to retire. On March 9, 2010, I submitted my retirement papers and began using my unexpended accrued vacation, making my actual retirement official in September 2010. I also submitted a memorandum to clarify that it was not the OAG investigation that caused me to retire but that the governor's office sought someone else for the post. During the months I was on pre-retirement leave, I considered those individuals I was fortunate to have worked with and who served as mentors.

Chapter 19 - Heroes, Mentors, and Friends

My expedition through the New York State Police would not have been possible without the help of heroes, mentors, and friends. This trek succeeded despite the efforts of those who stood against diversity, equity, and inclusion. I knew some of these folks, but many were unknown. This adventure was full of perils I needed to avoid and treasures I needed to gather. These mentors showed me the right pathway to avoid the inherent landmines, while those opposed to my membership in the NYSP either failed to point out these hazards or planted more. Trooper Richard Fisher was first among these welcoming officers, without whom I would not have made it through my first year as a trooper. Dick was righteous and honorable. He was, as mentioned, my "senior man," Field Training officer during my first thirty days as a rookie trooper. He quietly intervened to stop the microaggression I was experiencing during my training at SP Allegany when another trooper's idea of a "funny" play-on word sounded when dispatching me to a call for service. This trooper would use my middle name, Juan, which sounds like "one," Juan Zero Two Seven versus One Zero Two Seven. I knew I would face more micro-aggressive behaviors later, as I had while training with the SP Peekskill trooper. Trooper Fisher gave me good advice to paraphrase using a cliched civil rights mantra, but still valid: keep your eye on the prize.

Trooper Fisher was also right about my ability to drive on the rural roads of western New York. I had a half dozen troop car-deer accidents, and I lost a few vacation days as a penalty to pay for my error. I nearly lost several days after having crashed a brand-new police vehicle into several road signs to avoid "T-boning" an elderly woman who drove through a stop sign a T-intersection directly in front of me. I had seen the woman at the stop sign, and she looked at me when she suddenly pulled away from the stop sign and directly into my path. When Zone Sergeant McCole pulled up, his first comment was, "I hope you have vacation days saved up. It looks like you will lose some more." I told him it was not my fault. I asked him to please interview the elderly lady I did not T-bone by spiking the brakes and veering sharply to the right, striking some traffic control sign, like the stop sign she did not obey. The sergeant interviewed the woman, who acknowledged the accident was her fault. She said she had been going to her attorney's office to update her will and was distracted. For a while, I had the nickname "Perez, the deer slayer." Sergeant McCole was a no-nonsense supervisor who always treated me fairly and held me accountable for errors. After interviewing the woman, he marched over to me with a stern look as if he did not believe the story. Sergeant McCole stared at me for a very uncomfortable moment and then smiled. "You are one lucky son of a bitch," he said laughingly. Then McCole said it was ironic the woman was going to her attorney's office to rewrite her will. He suggested she make me one of her beneficiaries as I had nearly sacrificed my life for hers. He gave me a fatherly pat on my shoulder and said, "Now we have to convince the major not to punish you by taking vacation days away." "You did wreck a brand new Troop car."

The strange thing was that I had not noticed the plate number on it when I retrieved it from troop headquarters in Batavia, New York. It was the same plate number the obese trooper at SP Allegany used when he would dispatch calls for service to me: 1027, or as he would have said to annoy me, "Juan Zero Two Seven." I started laughing; that was the true irony of the event. The sergeant asked, "What the fuck are you laughing about?" I answered, "Nothing; I am just nervous and hope the 'old man' believes it was not my fault and lets me keep my vacation days." Perez, the deer slayer, became the destroyer of signs.

Charles McCole, Bruce Roloff, and several others were among the White troopers and supervisors I met who were incredibly generous mentors. They were among the culturally competent men and women in the state police who helped guide my career. They unflinchingly stood for integrity, and character was critical to being a good trooper. They moved past the societal and organizational systemic racism to promote diversity and inclusion. This help sometimes came from the agency's top leaders: for instance, several superintendents, like the late Thomas A. Constantine, James W. McMahon, and the late Harry J. Corbitt.

- Gov. Mario M. Cuomo appointed Thomas A. Constantine to be the tenth superintendent of the New York State Police on January. 2, 1987. He was the first superintendent in thirty years to rise through the ranks; he undertook a division-wide review of all NYSP operations and procedures.[421] He approved my first commission and several other promotions before he retired.
- On April 4, 1994 Governor Mario Cuomo appointed James W. McMahon as the 11th superintendent of the Division. On December. 28, 1994, Gov. George E. Pataki reappointed Superintendent McMahon to lead the state police; the Senate reconfirmed him on June 13, 1995.[422] He promoted me to major, inspector, and then lieutenant colonel-BCI.
- Harry J. Corbitt served twenty-five years with the New York State Police (NYSP) before his retirement in 2004. Governor David A. Paterson asked him to return to service as superintendent of the state police. He was confirmed by the NYS Senate and appointed on April 16, 2008.

Superintendent Corbitt was the first African American in the state police's history to hold the agency's highest rank.[423] He appointed me as the first deputy superintendent and Anthony Ellis as the colonel in charge of the Internal Affairs Bureau. This promotion also made history. I became the first Nuyorican to serve at this rank, and Tony became the third man of Color to serve as the chief inspector, a position that Harry Corbitt and I also held a few years earlier. He, Tony, and I broke the glass ceiling, creating the most diverse senior leadership in the history of the NYSP. Because so much had changed during the four years Harry was retired. I had broad experience in the BCI and was serving as the Field commander. He asked me to be more active in helping him lead the state police than other superintendents had of their first deputy. I was honored to serve in this role.

Ellis was a highly respected state police leader. During his tenure with the NYSP, he was assigned to the NY State Park Police as its interim leader to help clean up some inefficiencies and other internal problems this agency faced. I never got to be a park ranger, as I first hoped when I took what I thought was the Ranger's entrance exam. Tony, a peer mentor and a lifelong friend, became a top ranger between August 1999 and February 2003. Then, in December 2003, he was reassigned to the NY State Parole to correct some disciplinary issues within its ranks. Soon after returning to the Division, he became the chief inspector in 2008.

I must acknowledge that Superintendent Corbitt was the first fully appointed man of Color to serve as a major general in the Division. Still, he was not the first African American to lead the state police. Acting Superintendent (First Deputy Superintendent) Preston Felton was the first Black leader of the state police. The New York State Senate did not confirm Superintendent Felton. He held the rank of brigadier general until he retired before leaving the NYSP; Superintendent Felton appointed me as the Field commander (third highest position and third in the succession line for the superintendent post). This promotion cracked the glass ceiling, although it did not break. I, too, served as acting superintendent for the first time when Felton retired and then again when the late superintendent Corbitt retired.[424] Several other commissioned officers I worked for shared their social capital and helped me advance in my career.[425] I owe a profound gratitude to them because without these individuals, I would not have survived my first 18 months, let alone more than twenty-nine years in the police.

I thank the late Theodore "(Teddy")" Cook III.[426] Throughout my career in the state police, his mentorship allowed me to thrive in an agency that would not have hired me before he went from senior investigator to Technical Lieutenant - Affirmative action officer. During the height of the Civil Rights movement of the late 1960s, the state police recruited a few dozen African Americans and Latinos, hiring only fifteen or so from that group. Most did not stay, and the state police, for the next two decades or so, did not hire any men of Color. Yet, some men of Color hired back then remained on the job for decades. Two became commissioned officers whom I met at the academy. They became my mentors and were heroes to many of us.

In 1974, the New York State Police four women entered and graduated from the NYSP academy, and it was the first time in the history of the state police that women had successfully become troopers. Carol J. Johnston, Carol A. Desell, Maureen P. Gordinier, and Regina M. Robbins made history as the first women to complete the academy training.[427] The decision to hire women came in the wake of the "1974 Equality Act [that] proposed to amend the Civil Rights Act of 1964 to include prohibition of discrimination on the basis of sex, sexual orientation, and marital status in federally assisted programs, housing sales, rentals, financing, and brokerage services."[428] The Equality Act did not come to a vote in 1974. The U.S. House of Representatives did pass it in 2021, but not the Senate.[429] Change does not come easily. Consider the state police, established more than one hundred years ago because of the work of Katherine Mayo and Moyca Newell. They advocated for a state police force after the 1913 robbery and murder of Sam Howell, one of Newell's construction foremen in Westchester County, and the fact that the local police had no one under arrest, even though he had named them before his death. The state police was created four years later, in 1917.[430] Fifty-seven years later, the first four women troopers joined and graduated from the New York State Police Academy. It would take nearly four more years for the first Black female to enter and graduate from the NYSP academy, Pamela Sharpe. Judge Foley's mandate for all its limitations succeeded in bringing more women of Color, even though the percentage of women was only 10 percent, which did not reflect the number of women in New York. More than 150 police departments recently signed the thirty-by-thirty pledge, an effort affiliated with the New York University School of Law's Policing Project and the National Association of Women Law Enforcement Executives. By signing the thirty-by-thirty pledge, the state police aim to raise the percentage of female recruits to 30 percent by 2030. It also agrees to have bias-free policies, an inclusive culture, and promote equitable hiring.[431]

During my academy training session, Lieutenant John Heritage and Technical Lieutenant Theodore Cook III were African American commissioned officers, both making history as a result. Lieutenant Heritage taught NYSP Rules and Regulations. Heritage and Cook were among the original troopers of Color hired in the 1960s. He was one of eight men of Color represented by the U.S. Justice Department in the United States v. State of NY, 475 F. Supp. 1103 (N.D.N.Y 1979).[432] The court upheld his and two of the other plaintiffs' claims.

> "Of the eight individual claims, three are upheld. Having been found to have suffered discrimination, Timothy K. Roberts, a Binghamton police officer, is to be offered appointment as a trooper. trooper Lewis P. Steverson is to be offered appointment to the Bureau of Criminal Investigation (B.C.I.) of the New York State Police. John W. Herritage, [sic – Heritage], of the B.C.I. is to be offered a promotion to the position of Senior Investigator in the BCI."

In this decision, Judge Foley wrote:

> "to the objectives of this action, it is important to preliminarily note that all human beings are by nature free, equal and independent. When joined in a democratic society, they place a trust in their government to act for the public good. In this case, the public good is the benefits that flow from a state police force reasonably representative of the public it serves."[433]

Many police agencies have yet to achieve this goal, although Judge Foley thought the NYSP had and lifted his order; many believed it was a premature relief from his edict.[434] From that moment on, the state police slowly began to return to a point where it was again not "reasonably representative of the public it serves."[435] Superintendent Constantine wisely disagreed with the decision handed down by Judge Foley. He told New York Times reporter Philip S. Gutis:

> "The superintendent of the state police, Thomas Constantine, said he was disappointed that Judge Foley had not agreed to his request that the quotas for Black and Hispanic troopers be maintained but reduced to about 20 to 25 percent of each training class, from the 40 percent mandated in 1979. "It would have been an easier transition," Mr. Constantine said in a telephone interview."[436]

Superintendent Constantine in the same interview, said:

> "There is a tremendous benefit to having your police agency mirror society so that all parts of society feel that they are represented by the police force."[437]

According to the most recent data from the U.S. Census for New York State, 68.6 percent are White, 19.7 percent are Hispanic or Latino, 17.7 percent are Black or African American, and 9.6 percent are Asians. New Yorkers who claim two or more races are 2.8 percent, American Indians and Alaskans are 1 percent of New York, and Native Hawaiian and other Pacific Islanders are .01 percent of the state's population. Additionally, female persons are 51.1 percent of New York's population.[438] The New York State Division of Criminal Justice Services, as reported by Nydatabases.com, the state police ethnic and gender diversity as of 2020 was 67.5 percent White, followed by Black or African American 2.7 percent, Hispanics 3.6 percent, Asian/Pacific Islander 0.8, American Indian/Alaskan Native 0.2 and finally Unknown ethnicity 25.2 percent.[439] Finally, females are 18.7 percent of the members of the NYSP.[440] These numbers reflect the

New York State Police is not "reasonably representative of the public it serves." Why has this happened? What are we going to do about it?

Judge Foley's last decision allowed the Division to gradually become less diverse in the decades after he dropped the 50-40-10 hiring quota he imposed in 1979. Thirty-seven years later, in an Op-Ed commentary I wrote for the Albany Times Union, I expressed my concerns about the decreasing diversity within the ranks of the state police and the comments made by the retiring first counsel for the NYSP:

> "However, the comments made by the retiring first counsel for state police left me questioning what should be considered success. Thomas Capezza said his most memorable achievement was getting the agency out from under a consent decree that required it to change its exclusionary and discriminatory hiring practices, which severely limited the numbers of men of color and women in the state police. I view this "memorable achievement" not as one that should be lauded, but one that should raise concerns given the current state of affairs with police and the communities they serve."[441]

The June 1, 2021, Associated Press article, "Still on the farm: NY state police struggles to diversify." The acting superintendent said:

> "You can't just keep doing the same thing and expect different results," acting Superintendent Kevin Bruen said in an interview. "We patrol the state, so our ethnic breakdown should roughly mirror that. To say it's a priority for me would be an understatement."[442]

Sadly, changing this reality was what Theodore Cook, Harry Corbitt, Anthony Ellis, John Heritage, Pamela Sharpe, Arthur Taggart, and I hoped to accomplish. That goal remains, albeit it seems far off into the future; it is one of the reasons I embarked on telling our story. The stories of retired Investigator Michael Marin, retired trooper Lethonia Miller, and recently retired Senior Investigator Kim Bryson, all of whom are African American, are evidence of the continuing issues of bigotry within the agency. Their very recent experiences decry the unfulfilled promise of the current Division's Diversity Statement.[443]

> "Michael Marin, recalled a white colleague admonishing him in 2008 to "take the cotton you've been picking out your ears."

> "Lethonia Miller filed a complaint against a white supervisor for using racial slurs more than a dozen times in his presence. He said, "The culture in the state police was systemically racist."

> "Kim Bryson, a senior state police investigator on Long Island, provided AP a copy of an image a white colleague hung in her office. Superimposing her face on that of a Black woman at work in a kitchen, it was captioned "House of Chitlins" a reference to food scraps given to slaves.[444]

The state police must do more to become a diverse, inclusive, and welcoming agency. As a recruit, I worked to learn more about the state police. I sat in the academy's classroom listening to this courageous Black state police lieutenant. John Heritage had passed the arduous written examinations for the permanent ranks of sergeant and lieutenant. He served as our instructor for the rules and regulations course. He was a tall, handsome man who exuded confidence and a sense of defiance as he taught. The class was the first course we had to take: to study and memorize portions of the enormous administrative manual and the equally dense Field manual. Some years later, Senior Investigator Taggart, from Buffalo, told me that when Lieutenant Heritage was a trooper in Troop A, some White judges would not let him into their home offices for the after-hours arraignment of prisoners. Heritage had to endure constant instances of racist attitudes throughout his career.

Sadly, an apparent source of conflict between two of my mentors, Heritage and Cook, was the distinction between a "permanently" ranked commissioned officer and a "technical" commissioned officer. Rank in any military or paramilitary organization is highly significant. The difference between permanent ranks and technical ranks was also significant in the NYSP culture because each type of rank was also different in its perceived prestige. There was a visual difference in the rank insignia. The single bar on each shoulder pad of the uniform blouse or collar of a uniform shirt was light brass-colored for technical lieutenants; for permanently ranked lieutenants, the bar was silver-colored. A permanently ranked lieutenant had to be a permanently ranked sergeant who had successfully passed the sergeant's written exam, qualifying them for the lieutenant's promotional examination. There was also a requirement to have been at sergeant rank for at least two years, which often turned out to be four years because of exam schedules. A technical lieutenant, by contrast, did not have to have had the permanent designation of sergeant. To become a technical lieutenant, your tenure as a trooper played a role, and you needed an identified ability in a specialty. I explain this because Lieutenant Cook had been a highly skilled senior investigator, and part of this new job was investigating allegations of discrimination. However, he needed training, experience, or technical expertise in affirmative action issues, statutes, and law, which the Division did not provide. The entire organization assumed this technical lieutenant got promoted because of the accident of his birth as a Black man. The rest of the academy staff, from the commissioned officers to the cohort counselors, were White men except for two other African American troopers and two female troopers.

These hiring efforts affirmed that my decision to join this police force held the real potential of giving my family a chance to have a better life if I could survive the first six months and beyond. Frankly, I had no choice; it was a chance to succeed or for my family to stay in poverty and possibly end up homeless.

Chapter 20 - The Color of Law

While grateful for the opportunity this career path afforded my family and me, I had been unaware of some of the tragic history of policing in America. Since the very first days of policing in this nation, America has seen police departments and their practices go through cycle after cycle of inequality and inequity while at the same time striving to professionalize and become fairer. The history of policing is complex and often troubling. The Code of Hammurabi and Mosaic law are the first cornerstones of policing.[445] Peisistratus (605–527 BCE) created the first form of systemic policing. He established a guard system, a watchtower, and highways to protect himself.[446] Augustus Caesar (27 BCE) created the Praetorian Guard and "urban cohort."[447] Most textbooks on modern policing cite August Vollmer as the father of modern American policing.[448] Before Vollmer's influence, policing took two paths in US history, one in the northern states and another in the southern ones.

Policing in the South included, "Slave Patrols."[449] Some sources suggest the Carolinas started the first formal slave patrol in 1704. These patrols had three functions:

(1) to chase down, apprehend, and return to their owners, runaway slaves;
(2) to provide a form of organized terror to deter slave revolts; and
(3) to maintain a form of discipline for slave-workers who were subject to summary justice, outside of the law, if they violated any plantation rules.[450]

However, its origins are much earlier; an example of Slave Patrol's roots is in the story of John Punch. In 1640, an African and two other indentured servants, a Dutchman and a man of Scottish descent, ran away from the landowner who had contracted them, only to get caught days later. The Virginia judicial records show that all three indentured received thirty lashes each. The court extended Dutchman and Scot indentured servitude by four years. Tragically and mercenarily, it made John Punch's servitude last for the rest of his life, making Punch the first person subjected to life-long slavery as a judicial sentence for daring to seek freedom! The case also became the first time the alleged or convicted perpetrators' race was a factor in sentencing decisions. We now know how that evolved throughout this nation's criminal justice system.[451] It creates a flawed and generationally devasting legal foundation for lifetime servitude. It served as a cornerstone for other Virginia laws that followed, like the 1662 law that made "hereditary" slavery. In that case, an enslaved African woman raped by a White "Englishman" suffered an even more significant injury. The child born because of that crime inherited the mother's status as an enslaved person for life, like John Punch.[452] A few years later, in 1705, a newly enacted law declared all "non-Christian" servants brought to the colonies would automatically become enslaved persons.[453]

During Reconstruction after the Civil War, vigilante-style organizations evolved in Southern police departments to control formerly enslaved people working as sharecroppers. They also enforced "Jim Crow" segregation laws, denying the folks equal rights and access to the political system.[454]

Dr. Gary Potter, a professor at Eastern Kentucky University, remarks in his treatise on early policing in America:

> "Early American police departments shared two primary characteristics: they were notoriously corrupt and flagrantly brutal. This should come as no surprise in that police were under the control of local politicians. The local political party ward leader in most cities appointed the police executive in charge of the ward leader's neighborhood. The ward leader, also, most often was the neighborhood tavern owner, sometimes the neighborhood purveyor of gambling and prostitution, and usually the controlling influence

over neighborhood youth gangs who were used to get out the vote and intimidate opposition party voters. In this system of vice, organized violence, and political corruption it is inconceivable that the police could be anything but corrupt (Walker 1996). Police systematically took payoffs to allow illegal drinking, gambling, and prostitution. Police organized professional criminals, like thieves and pickpockets, trading immunity for bribes or information. They actively participated in vote-buying and ballot-box-stuffing. Loyal political operatives became police officers. They had no discernable qualifications for policing and little if any training in policing. Promotions within the police departments were sold, not earned. Police drank while on patrol, they protected their patron's vice operations, and they were quick to use peremptory force. Walker goes as far as to call municipal police "delegated vigilantes," entrusted with the power to use overwhelming force against the "dangerous classes" as a means of deterring criminality."[455]

The capture and return of escaped enslaved person have been part of the nation's ugly legacy since 1643, and even colonies like Maryland, New York, and Virginia have versions of this enforcement policy. The Fugitive Slave Act of 1793 and the strengthened version of 1850 further codified this act, requiring the northern states' law enforcement officials to turn captured enslaved persons back to states and enslaver they had fled.[456] In June 1864, Congress repealed the law.[457]

In the 1830s, police departments first appeared in the United States in the northern states. In 1838, Boston launched the first American police force, followed by New York City in 1845, Chicago in 1851, New Orleans and Cincinnati in 1853, Philadelphia in 1855,

Newark, New Jersey, and Baltimore in 1857. By the 1880s, all major U.S. cities had police forces in place.[458]

Police agencies did not behave as servants of all the people. Police often did not serve the poor, the disenfranchised, and the powerless. Today's examples are civilians' wrongful deaths, especially people of Color, at police officers' hands. Legitimate claims of police abusing their authority, particularly in poor neighborhoods and communities of Color, have often resulted in demands for reform. Some cities and their police department have reluctantly implemented these reforms but have soon forgotten them once the media and the community demanding these changes stopped paying attention. The failures of these efforts to comprehensively reform all police agencies across the decades have eroded community trust. There is a "legitimacy deficit."[459] This deficit is a major issue discussed in the "Final Report of the President's Task Force on 21st Century Policing."[460] I, too, experienced a lack of trust in police and generally felt the only validity police had depended on fear and intimidation. Although becoming a trooper was serendipitous, I decided to pursue this career, and despite the state police's history, I was determined to be a change agent. The first step was to decide how I would define my role as a law enforcement officer.

Once I joined the state police, I vowed to be a "Peace Officer" for social justice and not a "warrior" engaged in a war on crime. I understand and continue to recognize that individuals who violate the law must face just and effective prosecution. I fulfilled my duties as a police officer, vigorously enforcing the law. I did so while not forgetting where I came from and ensuring my continued commitment to social justice and equity. Doing this became increasingly difficult as I learned more about the structural inequities and discriminatory laws that negatively impacted communities of Color. Do I enforce those laws or not? I did the latter whenever possible and advocated to change those discriminatory laws or practices. I used discretion, as mentioned during the deer jacking incident involving a family experiencing the hardships of rural poverty. The father shot a deer out of season and at night because they were hungry. I had no desire to act like the Sheriff of Nottingham (i.e., protecting the "King's" deer while a family went hungry). I helped translate the "Miranda" warning into Spanish. I read the first version; I saw that the drafters used the Spanish word for interrogation, not realizing that in some South American countries, individuals subjected to police interrogation would be tortured or "disappeared" (killed). I suggested they use "entrevista" (interview) instead because it was less likely to cause fear and may elicit greater compliance during encounters with troopers, keeping both the officer and the detainee safe.

The struggle for social justice, the urgency of protecting communities of Color, and the need for those committed to protecting their fellow citizens' human rights began centuries ago. People who understand that someone must speak for those who cannot speak for themselves lead the struggle because the amplified speakers of the "system" trumpet the message of disconnection and hopelessness too loudly. The tragic staining of our nation by the blood of people not protected by their police and, worse, instances where the police were directly involved in atrocities. Slave patrols started this horrible history. We need only consider the following cases where either the police ignored the lynching of innocent people of Color and the destruction of entire communities or were involved. Many police departments and its officers enforcement of "Black Codes" and "Jim Crow Laws" in the 19th century.[461] The 1865 forced expulsion of Chinese people from California and the Pacific Northwest.[462] The 1921 Tulsa Race Massacre.[463] The forced displacement and internment of Japanese Americans during World War II.[464] Also consider the most recent wound to our body politic, the clearing of "Black Lives Matter" protestors from Lafayette Square, Washington, DC. January 6 demonstrates the difference between how people of Color were and are treated by some in law enforcement and how police engage White people.[465]

Police must, no, we all must defend those who often lack the skills, resources, or tools needed to safeguard themselves against the criminals who prey on them. Moreover, we must work to reverse institutional discrimination that has allowed the criminal justice system to treat poor people, marginalized groups, and their neighborhoods all too often abusively. We knowingly and willingly must be prepared to walk the gauntlet formed by those opposed to social justice. We cannot forget the courage and determination of the civil rights advocates who walked across the Edmund Pettus Bridge and the onslaught they faced from the police that awaited them on that "Bloody Sunday."[466] On that fateful day an infamous moment is capture by the news media of an Alabama State trooper severely injuring the late Congressman John Lewis as he engaged in, "Good Trouble," peacefully protesting on March 7, 1965.[467]

We must be ready to speak for and protect our neighbors who are disenfranchised, disconnected, and discriminated against in our society. We should reach deep into our communities and shine a light on the path out of despair and poverty. We must turn on our flashlights and help our young brothers and sisters get their lamps.

The United States again finds itself facing "civil disobedience" demonstrations, justifiable peaceful uprisings, and tragically violent riots because of its continued failure to fully actualize the promise of freedom, justice, equality, and equity for all the people living on this land. Our failure as a nation to bridge these gaps equitably, to dismantle the structural inequities built into our government, starting with our Constitution, albeit already amended for the better with the passage of the 13th, 14th, 15th, and 19th amendments. The Constitution is a powerful yet incomplete declaration of human rights for "We," the people, all the people. The drafters intentionally ignored the full expression of the phrase "We the People" proclaimed by this internationally cherished document. Proof of this deliberate marginalization in the terms used in section two of the Constitution, "excluding Indians not taxed" and "three-fifths of other Persons." John Adams ignored his wife, Abigail Adams's appeal, "Remember the Ladies;" women were also not recognized as citizens of this republic.[468]

Many Americans hoped the first bi-ethnic president's election in 2008 would move America to a "post-racial" era. We prayed that President Obama would reawaken and reinstitute Presidents Franklin Roosevelt's, John F. Kennedy's, and Johnson's policies and goals as they tried to help poor Americans and communities of Color. In recent surveys, Americans expressed a worsening of relations between the ever-growing population of Color and the shrinking White majority.[469] There are African Americans, Asians, Latinos, Indigenous people, and poor people who still fear and resent the police. They continue to suffer the abuse of power by some police officers and departments. Across the country, marginalized communities live in poverty with deleterious consequences in fear of criminals and the police who are supposed to protect them from those criminals. In cities like Ferguson, New York, Cleveland, Minneapolis, and many other locations across America, recent deaths of people of Color at police hands remind everyone that America has not resolved its racist legacy.

That is not to say there have not been improvements in "race relations" in the United States. Obama's election, the appointment of Eric Holder to U.S. attorney general, and the many other men and women of Color who have won high office in federal, state, and local government are significant facts. As President Obama rescued the nation from the Great Recession by bailing out the automobile industry and the Federal Reserve propped up some large investment banks, many communities of Color and poor people wondered when their rescue would arrive. However, the hope for progress in race relations and increased economic development in these communities was elusive and often illusory.[470]

The increased diversity of our government did not change the lives of many Black, Hispanic, or Indigenous people living with poverty, financial instability, and limited educational opportunities. They did not end the abuse of power by some police officers and departments. During President Obama's first term, there was a lack of sustainable economic improvement in poor communities. That, coupled with the continuing violations of fair policing, taints the heroic and compassionate work many of America's police officers perform every day, including those who have given their lives in the pursuit of justice. Let us not forget that most police officers run towards danger in response when criminals or terrorists engage in their unlawful actions. Consider the police actions during 9/11 or, more recently, on January 6, 2020. Nevertheless, these acts of heroism do not in any way excuse centuries-old wounds and current injuries still inflicted on Black, Brown, and Indigenous women and men caused by the unlawful, unjustifiable, and horrendous murders by some police officers across the nation. I stand with millions of Americans who deeply grieve the deaths of our neighbors killed by those sworn to protect anyone in their charge. Police reform is needed now more than ever before. We must continue to have an open dialogue about race and Color because it still matters![471]

We cannot allow our cultural, ethnic, political, and philosophical differences to continue to delay this emotionally charged conversation. We cannot allow those differences to prevent the enactment and enforcement of laws that are just and equitable. Our behavior as citizens, and the behavior we demand from our police, must stand on truth, justice, integrity, and equity, which then trumps our differences. We must find beauty and hope in our similarities, aspirations, and humanity. It is unnecessary to shed our individual and collective identities, cultures, and ethnicities to have this discussion. Nor should we think the delivery of justice means surrendering who we are to fulfill our duties as citizens of this nation. Our authentic selves and cultural uniqueness can remain intact during these challenging but necessary conversations.

As we search for solutions, many previously tried remedies will surface, such as cultural sensitivity training, better minority recruitment efforts, and stricter accountability of police and the criminal justice system. We should ban the death penalty because it is flawed in many ways. Moreover, we cannot reverse the outcome of death once the syringe, the bullet, the gas, and the electric current are applied.[472] Reports of severe suffering from the various methods administered in the death chamber appear to violate the Eighth Amendment, which prohibits cruel and unusual punishments. Consider two botched executions in Oklahoma that used lethal injections. Clayton D Lockett in 2014 and John Marion Grant in 2021, convicted of murder, died in agony after the medical cocktail allegedly created to provide a more humane death. Grant and Lockett: Grant killed a prison cafeteria worker, and Lockett shot a nineteen-year-old woman and buried her alive.[473]

Furthermore, because of systemic racism and class bias embedded in the process, the death penalty is inequitably applied. African

Americans compose 42 percent of inmates on death row and 34 percent of those executed, while they are only 13 percent of the U.S. population. Seventy-five percent of executions were in cases with White victims. In states like Georgia, people convicted of killing White victims are seventeen times more likely to be executed than those convicted of murdering Black victims. Additionally, mental health experts estimate that at least 20 percent of the inmates on death row have a severe mental illness. The inequity in administering the death penalty also exists for poor people. Those who cannot afford an effective lawyer are often appointed one who is underpaid, overworked, and inexperienced in death penalty cases.[474] Let us not forget these tragic and unjust systems; we must act to end these practices because history tells us that America's attention will drift away from this crisis to another.

Upon colonization of the Americas, many Europeans ignored the genocide of the aboriginal people, and the destruction of their culture and societies remained silent. Many stayed silent as slavery expanded from Jamestown, Virginia, to other states and territories within the United States. When Presidents accepted the idea of "Manifest Destiny," essentially that God ordained its expansion from sea to sea, they forcibly displaced or, far worse, killed Indigenous people to secure more land.[475] For years, many White citizens remained silent in the face of police brutality inflicted on their fellow Black, Brown, Asian, and Indigenous citizens because it was not happening in their communities. When convicted former police officer Derek Chauvin murdered George Floyd, the police officers at the scene said and did nothing. We must end this silence to have a more just and "perfect union."

Consider the poem:

> First they came for the Communists
> And I did not speak out
> Because I was not a Communist
> Then they came for the Socialists
> And I did not speak out
> Because I was not a Socialist

Then they came for the trade unionists
And I did not speak out
Because I was not a trade unionist
Then they came for the Jews
And I did not speak out
Because I was not a Jew
Then they came for me
And there was no one left
To speak out for me.
Martin Niemöller, German Protestant Pastor,
1892 – 1984 [476]

In the George Floyd case it was the courageous act of a Black female teenager who videoed the horrendous tragedy to awaken citizens of this nation and around the world. We need more acts of courage and resistance to racist police and systemic racist policing policies. Speaking out is not enough; we must use the power of our franchise to vote for lasting change. Courageous citizens videoing police does not diminish the devastating impact of police abuse on the individuals, their families, and the communities who are the victims of this abuse of power by bad policing and structural inequities deeply rooted in America's law enforcement policies and procedures. We also need government officials who agree to stop police from abusing their powers, who will prosecute them when appropriate, and who are committed to social justice.

The anguish, grief, and fear experienced by the victims of unlawful police violence because of the centuries African Americans, Latinx, Native Americans, and other marginalized communities have suffered because of these abuses of authority. There must be zero tolerance for police abuse of power. Like all US citizens, police are not above the law, and the people they serve are not below the law.[477] Yet, for hundreds of years, only a few police were held accountable or prosecuted for their criminal behavior. Consider the analysis of a collaborative research project, "Mapping Police Violence." They reported that "97% of people killed by police in 2021 were killed by police shootings."[478]

When the police have violated our constitutional rights of the presumption of innocence and due process by acting as judge, jury, and executioner, we must hold them accountable, appropriately prosecuted, and sentenced accordingly. We also need to understand the impact of qualified immunity on police and other governmental officials. Often misunderstood, qualified immunity is a judicial doctrine that arose out of the Ku Klux Klan Act of 1871 to address the surge of racial violence during Reconstruction. When White vigilante groups, including the Ku Klux Klan, were viciously attacking freed Black Americans and any White citizens aiding them. This policy occurred when law enforcement officials did not merely ignore but, at times, were actively participating in the violence.[479] This decree provided the federal right to the victims of racial violence to sue state and local governments for violating their newly enacted Constitutional rights of the Fourteenth Amendment.[480] The Supreme Court, through a series of decisions starting in 1961, expanded it to protect government officials, including police, from lawsuits brought against them under different standards, like the notion of "good faith." Was the officer acting under the "color of law," or would a "reasonable officer" view the constitutional violation as a "clearly established" doctrine?[481] Some argue that Qualified immunity is essential to keep police from becoming bankrupt, keep police morale high, and protect recruitment efforts by police departments. On the other side of the argument concerning this doctrine, some see these reasons as an attempt to avoid accountability. In her book, "Shielded," law professor Joanna Schwartz at the University of California, Los Angeles, examines how our legal system protects police, regardless of the outcomes, with insightful analyses about subjects ranging from qualified immunity to no-knock warrants. She reveals how a law initially intended to protect African Americans freed from slavery during the Jim Crow era turned into a weapon wielded against all of us.[482]

This abuse of immunity protection has begun to change because of the "Black Lives Matter" movement. It is shown most poignantly in 2021 by the conviction of former police officer Derek Chauvin for the murder of George Floyd.[483] Slowly, painfully slowly, the pace of holding police officers accountable for their murderous actions has begun to speed up. In 2021, there are about 725,000 sworn law enforcement officers in the United States.[484] In 2019, there were 55,800,880 police encounters with American citizens, while many of these encounters were managed fairly and professionally by the police.[485] Far too many have ended with officers abusing their authority, sometimes with deadly results. Between 2005 and 2020, according to a report published this year by Statista Research Department, of the 42 nonfederal police officers convicted following their arrest for murder due to an on-duty shooting, five received a conviction of murder. Yet, the most common lower offense of manslaughter occurred in the 11 officer convictions.[486] A vastly different outcome occurred in the Derek Chauvin case; a guilty verdict on all the criminal charges was rendered, including the most serious for murder in the second degree.

This deadly abuse of the authority we grant police officers must end. We need a justice system that is just for all people inside our borders. Indeed, we may not be able to eradicate accidental police shootings. Still, we can do a much better job of preventing unlawful police shootings of our citizens through proper recruitment, training, and stricter accountability. Police in the US shoot and kill more people of Color than they do White citizens.

In a report by Prison Policy Initiative titled "Not just "a few bad apples": U.S. police kill civilians at much higher rates than other countries." Their analysis is that police shootings of civilians in the US are not random or accidental. They are a systemic problem that happens on a scale far more significant than that of other wealthy nations.[487] Police in the United States kill more civilians than any of the European countries and Japan.

Far too many get it wrong in the current militarized police culture and its ensuing practices. Part of the problem is that most police agencies model their structure and behavior on the military. While no one wants this, the military leaders understand there are acceptable casualties in combat. One crucial objective in war is to have fewer casualties than the enemy. While commanders, and most importantly, soldiers, want to come home alive and in one piece, all know some will not. In police work, though, there is no acceptable level of casualty. All police officers expect to get home at the end of their tour. This reality may cause some officers to rush to judgment when they feel the individual they are engaging is a deadly threat to the officer or a third person, actual or imagined. Taint those fears with an implicit or explicit bias toward the person police are supposed to serve, and the outcome is almost assured to be fatal.

A neutral third party must conduct a thorough analysis of the militarization of policing to figure out which agencies need the equipment and tactics and which do not. What should also change is how police departments recruit, evaluate background investigations, and select and train both initial and in-service officers to ensure their reason for joining and remaining on the force is not about aggrandizement and power. Instead, hire and retain individuals who honestly believe in serving their community equitably, serving with compassion and without biases inherent in some law enforcement officers.[488] Another concern regarding the militarization of policing is armies have enemies; police must not view the people they serve as their enemies. Moreover, consider what can happen when the police culture of a particular department labels a community as the enemy. It heightens the possibility of using deadly physical force when de-escalation and less force are the more appropriate responses. Add to this the increasing number of White supremacists and far-right militants joining police departments over the past eighteen years, as predicted by scholars and the FBI.[489]

Of course, concerning deadly force, police are human. The hardest thing to do when threatened or engaged in a firefight or when they believe their lives are in jeopardy is not to emotionally respond to the person threatening them as their enemy.[490] Police using military equipment and tactics are necessary when criminals or terrorists use these weapons and tactics to complete their criminal or terroristic enterprise. Ordinary citizens, common criminals, and others are not the enemy; they are our fellow citizens. When police view them as the enemy, it has led to tragic and wrongful deaths. Eliminating this misperception caused by the incorrect modeling of military culture is a significant aspect of the systemic changes needed within law enforcement.

However, those looking to reform policing who propose demilitarization by restricting or removing equipment or tactics are misguided. Small rural police agencies may not need armored personnel vehicles, SWAT, or other military-type equipment, but larger metropolitan police departments need these capabilities. Police agencies, from their start, have used the military's structure, ranking hierarchy, and tactics. The New York State Police is an example of this, and its founder based the New York State Troopers on the US Army Manual.

Most police departments around the world also model themselves after the military. Again, the militarization of police is concerning. The solution to this complex situation is ensuring departmental leadership has fully vetted the need for this equipment and decides how, why, and when to deploy this equipment and tactics. Are their officers sufficiently trained in the use of these? An essential aspect of the solution is recruitment practices. It is time for an impartial commission, like the International Association of Chiefs of Police and the various other police associations, to investigate the recruitment practices of police departments as was done by the Justice Department concerning the NYSP discriminatory hiring practices. Another review should consider looking at weeding out White supremacists, racists, misogynists, or individuals who are simply looking for the power and prestige associated with the job.

We can change how and why we recruit police candidates. Most policing agencies' web pages and recruitment materials feature police officers holding high-powered military weapons, helicopters, and K9 officers, focusing on the para-military action segments of policing. New Zealand's analysis of how they were perceived by the community, particularly by the Indigenous Māori, Pasifika people, and women, made them change their recruitment strategy.[491] They embarked on a very sophisticated, progressive, service-based recruitment campaign that focused on the community service aspect of policing. They used actual officers, ensuring these officers reflected the diversity of New Zealand's population. They minimized the para-military part of policing. Their initiative was quite successful:

- Thirty percent increase in applications.
- Forty-one percent of applications were female.

- Forty-five percent of applications were Maori/Pacific Islanders.
- One hundred percent increase in number of people who believe "care" is a trait NZ Police are looking for in candidate police officers.
- Application targets exceeded by more than 60 percent.
- About 51 Million views across social media globally.
- Eighty-three percent new applications were Female, Maori, Asian, and Pasifika.
- About 65.5 percent of applications were eighteen to twenty-nine years old.[492]

I cannot entirely agree with the premise of a "broken" criminal justice system. No, it works as intended when considering its history and purpose. Yet again, consider the purpose of Slave Patrols and what Dr. Gary Potter, professor at Eastern Kentucky University, stated in his treatise on early American policing:

> "By the end of 19th century municipal police departments were firmly entrenched in the day-to-day political affairs of big-city political machines. Police provided services and assistance to political allies of the machine and harassed, arrested, and interfered with the political activities of machine opponents. This was a curious dichotomy for an ostensibly crime-controlled organization. Political machines at the turn of the century, were in fact the primary modality through which crime was organized in urban areas. Politicians ran or supervised gambling, prostitution, drug distribution and racketeering. In fact, organized crime and the dominant political parties of American cities were one in the same. Politicians also employed and protected the many white-youth gangs that roamed the cities, using them to intimidate opponents, to get

out the vote (by force if necessary), and to extort "political contributions" from local businesses. At the dawn of the 20th century, police were, at least de facto, acting as the enforcement arm of organized crime in virtually every big city."[493]

We need meaningful reform, not its abolition or de-funding. We can divert some of its funding to pay professional civilian first responders to help police with nonviolent offenses and incidents arising from mental health issues, drug addiction, or homelessness. Several states are implementing this strategy.[494]

I recommend the US Justice Department, the International Association of Chiefs of Police (IACP), and various other police associations include psychological evaluations and integrity tests in their in-service training sessions to determine the mental and emotional fitness of police officers. These tests should also include police leaders. Criminal justice training should also consist of "Adverse Childhood Experiences" (ACES), "Trauma-Informed Care" (TIC), and "Implicit Bias" (IMB) during the police officers, correction officials, and prosecutors careers.

TIC and its related phenomena, "Vicarious Trauma (VT)" and "Traumatic Stress (TS)," must be part of a comprehensive organizational approach to keep the police department and its officers healthy.[495] TIC will help agencies and their officers understand trauma and its effect on crime victims, alleged perpetrators, and investigating officers. It will build community trust, facilitating investigations and potentially reducing repeated criminality by enlisting a community's cooperation. It will help ensure traumatized individuals get community services and mental health support. Had I known these, I may have been better able to address the trauma of the woman who lost her daughter because of the milk truck fatal accident and handle "VT's" impact on me (I still tear up when I remember this case.) It may have reduced the amount of "TS" I accumulated. Suppose I had received training in coping and healing self-care techniques. In that case, I might have been able to handle the post-traumatic stress I experienced while watching the unlawful attacks on the Capital

Police during the January 6 riots. This event reminded me of the 1992 and 1997 tax protest riots I lived through.[496]

More importantly, for many police officers, their families, and society, implementing these healing strategies may reduce the tragically high rate of suicides among police officers. According to the Police Executive Research Forum, more police die by suicide than feloniously or accidentally.[497] In a heartbreaking, albeit sadly understandable, application of respecting privacy or downright shame, USA Today reported in an article published on October 14, 2021, "4 police died by suicide after the Capitol riot; it's the reason their names won't be memorialized."[498] Should these deaths be considered line-of-duty deaths and honored as such? While more data and analysis are needed, many, as I do, argue yes![499]

In addition, these training programs should be part of in-service for the criminal justice system and departmental leadership teams. Several police departments in New York State have implemented implicit bias training for their officers. In 2016, the city of Albany, New York, began implicit bias for its officers, embarked on a communitywide conversation about this training, and offered the training to community members interested in receiving this training.[500] I attended several of these sessions in Albany as part of Albany's Mayor's Ad Hoc Equity Task Force. In 2018, New York City's police department also began implicit training for its officers. While its efficacy in changing behavior is still undetermined, it is a significant effort to create more unbiased policing.[501]

Understanding the importance of mental health, ACES, and TIC in policing compelled the IACP in 2019 to recommend all police departments consider training their officers in these practices. The IACP, in their publication "The Police Chief," authored an article titled "Increasing Empathy Through Trauma-Informed Policing." The authors of the paper were not naïve in making the recommendations that by using ACERS and TIC, officers might become more empathic to the people they serve:

> "For some in law enforcement, transitioning
> from traditional law enforcement responses to

using a trauma-responsive lens will be a significant shift, but infusing greater empathy in police
settings will allow the profession to reap the benefits experienced in multiple other settings such
as healthcare and education."[502]

I also recommend police departments do what the Federal
Aviation Administration (FAA) requires pilots to undergo Aviation
Medical Examiner (AME) tests every six or twelve months, depending on the pilot's age, which includes questions regarding mental
fitness.[503] The Department of Justice should consider creating a
national database to standardize and track police disciplinary action
and termination of police officers. So departments looking to hire
officers can refer to this data when conducting background checks
on potential candidates.

I also agree with the recommendations offered by Richard
Meadow in an article he wrote for the Police Brutality Center:

- To reduce fatal police encounters and increase public safety,
  Congress and all 50 states should pass police reform bills to
  provide the following interventions:
  œ Improve use of force standards, including rules man-
     dating when law enforcement officers can and cannot
     use deadly force
  œ Collect and publish detailed data on officer arrests, use
     of force injuries and deaths, and racial bias data during
     police stops
  œ Ensure independent and transparent investigations
     into all cases of excessive force and severe misconduct
     to ensure that officers are held accountable for their
     actions
  œ License and track "wandering officers" to prevent
     agencies from hiring officers dismissed for misconduct
     by other agencies[504]

We can increase the criminal justice system's diversity and inclusiveness. Ensuring police agencies, prosecutorial entities, the judicial system, and correctional institutions reflect America's diversity. Yet the jury is still out regarding whether having more African Americans, Hispanics, Native Americans, Asians, and other representatives from marginalized communities will reduce police abuses.[505] An article by NBC News reported on a scientific review conducted involving the Chicago Police Department called "The role of officer race and gender in police-civilian interactions in Chicago."[506] Regina Russell, co-chair at the Chicago Alliance Against Racist and Political Repression said this:

> "It was exciting to watch this demographic shift happen in real-time. However, she said, 'Just increasing diversity isn't going to fix this…' She and other local activists want to see more body cameras, community oversight of police, stringent use of force policies and more consequences for police officers who do harm while on the job."

Others, like Erika Maye, a senior leader for the nonprofit civil rights organization "Color of Change," say pushes for diversity are a misstep. "They don't go deep enough or tackle the root issues," she said. "Police violence is not an issue of representation."[507]

Consider the unjustified and illegal brutal murder of a Memphis motorist that occurred on the evening of January 7, 2023. Five African American police officers killed a Black motorist.[508]

There are numerous studies on both sides of this issue. Yet, most of these reviews adhere to the premise that the diversity of a police department enhances community policing, and some go as far as to say that diversity leads to empathic policing. Another article by Mark B. Baer, Esq., published in Psychology Today: "Police Officer

Diversity Status Impacts Their Perceptions -Whether a police officer falls within the dominant culture impacts perspective." He asserted:

> "Empathy can be a transformative tool for deconstructing unconscious biases and building understanding between people of different backgrounds. What does diversity within the police force have to do in that regard? "Integration and assimilation are very positive things because they enable people to see other perspectives, which is the core of empathy." Furthermore, "empathy is an amazing form of bias reduction and in keeping your biases in check."[509]

I feel, as many do, including the International Association of Police Chiefs, that the system needs to increase its diversity to reflect our community, knowing it is only one of the many steps we need to take to make policing fairer for all citizens, particularly in marginalized communities.[510] We should add de-escalation training and tactics to the tool chests police can employ before reaching for tasers or their sidearm.[511] Another training source to enhance de-escalation techniques and tactics is "aha–Process's Tactical Communication for First Responders."[512]

American citizens, all of us, need a criminal justice system that is fair, professional, and committed to serving their communities with integrity. We need to examine our existing laws, governmental rules, and regulations and those proposed to ensure they are morally just. We must ensure officers are not placed in untenable positions enforcing unjust laws or, because of laws like "Jim Crow" laws and other more recent unjust statutes.[513] I hope my journey has shed some light on the challenge of lifting oneself out of poverty. And how police can either play a positive role in that endeavor or continue to be the lethal arm of oppression. I pray for the former, will speak out, and take whatever legal action I can against the latter. "Protect and Serve" should mean just that!

We face a dilemma regarding the motto "Protect & Serve," in a 2005 Supreme Court case—Castle Rock v. Gonzales, No. 04-278, a domestic violence case, the court ruled, "The police did not have a constitutional duty to protect a person from harm, even a woman who had obtained a court-issued protective order against a violent husband making an arrest mandatory for a violation."[514] In another case, this one involving the horrendous massacre on February 14, 2018, at Marjory Stoneman Douglas High School in Parkland, Florida, the judge decided:

> "Broward County Circuit Judge Patti Englander Henning disagreed, ruling that Peterson—on duty as the school's resource officer—had a duty to protect the students inside Marjory Stoneman Douglas High School instead of cowering out-side the building while 34 were shot, 17 of whom died."[515]

In another article by Eric P. Daigle and Steve "Pappy" Papenfuhs for Police-1, they wrote:

> "The so-called public duty doctrine provides that absent a special relationship between the govern-mental entity and the injured individual, the governmental entity will not be liable for injury to an individual… the governmental entity owes a duty to the public in general. The doctrine has been commonly described by the oxymoron, 'duty to all, duty to none."[516]

They added:

> "Law enforcement personnel are moral and hon-orable public servants. Most sworn officers take their oaths of office as a solemn pledge - a pledge to safeguard life and property. Officers lose their

lives every day attempting to fulfill this oath. Officers, however, often put themselves at risk because they incorrectly believe that they have a duty to act when, in fact, no such duty exists. Officers must balance the pros and cons of acting against the rights, responsibilities, and the limitations of the profession imposed upon them by the Constitution, statute, and case law."[517]

Notwithstanding this legal opinion, I sincerely believed in the solemn oath and the duty to protect and serve throughout my career. I still do.

At the end of my career, I gathered my memorabilia and thought about what I had accomplished. Had I made a difference? My immediate and extended family were no longer in poverty. I had managed to address instances of racism, like the infamous road in Allegany County, racism in Wellsville's school system, and changing the language on the Miranda card the state police used. In cases I handled, I treated suspects and those I arrested the way I would have wanted my mother treated fairly and with as much dignity as the ignominious situation would allow. During the crack cocaine crisis in the 1990s, I ensured the investigations focused on the violent narco-traffickers. I did my best to treat my Indigenous cousins fairly, even when their rightful protests turned into violent riots. I did not use the horrendous tactics suggested by a colonel during the tax protests. While the work to diversify the NYSP and other departments remains incomplete, I will continue to advocate for it. I walked out the doors of the state police headquarters, proud of what I had done and with my head held high.

Today, I am deeply grateful to my former colleagues and current officers on the streets for serving with honor and integrity.

Thank you for your service!

Notes

Title

1   Wilfred Guerron, CHARAS and The Reimagination of Loisaida, https://www.latinxproject.nyu.edu/intervenxions/charas-and-the-reimagination-of-loisaida, October 13, 2020, accessed December 31, 2023

Prologue

2   The Seneca Nation of Indians, (website), (n.d.), hppts://sni.org/, accessed July 5, 2016.

3   "Tax War between New York State, Indians Heats up, Blocks Traffic," Los Angeles Times, https://www.latimes.com/archives/la-xpm-1992-07-17-mn-3500-story.html, accessed July 5, 2016.

4   Pedro Perez, Personal Files, accessed July 5, 2016.

5   "The Rise and Fall of Jim Crow," Thirteen.org, hppts://www.thirteen.org/wnet/jimcrow/, accessed July 5, 2016.

6   John Creamer, "Inequalities Persist despite Decline in Poverty for All Major Race and Hispanic Origin Groups," U.S. Census Bureau, hppts://www.census.gov/library/stories/2020/09/poverty-rates-for-blacks-and-hispanics-reached-historic-lows-in-2019.html, accessed April 27, 2021.

7   Chairman Alan Greenspan, "Chairman Alan Greenspan's Speech at the Federal Reserve Bank of Kansas City's Annual Symposium, Jackson Hole, Wyoming," Federal Reserve, August 28, 1998, hppts://www.federalreserve.gov/boarddocs/speeches/1998/19980828.htm, accessed April 27, 2021.

8   "Mission and Values," New York State Police, hppts://troopers.ny.gov/mission-and-values, accessed November 17, 2023.

9   Monnica T. Williams, "Colorblind Ideology Is a Form of Racism," Psychology Today, December 27, 2011, hppts://www.psychologytoday.com/us/blog/culturally-speaking/201112/colorblind-ideology-is-form-racism, accessed July 5, 2020.

10   Ibid.

11   Bruce Jackson, "ATTICA: An Anniversary of Death," September 9, 1999, hppts://www.acsu.buffalo.edu/~bjackson/attica.htm, accessed June 6, 2016.

[12] Attica, The Movie, https://www.imdb.com/title/tt12482898/?ref =ext_shr_lnk, accessed December 22, 2023.

[13] David R. Roediger, Working Toward Whiteness: How America's Immigrants Became White: The Strange Journey from Ellis Island to the Suburbs (New York: Basic Books, 2018), hppts://www.harvard.com/book/working_toward_whiteness_how_americas_immigrants_became_white_the_strange_j/, accessed June 6, 2016.

[14] Christopher Munsey, "But Not All Americans Benefited Equally," Monitor on Psychology, no. 10 (November 2010): 57, hppts://www.apa.org/monitor/2010/11/gi-bill.aspx, accessed June 17, 2016.

[15] "#The4thBox Resources," Center for Story-based Strategy, hppts://www.storybasedstrategy.org/the4thbox-resources, accessed June 18, 2016.

[16] Ibid.

Use of Terminology

[17] Kamala Kelkar, "How a Shifting Definition of 'White' Helped Shape U.S. Immigration Policy," PBS NewsHour, hppts://www.pbs.org/newshour/nation/white-u-s-immigration-policy, accessed March 16, 2020.

[18] "Race Is Not Genetic," Understanding Race hppts://understandingrace.org/race-is-not-genetic/, accessed June 18, 2016.

[19] Patrick Zylberman, "Marius Turda and Paul J Weindling (Eds), Blood and Homeland: Eugenics and Racial Nationalism in Central and Southeast Europe, 1900–1940, Budapest and New York, Central European University Press, 2007, Pp. Ix, 467, £13.95 (Paperback 978-963-7326-81-3).," Medical History 53, no. 2 (April, 2009): 294–95, https://doi.org/10.1017/s0025727300003689, accessed March 16, 2020.

[20] "Human Variation," Understanding Race, hppts://www.understandingrace.org/resources/glossary.html#humanvariation, accessed March 16, 2020.

[21] "Eugenics And Physical Anthropology (1890-1930)," Understanding Race, https://understandingrace.org/history/science/eugenics-and-physical-anthropology-1890-1930/, accessed March 16, 2020.

[22] Marcus L. Martin et al., "Report to President Teresa A. Sullivan," University of Virginia, 2018, hppts://slavery.virginia.edu/wp-content/uploads/2021/03/PCSU-Report-FINAL_July-2018.pdf, accessed July 11, 2020.

23 Marcus L. Martin et al., "Report to President Teresa A. Sullivan," University of Virginia, 2018, hppts://www.tjheritage.org/jefferson-and-slavery, accessed July 11, 2020.

24 Fessenden, "Thomas Jefferson Conducted Early Smallpox Vaccine Trials," Smithsonian Magazine, February 4, 2015, hppts://www.smithsonianmag. com/smart-news/thomas-jefferson-conducted-early-smallpox-vaccine-trials-180954146/, accessed July 11, 2020.

25 "Thomas Jefferson's List of Slave Vaccinations, April–May 1816," Founders Online, hppts://founders.archives.gov/documents/Jefferson/03-09-02-0482, accessed July 11, 2020.

26 History.com Editors, "Sally Hemings," History, January 28, 2010, hppts:// www.history.com/topics/slavery/sally-hemings, accessed July 11, 2020.

27 "George Washington's Will," George Washington's Mount Vernon, hppts:// www.mountvernon.org/library/digitalhistory/digital-encyclopedia/article/ george-washington-s-will/, accessed July 11, 2020.

28 Maureen Corrigan, "'Master' Jefferson: Defender of Liberty, Then Slavery," WPRL, hppts://www.wprl.org/2012-10-18/master-jefferson-defender-of-liberty-then-slavery, accessed July 11, 2020.

29 Yohuru Williams, "Why Thomas Jefferson's Anti-Slavery Passage Was Removed from the Declaration of Independence," History, June 29, 2020, hppts://www. history.com/news/declaration-of-independence-deleted-anti-slavery-clause-jefferson, accessed July 11, 2020.

30 Dave Benner, "Jefferson and the Barbary Pirates," Abbeville Institute, January 26, 2016, hppts://www.abbevilleinstitute.org/jefferson-and-the-barbary-pirates/, accessed July 11, 2020.

31 "The United States and the Haitian Revolution, 1791–1804," Office of the Historian, hppts://history.state.gov/milestones/1784-1800/haitian-rev, accessed July 11, 2020.

32 Thomas Jefferson Heritage Society, "Jefferson and Slavery." hppts://www. tjheritage.org/jefferson-and-slavery, accessed July 11, 2020.

33 Me Too. Movement, hppts://metoomvmt.org/, accessed July 11, 2020.

34 "Black Lives Matter Announces Support for The People's Response Act," Black Lives Matter, hppts://blacklivesmatter.com/news/, accessed July 11, 2020.

35 Lydia Millet, "Native Lives Matter, Too," The New York Times, October 13, 2015, hppts://www.nytimes.com/2015/10/13/opinion/native-lives-matter-too.html, accessed July 11, 2020.

[36] Elise Hansen, "The Forgotten Minority in Police Shootings," CNN, November 13, 2017, hppts://www.cnn.com/2017/11/10/us/native-lives-matter/index.html, accessed July 11, 2020.

[37] Ibid.

[38] Who Is Most At Risk For Police Violence? Kera news, Lisa Dunn, August 6, 2020 https://www.keranews.org/2020-08-06/who-is-most-at-risk-for-police-violence, accessed August 11, 2020.

[39] Pamela Paul, "Reflections on Stephen L. Carter's 1991 Book, 'Reflections of an Affirmative Action Baby,'" The New York Times, May 25, 2023 hppts://www.nytimes.com/2023/05/25/opinion/columnists/affirmative-action-stephen-carter.html, accessed May 26, 2023.

[40] Lori L. Tharps. "The difference between racism and colorism.", Time, October 6, 2016, hppts://time.com/4512430/colorism-in-america/, accessed July 8, 2020.

[41] Alan H. Goodman, Yolanda T. Moses, and Joseph L. Jones, "Histories of Race, Difference, and Racism," in Race: Are We So Different?, ed. Alan H. Goodman, Yolanda T. Moses and Joseph L. Jones (London: John Wiley & Sons, Ltd, 2012), hppts://onlinelibrary.wiley.com/doi/abs/10.1002/9781118233023.part1, accessed July 11, 2020.

[42] Samara Lynn, "Controversial Group ADOS Divides Black Americans in Fight for Economic Equality," ABC News, January 19, 2020, hppts://abcnews.go.com/US/controversial-group-ados-divides-black-americans-fight-economic/story?id=66832680, accessed April 2, 2021.

[43] Rachelle Hampton, "'People of Color' Was Once a Sign of Respect. But It's Becoming a Cop-out for the Powerful.," Slate, February 13, 2019, hppts://slate.com/human-interest/2019/02/people-of-color-phrase-history-racism.html, accessed May 11, 2019.

[44] N. Jamiyla Chisholm, "What's the Right Term: POC, BIPOC, or Neither?," YES! Magazine, October 8, 2020, hppts://www.yesmagazine.org/social-justice/2020/10/08/poc-bipoc-or-neither, accessed October 10, 2020.

[45] Ibid.

[46] "Martin Luther King, Jr.," National Archives, last reviewed February 2, 2022, hppts://www.archives.gov/nyc/exhibit/mlk, accessed August 6, 2022.

[47] Leah Asmelash, "Just 4% of Hispanic or Latino People Prefer the Term 'Latinx,' New Gallup Poll Finds," CNN, August 5, 2021, hppts://www.cnn.com/2021/08/05/us/Latinx-gallup-poll-preference-trnd/index.html, accessed August 7, 2022.

48 Edward Schumacher-Matos, "On Race: The Relevance of Saying 'Minority,'" NPR, August 29, 2011, hppts://www.npr.org/sections/ombudsman/2011/08/29/140040441/covering-race-considering-journalists-use-of-minority, accessed May 2, 2016.

49 Jonathan Vespa, David M. Armstrong, and Lauren Medina, "Demographic Turning Points for the United States: Population Projections for 2020 to 2060," US Census Bureau, February 2020, hppts://www.census.gov/library/publications/2020/demo/p25-1144.html, accessed September 22, 2022.

50 Robert B. Porter. "Building a New Longhouse: The Case for Government Reform within the Six Nations of the Haudenosaunee", Buffalo Law Review 46, no. 3 (1998): 805–945, hppts://digitalcommons.law.buffalo.edu/buffalolawreview/vol46/iss3/6/, accessed September 22, 2022.

51 History.com Editors, "Christopher Columbus," History, November 9, 2009, hppts://www.history.com/topics/exploration/christopher-columbus, accessed August 24, 2022.

52 Michael Isikoff and Sharon LaFraniere, "FBI Settles Black Agents' Discrimination Charges," Washington Post, January 27, 1993, hppts://www.washingtonpost.com/archive/politics/1993/01/27/fbi-settles-black-agents-discrimination-charges/a7843576-35af-47fe-b5a4-7c4cf13d347d/, accessed December 12, 2020.

53 Sam Briger, "Documentary Exposes How the FBI Tried to Destroy MLK with Wiretaps, Blackmail," NPR, January 18, 2021, hppts://www.npr.org/2021/01/18/956741992/documentary-exposes-how-the-fbi-tried-to-destroy-mlk-with-wiretaps-blackmail, accessed September 27, 2022.

54 United States v. State of NY, 475 F. Supp. 1103 (N.D.N.Y 1979), https://law.justia.com/cases/federal/district-courts/FSupp/475/1103/1688027/, accessed April 216, 2016.

55 Steve Bradt, "'One-Drop Rule' Persists," Harvard Gazette, December 9, 2010, hppts://news.harvard.edu/gazette/story/2010/12/one-drop-rule-persists/, accessed September 27, 2022.

56 "Enactment of Hereditary Slavery Law Virginia 1662-ACT XII," NPS.gov, hppts://www.nps.gov/ethnography/aah/aaheritage/Chesapeake_pop2.htm, accessed January 4, 2022.

57 Erin Blakemore, "How Dolls Helped Win Brown v. Board of Education," History, March 27, 2018, hppts://www.history.com/news/brown-v-board-of-education-doll-experiment, accessed April 29, 2021.

58 Lindsey Craig, "Racial Bias May Begin in Babies at Six Months, U of T Research Reveals," University of Toronto, April 11, 2017, hppts://www.utoronto.ca// news/racial-bias-may-begin-babies-six-months-u-t-research-reveals, accessed April 29, 2021.

59 Kwame Anthony Appiah, "The Case for Capitalizing the B in Black," The Atlantic, June 18, 2020, hppts://www.theatlantic.com/ideas/archive/2020/06/ time-to-capitalize-blackand-white/613159/, accessed January 18, 2021.

60 "Capitalization Conventions - Framework Design Guidelines," Microsoft, hppts://docs.microsoft.com/en-us/dotnet/standard/design-guidelines/ capitalization-conventions, accessed October 4, 2023.

61 New York State Police (website), hppts://troopers.ny.gov/, accessed March 24, 2016.

Chapter 1 - My Daughter's Eyes

62 Eric Ferrara, "A Brief History of Public Housing on the Lower East Side," Lower East Side History Project, March 7, 2013, hppts://www.leshp.org/blog/ a-brief-history-of-public-housing-on-the-lower-east-side/, accessed March 3, 2021.

63 Pedro Perez, Personal Files, accessed July 5, 2016.

64 Erik Erikson's Stages of Psychosocial Development simplypsychology.org/Erik-Erikson.html by Saul McLeod, updated 2018, hppts://basics.nami.org/docs/ simplypsychology.org-Erik-Erikson.pdf, accessed April 16, 2019.

65 Donald Waldrip, "A Brief History of Magnet Schools," Magnet Schools of America, hppts://magnet.edu/brief-history-of-magnets, accessed December 2, 2017.

66 Andrew Griffiths, "Mas Oyama – Founder of Kyokushin Karate," History of Fighting, hppts://www.historyoffighting.com/mas-oyama.php, accessed December 2, 2017.

67 John Samples, "Limiting Government, 1980–2010," Cato Institute, March/ April 2010, hppts://www.cato.org/policy-report/marchapril-2010/limiting-government-1980-2010, accessed December 2, 2017.

68 The Chief (website), hppts://thechiefleader.com/, accessed April 5, 2020.

Chapter 2 - Leap of Faith

69 Ibid.

70 United States v. State of NY, 475 F. Supp. 1103 (N.D.N.Y 1979)hppts://law. justia.com/cases/federal/district-courts/FSupp/475/1103/1688027/, accessed December 2, 2017.

71 Ibid.

72 George L. Kelling and Mark Moore, The evolving strategy of policing (No. 4) (US Department of Justice, Office of Justice Programs, National Institute of Justice, 1989), hppts://www.sagepub.com/sites/default/files/upm-binaries/50819_ch_1.pdf, accessed December 3, 2017.

73 Pedro Perez, Personal Files, accessed July 5, 2016.

74 Pictorial Press Ltd, "School Begins: Cartoon from American Satirical Magazine Puck on 25 January 1899 Showing Uncle Sam Teaching the Newly Liberated Territories in the Front Row the Elements of Self Government," Alamy, hppts://www.alamy.com/stock-photo-school-begins-cartoon-from-american-satirical-magazine-puck-on-25-129650250.html, accessed July 7, 2017.

75 Damon Young, "The Definition, Danger and Disease of Respectability Politics, Explained," The Root, March 21, 2016, hppts://www.theroot.com/the-definition-danger-and-disease-of-respectability-po-1790854699?, accessed July 7, 2017.

76 María Sánchez Diez, "The True Origin of the Word 'Spic,' the Racist Insult Aimed at Hispanics," Univision, June 8, 2017, hppts://www.univision.com/univision-news/united-states/the-true-origin-of-the-word-spic-the-racist-insult-aimed-at-hispanics, accessed July 7, 2017.

77 Eli Watkins and Abby Phillip, "Trump Decries Immigrants from 'Shithole Countries' Coming to US," CNN, January 12, 2018, hppts://www.cnn.com/2018/01/11/politics/immigrants-shithole-countries-trump/index.html, accessed September 9, 2022.

78 Larry Rohter, "Joe Cuba, Bandleader Known as the Father of Latin Boogaloo, Dies at 78," The New York Times, February 18, 2009, hppts://www.nytimes.com/2009/02/18/arts/music/18cuba.html, accessed August 23, 2022.

79 Paul Sorene, "Huey P. Newton and the Black Panther Party: A Picture Story," Flashbak, February 18, 2013, hppts://flashbak.com/huey-p-newton-and-the-black-panther-party-a-picture-story-13283/, accessed December 5, 2020.

80 Huey P. Newton "Revolutionary Suicide," Internet Archive, April 1, 1995, hppts://archive.org/details/Revolutionarysuicidehuey/mode/2up, accessed December 5, 2020.

81 John Kane, "Senecas Clash with Police Over Tax Ruling (July 17, 1992)," Native Pride, July 17, 2012, hppts://letstalknativepride.blogspot.com/2012/07/senecas-clash-with-police-over-tax.html, accessed December 5, 2020.

82 Connie Kargbo, "Puerto Rican Radical Group Young Lords Retake NYC in Museum Exhibit," PBS NewsHour, September 19, 2015, hppts://www.pbs.org/newshour/arts/puerto-rican-radical-group-young-lords-retake-new-york-city-multi-museum-exhibit, accessed December 5, 2020.

83 "Elaine Brown's 'Seize the Time,' 1969: Smithsonian Year of Music Object of the Day, October 5," Smithsonian Music, October 5, 2019, hppts://music.si.edu/story/elaine-browns-seize-time-1969-smithsonian-year-music-object-day-october-5, accessed December 5, 2020.

84 Randolph Walters, "MLK Day Reflection: The Fierce Urgency of Now," Eastern University, January 15, 2021, hppts://www.eastern.edu/news/mlk, accessed December 5, 2021.

85 Rosalind Dixon, "Why Supreme Court Justices Need Term Limits," The New York Times, hppts://www.nytimes.com/2021/12/31/opinion/supreme-court-term-limits.html, accessed December 31, 2021.

86 Barry C. Feld, "Race, Politics, and Juvenile Justice: The Warren Court and the Conservative Backlash." Minn. L. Rev. 87 (May 2003): 1447–1578. hppts://www.ojp.gov/ncjrs/virtual-library/abstracts/race-politics-and-juvenile-justice-warren-court-and-conservative, accessed December 21, 2021.

87 Desmond Brown, "10 Reasons Why Cutting Poverty Is Good for Our Nation," Center for American Progress Action, December 6, 2011, hppts://www.americanprogressaction.org/article/10-reasons-why-cutting-poverty-is-good-for-our-nation/, accessed December21,2021.

Chapter 3 - Affirmative Action Trooper

88 "History: 1970s," New York State Police, hppts://www.troopers.ny.gov/Introduction/History/1970s/, accessed December 12, 2020.

89 "Title VII of the Civil Rights Act of 1964," US Equal Employment Opportunity Commission, 2023, hppts://www.eeoc.gov/statutes/title-vii-civil-rights-act-1964, accessed December 12, 2020.

90 Michael Oreskes, "State Police Win Suit Over Bias At Academy," The New York Times, hppts://www.nytimes.com/1984/09/25/nyregion/state-police-win-suit-over-bias-at-academy.html, accessed September 9, 2022.

91 United States v. State of NY, 593 F. Supp. 1216 (1984), hppts://www.leagle.com/decision/19841809593fsupp121611625.xml, accessed September 9, 2022.

92 Ibid.

93 Ibid.

Chapter 4 - Stories of Interpersonal Racism

94 N'dea Yancey-Bragg, "What Is Systemic Racism? Here's What It Means and How You Can Help Dismantle It," USA TODAY, January 29, 2021, hppts://www.usatoday.com/story/news/nation/2020/06/15/systemic-racism-what-does-mean/5343549002/, accessed September 16, 2022.

95 Pamela Paul, "Reflections on Stephen L. Carter's 1991 Book.".hppts://www.nytimes.com/2023/05/25/opinion/columnists/affirmative-action-stephen-carter.html, accessed July 11, 2020.

96 "Court Rules Height-Weight Requirement for Job May Discriminate against Women," The New York Times, June 28, 1977, hppts://www.nytimes.com/1977/06/28/archives/court-rules-heightweight-requirement-for-job-may-discriminate.html, accessed September 16, 2022.

97 Eldridge Cleaver, Soul on Ice (New York: Delta, 1968), hppts://archive.org/details/soul-on-ice-by-eldridge-cleaver/page/14/mode/2up, accessed July 17, 2017.

98 Michael J. Pfeifer, "Pfeifer on Woodward, 'the Strange Career of Jim Crow: A Commemorative Edition,'" H-South, May, 2003, hppts://networks.h-net.org/node/512/reviews/699/pfeifer-woodward-strange-career-jim-crow-commemorative-edition, accessed July 17, 2017.

99 Paulo Freire, Pedagogy of the Oppressed, 30th Anniversary ed. (London: Continuum, 2005), hppts://envs.ucsc.edu/internships/internship-readings/freire-pedagogy-of-the-oppressed.pdf, p. 44, accessed July 20, 2017.

100 IBID.

101 "Irish Political Cartoons," Victoriana, hppts://www.victoriana.com/history/irish-political-cartoons.html, accessed September 13, 2022.

[102] Joel Williamson, The Crucible of Race: Black-White Relations in the American South Since Emancipation (New York: Oxford University Press, 1984), hppts://archive.org/details/crucibleofracebl0000will/page/n599/mode/2up?view=theater, p. 111-179, accessed July 7. 2017.

[103] William DeLong, "Frank Serpico: The Unbelievable True Story behind Al Pacino's Iconic Role," All That's Interesting, November 29, 2021, hppts://allthatsinteresting.com/frank-serpico, accessed December 17, 2021.

[104] Albany Times Union, "Theodore A. Cook III," Legacy, May 2, 2013, hppts://www.legacy.com/us/obituaries/timesunion-albany/name/theodore-cook-obituary?id=4981309, accessed December 5, 2016.

[105] United States v. State of NY, 475 F. Supp. 1103 (N.D.N.Y 1979), hppts://law.justia.com/cases/federal/district-courts/FSupp/475/1103/1688027/, accessed July 17, 2017.

[106] Peggy McIntosh, "White Privilege and Male Privilege: A Personal Account of Coming to See Correspondences Through Work in Women's Studies," in Re-visioning Family Therapy: Addressing Diversity in Clinical Practice, ed. Monica McGoldrick and Kenneth V. Hardy (New York: The Guilford Press, 2019), 215–225, hppts://psycnet.apa.org/record/2019-25170-015, accessed January 21, 2021.

[107] Gustavo Arellano, "What's the History of the Words Wetback, Beaner and Spic?" OC Weekly, May 25, 2017, hppts://www.ocweekly.com/whats-the-history-of-the-words-wetback-beaner-and-spic-8133003/, accessed January 21, 2021.

Chapter 5 - Dancing in the Parking Lot

[108] "History: 1917-1929," New York State Police, hppts://Troopers.ny.gov/Introduction/History/1917-1929/, accessed March 24, 2016.

[109] Van de Water and Frederic Franklyn, Grey Riders: The Story of the New York State Troopers (New York: Putnam's Sons, 1922), hppts://archive.org/details/greyridersstoryo00vand/page/n81/mode/2up, p. 82, accessed September 9, 2022.

[110] Lorraine Boissoneault, "Martin Luther King Jr.'s Assassination Sparked Uprisings in Cities across America," Smithsonian Magazine, April 3, 2018, hppts://www.smithsonianmag.com/history/martin-luther-king-jrs-assassination-sparked-uprisings-cities-across-america-180968665/, accessed December 12, 2017.

[111] Joseph M. Murphy, "Santeria," Encyclopedia Britannica, December 8, 2023, hppts://www.britannica.com/topic/Santeria, accessed December 12, 2017

Chapter 6 - The Road of Shame

[112] "More History of Olean," City of Olean, hppts://cityofolean.org/history/more-history-of-olean/, accessed December 19, 2017.

[113] US Census, Historical Poverty Tables: People and Families - 1959 to 2022, Current Population Survey (CPS), https://www.census.gov/data/tables/time-series/demo/income-poverty/historical-poverty-people.html, assessed December 19, 2017.

[114] Stephen Sweet, "Oil and Gas in Allegany County History," Allegany County Historical Society, hppts://www.alleganyhistory.org/culture/industry/oil-gas/3510-oil-and-gas-in-allegany-county-history, accessed December 19, 2017.

[115] "History," Seneca Nation of Indians hppts://sni.org/culture/history/, accessed December 19, 2017.

[116] "Historical Markers Listing 2018," Association of Public Historians of New York State, hppts://www.aphnys.org/wp-content/uploads/2018/07/Historical-Markers-Listing-2018-07.pdf, accessed December 23, 2017.

[117] "New York State's Days of Oil Glory," The New York Times, January 7, 1985, Sec. A, 16, hppts://www.nytimes.com/1985/01/07/opinion/l-new-york-state-s-days-of-oil-glory-194196.html, accessed January 3, 2018.

[118] Town of Bolivar (website), hppts://www.townofbolivar.com/, accessed January 3, 2018.

[119] "Confederate Flag," ADL, hppts://www.adl.org/education/references/hate-symbols/confederate-flag, accessed January 15, 2021.

[120] Pedro Perez, Personal Files, accessed July 5, 2016.

[121] Helen C. Phelan, "And Why Not Every Man," Open Library, June 30, 2011, hppts://openlibrary.org/works/OL15813601W/And_why_not_every_man, accessed January 15, 2021.

[122] "Underground Railroad," Allegany County Historical Society, hppts://gallery2.alleganyhistory.org/gallery/Maps/Underground%20Railroad/index.html, accessed January 15, 2021.

[123] New York State Finally Renames "N*gger Lake," Ross Scarano, June 22, 2011, https://www.complex.com/pop-culture/a/ross-scarano/new-york-state-finally-renames-ngger-lake, accessed January 15, 2021.

124 There's hundreds of racist place names across the U.S. Here's why it's hard to change them. https://www.vice.com/en/article/vbaaey/theres-hundreds-of-racist-place-names-across-the-us-heres-why-its-hard-to-change-them, Emma Ockerman, January 4, 2019, accessed January 15, 2021.

Chapter 7 - Deer Jacking-Unseen Poverty

125 Ken Moran, "A 'Dark Night' for Deer Jackers," New York Post, December 19, 2010, hppts://nypost.com/2010/12/19/a-dark-night-for-deer-jackers/, accessed February 20, 2021.

Chapter 8 - A Uniform without a Shield

126 Gabriel Pogrund, "How White Supremacists Split a Quiet Rust Belt Town," The Washington Post, July 28, 2018, hppts://www.washingtonpost.com/politics/how-white-supremacists-split-a-quiet-rust-belt-town/2018/07/28/15a7e414-85df-11e8-8f6c-46cb43e3f306_story.html, accessed February 14, 2021.

127 "Allegany, New York (NY) Poverty Rate Data - Information about Poor and Low-Income Residents," City-data.com, hppts://www.city-data.com/poverty/poverty-Allegany-New-York.html, accessed February 15, 2021.

128 Robert J. Mcguire, "Homicide Analysis - New York City, 1981," Office of Justice Programs, 1981, hppts://www.ojp.gov/ncjrs/virtual-library/abstracts/homicide-analysis-new-york-city-1981, accessed February 15, 2021.

129 Richard Rothstein, Liveright Publishing, (May 2, 2017), The color of law, a forgotten history of how our government segregated America (1st ed.). New York, accessed February 15, 2021.

130 "Single Family Housing Guaranteed Loan Program," Rural Development, hppts://www.rd.usda.gov/programs-services/single-family-housing-guaranteed-loan-program, accessed July 25, 2017.

Chapter 9 - Doors Open

131 The New Yorker, "Malcolm Gladwell Discusses Tokens, Pariahs, and Pioneers - The New Yorker Festival," YouTube video, 2:49, November 8, 2013, hppts://youtu.be/rW888do1awo?si=6iy47kwQ9qLEaszY, accessed July 25, 2017.

132 Ibid.

133 History.com Editors, "Munich Massacre," History, May 24, 2021, hppts://www.history.com/topics/1970s/munich-massacre-olympics, accessed November 14, 2022.

134 Sarah Pruitt, "How the Iran Hostage Crisis Became a 14-Month Nightmare for President Carter and the Nation," History, November 4, 2014, hppts://www.history.com/news/background-to-the-iran-hostage-crisis, accessed June 22, 2023.

135 Pedro Perez, Personal Files, accessed July 5, 2016.

136 Pedro Perez, Personal Files, accessed July 5, 2016.

137 Pedro Perez, Personal Files, accessed July 5, 2016.

138 "Defendant Who Fled Murder Trial Is Seized," The New York Times, May 24, 1984, Sec. B, 8, hppts://www.nytimes.com/1984/05/24/nyregion/defendant-who-fled-murder-trial-is-seized.html, accessed July 18, 2017.

139 William Shakespeare – "Band of Brothers" Speech from Henry V https://genius.com/William-shakespeare-band-of-brothers-speech-from-henry-v-annotated, accessed July 18, 2017

Chapter 10 - Santa Claus

140 Pedro Perez, Personal Files, accessed July 5, 2016.

141 "The History and Culture of the Iroquois," Native Hope, November 6, 2022, hppts://blog.nativehope.org/the-history-and-culture-of-the-iroquois, accessed November 25, 2022.

142 The Editors of Encyclopedia Britannica, "Iroquois," Encyclopedia Britannica, December 7, 2023, hppts://www.britannica.com/topic/Iroquois-people, accessed December 10, 2023.

143 David Sommerstein, "At U.S.-Canada Border Reservation, Mohawks Say They Face Discrimination," NPR, October 28, 2017, hppts://www.npr.org/2017/10/28/560436303/at-u-s-canada-border-reservation-mohawks-say-they-face-discrimination, accessed January 10, 2021.

144 The Editors of Encyclopedia Britannica, "Iroquois Confederacy," Encyclopedia Britannica, hppts://www.britannica.com/topic/Iroquois-Confederacy, accessed January 10, 2021.

145 Rick Hill, "Choosing Sides: Divided Loyalties in the War of 1812," American Indian 13, no. 4 (Winter 2012), hppts://www.americanindianmagazine.org/story/choosing-sides-divided-loyalties-war-1812, accessed January 1, 2021.

[146] "Border Crossing Rights under the Jay Treaty," Pine Tree Legal Assistance, last edited September 2016, hppts://www.ptla.org/border-crossing-rights-jay-treaty, accessed January 10, 2021.

[147] Robert N. Wells Jr., et al., "Community Mobilization and Leadership Development on the St. Regis (Akwesasne) Mohawk Reservation," paper presented at the Southwestern Sociological Association 1974 Annual Meetings, March 29, 1974, ERIC, ED 088 625, hppts://files.eric.ed.gov/fulltext/ED088625.pdf, accessed January 15, 2021

[148] AP, "Slot Machines Seized at Indian Reservation," The New York Times, December 17, 1987, Sec. B, 17, hppts://www.nytimes.com/1987/12/17/nyregion/slot-machines-seized-at-indian-reservation.html, accessed September 25, 2022.

[149] "DOI Gaming Regulations," National Indian Gaming Commission, hppts://www.nigc.gov/general-counsel/doi-gaming-regulations, accessed September 25, 2022.

[150] "Mohawk Violence Escalates; Two Killed in Gun Battles - UPI Archives," UPI, May 1, 1990, https://www.upi.com/Archives/1990/05/01/Mohawk-violence-escalates-two-killed-in-gun-battles/6874641534400/, accessed September 25, 2021.

[151] David Treadwell and Lisa Phillips, "Police Patrol Indian Reservation After Slayings: Mohawks: Cuomo Refuses to Send in Troops. A Key Aide Will Meet with Tribal Leaders and Canadian Officials. - Los Angeles Times," Los Angeles Times, May 3, 1990, hppts://www.latimes.com/archives/la-xpm-1990-05-03-mn-457-story.html, accessed September 25, 2022.

[152] Ibid.

[153] The Interior Department and The Indian Affairs Bureau, "Indian Gaming," Federal Register, August 13, 1999, hppts://www.federalregister.gov/documents/1999/08/13/99-20931/indian-gaming, accessed July 13, 2020.

[154] Curt H. Stiles, Carlos L. Rodriguez, and Craig S. Galbraith, "American Indian Collectivism," Property and Environment Research Center, June 1, 2006, hppts://www.perc.org/2006/06/01/american-indian-collectivism/, accessed October 2, 2020.

[155] "My Tribal Area," U.S. Census Bureau, hppts://www.census.gov/tribal/?st=36&aianihh=3320, accessed January 20, 2021.

[156] "What Drives Native American Poverty? Institute for Policy Research," Northwestern University, February 24, 2020, hppts://www.ipr.northwestern.

edu/news/2020/redbird-what-drives-native-american-poverty.html, accessed January 13, 2021.

157 "Striving to Achieve Helping Native American Students Succeed," National Conference of State Legislatures, 2008, hppts://documents.ncsl.org/wwwncsl/LegislativeStaff/Quad-Caucus/strivingtoachieve.pdf, accessed January 24, 2021.

158 Mark Hugo Lopez, Jens Manuel Krogstad and Antonio Flores, "Most Hispanic Parents Speak Spanish to Their Children, but This Is Less the Case in Later Immigrant Generations," Pew Research Center, April 2, 2018, hppts://www.pewresearch.org/fact-tank/2018/04/02/most-hispanic-parents-speak-spanish-to-their-children-but-this-is-less-the-case-in-later-immigrant-generations/, accessed October 1, 2022.

159 Cydney Adams, "The Man behind the Marijuana Ban for All the Wrong Reasons," CBS News, November 17, 2016, hppts://www.cbsnews.com/news/harry-anslinger-the-man-behind-the-marijuana-ban/, accessed October 1, 2022.

160 "Rates of Drug Use and Sales, by Race; Rates of Drug Related Criminal Justice Measures, by Race," The Hamilton Project, October 21, 2016, hppts://www.hamiltonproject.org/charts/rates_of_drug_use_and_sales_by_race_rates_of_drug_related_criminal_justice, accessed October 7, 2022.

161 Devika Girish, "'Crack: Cocaine, Corruption & Conspiracy' Review: A Brisk Look Back at a Crisis," The New York Times, January 12, 2021, hppts://www.nytimes.com/2021/01/12/movies/crack-cocaine-corruption-conspiracy-review.html, accessed October 7, 2022.

162 Ibid.

163 "A Social History of America's Most Popular Drugs," PBS, hppts://www.pbs.org/wgbh/pages/frontline/shows/drugs/buyers/socialhistory.html, accessed October 10, 2022.

164 Nick Schager, "Netflix Doc Alleges CIA Flooded Black Communities with Crack," The Daily Beast, January 5, 2021, hppts://www.thedailybeast.com/netflix-doc-alleges-cia-flooded-black-communities-with-crack, accessed October 10, 2022.

165 History.com Editors, "Just Say No," History, May 31, 2017, hppts://www.history.com/topics/1980s/just-say-no, accessed October 10, 2022.

166 History.com Editors, "Iran-Contra Affair," History, August 10, 2017, hppts://www.history.com/topics/1980s/iran-contra-affair, accessed October 10, 2022.

167 Beatrice Loayza, "'The War on Drugs Funded Policing': Behind a Netflix Documentary about Crack," The Guardian, January 13, 2021, hppts://www.

theguardian.com/film/2021/jan/12/crack-cocaine-corruption-conspiracy-stanley-nelson-netflix, accessed October 10, 2022.

168 "Criminal Procedure Law Section 700.30," New York Public Law, last modified September 22, 2014, hppts://newyork.public.law/laws/n.y. criminal procedure law sec. 700.30, January 13, 2021.

169 Merriam-Webster, s.v. "Spanglish (n.)," hppts://www.merriam-webster.com/dictionary/Spanglish, accessed July 20, 2019.

170 "Nuyoricans," Encyclopedia.com, hppts://www.encyclopedia.com/social-sciences/applied-and-social-sciences-magazines/nuyoricans, accessed October 6, 2022.

171 Calvin Sims, "Cuomo Budget Cuts May Open New Gaps for Municipalities," The New York Times, January 22, 1992, Sec. B, 6, hppts://www.nytimes.com/1992/01/22/nyregion/cuomo-budget-cuts-may-open-new-gaps-for-municipalities.html, accessed July 20, 2019.

172 "Narcotics," Chautauqua County Sheriff's Office, hppts://www.sheriff.us/drugtaskforce, accessed January 21, 2021.

173 Pedro Perez, Personal Files, accessed July 5, 2016.

174 Jim Mustian and Camille Fassett, "NY State Police Struggles to Diversify amid National Reckoning. Check Our Database," Democrat and Chronicle, June 4, 2021, hppts://www.democratandchronicle.com/story/news/2021/06/04/database-ny-state-police-diversity/7534745002/, accessed June 4, 2021.

175 Ibid.

176 Peggy McIntosh, "White Privilege and Male Privilege," hppts://www.nationalseedproject.org/images/documents/White Privilege and Male Privilege Personal Account-Peggy McIntosh.pdf, accessed January 1, 2021.

177 Peggy McIntosh, "White Privilege: Unpacking the Invisible Backpack," Mentored Research Project - Harvard Global Health Program, 2013, hppts://www.hsph.harvard.edu/wp-content/uploads/sites/122/2013/08/White-Privilege-Unpacking-the-Invisible-Knapsack.pdf, accessed January 21, 2021.

Chapter 11 - Operation Crackdown

178 "Violent Crime in the City of Good Neighbors," Regional Institute, University at Buffalo, February 2007, hppts://ubwp.buffalo.edu/ubri/wp-content/uploads/sites/3/2014/12/Violent-Crime-in-the-City-of-Good-Neighbors-Policy-Brief.pdf, accessed June 13, 2020.

179 "A Brief History of Civil Rights in the United States," Howard University, last updated January 2019, hppts://library.law.howard.edu/civilrightshistory/blackrights/massincarceration, accessed July 13, 2020.

180 Ibid.

181 Ashley Nellis, "Mass Incarceration Trends," The Sentencing Project, January 2023, hppts://www.sentencingproject.org/app/uploads/2023/01/Mass-Incarceration-Trends.pdf, accessed July 13, 2023.

182 Alex Harocopos and Mike Hough, "Drug Dealing in Open-Air Markets," Office of Justice Programs, January 2005, hppts://www.ojp.gov/ncjrs/virtual-library/abstracts/drug-dealing-open-air-markets, accessed March 4, 2021.

183 Stanton E. Samenow, "Crime Causes Poverty," Psychology Today, December 24, 2014, hppts://www.psychologytoday.com/us/blog/inside-the-criminal-mind/201412/crime-causes-poverty, accessed March 4, 2021.

184 Ibid

185 Mireya Navarro, "After a Stray Shot: A Girl's Family Seeks Meaning in a Random Loss," The New York Times, August 26, 1990, hppts://www.nytimes.com/1990/08/26/nyregion/after-a-stray-shot-a-girl-s-family-seeks-meaning-in-a-random-loss.html, accessed March 4, 2021.

186 "Open-Air Drug Markets: Analyzing the Details and Closing off Opportunities," ASU Center for Problem-Oriented Policing, hppts://popcenter.asu.edu/sites/default/files/madensen.mills .drug_markets4.pdf, accessed March 4, 2021.

187 '92 City Homicides Took Toll on Young Most Point Fingers at Drugs, Guns, Gangs, Buffalo News, Jan 3, 1993 hppts://buffalonews.com/news/92-city-homicides-took-toll-on-young-most-point-fingers-at-drugs-guns-gangs/article_57bde7a4-f269-5a8a-9901-, accessed February 5, 2021.

188 Anna Blatto, "A City Divided: A Brief History of Segregation in Buffalo," Partnership for the Public Good, May 7, 2018, hppts://ppgbuffalo.org/buffalo-commons/library/resource:a-city-divided-a-brief-history-of-segregation-in-buffalo-1/, accessed February 5, 2021.

189 The Editors of Encyclopedia Britannica, "Jay Treaty," Encyclopedia Britannica, hppts://www.britannica.com/event/Jay-Treaty, November 12, 2023.

190 Pedro Perez, Personal Files, accessed July 5, 2016.

191 Johnny Cash, "As Long As the Grass Shall Grow," track 1 on Bitter Tears: Ballads of the American Indian, produced by Don Law and Frank Jones, 1964, in Genius, hppts://genius.com/Johnny-cash-as-long-as-the-grass-shall-grow-lyrics, accessed June 15, 2020.

[192] K. W., "What Sovereignty Means for America's Indian Tribes," The Economist, July 16, 2018, hppts://www.economist.com/the-economist-explains/2018/07/16/what-sovereignty-means-for-americas-indian-tribes, accessed June 15, 2020.

[193] United States Code: Government of Indian Country and Reservations, 25 U.S.C. §§ 216-265, hppts://uscode.house.gov/view.xhtml?path=/prelim@title25/chapter6&edition=prelim, accessed February 1, 2021.

[194] Rob Capriccioso, "Illuminating the Treaties That Have Governed U.S.-Indian Relationships," Smithsonian Magazine, August 21, 2014, hppts://www.smithsonianmag.com/smithsonian-institution/treaties-governed-us-indian-relationships-180952443/, accessed February 1, 2021.

[195] Sebastian Murdock, "Donald Trump Helps Suffering Puerto Ricans by Throwing Paper Towels at Them," HuffPost, October 3, 2017, hppts://www.huffpost.com/entry/donald-trump-helps-suffering-puerto-ricans-by-throwing-paper-towels-at-them_n_59d3db64e4b0218923e5b4f7, accessed February 1, 2021.

[196] History.com Editors, "Selma to Montgomery March," History, January 28, 2010, https://www.history.com/topics/black-history/selma-montgomery-march, accessed September.20, 2022.

[197] John McCormack, Ivor Novello, and Oliver Gilbert, "Ivor Novello - Keep the Home Fires Burning ('till the Boys Come Home) Lyrics," Lyrics.com, hppts://www.lyrics.com/lyric/5583359/Ivor+Novello/Keep+the+Home+Fires+Burning+%28%27Till+the+Boys+Come+Home%29, accessed October 5, 2022.

[198] Henry Louis Taylor, Jr., "A Historical Overview of Blacks in the Fruit Belt: The Continuing Struggle to Build a Vibrant Community," University at Buffalo Center for Urban Studies, School of Architecture and Planning, hppts://ubwp.buffalo.edu/aps-cus/wp-content/uploads/sites/16/2015/04/The-Rise-Fall-and-Rise-of-the-Fruit-Belt.pdf, accessed June.28, 2020.

[199] The Associated Press, "75 Arrested for Drug Deals in Buffalo Raid," The New York Times, August 20, 1992, hppts://www.nytimes.com/1992/08/20/nyregion/75-arrested-for-drug-deals-in-buffalo-raid.html, accessed October 9, 2022.

[200] Ibid.

[201] Ibid.

[202] James Cullen, "The History of Mass Incarceration," Brennan Center for Justice, July 20, 2018 hppts://www.brennancenter.org/our-work/analysis-opinion/history-mass-incarceration, accessed June 28, 2020.

[203] Arun Venugopal, "Black Leaders Once Championed the Strict Drug Laws They Now Seek to Dismantle," WNYC, August 16, 2013, hppts://www.wnyc.org/story/312823-black-leaders-once-championed-strict-drug-laws-they-now-seek-dismantle/, accessed June 22, 2020

[204] The Speed of Trust (website), hppts://www.speedoftrust.com/, accessed June 22, 2020.

[205] National Commission on Law Observance and Enforcement, "Report on the Enforcement of the Prohibition Laws of the United States," Department of Justice, January 7, 1931, 78–86, hppts://www.ojp.gov/pdffiles1/Digitization/44540NCJRS.pdf, p. 78 – 86, accessed June 22, 2020.

[206] History.com Editors, "Kerner Commission Report Released," History, July 21, 2010, hppts://www.history.com/this-day-in-history/kerner-commission-report-released, accessed February 19, 2021.

[207] President's Task Force on 21st Century Policing, "Final Report of the President's Task Force on 21st Century Policing," Office of Community Oriented Policing Services, May 2015, hppts://cops.usdoj.gov/pdf/taskforce/taskforce_finalreport.pdf, accessed February 19, 2021.

Chapter 12 - A Bridge toward Change

[208] Matthew A. McIntosh, "The Praetorian Guard in Ancient Rome: Protection and Imperial Intelligence," Brewminate, June 4, 2020, hppts://brewminate.com/the-praetorian-guard-in-ancient-rome-protection-and-imperial-intelligence/, accessed February 13, 2021.

[209] The Power of Exclusion: Dismantling the "Good Ol' Boys" Network, https://greaterdiversity.com/7085-2/, accessed January 1, 2021.

[210] Pedro Perez, Personal Files, accessed July 5, 2016.

[211] "FBI National Academy," Federal Bureau of Investigation, September 28, 2012, hppts://www.fbi.gov/news/stories/fbi-national-academy, accessed December 24, 2020.

[212] Pedro Perez, Personal Files, accessed July 5, 2016.

[213] The Editors of Encyclopedia Britannica, "Mason-Dixon Line," Encyclopedia Britannica, July 20, 1998, hppts://www.britannica.com/place/Mason-and-Dixon-Line, accessed December 26, 2020.

[214] Becky Little, "Slavery Persisted in New England until the 19th Century," History, June 29, 2020, hppts://www.history.com/news/slavery-new-england-rhode-island, accessed December.26, 2020.

[215] Joshua J. Mark, "Slavery in Colonial America," World History Encyclopedia, June 19, 2023, hppts://www.worldhistory.org/article/1739/slavery-in-colonial-america/, accessed December 26, 2020.

[216] Morris-Suzuki Tessa "The AINU: Beyond the Politics of Cultural Coexistence," Cultural Survival, April 2, 2010, hppts://www.culturalsurvival.org/publications/cultural-survival-quarterly/ainu-beyond-politics-cultural-coexistence, accessed December 31, 2020.

[217] James McGrath Morris, "Occupation Babies: Mixed-Race Japanese Children," Wonders & Marvels, February 28, 2015, hppts://www.wondersandmarvels.com/2015/02/occupation-babies-mixed-race-japanese-children.html, accessed October 06, 2022.

[218] "Whereas Japanese Enthusiastically Embraced Cultural Mixing with the U.S., They Rejected Biological Mixing Outright, Seeing Mixed-Race Babies as a Threat to Their Racial Purity and Tantamount to an Assault on the Japanese Race Itself," Mixed Race Studies, hppts://www.mixedracestudies.org/?p=62456, accessed October 6, 2022.

[219] Alexis Clark, "Why Mixed-Race Children in Post-WWII Germany Were Deemed a 'Social Problem,'" History, June 3, 2021, hppts://www.history.com/news/mixed-race-babies-germany-world-war-ii, accessed October 6, 2022.

[220] History.com Editors, "Loving v. Virginia: 1967 & Supreme Court Case," HISTORY, November 17, 2017, hppts://www.history.com/topics/civil-rights-movement/loving-v-virginia#the-loving-v-virginia-supreme-court-case, accessed October 6, 2022.

[221] Yukihiko Kitagawa, "Homeless Policy as a Policy for Controlling Poverty in Tokyo: Considering the Relationship between Welfare Measures and Punitive Measures," Critical Sociology 47, no. 1 (May 2020): 91–110, hppts://journals.sagepub.com/doi/full/10.1177/0896920520921494, accessed October 6, 2022.

[222] "Enter the Dragon Quotes," Movie Quotes, hppts://www.moviequotes.com/s-movie/enter-the-dragon/, accessed January 15, 2021.

223 Pedro Perez, Personal Files, accessed July 5, 2016.

224 "History: 1990s," New York State Police, hppts://www.troopers.ny.gov/Introduction/History/1990s/, accessed January 17, 2021.

225 "Interstate Highway System," Eisenhower Presidential Library, hppts://www.eisenhowerlibrary.gov/research/online-documents/interstate-highway-system, accessed January 17, 2021.

226 Ibid.

227 New York State Police, "History: 1990s," hppts://www.troopers.ny.gov/Introduction/History/1990s/, accessed January 17, 2021.

228 Andrew M. Cuomo and Michael C. Green, "Operation Impact Annual Report - 2013," New York State Division of Criminal Justice Services, 2013, hppts://www.criminaljustice.ny.gov/crimnet/ojsa/impact/2013annualreport.pdf, accessed January 17, 2021.

229 "James W. McMahon," New York State Police, accessed January 25, 2022, hppts://troopers.ny.gov/james-w-mcmahon, accessed January 25, 2022.

230 Pedro Perez, Personal Files, accessed July 5, 2016.

Chapter 13 - Red Beans and Rice

231 United States v. State of NY, 475 F. Supp. 1103 (N.D.N.Y 1979), hppts://www.leagle.com/decision/19791578475fsupp110311422.xml, accessed June 29, 2023.

232 Ibid.

233 Ibid.

234 Ibid.

235 Michael Oreskes, STATE POLICE WIN SUIT OVER BIAS AT ACADEMY, hppts://www.nytimes.com/1984/09/25/nyregion/state-police-win-suit-over-bias-at-academny.html, accessed February 7, 2021.

236 Ibid.

237 "Correction Officer and Deputy Sheriff-Officer 60-081," GovernmentJobs.com, hppts://www.governmentjobs.com/careers/erieco/jobs/3735946/correction-officer-and-deputy-sheriff-officer-60-081?pagetype=jobOpportunitiesJobs, accessed October 11, 2022.

238 Cecil Adams, "In the Old Lone Ranger Series, What Did 'Kemosabe' Mean?," The Straight Dope, July 18, 1997, hppts://www.straightdope.com/21342134/

in-the-old-lone-ranger-series-what-did-kemosabe-mean, accessed October 12, 2022.

239 Oxford English Dictionary, s.v. "Frenemy (n.)," hppts://www.oed.com/view/Entry/273014, accessed October 12, 2022.

240 Albert S. Kurek, The Troopers Are Coming: New York State Troopers 1917-1943 (London: Rooftop Publishing, 2007), 27–28, hppts://books.google.com/books?id=e3d9tTxg1N8C&lpg=PA9&dq=george%20fletcher%20chandler&pg=PA27#v=onepage&q=george%20fletcher%20chandler&f=true, accessed April 19, 2021.

241 Douglas Longshore, "Color Connotations and Racial Attitudes," Journal of Black Studies 9, no. 4 (June 1979): 183–97, hppts://doi.org/10.1177/002193477900900403, accessed April.19, 2021.

242 The Racial Slur Database, "Races," hppts://www.rsdb.org/races, accessed April 19, 2021.

243 The Free Dictionary, "In Loco Parentis," hppts://legal-dictionary.thefreedictionary.com/In+loco+parentis, accessed February 14, 2021.

244 "Deprivation of Rights under Color of Law," Civil Rights Division, U.S. Department of Justice, hppts://www.justice.gov/crt/deprivation-rights-under-color-law, accessed October 13, 2022.

245 Elizabeth Nix, "Who Was the Real Horatio Alger?," History, November 10, 2016, hppts://www.history.com/news/was-horatio-alger-a-real-person, accessed February 13, 2021.

246 Livia Gershon, "How Stereotypes of the Irish Evolved from 'Criminals' to Cops," History, December 18, 2017, hppts://www.history.com/news/how-stereotypes-of-the-irish-evolved-from-criminals-to-cops, accessed October 19, 2022.

247 "Official English Is Not English Only," ProEnglish, hppts://web.archive.org/web/20080106103635/hppts://www.proenglish.org/notenglishonly.html, accessed October 22, 2022.

248 Merriam-Webster, s.v. "Honcho (n.)," hppts://www.merriam-webster.com/dictionary/honcho, accessed October 22, 2022.

249 Karen Dolan, "Criminalization of Race and Poverty," Institute for Policy Studies, hppts://ips-dc.org/criminalization-of-race-and-poverty/, accessed February 13, 2021.

250 "Investigation of the Ferguson Police Department," United States Department of Justice Civil Rights Division, March 4, 2015, hppts://www.justice.gov/sites/

default/files/opa/press-releases/attachments/2015/03/04/ferguson_police_department_report.pdf, accessed February 13, 2021.

251 Katie Cowart, "A History of Colorism Sheds Light on Discrimination Today," Franklin College of Arts and Sciences, September 22, 2021, hppts://www.franklin.uga.edu/news/stories/2021/history-colorism-sheds-light-discrimination-today, accessed September 23, 2021.

252 David A Love, "Portland Shows That White Allies Can Play a Vital Role in Social Justice Movements," The Washington Post, August 5, 2020, hppts://www.washingtonpost.com/outlook/2020/08/05/portland-shows-that-white-allies-can-play-vital-role-social-justice-movements/, accessed January 21, 2021.

Chapter 14 - The Fires Burned

253 "Department of Taxation and Finance of New York, Et Al., Petitioners V. Milhelm Attea & Bros., Inc., etc., et al.," Legal Information Institute, hppts://www.law.cornell.edu/supremecourt/text/512/61, accessed June 30, 2023.

254 Pedro Perez, Personal Files, accessed July 5, 2016.

255 "The History of the Olympic Flame," Olympics, October 24, 2017, hppts://olympics.com/en/desktop/news/CH/the-history-of-the-olympic-flame, accessed April 16, 2021.

256 Pedro Perez, Personal Files, accessed July 5, 2016.

257 Pedro Perez, Personal Files, accessed July 5, 2016.

258 Pedro Perez, Personal Files, accessed July 5, 2016.

259 Pedro Perez, Personal Files, accessed July 5, 2016.

260 Pedro Perez, Personal Files, accessed July 5, 2016.

Chapter 15 - Major Perez Off the Rez

261 "Seneca Nation Oil Process in New York State," New York History, hppts://nyhistoric.com/2013/10/seneca-oil-spring/, accessed December 23, 2020.

262 Ibid.

263 "Indigenous Appalachia," West Virginia University, hppts://indigenousappalachia.lib.wvu.edu/peoples/native-nations/seneca, accessed December 23, 2020.

264 "Tonawanda Band of Seneca Indians," LiquiSearch, https://www.liquisearch.com/tonawanda_band_of_seneca_indians/history, accessed December 23, 2020.

[265] "List of Federal and State Recognized Tribes," National Conference of State Legislatures, hppts://www.ncsl.org/research/state-tribal-institute/list-of-federal-and-state-recognized-tribes.aspx#ny, accessed January 20, 2021.

[266] "NY Land Claims," U.S. Department of the Interior, July 14, 2015, hppts://www.doi.gov/ocl/ny-land-claims, accessed April 1, 2021.

[267] "Search Federally Recognized Tribes," Indian Affairs, hppts://www.bia.gov/service/tribal-leaders-directory/federally-recognized-tribes, accessed November 23, 2023.

[268] "Native American Boarding Schools and Education History," Native Hope, September 12, 2023, hppts://blog.nativehope.org/native-american-boarding-schools-and-education-history, accessed September 20, 2023.

[269] "Thomas Asylum for Orphan and Destitute Indian Children (Cattaraugus Indian Reservation, N.Y.)," Social Networks and Archival Context, hppts://snaccooperative.org/view/87748454, accessed November 30, 2023.

[270] Ibid.

[271] Jacob Soboroff, "More than 2,100 Children Separated at Border 'Have Not yet Been Reunified,' Biden Task Force Says," NBC News, June 8, 2021, hppts://www.nbcnews.com/politics/immigration/more-2-100-children-separated-border-have-not-yet-been-n1269918, accessed October 18, 2022.

[272] The Editors of Encyclopedia Britannica, "Sovereignty," Encyclopedia Britannica, hppts://www.britannica.com/topic/sovereignty/Sovereignty-and-international-law, accessed October 19, 2022.

[273] "Sovereignty," Milwaukee Public Museum, hppts://www.mpm.edu/index.php/educators/wirp/nations/sovereignty, accessed October 19, 2022.

[274] Ibid.

[275] "678. The General Crimes Act—18 U.S.C. § 1152," U.S. Department of Justice, hppts://www.justice.gov/archives/jm/criminal-resource-manual-678-general-crimes-act-18-usc-1152, accessed October 19, 2022.

[276] United States Code: Government of Indian Country and Reservations, 25 U.S.C. §§ 216-265, hppts://uscode.house.gov/view.xhtml?path=/prelim@title25/chapter6&edition=prelim, accessed February 1, 2021.

[277] Mariel Jackson, "Racial Identity in Policing Is More Complicated than We Think," McCourt School of Public Policy, July 5, 2022, hppts://mccourt.georgetown.edu/news/racial-identity-in-policing/, accessed July 22, 2022.

[278] "Former Seneca President Rob Porter for Governor of New York?," The Buffalo Chronicle, April 8, 2017, hppts://buffalochronicle.com/2017/04/08/

republicans-should-run-former-seneca-president-rob-porter-for-governor/, accessed January 22, 2021.

279 "Treaty with the Seneca, 1842," Tribal Treaties Database, hppts://treaties. okstate.edu/treaties/treaty-with-the-seneca-1842-0537, accessed January 22, 2021.

280 Ibid.

281 Guy Rolnik, "140 Years of Antitrust: The Evolution of Economic Language Related to Trusts and Antitrust," ProMarket, July 24, 2020, hppts://promarket. org/2016/10/25/140-years-antitrust2/, accessed January 27, 2021.

282 Ibid.

283 Ibid.

284 "Seneca Nation Leaders Should Share The Wealth", Buffalo News, May 27, 2004, hppts://buffalonews.com/news/seneca-nation-leaders-should-share-the-wealth/article_ddb128d5-4a0b-5476-9fd2-cc848f88a0b2.html, accessed February 20, 2021.

285 Robert Odawi Porter, "Jurisdictional Relationship Between the Iroquois and New York State," New York Federal-State-Tribal Courts Forum, 1990, hppts://www.nyfedstatetribalcourtsforum.org/listeningconference/pdfs/RobertOdawiPorterJurisdictional.pdf, accessed January 23, 2021.

286 "Oklahoma v. Castro-Huerta, 597 U.S. ___ (2022)," Justia U.S. Supreme Court, hppts://supreme.justia.com/cases/federal/us/597/21-429/, accessed October 20, 2022.

287 Donald L. Fixico, "When Native Americans Were Slaughtered in the Name of 'Civilization,'" History, March 2, 2018, hppts://www.history.com/news/native-americans-genocide-united-states, accessed October 20, 2022.

288 Paulo Freire, Pedagogy of the Oppressed, translated by M. B. Ramos (New York, NY: Continuum, 2000), hppts://www.historyisaweapon.com/defcon2/pedagogy/pedagogychapter1.html, accessed January 25, 2021.

289 Ibid.

290 Ibid.

291 State Court Told It Has No Jurisdiction Over Senecas' Dispute, Buffalo News, November 1997, hppts://buffalonews.com/news/state-court-told-it-has-no-jurisdiction-over-seneca-dispute/article_6bfebb7e-5354-59ef-8184-92f8fa387844.html, accessed January 25, 2021.

292 Averi Harper, "Capitol Attack Conjures American Legacy of Racial Violence," ABC News, January 19, 2021, hppts://abcnews.go.com/Politics/capitol-attack-

conjures-american-legacy-racial-violence/story?id=75331177, accessed January 25, 2021.

293 John Kifner, "Tribal Shootout: Rival Factions behind Conflict," The New York Times, April 3, 1995, hppts://www.nytimes.com/1995/04/03/nyregion/tribal-shootout-rival-factions-behind-conflict.html, accessed January 29, 2021.

294 Ibid.

295 Ibid.

296 Associated Press, "Two Seneca Indian Factions Clash over Political Control; 3 Killed," Los Angeles Times, March 5, 2019, hppts://www.latimes.com/archives/la-xpm-1995-03-26-mn-47360-story.html, accessed October 24, 2022.

297 Tribal Shootout: Rival Factions Behind Conflict, hppts://www.nytimes.com/1995/04/03/nyregion/tribal-shootout-rival-factions-behind-conflict.html, accessed October 24, 2022.

298 "Cause, Mechanism, and Manner of Death," Crime Museum, hppts://www.crimemuseum.org/crime-library/forensic-investigation/cause-mechanism-and-manner-of-death/, October 24, 2022.

299 Witness Questions Grand Jury Probe of Olean Man's Death, Buffalo News, December 2, 1995, https://buffalonews.com/news/witness-questions-grand-jury-probe-of-olean-mans-death/article_112311c7-66ab-5898-b42a-f9d5115fe93e.html, accessed February 1, 2021.

300 Haggerty v. Himelein, 89 N.Y.2d 431, 677 N.E.2d 276, 654 N.Y.S.2d 705 (1997), hppts://www.law.cornell.edu/nyctap/I97_0004.htm, accessed February 5, 2021.

301 Dr. Michael Baden (website), hppts://www.drmichaelbaden.com/, accessed February 5, 2021.

302 Pedro Perez, Personal Files, accessed July 5, 2016.

303 6 Guilty In King Death Enter Pleas In 1994 Fatal Beating Outside Olean Coffee Shop, Buffalo News, August 26, 1997, hppts://buffalonews.com/news/6-guilty-in-king-death-enter-pleas-in-1994-fatal-beating-outside-olean-coffee-shop/article_30445205-9157-5ac8-af8b-2fbc3adb294a.html, accessed February 2, 2021.

304 Leader In Fatal Attack On Kevin King Sentenced, Buffalo News, January 30, 1999, hppts://buffalonews.com/news/leader-in-fatal-attack-on-kevin-king-sentenced/article_4533e9c3-dc2c-5ca2-a3af-622dee3092e7.html, accessed February 5, 2021.

[305] Robert D. McFadden, "Seneca Feud Boils over; 3 Are Slain," The New York Times, March 26, 1995, Sec. A, 41, hppts://www.nytimes.com/1995/03/26/nyregion/seneca-feud-boils-over-3-are-slain.html, accessed February 3, 2021.

[306] Two Seneca Indian Factions Clash Over Political Control; 3 Killed, L.A. Times Archives, March 26, 1995, hppts://www.latimes.com/archives/la-xpm-1995-03-26-mn-47360-story.html, accessed February 3, 2021.

[307] Bowen v. Doyle, 230 F.3d 525 (2d Cir. 2000), hppts://law.justia.com/cases/federal/appellate-courts/F3/230/525/587656/, accessed December 21, 2022.

[308] Bowen v. Doyle, 880 F. Supp. 99 (W.D.N.Y. 1995), hppts://law.justia.com/cases/federal/district-courts/FSupp/880/99/1408551/, accessed February 5, 2021.

[309] Bowen v. Doyle, 230 F.3d 525 (2d Cir. 2000), hppts://law.justia.com/cases/federal/appellate-courts/F3/230/525/587656/, accessed February 5, 2021.

[310] Ibid.

[311] State Court Told It Has No Jurisdiction Over Senecas' Dispute, Buffalo News, May 27, 2004, hppts://buffalonews.com/news/state-court-told-it-has-no-jurisdiction-over-seneca-dispute/article_6bfebb7e-5354-59ef-8184-92f8fa387844.html, accessed February 6, 2021.

[312] Joseph J. Heath, "Review of the History of the April 1997 Trade and Commerce Agreement Among the Traditional Haudenosaunee Councils of Chiefs and New York State and the Impact Thereof on Haudenosaunee Sovereignty," Buff. L. Rev. 46 (1998): 1011, hppts://heinonline.org/HOL/LandingPage?handle=hein.journals/buflr46&div=32&id=&page=, accessed February 6, 2021.

Chapter 16 - My Cousins - History, Identity, Sovereignty, what did I learn?

[313] Puerto Ricans Got U.S. Citizenship 100 Years Ago-But Their Identity Remains Fraught, https://www.smithsonianmag.com/history/100-years-ago-puerto-ricans-got-us-citizenship-it-only-made-things-more-complicated-180962412, accessed February 15, 2021

[314] "Constitutional Amendments, Treaties, and Major Acts of Congress Referenced in the Text," U.S. Government, hppts://www.moderntreatise.com/current-affairs/2021/7/20/nations-within-a-nation-the-politics-of-american-peoplehood, accessed October 27, 2022.

[315] "House of Representatives Staff Analysis: CS/HM 147 – Status of Puerto Rico (2018)," hppts://www.flsenate.gov/Session/Bill/2018/147/Analyses/h0147c. GAC.PDF, accessed February 15, 2021.

[316] "LatinX Genocide," Dartmouth Journeys, <u>Population Control in Puerto Rico – Latinx Genocide (dartmouth.edu)</u>, accessed July 17, 2017.

[317] Shannon Collins, "Puerto Ricans Represented throughout U.S. Military History," U.S. Department of Defense, October 14, 2016, hppts://www. defense.gov/Explore/News/Article/Article/974518/puerto-ricans-represented-throughout-us-military-history/, accessed February 15, 2021.

[318] "Treaties," Seneca Nation of Indians, hppts://sni.org/culture/treaties/, accessed January 30, 2021.

[319] "An Issue of Sovereignty," National Conference of State Legislatures, accessed April 1, 2021, hppts://www.ncsl.org/research/state-tribal-institute/an-issue-of-sovereignty.aspx, accessed April 1, 2021.

[320] Samar Khurshid, "'They're Conditioned to Just Ignore or Erase Us': Native Americans in New York Fear Another Census Undercount," Gotham Gazette, March 9, 2020, hppts://www.gothamgazette.com/state/9189-goverment-conditioned-ignore-or-erase-us-native-americans-in-new-york-2020-census-undercount, accessed January 15, 2021.

[321] "Today in History - June 2," The Library of Congress, hppts://www.loc.gov/item/today-in-history/june-02/, accessed January 15, 2021.

[322] Olivia B. Waxman, "'It's a Struggle They Will Wage Alone.' How Black Women Won the Right to Vote," Time, August 14, 2020, hppts://time.com/5876456/black-women-right-to-vote/, accessed February 15, 2022.

[323] Andrea Faville, "A Civil Rights History: Latino/Hispanic Americans," Knight Chair in Political Reporting, hppts://knightpoliticalreporting.syr.edu/?civilhistoryessays=a-civil-rights-history-latinohispanic-americans, accessed February 15, 2022.

[324] "History of Federal Voting Rights Laws," U.S. Department of Justice, hppts://www.justice.gov/crt/history-federal-voting-rights-laws, accessed January 21, 2021.

[325] "Fighting Voter Suppression," American Civil Liberties Union, (aclu.org,) https://www.aclu.org/issues/voting-rights/fighting-voter-suppression, accessed May 9, 2021.

[326] Sam Levine, "US Supreme Court Deals Blow to Voting Rights by Upholding Arizona Restrictions," The Guardian, July 1, 2021, hppts://www.theguardian.

com/us-news/2021/jul/01/us-voting-rights-supreme-court-arizona, accessed October 28, 2022.

Chapter 17 - The Thruway Again, a Bridge to Nowhere

[327] Department of Taxation and Finance of N. Y. v. Milhelm Attea & Bros., 512 U.S. 61 (1994), hppts://supreme.justia.com/cases/federal/us/512/61/, accessed February 24, 2021.

[328] Ibid.

[329] Heath, "Review of the History of the April 1997 Trade," hppts://heinonline. org/HOL/LandingPage?handle=hein.journals/buflr46&div=32&id=&page=, accessed February 24, 2021.

[330] ShareAmerica, "Sovereignty: What It Means and What It Doesn't," ShareAmerica, September 23, 2019, hppts://share.america.gov/sovereignty-what-it-means-and-what-it-doesnt/, accessed December 22, 2022.

[331] "Seneca Nation Leaders Should Share The Wealth", Buffalo News, May 27, 2004, hppts://buffalonews.com/news/seneca-nation-leaders-should-share-the-wealth/article_ddb128d5-4a0b-5476-9fd2-cc848f88a0b2.html, accessed February 20, 2021.

[332] Stiles, Rodriguez, and Galbraith, "American Indian Collectivism," The Property and Environment Research Center (PERC), June 1, 2006, hppts://www.perc. org/2006/06/01/american-indian-collectivism/, accessed February 20, 2021.

[333] Buffalo Law Review, October 1, 1998, hppts://core.ac.uk/reader/236355281, accessed February 27, 2021.

[334] Ibid.

[335] Tribune News Services, "Tax Protest Turns into a Scuffle as Indians Briefly Block Thruway," Chicago Tribune, April 21, 1997, hppts://www.chicagotribune. com/news/ct-xpm-1997-04-21-9704210094-story.html, accessed March 9, 2021.

[336] Pedro Perez, Personal Files, accessed July 5, 2016.

[337] Pedro Perez, Personal Files, accessed July 5, 2016.

[338] "Interstate Highway System," Eisenhower Presidential Library, hppts:// www.historynet.com/president-dwight-eisenhower-and-americas-interstate-highway-system/, accessed March 9, 2021.

[339] Biography.com, March 29, 2021 https://www.biography.com/political-figures/ eugene-bull-connor, accessed March 9, 2021.

340 Alexis Clark, "The Children's Crusade: When the Youth of Birmingham Marched for Justice," HISTORY, October 14, 2020, hppts://www.history.com/news/childrens-crusade-birmingham-civil-rights, accessed October 16, 2022.

341 Statement To Governor George E. Pataki - State of New York Haudenosaunee, hppts://sisis.nativeweb.org/mohawk/mar3197.html, accessed October 18, 2022.

342 Smokin' Joe' To Make His Own Cigarettes, hppts://buffalonews.com/news/smokin-joe-to-make-his-own-cigarettes/article_561fc087-4521-5b70-96d1-2249c445342c.html, accessed October 18, 2022.

343 N.Y to Tax Native American Sales of Tobacco and Gas, Convenience Store News, September 15, 2003, hppts://csnews.com/ny-tax-native-american-sales-tobacco-and-gas, accessed October 18, 2022.

344 New York State Department of Taxation and Finance v. Bramhall (1997), hppts://caselaw.findlaw.com/court/ny-supreme-court-appellate-division/1065090.html, accessed October 18, 2022.

345 Pedro Perez, Personal Files, accessed July 5, 2016.

346 Settlers in Support of Indigenous Sovereignty (SISIS), hppts://sisis.nativeweb.org/seneca/apr27sch.html, accessed October 19, 2022.

347 Ibid.

348 Tire Fires Blamed In Expressway Fatality, Buffalo News, Gene Warner and Agnes Palazzetti, Apr 9, 1997 hppts://buffalonews.com/news/tire-fires-blamed-in-expressway-fatality/article_2af4a289-c4bd-5457-a4a5-d41f2e0e0e50.html, accessed March 21, 2021.

349 Ibid.

350 Ibid.

351 Raymond Hernandez, "Pataki to Seek Some Taxes on Cigarettes Indians Sell," The New York Times, February 12, 1997, hppts://www.nytimes.com/1997/02/12/nyregion/pataki-to-seek-some-taxes-on-cigarettes-indians-sell.html, accessed October 29, 2022.

352 The Associated Press, "Protesters Block Road over Indian Taxes," The New York Times, April 14, 1997, hppts://www.nytimes.com/1997/04/14/nyregion/protesters-block-road-over-indian-taxes.html, accessed March 28, 2021.

353 Tribune News Services, "Tax Protest Turns into a Scuffle," April 21, 1997, hppts://www.chicagotribune.com/news/ct-xpm-1997-04-21-9704210094-story.html, accessed March 28, 2021.

[354] Letter From Seneca President Mike Schindler To US President Bill Clinton), April 29 1997, hppts://sisis.nativeweb.org/seneca/apr27sch.html, accessed March 28, 2021.

[355] Pedro Perez, Personal Files, accessed July 5, 2016.

[356] Pedro Perez, Personal Files, accessed July 5, 2016.

[357] Pedro Perez, Personal Files, accessed July 5, 2016.

[358] Tribune News Services, "Tax Protest Turns into a Scuffle," April 21, 1997, hppts://www.chicagotribune.com/news/ct-xpm-1997-04-21-9704210094-story.html, accessed March 29, 2021.

[359] "Arthur O. Eve," Uncrowned Community Builders, accessed October 30, 2022, hppts://uncrownedcommunitybuilders.com/person/arthur-o-eve, accessed October 30, 2022.

[360] "Who Is Arthur O. Eve?," Office of Academic Diversity Initiatives, accessed October 30, 2022, hppts://oadi.cornell.edu/signature-programs/eop-heop/what-are-eopheop/who-arthur-o-eve, accessed October 30, 2022.

[361] "Arthur O. Eve," University of Buffalo, accessed October 9, 2022, hppts://www.buffalo.edu/eoc/about-us/detailedbeochistory/artoeve.html, accessed October 9, 2022.

[362] Pedro Perez, Personal Files, accessed July 5, 2016.

[363] "23 Indians Arrested in Protest over Taxes," The New York Times, May 19, 1997, Sec. B, 5, hppts://www.nytimes.com/1997/05/19/nyregion/23-indians-arrested-in-protest-over-taxes.html, accessed March 31, 2021.

[364] "N.Y. Penal Law § 205.30 – Resisting Arrest," New York Public Law, last modified September 22, 2014, hppts://newyork.public.law/laws/n.y._penal_law_section_205.30, accessed April 2, 2021.

[365] "Kerner Commission," HistoryLabs, hppts://policing.umhistorylabs.lsa.umich.edu/s/detroitunderfire/page/kerner-commission, accessed October 31, 2022.

[366] Papineau v. Parmley, 465 F.3d 46 (2d Cir. 2006), hppts://case-law.vlex.com/vid/papineau-v-parmley-docket-894104951, accessed October 31, 2022.

[367] John O'Brien, "Head of State Police Testifies at Boisterous Trial over 1997 Indian Tax Protest," Syracuse, September 27, 2016, hppts://www.syracuse.com/crime/2016/09/head_of_state_police_testifies_at_boisterous_trial_over_1997_indian_tax_protest.html, accessed April 5, 2021.

[368] Syracuse, "New York State Troopers Subdue Native American Tax Protester in 1997 Near Syracuse," YouTube video, 0:39, October 17, 2016, hppts://youtu.be/KZ4NWfO2jR8?si=eYHb953n3fBvX1mv, accessed April 2, 2021.

[369] John O'Brien, "State Police Investigator Probing Brutality at Indian Nation Says He Was Muzzled," Syracuse, August 5, 2012, hppts://www.syracuse.com/news/2012/08/state_police_investigator_prob.html, accessed October 31, 2022.

[370] Ibid.

[371] Ibid.

[372] Ibid.

[373] John O'Brien, "New State Police Boss Led Response to 1997 Indian Protest That Ended in $2.7m Settlement," Upstate New York, August 1, 2016, https://www.newyorkupstate.com/news/2016/08/new_head_of_state_police_led_response_to_1997_indian_protest_that_ended_in_27m_s.html, accessed April 5, 2021.

[374] "Police Investigation Supervisor Admits Faking Fingerprints," The New York Times, July 30, 1993, Sec. B, 5, hppts://www.nytimes.com/1993/07/30/nyregion/police-investigation-supervisor-admits-faking-fingerprints.html, accessed May 16, 2022.

[375] Dale Gardner, "New York Police Falsify Evidence," Prison Legal News, October 15, 1994, hppts://www.prisonlegalnews.org/news/1994/oct/15/new-york-police-falsify-evidence/, accessed May 16, 2022.

[376] Admin, "New York State Police Troop C Scandal," Police Wiki, March 29, 2018, hppts://policewiki.blogspot.com/2018/03/new-york-state-police-troop-c-scandal.html, accessed May 16, 2022.

[377] Executive Office of the President President's Council of Advisors on Science and Technology, "Report to the President Forensic Science in Criminal Courts: Ensuring Scientific Validity of Feature-Comparison Methods," The White House, September 2016, hppts://obamawhitehouse.archives.gov/sites/default/files/microsites/ostp/PCAST/pcast_forensic_science_report_final.pdf, accessed May 17, 2022.

[378] FindLaw Staff, "Fingerprints: The First ID," Findlaw, September 13, 2023, hppts://www.findlaw.com/criminal/criminal-procedure/fingerprints-the-first-id.html, accessed May 19, 2022.

[379] Bradford T. Ulery et al., "Measuring What Latent Fingerprint Examiners Consider Sufficient Information for Individualization Determinations," PLOS

ONE 9, no. 11 (November 2014): e110179, https://doi.org/10.1371/journal. pone.0110179, accessed May 20, 2022.

380 Ibid.

381 "Y2K Bug," National Geographic Society, hppts://education.nationalgeo-graphic.org/resource/Y2K-bug, accessed December 22, 2022.

382 "Disaster Mortuary Operational Response Teams," ASPR, hppts://aspr.hhs. gov/NDMS/Pages/dmort.aspx, accessed November 1, 2022.

383 Yasmine Leung, "Who Was the Last Survivor of 9/11 to Be Found and How Many People Died?," HITC, September 10, 2021, hppts://www.hitc.com/ en-gb/2021/09/10/who-was-the-last-survivor-of-9-11-to-be-found-and-how-many-people-died/, accessed August 30, 2022.

384 Nathan Place, "How Many People Died in 9/11?," The Independent, September 11, 2023, hppts://www.independent.co.uk/news/world/americas/9-11-september-11-what-happened-b2164404.html, accessed November 2, 2023.

385 Ibid.

386 New York State Police, Wall of Honor - Honoring Troopers who have died in the line of duty, https://troopers.ny.gov/wall-honor, accessed November 2, 2023.

387 "Ralph 'Bucky' Phillips Manhunt," New York State Police, accessed November 2, 2022, hppts://troopers.ny.gov/ralph-bucky-phillips-manhunt, accessed November 2, 2022.

388 Staff Writer, "State Police Report Criticizes Handling of Phillips Manhunt," Times Herald-Record, May 18, 2007, hppts://www.recordonline.com/story/ news/2007/05/18/state-police-report-criticizes-handling/528956760007/, accessed November 3, 2022.

389 Mike Goodwin, "Bucky Phillips Gave State Police a Critique of Their Manhunt Tactics," Crime Confidential, June 7, 2009, hppts://blog.timesunion.com/ crime/bucky-phillips-gave-state-police-a-critique-of-their-manhunt-tactics/1516/, accessed November 3, 2022.

390 Ibid.

391 "Notice of Reasonable Cause: Preston Felton," New York State Joint Commission on Public Ethics, December 2017, hppts://ethics.ny.gov/system/ files/documents/2017/12/preston-feltonnotice-reasonable-cause.pdf, accessed November 6, 2022.

392 Ibid.

[393] Danny Hakim, "Spitzer's Staff Misused State Police, Report Says," The Boston Globe, July 24, 2007, hppts://archive.boston.com/news/nation/articles/2007/07/24/spitzers_staff_misused_state_police_report_says/, accessed November 6, 2022.

[394] Danny Hakim, "Spitzer's Staff Misused Police, Report Finds," The New York Times, July 23, 2007, hppts://www.nytimes.com/2007/07/23/nyregion/23cnd-spitzer.html, accessed November 6, 2022.

[395] Ibid.

[396] "Eliot Spitzer Resigns," Intelligencer, March 12, 2008, hppts://nymag.com/intelligencer/2008/03/eliot_spitzer_resigns.html, accessed November 6, 2022.

[397] "Mann Act," Legal Information Institute, hppts://www.law.cornell.edu/wex/mann_act, accessed November 7, 2022.

[398] Danny Hakim and William K. Rashbaum, "No Federal Prostitution Charges for Spitzer," The New York Times, November 6, 2008, hppts://www.nytimes.com/2008/11/07/nyregion/07spitzer.html, accessed November 7, 2022.

[399] Ibid.

[400] "Mann Act," Public Broadcasting Service, hppts://www.pbs.org/kenburns/unforgivable-blackness/mann-act, accessed November 07, 2022.

[401] "Harry J. Corbitt," New York State Police, hppts://troopers.ny.gov/harry-j-corbitt, accessed November 07, 2022.

[402] "Glenn Valle Testimony," The New York Times Web Archive, July 31, 2012. hppts://archive.nytimes.com/www.nytimes.com/interactive/2012/07/31/nyregion/07312012-cuomo-document.html, accessed November 10, 2022.

[403] Danny Hakim, "Cuomo Said to Have Dissuaded Lawyer Use by Witnesses in 2008 State Police Inquiry," The New York Times, July 31, 2012, hppts://www.nytimes.com/2012/07/31/nyregion/cuomo-said-to-have-dissuaded-lawyer-use-by-witnesses-in-2008-state-police-inquiry.html, accessed November 10, 2022.

[404] Perdido Street School: July 2012. https://perdidostreetschool.blogspot.com/2012/07/, accessed November 10, 2022.

[405] Jeremy W. Peters, "Paterson Says He Feared Exposure by State Police," The New York Times, May 3, 2008, hppts://www.nytimes.com/2008/05/03/nyregion/03paterson.html, accessed November 10, 2022.

[406] Ibid.

[407] Ibid.

[408] Joseph Spector, "State Police Superintendent: 'I Never Heard of a Rogue Unit,'" Democrat and Chronicle, May 27, 2008, hppts://www.democratandchronicle. com/story/news/politics/blogs/political-scene/2008/05/27/state-police-superintendent-i-never-heard-of-a-rogue-unit/2253907/, accessed November 10, 2022.

[409] Nicholas Confessore and Jeremy W. Peters, "Governor's Aide Had 'Late-Filing Syndrome,' Lawyer Says," The New York Times, October 23, 2008, hppts://www. nytimes.com/2008/10/23/nyregion/23obyrne.html?searchResultPosition=8, accessed November 10, 2022.

[410] Brendan Scott, "Paterson's Chief of Staff O'Byrne Resigns under Pressure," New York Post, October 24, 2008, hppts://nypost.com/2008/10/24/patersons-chief-of-staff-obyrne-resigns-under-pressure/, accessed November 10, 2022.

[411] "Total Number of Terrorist Attacks in the United States 1995-2020," Statista, August 1, 2023, hppts://www.statista.com/statistics/591079/number-of-terrorist-attacks-in-united-states/, accessed November 12, 2022.

[412] Chris Canipe and Travis Hartman, "A Timeline of Mass Shootings in the U.S.," Reuters, March 23, 2021, hppts://graphics.reuters.com/USA-GUNS/MASS-SHOOTING/nmovardgrpa/, accessed November 14, 2022.

[413] Fredric U. Dicker, "Ex-State Cop Boss Admits Troopergate Role," New York Post, November 25, 2009, hppts://nypost.com/2009/11/25/ex-state-cop-boss-admits-troopergate-role/, accessed November 7, 2022.

[414] Final Report of Investigation into the response by the NYSP, hppts://ag.ny.gov/ sites/default/files/press-releases/archived/report.final.pdf, accessed November 15, 2022.

[415] "Driving While Black: Racial Profiling on Our Nation's Highways," American Civil Liberties Union, hppts://www.aclu.org/report/driving-while-black-racial-profiling-our-nations-highways, accessed November 17, 2022.

[416] German Lopez, "Black Parents Describe 'The Talk' They Give to Their Children about Police," Vox, August 8, 2016, hppts://www.vox.com/2016/ 8/8/12401792/police-black-parents-the-talk, accessed November 17, 2022.

[417] Final Report Investigation into the by the NYSP, hppts://ag.ny.gov/sites/ default/files/press-releases/archived/report.final.pdf, accessed November 17, 2022.

[418] "News from Independent Counsel Judith S. Kaye," New York State Attorney General, July 28, 2010, hppts://ag.ny.gov/press-release/2010/news-independent-counsel-judith-s-kaye-0, accessed November 17, 2022.

[419] FOX Sports, "Patterson Pays $62K Fine over Yanks Tickets," FOX Sports, February 4, 2011, https://www.foxsports.com/stories/mlb/patterson-pays-62k-fine-over-yanks-tickets, https://www.cnn.com/2010/POLITICS/12/20/new.york.governor.tickets/index.html accessed November 17, 2022.

[420] Judith Kaye's Report of Investigation – Governor acquisition of 2009 World Series Tickets, hppts://ag.ny.gov/sites/default/files/reports/report.final.pdf, accessed November 17, 2022.

[421] "Thomas Constantine," New York State Police, hppts://troopers.ny.gov/thomas-constantine, accessed November 17, 2022.

[422] New York State Police, "James W. McMahon," hppts://troopers.ny.gov/james-w-mcmahon, accessed November 17, 2022.

[423] New York State Police, "Harry J. Corbitt," hppts://troopers.ny.gov/harry-j-corbitt, accessed November 17, 2022.

[424] Albany Times Union, "Harry Corbitt Obituary (1947 - 2019)," Legacy, May 9, 2019, hppts://www.legacy.com/us/obituaries/timesunion-albany/name/harry-corbitt-obituary?id=5038536, accessed November 17, 2017.

[425] "Evolution of Social Capital," Institute for Social Capital hppts://www.socialcapitalresearch.com/literature/evolution/, accessed June 17, 2016.

[426] Albany Times Union, "Theodore A. Cook III, hppts://www.legacy.com/us/obituaries/timesunion-albany/name/theodore-cook-obituary?id=4981309, accessed December 17, 2017.

[427] "First Women Graduate from the New York State Police Academy," New York State Police, https://troopers.ny.gov/first-women-graduate-new-york-state-police-academy, accessed April 2, 2021.

[428] H.R.14752 - Equality Act 93rd Congress (1973-1974), hppts://www.congress.gov/bill/93rd-congress/house-bill/14752, accessed April 2, 2021.

[429] Daniella Diaz and Annie Grayer, "House Passes Equality Act Aimed at Ending Discrimination Based on Sexual Orientation and Gender Identity," CNN, March 16, 2021, hppts://www.cnn.com/2021/02/25/politics/equality-act-passes-house/index.html, accessed April 2, 2021.

[430] "About New York State Police," New York State Police, hppts://troopers.ny.gov/about-new-york-state-police, accessed November 1, 2022.

[431] Sarah K. Estill, "30x30 Initiative: Why We Need More Women in Policing and How to Achieve It," COPS Office, March 2021, hppts://cops.usdoj.gov/html/dispatch/03-2021/initiative.html, accessed November 1, 2022.

[432] United States v. State of NY, 475 F. Supp. 1103 (N.D.N.Y 1979). hppts://law. justia.com/cases/federal/district-courts/FSupp/475/1103/1688027/, accessed May 16, 2022.

[433] Ibid.

[434] Philip S. Gutis, "Judge Drops Hiring Quotas for New York State Police," The New York Times, May 14, 1989, hppts://www.nytimes.com/1989/05/14/ nyregion/judge-drops-hiring-quotas-for-new-york-state-police.html, February 7, 2021.

[435] Ibid.

[436] Ibid.

[437] Ibid.

[438] "QuickFacts: New York; United States," United States Census Bureau, February 7, 2022, hppts://www.census.gov/quickfacts/fact/table/NY,US/PST045222, February 7, 2022.

[439] Andrew M. Cuomo and Lola W. Brabham, "2020 New York State Workforce Management Report," Department of Civil Service, 2020, hppts://www.cs.ny. gov/businesssuite/docs/workforceplans/2020.pdf, accessed February 7, 2022.

[440] Ibid.

[441] Pedro Perez, "Commentary: Diversity in State Police Ranks Still Not What It Should Be," Times Union, September 26, 2016, hppts://timesunion. com/tuplus-opinion/article/Commentary-Diversity-in-State-Police-ranks-still-9284032.php, accessed February 15, 2022.

[442] Jim Mustian and Camille Fassett, "'Still on the Farm': NY State Police Struggles to Diversify," NBC New York, June 1, 2021, hppts://www.nbcnewyork.com/ news/local/still-on-the-farm-ny-state-police-struggles-to-diversify/3083226/, accessed February 15, 2022.

[443] New York State Police, Diversity Statement, https://troopers.ny.gov/system/ files/documents/2021/10/diversity-statement.pdf, accessed February 15, 2022.

[444] Jim Mustian and Camille Fassett, "'Still on the Farm': NY State Police Struggles to Diversify," NBC New York, June 1, 2021, hppts://www.nbcnewyork.com/ news/local/still-on-the-farm-ny-state-police-struggles-to-diversify/3083226/, accessed February 15, 2022.

Chapter 20 - The Color of Law

445 Tiffany Morey and Kate McLean, "Policing in Ancient Times," in Introduction to the US Criminal Justice System, eds. Alison S. Burke, David Carter, Brian Fedorek, Tiffany Morey, Lore Rutz-Burri, and Shanell Sanchez (New York: Pennsylvania State University, 2019), hppts://psu.pb.unizin.org/criminaljusticemclean/chapter/5-1-history-of-policing/, accessed October 8, 2022.

446 Ibid.

447 Ibid.

448 Ibid.

449 Denise Oliver Velez, "Dred Scott, Slave Catchers and Slave Patrols," Daily Kos, July 17, 2016, hppts://www.dailykos.com/stories/2016/7/17/1546840/-Dred-Scott-slave-catchers-and-slave-patrols, accessed October 8, 2022.

450 "Slave Patrols: An Early Form of American Policing," National Law Enforcement Officers Memorial Fund, hppts://nleomf.org/slave-patrols-an-early-form-of-american-policing/, accessed November 22, 2020.

451 Jbkatz, "Punch, John – First 'Official' Slave in America," Amazing Black History, January 20, 2022, hppts://amazingblackhistory.com/2022/01/20/punch-john-first-official-slave-in-america/, accessed September 27, 2022.

452 "Enactment of Hereditary Slavery Law Virginia 1662-ACT XII," National Park Service, hppts://www.nps.gov/ethnography/aah/aaheritage/Chesapeake_pop2.htm, accessed September 27, 2022.

453 Robert Beverley, "Of the Servants and Slaves in Virginia," in The History of Virginia (London: B. and S. Tooke, 1705), 235–239, hppts://nationalhumanitiescenter.org/pds/amerbegin/power/text8/BeverlyServSlaves.pdf, accessed September 27, 2022.

454 Gary Potter, "The History of Policing in the United States, Part 1," EKU Online, June 25, 2013, hppts://plsonline.eku.edu/insidelook/history-policing-united-states-part-1, accessed November 22, 2020.

455 Ibid.

456 History.com Editors, "Fugitive Slave Acts," History, December 2, 2009, hppts://www.history.com/topics/black-history/fugitive-slave-acts, accessed October 2, 2022.

457 Don E. Fehrenbacher and Ward M. McAfee, The Slaveholding Republic: An Account of the United States Government's Relations to Slavery

(New York: Oxford Academic, 2002), hppts://doi.org/10.1093/acprof: oso/9780195158052.001.0001, accessed October 2, 2022.

[458] Gary Potter, "The History of Policing in the United States, Part 1," EKU Online, June 25, 2013, hppts://plsonline.eku.edu/insidelook/history-policing-united-states-part-1, accessed October 2, 2022.

[459] Monica C. Bell, "Police Reform and the Dismantling of Legal Estrangement," Yale Law Journal, no. 126 (2017): 2058, hppts://www.yalelawjournal.org/essay/police-reform-and-the-dismantling-of-legal-estrangement, accessed December 11, 2020.

[460] President's Task Force on 21st Century Policing, "Final Report," hppts://cops.usdoj.gov/pdf/taskforce/taskforce_finalreport.pdf, accessed December 11, 2020.

[461] History.com, Nadra Kareem Nittle, How the Black Codes Limited African American Progress After the Civil War, October 1, 2020, https://www.history.com/news/black-codes-reconstruction-slavery, accessed January 22, 2022.

[462] Cui, D. Driven Out: The Forgotten War against Chinese Americans. Int. Migration & Integration 10, 479–482 (2009), hppts://link.springer.com/article/10.1007/s12134-009-0115-y, accessed January 22, 2022.

[463] History.com Editors, "Tulsa Race Massacre," History, March 8, 2018, hppts://www.history.com/topics/roaring-twenties/tulsa-race-massacre, accessed January 22, 2022.

[464] "Japanese-American Internment," Harry S. Truman, hppts://www.trumanlibrary.gov/education/presidential-inquiries/japanese-american-internment, accessed September 22, 2022.

[465] Rachel Chason and Samantha Schmidt, "BLM Protest vs. Capitol Riot: Comparing Police Response," Washington Post, January 14, 2021, hppts://www.washingtonpost.com/dc-md-va/interactive/2021/blm-protest-capitol-riot-police-comparison/, accessed September 22, 2022

[466] "Selma to Montgomery - Bloody Sunday," U.S. National Park Service, hppts://www.nps.gov/semo/learn/historyculture/bloody-sunday.htm, accessed May 11, 2022.

[467] "Civil Rights Protesters Beaten in 'Bloody Sunday' Attack," History, hppts://www.history.com/this-day-in-history/bloody-sunday-civil-rights-protesters-beaten-selma, accessed May 23, 2022.

[468] "Remember the Ladies," Public Broadcasting Service, https://www.pbs.org/wgbh/americanexperience/features/adams-remember-ladies/, accessed May 23, 2022

[469] "Have race relations improved during Obama's presidency?," The Hill, Amie Parnes and Justin Sink, December 2, 2014, hppts://thehill.com/homenews/administration/225665-have-race-relations-improved-during-obamas-presidency/, accessed May 4, 2022.

[470] Pedro Perez, "America Needs to Resolve Racist Legacy," Times Union, January 17, 2015, hppts://www.timesunion.com/news/article/America-needs-to-resolve-racist-legacy-6021385.php, accessed September 10, 2022.

[471] Cornel West, Race Matters (London: Vintage, 1993), hppts://openlibrary.org/books/OL24866519M/Race_matters, accessed May 4, 2016.

[472] David Aaro, "Capital Punishment, Which States Have It and What Methods Do They Use?," Fox News, February 21, 2020, hppts://www.foxnews.com/us/capital-punishment-which-states-have-it-and-what-methods-do-they-use, accessed September 30, 2022.

[473] Yvonne Juris, "Horror Details of Botched Death Row Killings Show Inmates Suffered 'Drowning' and 'Died in Agony' as Prison.," The US Sun, March 10, 2022, hppts://www.the-sun.com/news/4865013/horror-details-botched-death-row-killings-john-grant/, accessed October 2, 2022.

[474] "Death Penalty," Equal Justice Initiative, hppts://eji.org/issues/death-penalty/, accessed October 2, 2022.

[475] History.com Editors, "Manifest Destiny," History, April 5, 2010, hppts://www.history.com/topics/westward-expansion/manifest-destiny#section_3, accessed September 29, 2022.

[476] Pastor Martin Niemöller, "First They Came," Holocaust Memorial Day Trust, https://www.hmd.org.uk/resource/first-they-came-by-pastor-martin-niemoller/, accessed January 25, 2022.

[477] Emily Ekins, "Policing in America: Understanding Public Attitudes toward the Police. Results from a National Survey," Cato Institute, December 7, 2016, hppts://www.cato.org/survey-reports/policing-america-understanding-public-attitudes-toward-police-results-national, accessed January 25, 2022.

[478] Mapping Police Violence (website), hppts://mappingpoliceviolence.org/, accessed February 15, 2022.

[479] Jennifer Taylor, Reconstruction in America: Racial Violence after the Civil War, 1865-1876 (Equal Justice Initiative, 2020), hppts://eji.org/report/reconstruction-in-america/freedom-to-fear/#resisting-economic-exploitation, accessed September 30, 2022.

480 "Qualified Immunity," American Bar Association, December 17, 2020, hppts://
www.americanbar.org/groups/public_education/publications/insights-on-law-
and-society/volume-21/issue-1/qualified-immunity/, accessed September 30,
2022.

481 Nimra Azmi, "The Supreme Court's Insidious Development of Qualified
Immunity," Just Security, March 15, 2021, hppts://www.justsecurity.org/70751/
the-supreme-courts-insidious-development-of-qualified-immunity/, accessed
September 30, 2022.

482 Joanna C. Schwartz, "The case against qualified immunity," Notre Dame L.
Rev. 93 (2017): 1797, hppts://scholarship.law.nd.edu/ndlr/vol93/iss5/2/,
accessed September 30, 2022.

483 Stephanie Pagones, "LIVE UPDATES: Former Minneapolis Cop Derek
Chauvin Found Guilty on All Charges in George Floyd's Death," Fox News,
April 20, 2021, hppts://www.foxnews.com/us/live-updates-derek-chauvin-
trial-sees-jury-deliberations-begin, accessed April 28, 2021.

484 US Crime & Justice Statistics and Data Trends: national crime rates, gun
background checks, corrections, and more, March 30, 2023, USA Facts,
https://usafacts.org/topics/crime-justice/, accessed October 28, 2023.

485 Richard Meadow, "Police Brutality Statistics: What the Data Says about Police
Violence in America," Police Brutality Center, October 24, 2023, hppts://
policebrutalitycenter.org/police-brutality/statistics/, accessed October 28, 2023.

486 Statista - Number of nonfederal police officers arrested for murder who have
been convicted between 2005 and 2020, by charge, June 2, 2023, hppts://
www.statista.com/statistics/1123386/convictions-police-officers-arrested-
murder-charge-us/, accessed October 28, 2023.

487 Alexi Jones and Wendy Sawyer, "Not Just 'a Few Bad Apples': U.S. Police Kill
Civilians at Much Higher Rates than Other Countries," Prison Policy Initiative,
June 5, 2020, hppts://www.prisonpolicy.org/blog/2020/06/05/policekillings/,
accessed February 15, 2022.

488 Brian Miller, "The Militarization of America's Police: A Brief History,"
Foundation for Economic Education, May 24, 2019, hppts://fee.org/articles/
the-militarization-of-americas-police-a-brief-history/, accessed May 11, 2021.

489 Sam Levin, "White Supremacists and Militias Have Infiltrated Police across
US, Report Says," The Guardian, August 28, 2020, hppts://www.theguardian.
com/us-news/2020/aug/27/white-supremacists-militias-infiltrate-us-police-
report, accessed February 15, 2022.

490 Tom Nolan, "Militarization Has Fostered a Policing Culture That Sets up Protesters as 'the Enemy,'" The Conversation, June 2, 2020, hppts://theconversation.com/militarization-has-fostered-a-policing-culture-that-sets-up-protesters-as-the-enemy-139727, accessed May 11, 2021.

491 "Part 6: Diversity, Inclusiveness, and Organisational Health," Office of the Auditor-General New Zealand, hppts://oag.parliament.nz/2017/police/part6.htm, accessed May 11, 2021.

492 Ibid.

493 Gary Potter, "The History of Policing in the United States, Part 4," EKU Online, February 11, 2022, hppts://ekuonline.eku.edu/blog/police-studies/the-history-of-policing-in-the-united-states-part-4/, accessed October 3, 2022.

494 Collaboration to Reduce Tragedy and Improve Outcomes: Law Enforcement, Psychiatry, and People Living With Mental Illness Nils Rosenbaum, M.D., Detective Matthew Tinney, Mauricio Tohen, M.D., Dr.P.H., June 2017, hppts://www.gocit.org/uploads/3/0/5/5/30557023/law-mental health article.pdf, accessed April 29, 2021.

495 Altovise Love-Craighead, "Building Trust through Trauma-Informed Policing," Vera Institute of Justice, December 20, 2016, hppts://www.vera.org/news/police-perspectives/building-trust-through-trauma-informed-policing, accessed June 24, 2023.

496 "New Tools for the Field | Where Do We Begin?," Office for Victims of Crime, hppts://ovc.ojp.gov/program/vtt/where-do-we-begin-contd/new-tools-field#new-tools-for-the-field, accessed June 24, 2023.

497 "An Occupational Risk: What Every Police Agency Should Do To Prevent Suicide Among Its Officers," Police Executive Research Forum, October 2019, hppts://www.policeforum.org/assets/PreventOfficerSuicide.pdf, accessed June 26, 2023.

498 Kevin Johnson, "4 Police Died by Suicide after the Capitol Riot; It's the Reason Their Names Won't Be Memorialized," USA TODAY, October 14, 2021, hppts://www.usatoday.com/story/news/politics/2021/10/14/police-suicides-should-line-duty-deaths-capitol-survivors-say/6093369001/?gnt-cfr=1, accessed June 26, 2023.

499 Luke Broadwater, "Congress Clears Bill to Make Officer Suicides Eligible for Death Benefits," The New York Times, August 2, 2022, ppts://www.nytimes.com/2022/08/02/us/politics/congress-officer-suicides-ptsd-benefits.html, accessed June 26, 2023.

500 Dave Lucas, "Citizens Meet with Police on Countering Implicit Bias," WAMC, June 14, 2016, hppts://www.wamc.org/capital-region-news/2016-06-14/citizens-meet-with-police-on-countering-implicit-bias, accessed April 30, 2021.

501 Robert E. Worden et al., "The Impacts of Implicit Bias Awareness Training in the NYPD," International Association of Chiefs of Police, July 2020, hppts://www.theiacp.org/sites/default/files/Research%20Center/NYPD%20Implicit%20Bias%20Report.pdf, accessed April 30, 2021.

502 Becky Haas et al., "Increasing Empathy through Trauma-Informed Policing," Police Chief Magazine, October 2021, hppts://www.policechiefmagazine.org/increasing-empathy-through-trauma-informed-policing/, accessed October 03, 2022.

503 "Pilot Mental Fitness," Federal Aviation Administration, hppts://www.faa.gov/newsroom/pilot-mental-fitness, accessed January 26, 2022.

504 Richard Meadow, "Police Brutality Statistics: What the Data Says About Police Violence in America, "Police Brutality Center, Police Brutality Center, June 27, 2022, https://policebrutalitycenter.org/police-brutality/statistics/, accessed October 03, 2022.

505 Sean Nicholson-Crotty, Jill Nicholson-Crotty, and Sergio Fernández, "Will More Black Cops Matter? Officer Race and Police-Involved Homicides of Black Citizens," Public Administration Review 77, no. 2 (February 2017): 206–16, hppts://onlinelibrary.wiley.com/doi/epdf/10.1111/puar.12734, accessed January 26, 2022.

506 Bocar Ba et al., "The Role of Officer Race and Gender in Police-Civilian Interactions in Chicago," Science 371, no. 6530 (February 12, 2021): 696–702, hppts://pubmed.ncbi.nlm.nih.gov/33574207/, accessed June 26, 2023.

507 The Associated Press, "Diversity in Law Enforcement May Improve Policing, Study Shows," NBC News, February 11, 2021, hppts://www.nbcnews.com/news/nbcblk/diversity-law-enforcement-may-improve-policing-study-shows-n1257515, accessed October 4, 2022.

508 Rick Rojas and Jessica Jaglois, "Video Captures Brutal Beating of Tyre Nichols," The New York Times, March 8, 2023, hppts://www.nytimes.com/live/2023/01/27/us/tyre-nichols-memphis#george-floyd-police-reform-memphis, accessed June 26, 2023.

509 Mark B. Baer, "Police Officer Diversity Status Impacts Their Perceptions," Psychology Today, January 31, 2017, hppts://www.psychologytoday.com/

us/blog/empathy-and-relationships/201701/police-officer-diversity-status-impacts-their-perceptions, accessed October 04, 2022.

510 John Letteney, "President's Message: The Time to Enhance Diversity Is Now," Police Chief Magazine, January 13, 2023, hppts://www.policechiefmagazine.org/presidents-message-the-time-to-enhance-diversity-is-now/, accessed April 29, 2021.

511 Gabrielle T. Isaza et al., "Evaluation of Police Use of Force De-escalation Training: Assessing the Impact of the Integrating Communications, Assessment, and Tactics (ICAT) Training Program for the University of Cincinnati, OH Police Division (UCPD)," University of Cincinnati, December 2019, hppts://www.theiacp.org/sites/default/files/Research%20Center/UCPD_ICAT%20Evaluation_Final.pdf, accessed April 30, 2021.

512 Ruby K. Payne and Jodi Pfarr, "Tactical Communication First Responder Edition," Presented at aha! Process 2020 Addressing the Challenges of Poverty Conference, hppts://www.ahaprocess.com/wp-content/uploads/2020/09/ACP2020-handout-Tactical-Communication.pdf, accessed April 30, 2021.

513 History.com Editors, "Jim Crow Laws," History, February 28, 2018, hppts://www.history.com/topics/early-20th-century-us/jim-crow-laws, accessed May 14, 2021.

514 Castle Rock v. Gonzales, 545 U.S. 748 (2005), hppts://www.law.cornell.edu/supremecourt/text/04-278, accessed October 4, 2022.

515 Matthew Clarke, "Police Not Required to Protect; Are They Required to Serve?," Criminal Legal News, April 12, 2019, hppts://www.criminallegalnews.org/news/2019/apr/12/police-not-required-protect-are-they-required-serve/, accessed October 4, 2022.

516 "Duty to All, Duty to None," DLG Learning Center, April 13, 2020, hppts://dlglearningcenter.com/duty-to-all-duty-to-none/#post-25581-endnote-2, accessed October 4, 2022.

517 Ibid.

About the Author

Pedro Perez is a distinguished leader who has championed social justice and equity throughout his illustrious career. With over twenty-nine years of experience in the New York State Police, Pedro has earned distinction as the highest-ranking Nuyorican in the history of the New York State Police. He rose through the ranks and achieved the Brigadier General rank, serving as acting superintendent. Pedro has consistently been committed to promoting diversity and inclusion by helping people from underprivileged backgrounds gain access to education, employment, and entrepreneurial opportunities. He has also served as the executive director for various nonprofit organizations and is passionate about assisting marginalized communities gain access to the resources necessary to improve their lives.